Vampire Films Aro

Vampire Films
Around the World

*Essays on the Cinematic
Undead of Sixteen Cultures*

Edited by JAMES AUBREY

McFarland & Company, Inc., Publishers
Jefferson, North Carolina

Library of Congress Cataloguing-in-Publication Data

Names: Aubrey, James, 1945– editor.
Title: Vampire films around the world : essays on the cinematic undead of
    sixteen cultures / edited by James Aubrey.
Description: Jefferson : McFarland & Company, Inc., Publishers, 2020. |
    Includes bibliographical references and index.
Identifiers: LCCN 2020039047 | ISBN 9781476676739 (paperback) ∞ |
    ISBN 9781476639864 (ebook)
Subjects: LCSH: Vampire films—History and criticism. | Dracula films—
    History and criticism. | Motion pictures—Social aspects.
Classification: LCC PN1995.9.V3 V36 2020 | DDC 791.43/675—dc23
LC record available at https://lccn.loc.gov/2020039047

British Library cataloguing data are available

ISBN (print) 978-1-4766-7673-9
ISBN (ebook) 978-1-4766-3986-4

Front cover: Lina Leandersson in the 2008 Swedish film *Let the Right One In*
(Magnolia Pictures/Photofest)

Printed in the United States of America

McFarland & Company, Inc., Publishers
  Box 611, Jefferson, North Carolina 28640
  www.mcfarlandpub.com

Table of Contents

Introduction

JAMES AUBREY

When my nine-year-old grandson asked me, "Are vampires real?" I thought for a moment and said, "No, but it's fun to pretend they are." When he is older I will elaborate, that people enjoy conjuring strange things, from scary creatures that we know are not real to superheroes we wish were so. With vampires we get to feel both hope and fear: the attractive idea of eternal life but one that is marked with pain, of pleasure that is accompanied by an addiction to blood, of extraordinary power that is accompanied by extraordinary vulnerability, and of exotic experiences that can leave one dead—or undead.

Stories about a middle state between life and death have circulated across recorded history, in forms as diverse as cultural imaginations. Nearly three thousand years ago Homer's Odysseus obtained advice from shades of the departed by luring them from the underworld—with blood. Modern ghosts, zombies, and vampires have little in common with Greek shades because revenants always reflect their different cultural times and places. Dr. Faustus uses Christian demonology to summon Mephistopheles—and Helen of Troy—for meetings in late medieval Europe. America's cute talking bedsheet, Casper the Friendly Ghost, is a holdover from the days of traditional winding-sheets that pre-dated the modern use of coffins, which have become a standard accessory in vampire movies. We imagine vampires that fit our surroundings, needs and aspirations, which will vary from person to person. Nina Auerbach nicely captures the idea in her book title *Our Vampires, Ourselves*.[1] Vampire films will vary from culture to culture in significant ways—hence this book.

Vampire films do have some general features in common, or they wouldn't fit the category, but it is not enough to call the vampire an archetype or to label its popularity as "world-wide" or "gone global."[2] One of the problems is that the novel *Dracula* has been so influential on subsequent vampire

1

lore that vampire films have acquired a cinema genre's reputation for sameness. Jeffrey Weinstock calls *Dracula* the Ur-text, the seminal story to which all other vampire stories are related because audiences have expectations based on that novel, even if they haven't read it.[3] That may be generally true, but different films use *Dracula* in different ways. For example, one scene that has inspired various vampire films is the moment when Stoker's Dr. Seward reports how Renfield, his mental patient and Dracula's devotee, displayed madness by "lying on his belly on the floor licking up, like a dog, the blood which had fallen from my wounded wrist."[4] The scene is visually arresting, so it has inspired moments in films as different as *Cronos* (Mexico, 1993), when a decent man who is being turned into a vampire by a mechanical device follows another man who has cut his hand at a party into the men's room so that he can pathetically lick up spilled blood after the man has left, and *Let the Right One In* (Sweden, 2008), when a young boy deliberately cuts his hand hoping to bond with a violent girl-vampire, only to see her threateningly drop to the floor and start licking up some of his blood that has fallen there.[5] Dracula's influence is indeed world-wide, but the resulting vampires are distinct.

Dracula may have become the go-to source for vampire lore, but the novel itself derives from earlier folklore and literature. The first recorded document of vampirism was the 1728 report, in German, of Peter Plogojowitz, a Serbian revenant who was said to have visited his wife and attacked nine villagers—ten weeks after his death and burial. When his grave was opened, says the investigator, "not without astonishment, I saw some fresh blood in his mouth which, according to the common observation, he had sucked from the people killed by him."[6] The earliest report of such vampirism in English was in 1734, from three travelers to Germany who wrote, "These Vampyres are supposed to be the bodies of deceased Persons, animated by evil Spirits, which come out of the Graves, in the Night time, suck the blood of many of the Living, and thereby destroy them."[7] This kind of belief seems to have been based on medieval ideas of demonic possession that might animate corpses, and many of Stoker's ideas were borrowed from such religion-inflected folklore from eastern Europe, reported in *The Land Beyond the Forest*, an 1888 travelogue about Transylvania by Emily Gerard, a Scottish novelist.[8] Among beliefs that have become associated with vampires are revenants (corpses that return), exsanguination (blood draining), transmission (infecting others), and apotropaics (warding against vampires). An anthropological examination of such beliefs and their possible origins is Paul Barber's *Vampires, Burial, and Death*, which reproduces the earliest attempts to document vampire activity and accounts for many beliefs as misunderstanding of how communicable diseases such as plague are transmitted, and others as misunderstanding of how corpses can decompose in varying conditions, including bleeding out of the mouth. Garlic and thorny hawthorne branches were expected to repel vampires as they do humans.[9]

Stoker was not writing in a literary vacuum. The folkloric reports soon inspired poems by Heinrich August Ossefelder (*Der Vampir*, 1748) and George Gordon, Lord Byron (*The Giaour*, 1813) as well as prose by John Polidori (*The Vampyre*, 1819), James Rymer (*Varney the Vampire*, 1845), and Sheridan Le Fanu (*Carmilla*, 1871). Bram Stoker took these works, along with the folklore, to a new level with *Dracula* (1897), from which twentieth-century film adaptations would fix many of his ideas in the Western popular consciousness as embodiments of evil, brought to seeming life on the screen by actors such as Max Schreck, Bela Lugosi, and Christopher Lee. As Western moviegoers became less religious in the latter half of the twentieth century, vampires became less evil and more sympathetic, particularly after what might be called the Anne Rice revolution; her *Interview with the Vampire* (1976) humanized them in a new way. Twenty-first century film and media are taking the vampire in still newer directions, with increasing irony—our vampires, our friends.

Rather than acknowledge his sources, Stoker has Dr. Van Helsing make the broad claim (in his unidiomatic English) that vampirism is a universal phenomenon: "[H]e is known everywhere that man has been. In old Greece in old Rome; he flourish in Germany all over, in France, in India, in the Cheronese [juncture of Greece, Bulgaria, and Turkey]; and in China, so far from us in all ways, there even is he, and the people fear him at this day."[10] It must be said that Stoker was taking some literary license: India, despite Van Helsing's claim, has no such vampires, possibly because Hindu cremation practices do not encourage belief in returning corpses. Nor are the Chinese vampires of *Mr. Vampire* (1985) anything like Count Dracula, as they hop with their arms extended forward unless halted by the application of a magical text to their foreheads. Even if vampire stories have lately become an increasingly global phenomenon, they vary widely from culture to culture—particularly if they are blended with local traditions. For that reason, the contributors to this book examine vampire films in their local and national cultural contexts to discover why the narratives are so distinctive. It is, after all, the differences rather than the similarities among vampire traditions that are most interesting, even if some supposed traditions are imported and have become cinematic clichés such as capes and fangs, while other traditions such as wooden stakes have evolved, from Remington rifles in Stoker's novel to sunlight grenades in *Blade II*. Thus, aspects of vampire lore have been adopted or rejected by twentieth-century filmmakers as that mass medium spread vampire variants across the Atlantic and around the world.

Stoker's *Dracula* is a Victorian novel, and his vampirism was part of the zeitgeist. Dracula's move from Transylvania to London is a reversal of the classic British colonial move to invade another country during Britain's period of imperial dominance—perhaps indirectly a sign of Victorian fear that the empire might strike back. *Dracula's* Mina Murray Harker embodies the 1890s idea of the New Woman—new not only in her familiarity with novelties such as typewriters and shorthand but also in her active engagement in the struggle against Dracula, even to the extent that she takes up arms in the final confrontation. It was perhaps masculine wariness of such newly independent women that led Rudyard Kipling to write a poem called *The Vampire*, published the same year as *Dracula*, in 1897, whose title character does not drain her victim's blood but uses her power of sexual attraction to deprive a male "fool" of family, fortune, and, finally, of life.[11] The poem inspired the 1915 film *A Fool There Was*, starring "The Vamp," Theda Bara. As vampire films have evolved, one Dracula trope that has disappeared is the vampire as aristocrat, with titles such as Count or Countess that signal power and social prestige. Dracula's rank gave him a kind of impunity similar to that of the historical seventeenth-century Countess Elizabeth Bathory, whose notorious bathing in the blood of young girls in hope to preserve her own youth has led her to become associated with vampires. Indeed, she may have inspired Stoker to imagine that Dracula could "grow younger … when that he can fatten on the blood of the living."[12] Dracula is the male provider for his three female companions, who are grateful to receive a live baby in a bag; the fact that they are often called Dracula's "wives" is a reminder that his castle is a parody of a proper Victorian home and marriage. Van Helsing's claim for the vampire's universalism is similar to James Frazer's method in *The Golden Bough* (1890), an over-ambitious, would-be key to all mythologies. Stoker's *Dracula* is not necessarily ours.

Some world vampire conventions have been inherited not from the novel *Dracula* but from its film adaptations. One of the first vampire films, *Nosferatu* (1922), was a loose, unauthorized adaptation of the novel. The film's idea that the vampire sleeps in a coffin is not in the novel. Nor is the Count's extreme aversion to sunlight, which he merely experiences as reduced power during the daytime. At the end of *Nosferatu* Count Orlok burns to death in the morning sunlight, defeated by a self-sacrificing German wife; but those deliberate differences from the novel were partly to avoid copyright infringement.[13] It is ironic that the film's innovative idea, that daylight is fatal to a vampire, has become a standard of vampire cinema—evidence of the novel's indirect influence through the movies. Even the notion that vampires seek out virgins as victims may have originated in the common misrepresentation of *Nosferatu's Book of the Vampire* in condensed subtitles that mistranslate "*Weib*" (woman or wife) as "maiden." Likewise the idea that human food makes vampires sick is a common trope in vampire films, but it has developed as a cinematic way to indicate blood addiction rather than a reference to anything in the novel. Dracula's use of blood as a symbol is borrowed from Judeo-Christian traditions, but vampire films have promoted the idea to a common place. When Renfield declares that "blood is life" he echoes a basic principle of Jewish food preparation laws set out in Deuteronomy. When Dracula forces Mina to drink from the wound in his side, Van Helsing refers to it as "baptism in blood," but Dracula's own description is more a parody of the Christian marriage vows: "And you, their best beloved one, are now to me flesh of my flesh; blood of my blood; kin of my kin; my bountiful wine press for a while; and shall be my companion and my helper."[14] The reference to Mina's blood as metaphorical wine further calls to mind the sacrament of Holy Communion. Hammer films made Technicolor-red blood its vampiric trademark, even in the opening credits to *The Horror of Dracula* (1957), which some critics have seen as political symbolism evoking the color of Communism in the Cold War.[15] So even in vampire stories without a religious context, blood can still be symbolic—ultimately of power, says Weinstock, and particularly power over death since vampires are surely, foremost, a fantasy of immortality.[16]

"We come to understand the world through stories," a teacher proposes in *Byzantium*. The moment is ironic, in that the teacher doesn't understand that the vampire story Elinor has written is true, but the proposition is valid enough. It is also a meta-cinematic comment on the story of *Byzantium* itself—or on any of these vampire films, any of which can help us better understand societal codes, taboos, border crossings, fears and desires—the world. And, as I proposed earlier, watching them is fun.

Australia. In the first essay, Graeme A. Wend-Walker not only critiques *The Caretaker* (2012), Australia's most recent contribution to vampire films, but also he traces the evolution of the vampire sub-genre from the 1974 comedy in which media folk-hero Barry McKenzie holds off Count von Plasma with a cross made of Foster's beer cans. *The Caretaker* could not be more different, a serious thriller in which a vampire is recruited to help defend an isolated, outback household, besieged during nights of the living dead and illustrating what Wend-Walker calls the "peculiar relationship" of land, culture, and genre in Australian cinema.

Canada. Vampire novels and ballet performances are seldom combined art forms, but film director Guy Maddin captures the two in a 75-minute, silent movie adaptation of *Dracula* as performed by the Royal Winnipeg Ballet company and shot mostly in black and white—with an exception made for red blood. Canadian Lorna Hutchison locates Maddin's *Dracula: Pages from a Virgin's Diary* (2003) in histories of the monstrous body and the grotesque, and further examines how the film highlights the story's sexual and colonial impulses.

China. After explaining that the phrase "hopping vampire" is a mistranslation of *geong si,* or "stiff corpse," adopted to help market the Hong Kong vampire movies that have preceded *Rigor Mortis* (2016), Fontaine Lien identifies the various traditions that the film draws on, from ghosts to black magic to martial arts. The resulting amalgamation of globalized style with local culture Lien calls a "perfect *geong si* revival for Hong Kong in the twenty-first century."

Germany. As Kai-Uwe Werbeck points out, the glamorous lesbian vampires of *We Are the Night* (*Wir sind die Nacht,* 2010) reflect Post-wall Berlin culture rather than the classic German vampires or more recent German horror cinema. Despite the glamour and power of the female vampires, Werbeck notes that the film overall has a heteronormative tendency.

India. Anurag Chauhan notes that Indian vampire films such as *Closed Door* (*Bandh Darwaza,* 1990) and *Bloody Dracula* (*Khooni Dracula,* 1992) are few and tend to be highly derivative, based on Western traditions, but nevertheless they endorse patriarchal, Indian family values.

Iran. U. Melissa Anyiwo's study of *A Girl Walks Home Alone at Night* (2014) considers its claim to be the first Iranian vampire film. Despite its having been filmed in a supposedly Iranian setting, in Farsi, director Ana Lily Amirpour has been quick to acknowledge her own status as a Westerner and that the film has a culturally ambiguous point of view.

Ireland and UK. From its title the film *Byzantium* (2012) doesn't sound like a vampire film, let alone an Irish one, but its vampires originate on a rocky island off the southwest coast of Ireland. The story features a mother vampire and her teenage daughter as they struggle between themselves but above all work to evade an all-male vampire Brotherhood that is determined to exterminate these female interlopers. I examine the film as a transformation of an English play about a troubled adolescent into an Irish myth with a feminist subtext—possibly the best and surely the most underrated vampire movie yet.

Italy. Perhaps deservedly underrated is horror-thriller director Dario Argento's *Dracula 3D* (2012), which, despite its sensationalism, Vincent Piturro shows to be a revealing document of contemporary Italian politics—and possibly worthy of more respect than it has received. He argues that the confluence of vampire history, Argento's own career arc, genre study, and recent Italian politics all conspire to add surprising depth to this intriguing, if hokey narrative.

Japan. Jade Lum examines how the film *Moon Child* (2003) uses the fantastic vampire and science fiction dystopias to open spaces for reflecting on gender dynamics within Japan. Through the lens of Japanese pop culture, *Moon Child* is able to push against and reshape hegemonic images of masculinity.

Korea. David John Boyd examines the film *Thirst* (2009) with respect to the *jiangshi* (or *geong si*) vampire tradition, the genre of domestic melodrama, so-called Asian extreme cinema, and even Continental philosophy. As a companion film to *The Wailing* (2017), *Thirst* and vampire films can be seen as expressions of cosmic pessimism.

Mexico. An early film by the now famous director Guillermo del Toro, *Cronos* (1990), set in Mexico City, raises questions about the ethics of immortality. An antiques dealer and his granddaughter discover a medieval device that resembles a scorpion, half clockwork and half organic, which extracts blood and changes its owner into a vampire. Roberto Forns-Broggi raises provocative questions about the device and its many symbolic values.

Morocco and USA. The vampires of Jim Jarmusch's *Only Lovers Left Alive* (2013) epitomize cool in a declining civilization. Both Tangier and Detroit are sites of urban decay that lead to the deaths of a human friend and of the admirable vampire Christopher Marlowe, centuries after he wrote the plays attributed to Shakespeare. As Wendolyn Weber points out, the whole postcolonial world is unworthy of this surviving vampire couple.

New Zealand. *What We Do in the Shadows* (2014) is a vampire film about misfits who are trying to be hip. The comedic tone of the mock-documentary differentiates it from most films about vampire friends or enemies. Charles Hoge locates the film in cinema traditions as well as in the culture of Wellington, North Island.

Serbia. Examining *The She-Butterfly* (*Leptirica*, 1973) and *A Holy Place* (*Sveto mesto*, 1990), directed by Djordje Kadijević, Tatjana Aleksić shows how the dangerous females in both of these Slavic films actually uphold social norms even as they avenge victims of male aggression and privilege.

Sweden. Widely praised as the world's best vampire movie, *Let the Right One In* (*Låt den rätte komme in*, 2008) underwent many changes from the Swedish novel it is based on, about a pedophile and a castrated, transvestite boy vampire who befriends a lonely twelve-year-old who is being bullied at I shows how, in ways different from the novel, Tomas Alfredson's film is a subtle and moody coming-of-age story as well as a tale of revenge, as well as a vampire story that (almost) unqueers its source material.

USA. Spike Lee's *Da Sweet Blood of Jesus* (2014) is a remake of Bill Gunn's *Ganja and Hess* (1973), with significant differences. Cheryl D. Edelson locates both films in the history of Black horror cinema, with attention to museology as a frame of reference for the art collection of Dr. Hess, the later film's lead African American vampire.

USA. *The Transfiguration* (2016) is different from other vampire films, as Cain Miller observes, in that its would-be vampirism functions as a construction of masculinity in response to the intersectional otherness of an oppressed, queer black male.

NOTES

1. Nina Auerbach, *Our Vampires, Ourselves*, University of Chicago Press, 1995.
2. Erik Butler, *Metamorphoses of the Vampire in Literature and Film: Cultural Transformations in Europe, 1732–1933*, Camden House, 2010, page 3; Stacey Abbott, *Celluloid Vampires: Life After Death in the Modern World*, University of Texas Press, 2007, page 3.
3. Jeffrey Weinstock, *Vampire Films: Undead Cinema*, Columbia University Press, 2010, page 17.
4. Bram Stoker, *Dracula*, 1897, edited by Glennis Byron, Broadview Press, 1998, pages 177–78.
5. The scene is, of course, also featured in adaptations of the novel such as Francis Ford Coppola's relatively faithful *Bram Stoker's Dracula* (USA, 1992), and the less faithful Andy Warhol and Paul Morrissey's *Blood for Dracula* (Italy, 1974), where Dracula licks the hymeneal blood of a rape victim off the floor.
6. Paul Barber, *Vampires, Burial, and Death: Folklore and Reality*, Yale University Press, 1988, quoted in its entirety on pages 6–7.
7. *Harlean Miscellany*, London, 1745, part 4, page 358 (cited in the Oxford English Dictionary).
8. Stoker's source was Emily Gerard's "Transylvanian Superstitions," *The Nineteenth Century*, July 1885, volume 18, pages 130–50, which she later incorporated into *The Land Beyond the Forest*, in 1888. Excerpts are reproduced in Appendix C of the Broadview Press *Dracula*, pages 439–50.
9. Barber, cited above, pages 63–64.
10. Stoker, cited above, Chapter 8, page 278. The reference to India may be based on Captain Sir Richard Burton's translation of the Sanskrit word *baital* as "vampire" in his 1870 book *Vikram and the Vampire, or, Tales of Hindu Devilry*, facsimile edition from Hardpress Publishing, no date, pages 38–40; however, the *baital* is not a revenant and does not suck blood. It is a Hindu demon that resembles a bat by hanging upside down by its feet, and it is associated with revenants by its ability to animate dead corpses, but its primary function in the book is analogous to that of Sheherezade in the *Arabian Nights*, as a narrator of tales to King Vikram.
11. Kipling's poem *The Vampire* was inspired by a painting titled *The Vampire*, by Philip Burne-Jones, of an exultant female kneeling over a male victim on a bed. Location of the original painting is not known, but a black-and-white reproduction in an 1897 exhibition catalogue from The New Gallery is held in the Frick Collection. The poem inspired by the painting begins "A fool there was" and narrates that fool's downfall, orchestrated by a seductress who ruins his life. During the following decade the poem with the picture circulated in America on a penny postcard and subsequently inspired the earliest vampire movies, both *The Vampire* in 1913 and *A Fool There Was* in 1915 starring Theda Bara as "The Vamp" and popularizing the idea that a *femme fatale* is a kind of vampire.
12. Stoker, page 278.
13. Rolf Giesen, *The Nosferatu Story: The Seminal Horror Film, Its Predecessors and Its Enduring Legacy*, McFarland, 2019, page 88.
14. Renfield's declaration is in Chapter 11, page 178; the parallel passage is in Deuteronomy 12:23; Van Helsing's comment is in Chapter 24, page 362; Dracula's effusion is late in Chapter 21, page 328.
15. Weinstock, cited above, pages 128–29.
16. James George Frazer, *The New Golden Bough*, edited by Theodor H. Gaster, S.G. Phillips, 1959.

Children of the Night in a Sunburnt Country

Aristocrats and Outback Vampires

GRAEME A. WEND-WALKER

"One cannot imagine a man-made monster or a werewolf," wrote Drake Douglas in 1966, "creating a panic in the garish world of Times Square. [...] Dracula would simply not stir up much of a commotion in the bloodsucking centers of Wall Street or Madison Avenue. These creatures belong," he insisted, "to the dimly lit, foggy back alleys of Victorian London."[1] As Nina Auerbach notes, Douglas's shortsighted grafting of "Stoker's character to Hammer's mythic Victorianland" reflected a broad tendency at the time to reduce vampires to a single, timeless, "weighty archetype, The Vampire."[2] Filmmakers since then have come to imagine all manner of locations for their blood-is-the-life villains and anti-heroes.[3] But if it was difficult at that time to imagine Dracula in the cities of modern America, it is little surprise that few thought to transplant his kind to the geographical antithesis of dark, damp Englishness, the southern hemisphere's "sunburnt country."[4]

This description of the Australian landscape comes, of course, from Dorothea Mackellar's "My Country." The poem—beloved of Australians, second only perhaps to "Waltzing Matilda"—expresses the speaker's love for her natural environment in all its glorious and often fearful majesty. This affection, however, is framed explicitly in contradistinction to the love that others have for England: it locates its reader at first among images of "green and shaded lanes," but only so as to emphatically displace these with the "wide brown land" which owns the stanzas to follow. In addressing itself, in its opening lines, to an outsider who cannot comprehend the speaker's love (as underlined at the end, "All you who have not loved her, / You will not understand"), the poem performs the partially divided sense of identity that was

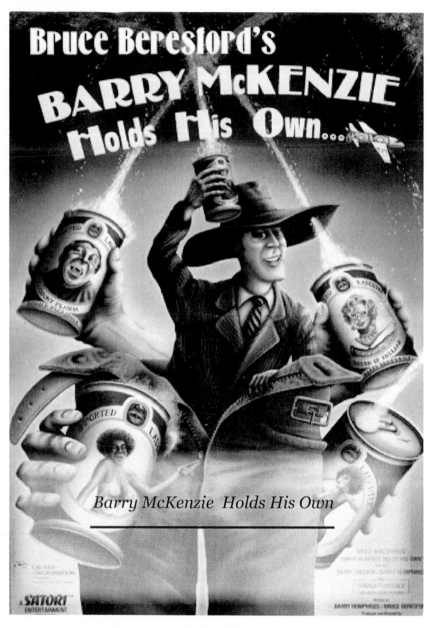

Barry McKenzie Holds His Own (1974). Late in this Australian spoof, vampire Count Erich von Plasma (Donald Pleasance), holding a German pistol, is defeated by Barry McKenzie (Barry Crocker) using an apotropaic made of Foster's beer cans in the shape of a cross, in order to save his aunt (Edna Everage) from captivity (which she thinks is part of her package tour) (Photofest).

characteristic of Australian culture through much of the twentieth century. The implied English reader implicitly positions the speaker's own voice *also* as an outsider's[5]; which is to say, the poem is the gentle rebuke of one who knows herself to be displaced from an English cultural center and who speaks back to that very displacement.[6]

These, then, are the twinned conditions under which the vampire enters Australia, as both a geographical and a cultural alien. Questions, of course, abound: Can the undead "live" in the "Dead Heart"? Do "down under" bats sleep right-side-up? It may, indeed, be difficult to imagine a vampire rousing much terror among inhabitants inured to the notion (as it is often joked) that everything around them can kill them; "Her beauty and her *terror*/The wide brown land for me!" proclaims Mackellar (my emphasis). Dracula is liable to find himself contending not with "soft dim skies" but "[t]he hot gold hush of noon"; he might well find the sunlight of a "pitiless blue sky" more disquieting than all the country's assembled snakes, sharks, and scream-inducing jellyfish.[7] At the same time, the sense of cultural displacement which long haunted Australian writers and artists inevitably meant that vampirism would become figured within—which is to say, would become a way of figuring—the cultural tension between Australia and Europe (and later, the United States). On the one hand, the conventionally marginalized condition of the vampire might stand for Australia's shunning by those who would claim the cultural daylight, and for the sense Australians long endured of their own benightedness. On the other, there is an evident vampirism in the disposition of old, imperial entities to regard this youthful and robust colony merely as something from which to extract material value without regard for the intrinsic value of its people.[8] For Australians, vampirism is at once both utterly alien and entirely familiar.

There have been, to date, six Australian feature films about vampires, and each of these—*Barry McKenzie Holds His Own* (1974), *Thirst* (1979), *Outback Vampires* (1987), *Bloodlust* (1992), *Reign in Darkness* (2002), and *The Caretaker* (2012)—can be seen negotiating in various ways these geographical and cultural tensions.[9] This essay will touch on all of them, but the focus will be on the first four, between which there emerges a peculiar relationship between the vampire genre, Australian film, and the culture that encompasses them.

The first thing to note here is that gothicism is considerably less prevalent in these films than one might expect. In Australia, "gothicism" has often been understood in relationship to the landscape; demonstrating that its terrors run deeper than burrowing funnel-web spiders, the somewhat loose category "Australian Gothic" has tended to locate the country's capacity to unsettle in the tragedies that befell those Europeans who first set out to explore the interior and in the dislocated condition of white people, generally,

in a land that was settled on a false claim to *terra nullius* and which consequently saw the figurative and literal erasure of its native inhabitants. Geoff
Stanton argues that Australian horror films are "rooted in the sturdy disquiet
born of early colonial misgivings":

> Our history was often scripted by pioneers who intended to subdue the land under
> harvests of principle and promise, but instead struck out for death and disaster. In
> fact, from the moment that the British declared Australia "empty," we were all
> headed for trouble. It is in this atmosphere that the Aussie horror movie has thrived
> and grown like bracket creep. It is the sheer space that stalks us, and a profound
> sense of alienation has long simmered in the darker core of our national conscious-
> ness.[10]

Filmmakers have explored this space through such films as *The Cars
That Ate Paris* (1974), *Picnic at Hanging Rock* (1975), *The Last Wave* (1977),
Long Weekend (1978), *Razorback* (1984), and *Wolf Creek* (2005). But vampires
cannot sit comfortably within the space of the Australian Gothic. Horror
arising from tensions with the pre-colonial landscape cannot easily accommodate non-indigenous lore. Anything but the vampire-like *Yara-ma-yha-
who* of Aboriginal mythology necessarily belongs to the colonizers, no matter
how distant its own origins, and must therefore stand against the land, not
in line with it. Dracula cannot make such an easy transition to Australia as
he does from the Carpathian Mountains to London, not just because the climate is different but because the land itself is already so hauntingly *other*. He
might, perhaps, at some point have taken up residence on a fog-shrouded
Tasmanian mountain; but if a distinctively Australian kind of gothicism cannot easily accommodate vampires, neither have Australian makers of vampire
films made much attempt to emulate any conventionally European form of
it. Perhaps due to sunshine's pivotal figuring within both vampire lore and
Australian self-conception, filmmakers have tended rather to embrace this
tension. "[W]hen Australians look for the values that shaped their national
character, they turn to the outback," notes Celeste Lipow MacLeod,[11] and
these filmmakers tend to present the "wide brown land" as Mackellar does,
as a symbol for a growing Australian resistance to the influence of its former
colonizer, as the soul of the country and its people. Almost all of these films
set a significant part of their action in the daylit bush, but unlike the above-
mentioned Australian Gothic films, the bush itself is rarely accorded any
capacity to disturb. This has, in any case, always been difficult to pull off:
"[N]ature fighting back" might seem "really exotic" to "an overseas audience,"
but it "seem[s] a little bit preposterous to an Australian audience. The landscape's very familiar; it doesn't look menacing," concluded *Long Weekend*'s
producer, Richard Brennan.[12] Filmmakers have generally avoided any temptation to see vampires sizzle in the hot Australian sun, and many revise vam-

pire lore to accommodate the setting. In the first three films, they are concerned not with the landscape's haunting of its white settlers but with the haunting of Australian culture by the imperial one looming over it.

The most culturally complex of these, *Barry McKenzie Holds His Own* (1974) emerges from a pivotal time in Australian cultural history and Australian film history in particular, and as the first vampire-themed feature from what was still to many "the Antipodes"—a place defined by its not being "here," by its being opposite to or an inversion of the familiar—its uniquely Australian deployment of the vampire motif sets the stage for much that follows. The vampire in this film does not come to Australia at all; most of the action, in fact, takes place among Australians in Europe, with the film only bookended by Australian scenes. It begins, as it will continue, with self-parody—an announcement from the "Australian Minister for Culture," who has a model of the Sydney Opera House on his desk and a Foster's Lager sign mounted prominently behind it. In the background is heard the distinctively plaintive whine of Australian ravens (colloquially, crows), which evokes for Australians not darkness but—as surely as any visual might—the image of an unrelenting sun beating down outside. The minister speaks warmly of the "Australian cultural renaissance which is sweeping the world," and with which the glories of Egypt, Greece, Italy, and France simply "cannot compare." He strolls to a bookcase on which rest volumes about great Australian artists—Boyd, Drysdale, Nolan—but the one he draws from the shelf is titled *Venomous Toads of Australia*.

Australia became a nation in 1901; Mackellar's poem, with its defiant sense of independence standing against an England it cannot dislodge from the center, was published just seven years later. In 1930, the country's most prominent literary critic, Nettie Palmer, lamented the absence of a strong, homegrown literary tradition:

> Three or four generations have not been enough to allow us to get thoroughly rooted in the soil. Waves of uncertainty sweep over us. Is this continent really our home, or are we just migrants from another civilization, growing wool and piercing the ground for metals, doomed to be dependent for our intellectual and aesthetic nourishment— our books, interpretations of art, theories of the social order, on what is brought to us by every mail from overseas?[13]

This sense of double consciousness reflected a tendency among Australians (one amplified by the English) to believe that Australia simply was not capable of producing art or literature of real cultural value. In 1950, A.A. Phillips named this phenomenon the "cultural Cringe." Part of the problem, Phillips felt, was that Australians were obliged to foreign touchstones: "The Australian writer cannot cease to be English even if he wants to. The nightingale does not sing under Australian skies; but he still sings in the literate Australian mind. It may thus become the symbol which runs naturally to the tip of the writer's pen; but he dare not use it because it has no organic relation with the Australian life he is interpreting." Nightingales, of course, were not the only "creatures of the night" not making music in Australia, and vampires run even less naturally to the page.[14]

Phillips wished for progress in "the art of being unself-consciously ourselves," and great efforts were made to this end in the 1970s through what became known as the "new nationalism," spearheaded in part by culturally attuned Prime Ministers John Gorton (1968–71) and, more emphatically, Gough Whitlam (1972–75) who, though from opposite sides of politics (ostensibly conservative and liberal, respectively)[15] greatly expanded funding for the arts and particularly film. Australian identity was in a state of redress, revision, flux, and renewal, and the establishment by the Gorton Government of the Australian Film Development Corporation in 1968 "as part of a last-ditch effort to rejuvenate the dormant Australian film industry" provided the right conditions for filmmakers to actively explore that double consciousness which had so long plagued Australian artistic production.[16]

The Adventures of Barry McKenzie (1972), written by Barry Humphries and directed by Bruce Beresford, was the first film fully financed by the Australian Film Development Corporation, and one of the first "Ozploitation" films, a subset of the Australian New Wave[17] Its sequel, *Barry McKenzie Holds His Own*, is also, on the surface of it, a broad farce variously lampooning both British and European society and the uncouth blunderings of Australians traveling there. But beneath its delight in vulgarity, the film also, as Pender observes, "vividly dramatises the anxiety and ambivalence inherent in the new nationalism and the post-imperial confusion experienced by Australians at this time."[18] Its use of vampire tropes emblemizes this search, at once deep, strained, and comically anarchic, for a sense of cultural identity. It begins where the previous film left off, with Barry, or Bazza (Barry Crocker), its lantern-jawed hero, dressed in his already old-fashioned 1950s-style double-breasted suit and floppy brown Akubra hat, returning from London to Sydney with his Aunt Edna (played by screenwriter Barry Humphries).[19] While stopped over in France, Aunt Edna is abducted by Eastern European agents and swifted away to Transylvania under directions from their literally vampiric leader, Count von Plasma (Donald Pleasance, who five years later would play Dr. Jack Seward to Frank Langella's vampire in John Badham's 1979 *Dracula*).[20] Plasma believes Edna's presence will help bolster his nation's tourist trade. But his assessment of her value overlooks everything distinctively Australian about her, and he sees only her seeming Englishness (he has mistaken the Australian housewife for the Queen of England). Among the film's multilayered satirical barbs lies the suggestion that people outside of Australia have difficulty locating that country as a nation in its own right, liable to think of it merely as an extension of England, or otherwise failing to distinguish between them at all.[21] Plasma comically misreads Edna's references to her suburban home life (she does not realize she has been abducted and thinks she is on a package tour), and when he realizes his error, she is taken to the cellar to have her blood drained into wine vats. Bazza and his mates eventually rescue her and destroy the Count with the aid of a crucifix made from Foster's beer cans—a gesture of defiance not only to vampires but also to any broader, non-native claims to cultural authority.

Barry Humphries was one of a number of Australian expat artists and intellectuals living in London at the time that he devised the Barry McKenzie films, which grew out of a comic strip he had been writing for the satirical British weekly *Private Eye*. As Tony Moore notes, the McKenzie character is derived from English stereotypes, "a modernization of the 'stage Australian,' a stock character that graced English music hall from the nineteenth century."[22] But Moore, following Pender, also notes "that Humphries had pioneered a reversal of the customary imperial gaze as early as 1963, 'treating the [London] locals as native specimens' and 'types' for the education of Australian audiences."[22] Thus, the beer-swilling, chundering (vomiting) bloke delivering an endless stream of colorfully crass Australian phrases was, on the one hand, both a mockery of certain Australian cultural dispositions and a celebration of them: that the film "celebrated the vulgarity of the Australian idiom," as Pender observes, "was significant because Australians had for so long been taught to regard their idiom, accent, syntax and vocabulary as ugly and inferior."[23] (As Barry enthuses, "[B]ack in Oz now, we've got culture up to our arseholes!") On the other hand, it was a critique of the way Australians were stereotyped abroad (even if the stereotypes were sometimes accurate) and a scathing review of the state of the former empire. Humphries, observes Pender, "poked fun at England as an impoverished country of would-be migrants to Australia, [...] ridicul[ing] the post-imperial realities of English life and the hollow pretences to bygone grandeur."[24] Plasma the vampire reflects this sense of decay, of an increasingly irrelevant aristocracy parasitic on the life of the common people, while simultaneously obliged to a kind of vampiric reciprocity as he, or it becomes dependent for its continued existence on its status as fodder for commerce. Hammer films had by this time shifted popular vampire sensibilities well into what Tim Kane calls the "Erotic Cycle,"[25] but the vampire Humphries and Beresford give us is pointedly Lugosiesque; against the backdrop of Christopher Lee's Dracula, Plasma seems especially stuffy and old-fashioned and pathetic in his need to trade on a more marketable aristocrat than himself. At the end of the film, Barry and Edna are greeted at the airport by Prime Minister Gough Whitlam, playing a cameo as himself:

PRIME MINISTER: Welcome, Barry. Australia is proud of you.
BARRY: Thank you very much, sir.
PRIME MINISTER: Dame Edna. Arise, Dame Edna.

One of Whitlam's first acts as Prime Minister had in fact been to end Australia's participation in the Imperial Honours system (albeit temporarily), so bestowing a "damehood" on Edna was "doubly ironic as he very clearly arrogates the imperial power to himself."[26]

The closing credits sequence restores the viewer to all that is good and uncomplicated in the world. Rolling over an image of the bright Australian countryside, it foregrounds the grave of Col "The Frog" Lucas who, before dying, had come to realize the terrible mistake he had made in forsaking Australia for European culture. His body is now restored to the true earth; the gravesite is not somber, but radiant in repose among golden, soft-rolling hills: in the words of poet Banjo Paterson, "a vision splendid of the sunlit plains extended," the soil as home of the Australian soul.[27]

In his travel book *In a Sunburned Country* (2000), Bill Bryson offers this observation: "One of the oddest things for an outsider to do is watch Australians assessing themselves. [...] They are an extraordinarily self-critical people. You encounter it constantly in newspapers and on television and radio—a nagging conviction that no matter how good things are in Australia, they are bound to be better elsewhere."[28] Paul Theroux saw something similar: that while the "Australian image abroad is one of swaggering confidence and contented good humor [...] in Australia itself there is nagging self-criticism, a constant theme of *What's wrong with us?*"[29] If Barry McKenzie the character embodies that swaggering confidence abroad, *Barry McKenzie* the film reflects, and engages with, the underlying self-doubt. Indeed, many Australians were mortally offended at how the film had characterized them, and "the poor critical reception of the film in Australia had disastrous consequences for director Bruce Beresford who was unable to find work for some time in Australia despite the boom in the Australian film industry."[30] Beresford, of course, would go on to international acclaim with film such as *Crimes of the Heart* (1981), *Tender Mercies* (1983), *Driving Miss Daisy* (1989), *Black Robe* (1991), and *Flint* (2017). Many other Australians were not offended at all: as Beresford puts it, "They thought it was an endorsement of their way of life. And in fact, in a funny kind of way [...] it was."

Thirst (1979), by contrast, is neither particularly swaggering nor self-critical, conveying a sense rather of Australians having grown confident in their cultural identity; another product of the New Wave, it has little in common with *Barry McKenzie*. Many of the narrative points of reference are the same though, with the threat once again coming from a nobility parasitic on ordinary Australians, which here too is represented in the coordinated abduction of an Australian woman to serve the interests of an elite. But where Aunt

Edna was valued only because she was mistaken for royalty, the Brotherhood is interested in Kate Davis only because she actually is a descendent of Countess Elizabeth Báthory—a status she has absolutely no use for or interest in. She is relieved, in fact, when she realizes that her abduction has something to do with her ancestry. "There's a legacy—That's it, isn't it?" she asks, laughing; "Look, you can have it. Please, take it!"

Through the first half of Australia's life as a nation, the identity of its people could barely be extracted from a sense of where they had come from. Among the upper-middle-class, "[n]one wanted to have convict ancestors, and few could be sure that some felon did not perch like a crow in the family tree"; convict ancestry was "a stain to be hidden"[31] even "a source of shame so powerful," as Babette Smith puts it, "that an entire society colluded in a decision not to discuss the subject."[32] The working class, meanwhile, and the large number of Australians descended from Irish transportees, "fostered the ennobling delusion that most Irish convicts had been sent to the Fatal Shore for political offenses,"[33] which is to say, they were not criminals so much as heroes who had resisted the oppressive English and been punished for it. When the convict archives became publicly accessible in 1951, Australians began to recover knowledge of their convict forebears, and by the 1970s convict heritage had become something to celebrate, with family historians "descend[ing] on the archives in droves."[34] Where *Barry McKenzie Holds His Own*, made early in the 70s, is set almost entirely in Europe, with its characters comically embroiled in the absurdities of the upper class, *Thirst*, from the end of the decade, is located wholly in Australia, and the vampire nobility is presented as an unwelcome intrusion entirely out of joint with the sense many Australians were coming to enjoy of their economic and cultural independence.

Kate Davis (Chantal Conouri) is a successful, independent woman running a business from her large, elegant, gated home where she lives with her maid, and where she enjoys visits from her muscular, mustachioed, architect boyfriend, Derek (Rod Mullinar), for sex and champagne by the fireplace. She is drugged and abducted by a secret society of international vampire nobles who want her blood, though in a different sense; their intention is to marry her to a certain Mr. Hodge and thus to see "the two greatest families reunited." (Where Kate reflects confidence in self-made prosperity, Hodge suggests that segment of the Australian populace which still identifies with the nation's former English masters.) Kate is flown by private jet to a sunny, remote airfield from which she is driven by Rolls Royce to the organization's country estate. "Welcome to the Brotherhood, Miss Davis—*Baroness*," she is greeted.

The Montsalvat artist colony outside of Melbourne provides the location, and though the Montsalvat Great Hall and Chapel are sufficiently gothic-inspired to have provided, under the right lighting, an appropriately atmospheric setting for a conventional vampire story, director Rod Hardy eschews any sense of the dim and musty for a sun-drenched relishing in the bright golds and greens of the surrounding Australian bush. As the nature of the Brotherhood is revealed to Kate, and the connection between vampirism and the aristocracy is shown to be more than metaphoric, the freedom of these "vampires" to move in the daylight becomes consonant with cultural superiority. "Vampire! We dislike that word," explains Mrs. Barker, Kate's chief abductor. "The Brotherhood is something far nobler than peasant superstitions have given it credit for. There's nothing supernatural about us, Kate." (They extract blood primarily by means of high-tech machinery, but use prosthetic fangs for ritual events in which a victim's neck is bitten and their blood drawn out.) Mr. Hodge (Max Phipps) steps in to clarify: "We're simply a superior race of people who have, over the centuries, proved that the drinking of the vital human essence confers youth and power. It's the ultimate aristocratic act."

Certain "that the old thirst will not have died out" in her, they are perplexed that she does not find this all wonderfully attractive. The remainder of the film consists in them employing whatever means necessary to induce her to accept what they see as her birthright, convinced that this "thirst" lies dormant in her and needs only to be reawakened. But they never succeed. They drug her and confine her to a dungeon-like room, put blood in her milk cartons, and slip her cappuccinos and baked goods with blood hidden beneath the froth and crusts. They give her hallucinogens so that she believes she is with Derek while Hodge, in fact, is raping her, forcing the union; and they torment her with a staged house-of-horrors ordeal in which doors are hacked at with axes, walls bend and crumble and rooms tilt, blood spurts from a showerhead, and her maid's face melts off.[35] She is driven "to the verge of insanity." Though they imagine at one point that the "conditioning" might have taken, nothing in the end is effective and she is unwilling and unable to accept what they still insist is her destiny.

The problem is that Kate has rather a different understanding of how class works. Not long after arriving at the "farm," she begins asking about the source of the blood that sustains the Brotherhood's 70,000-strong worldwide membership. "This is a farm, Kate, in the fullest sense," explains Barker, gesturing expansively toward the lethargic figures in patients' clothing wandering aimlessly around the sunny grounds; "One of many farms." But Kate remains concerned about these "donors," or "blood cows," as they are later called, particularly after she inadvertently selects a young woman to be her personal source of blood and a dazed young man approaches her to plead with her not to take too much. She presses Dr. Fraser (English actor David Hemmings), the only member of staff who seems genuinely concerned for her wellbeing, but his answer only reveals the ease with which the privileged package exploitation as a false ideal for the masses. As the following dialogue takes place, Kate and Fraser wander among "donors" lounging vacantly by the ornamental pool; elsewhere we see them playing lifeless games of badminton:

> FRASER: "Look around—Everybody's happy here. The farm's a bit like a.... It's a bit like a commune, really. It's all right, Kate. I wouldn't have it any other way."
> KATE: "Are they free to leave?"
> FRASER: "They can't leave."
> KATE: "Why not?"
> FRASER: "It's essential that they stay."

The myopic and self-serving needs of an old aristocratic order, *Thirst* suggests, are simply incompatible with the lives Australians now claim for themselves, and Australians are well beyond being persuaded that their lineage has any relevance. In the end, Kate begs to be admitted to the Brotherhood, but only because Dr. Fraser, seeming to help Kate escape from the farm, betrays her confidence; it seems that he, too, is of an aristocratic lineage, and when he has her trapped to himself, he fits his fangs. The "Brotherhood," it seems, is ultimately only an assemblage of individual greeds, but Kate will plead for entry to save herself from exsanguination.

Outback Vampires (1987), released in the American market as *The Wicked* (1991), is a considerably less serious, lower budget, made-for-TV effort that shares some of the genre-pilfering humor of *Barry McKenzie*. It is another Ozploitation piece; director Colin Eggleston, better known for the exceptional thriller *Long Weekend* (1979) in which the bush turns against a camping couple, seems concerned not so much with resolving vampire conventions to the Australian environment as delighting in the clash between them. The entire story takes places in the Australian countryside, and about half of it outdoors. Two young Aussie blokes, Nick (Richard Morgan) and Bronco (Brett Climo), are driving through the outback to a rodeo, singing cheerfully about "suckin' on a stubby" (consuming beer from a short bottle) and ready to laugh in the face of trouble. (A rubber shark hangs from the rearview mirror with a cigarette dangling from its jaws.) They pick up a female hitchhiker, Lucy, who is handy with a knife. When their car breaks down on a remote road (it has in fact been sabotaged by a hidden spring device), they wander through the bush until they come across three men filling in what appears to be a pit full of human bones. They are directed to the nearby town, or rather to its pub; the town seems to consist otherwise only of a disused railway station and a darkly looming house on the hill. The Lord Mayor, who wears garlic on his chain of office, tells them that there is no mechanic in town but that "Lord Alfred" will assist them. An old black limousine pulls up and "Frau Etzel" drives them to Terminus Manor, which does not seem quite so creepy up close ("Who's the decorator—Mary Poppins?" asks Bronco). The inside, however, is dark, and its suits of armor, skulls, cobwebs, and stuffed bear and bat assure us that we are in a horror movie—of sorts; the doorbell offers a wacky recorded greeting in the voice of Ed Wynn's Mad Hatter.

Sir Alfred Terminus (John Doyle) is our pallid Dracula figure, a mix perhaps of Christopher Lee and Gomez Addams. His wife Agatha (Maggie Blinco) wears a tiara and is also, somehow, Frau Etzel; their son George wears a garish tuxedo, has a disturbing laugh, and grows screaming roses; daughter Samantha (Antonia Murphy) is a shock-haired, ditsy nymphomaniac who was driven insane when beetles burrowed into her brain. A madwoman-in-the-attic type, she eats flies à la Renfield.[36] All speak with plummy, if not specifically English, accents. Nick and Lucy are polite but uncomfortable, while Bronco drinks too much Romanian vodka and breaks Alfred's stuffed vampire bat. They become separated, fall through trapdoors, and must fend off the attentions of Agatha, George, and Samantha, respectively. Strange activities involving coffins, electricity, and neck-biting are observed in the basement. Thunder and lightning make appearances. Eventually they escape but end up back in the house anyway, where they discover a factory in which bodies are processed into pâté. Samantha is humorously decapitated, George is set on fire, Agatha melts for no apparent reason, and our heroes escape once more before destroying Alfred, who has pursued them.

What actually is going on with this family of vampires is difficult to parse. Alfred explains on his guests' arrival that, while he was studying an indigenous culture in the Amazon they had all become infested with "a species of the nematode, [...] worms that live inside human intestines," and that due to the resulting ascariasis, they can now only consume "refined protein." ("Why, Alfred lost half his colon, but my rectum's the shortest now!" explains Agatha, helpfully.) Photos of the family on a boat, in shorts and Hawaiian shirts, possibly confirm this. Agatha later insists on detailing to Bronco her husband's scientific accomplishments in "biorhythmic blueprinting," which remains unexplained, but for which he had evidently been knighted. It is not clear, then, whether they *also* just happen to be hilarious vampires, or whether this is the tale of a brilliant scientist and his family who were tragically turned by worms into fanged people who can float in the air and tap-dance on the ceiling. Old Scot Jock, however (Andy Devine, earlier as one of the bone-buriers), insists the danger is real. The trio, making their daytime escape, declare, "Vampires can't live in sunlight!" and though Alfred had earlier *somewhat* shunned the light streaming through a window, chasing them into the sundrenched bush turns out not to be the obstacle they had imagined. His skin turns an ashy grey, which might be due to the sun; Lucy, taunting him, says his suntan is "ridiculous." But then, he also grows long black fingernails and becomes twenty feet tall, so it is difficult to say. Garlic bounces off of him and a crucifix has no impact: "I've always been an atheist," he says, a joke that makes more sense in a country where declared atheism is commonplace and the church is seen by many as another remnant of British colonialism. Alfred explodes into a shower of black goop when a bone from one of his victims is tossed at him. Worth noting is the occasional presence of a neck-biting crow, a rare (and not fully realized) gesture toward nature's gothic potential and an interesting twist on vampire bats. Bronco turns into one at the end.

To the extent that the film has any social commentary to offer amid its incoherent references to science, H.P. Lovecraft, *Soylent Green* (1973), *The Rocky Horror Picture Show* (1975), *Raiders of the Lost Ark* (1981) (and so on— not to mention the inexplicable appearance of a band which performs in Samantha's bedroom)—it is directed once again to issues of class. Whether their status is derived through blood or knighthood, the elite and aloof Terminus family represents an anachronistic aristocratic privilege that once again feeds on the bodies of a hapless common folk. This is amplified by the town's name: that "Yarralumla" is also the name of the Governor-General's residence in the Australian capital suggests that Sir Alfred is being likened to the Queen's representative in Australia. (The film was at one point called *Prince at the Court of Yarralumla*, making the association more explicit.) A bad taste lingered in many Australian mouths after the 1975 constitutional crisis (commonly known as the Dismissal) in which Prime Minister Gough Whitlam, champion of the cinematic arts, was sacked by the Governor-General—who was able to do so because of a (never before or since used) "reserve power" retained by the Queen's representative after Australia became self-governing. If it is true, as Theroux says, that "[n]o one is more mocking of Australia than the Australians themselves," they nonetheless reserve their greatest judgment for those interloping cultural forces that would subsume the nation to its former colonialist rulers.[37]

And so concludes, it would seem, Australia's cinematic preoccupation with aristocratic European vampires. In *Bloodlust* (1992), the shadow of Europe has been shaken off and the vampires are now entirely homegrown and thus free to become the story's (anti-)heroes. Young male vamp Tad and females Frank and Lear stalk the streets of Melbourne's underground, drinking, taking drugs, having sex, and killing people for kicks. After stealing three million dollars from a casino, they find themselves pursued by gangsters, a pair of corrupt cops, and a band of religious zealots: self-appointed vampire slayers in priest's robes, the leader of whom is actually the most ghoulish person in the film. But the peculiar thing about *Bloodlust*, culturally, is its obsession with the United States.

Australians have long had a love-hate relationship with American culture, which while enormously influential has at times threatened to drown out local voices, and the consequences of this clash are nowhere more apparent than in film. In the 1980s, the new 10BA tax incentives allowed investors a 150 percent tax concession on their investment in film, and this contributed to an explosion of cheap genre movies. Many of these fell "into an American-derivative pattern" (Barry), though "attempts to curry to the American market were often silly" (Brennan) and "made no sense culturally."[38] Some critics came to see genre films as "exclusively American."[39] The strain between these forces is strongly evident in *Bloodlust*, a low-budget film made after 10BA had been scaled back and government agencies, now grown wary of genre films, were less willing to provide funding. As George Miller explains, "It's much harder for a funding body to say, 'Here, we're giving taxpayers' money to genre movies'—because they're seen as imported films, not our culture." *Bloodlust*, which is clearly derivative, among other things, of Kathryn Bigelow's *Near Dark* (1987), does not seem to be clear as to which culture it is speaking from or to. One of the cops has, for no apparent reason, a (truly egregious) American accent, and the other makes half-hearted attempts at one. They drink Budweiser in their patrol car. When the leader of the zealots reappears at the end as a TV evangelist, he too has acquired this accent. Perhaps it means something that it is only the bad guys who are directly identified with America, but even Tad, while salivating over his gun collection (an American-feeling moment in itself), pronounces "Python" in the American manner (paɪ·θɑn, rather than paɪ-θən), and all of the bands contributing to the soundtrack are American, a lost opportunity given the vibrancy of the Melbourne music scene. There are a few gestures toward gothicism (an unoriginal use of Bach's Toccata and Fugue in D Minor), and though characters sometimes speak as if daylight were an issue, the film also seems confused on this point; the final act of the story moves, once again, to a rural farm in the daytime, where the various parties collide in a shoot-out.

In *The Caretaker* (2012), with the exception of a brief scene in a hospital, the entire story is located at a rural homestead upon which a number of unlikeable people converge. There is the romantically troubled couple who travel to the countryside to engage, apparently, in an uncommitted rehashing of Eggleston's *Long Weekend* (1978); the misogynist who, picking up another of that film's themes, come to a nearby pub to rouse the anger of disaffected men; and a doctor who has driven out to see a patient, the mother of Lester, the unnecessarily American caretaker of the property.[40] Vampirism is sweeping the country and it turns out to be mosquito-borne. Vampires do smoke and burn in the daylight here; they are, more or less, zombies that come out at night, and Lester has his stricken mother locked in her room (another madwoman-in-the-attic). The doctor, we discover, had already been bitten by the time he left the hospital and, as his transformation comes on and the nights find our cast holed up against growing waves of attacks (see *Night of the Living Dead* [1968]), he makes them a deal: If they will protect him from their kind during the day, he will protect them from his kind at night (*Blade* is also an influence here). Though the film is short on cultural metaphors, it is notable for its stunning cinematography of the natural environment, and particularly of the sky around dawn and dusk, though it is difficult to tell whether the influence here is earlier Australian films or the American *Near Dark* (1987)—from which *The Caretaker* also takes its driving-through-the-country-at-twilight opening sequence and scenes in which a newly-turned vampire throws up regular food, is shot in the stomach with a shotgun, and smokes in the sun. While the imagery of the sky and landscape does not serve much narrative purpose, it does locate the film within a now clearly established tradition: put vampires in the bush and bring this setting visually to the fore while suppressing its own capacity (gothic or otherwise) to disturb, so that it functions primarily to represent and reaffirm the story's sense of its own distinct Australianness. It is a tradition shaped in part by the demands of funding bodies which, striving "to foster a positive sense of national identity,"[41] expect the films they fund (as Phillip Adams puts it) to "smell 'eucalyptic.'" But it is a formula that by now seems drained of blood.

Reign in Darkness (2002) draws its inspiration—heavily—from *Blade* (1998) and *The Matrix* (1999). A biological engineer, who believes he is working on a cure for HIV, is accidentally infected with a virus. He discovers that the virus was created by a "Council" comprised of "the last of the pureblood vampires." When they send a bounty hunter after him, he decides that he will need to wear a special Kevlar vest and a long, black leather coat, and that he needs to acquire a lot of guns. Any sign of Australianness is intentionally erased, and almost everyone in the film puts on an American accent. (The remainder have British ones.)

But as frustrating (and sometimes embarrassing) as the Americanizing of Australian films can be, there are good reasons why producers of genre films have kept an eye on the international market. With the cultural policy underpinning film funding having "largely written off horror and other genres as debased production without cultural resonance and as an affront to 'quality' Australian cinema," genre filmmakers have had to rethink what constitutes success.[42] Because many Australian horror films "are produced on lean—indeed, at times very low—budgets," they are often able to "recoup production budgets—some from presales alone"; "a low-budget horror title can be released straight-to-DVD, marketed online and still make returns," and even "perform strongly in worldwide markets."[43] This has contributed to "non-culturally specific horror films compris[ing] the largest proportion of local horror output—titles without a distinctly Australian identity in the marketplace."[44] This raises questions about how such films should be identified culturally. Mark

ANNA KATE BURGESS   CLINT DOWDELL   COLIN MACPHERSON   LEE MASON   MARK WHITE

What happens when the thing you fear most is all that can save you?

the
CARETAKER

BEST FEATURE
STIFF
2012

REVELATION
PERTH
FILM FESTIVAL
2012

BEST FEATURE
DCIFF
2012

The Caretaker (2012). A group of humans in a farmhouse in Australia, under siege by vampires, hires the newly turned, formerly Dr. Grainger (Mark White), to protect them each night. At the end the farmer survives but two humans who have been turned commit vampire suicide by deliberately exposing themselves to the intense outback sunlight.

David Ryan notes that, "as the Australian film industry becomes increasingly integrated into a global audiovisual sector, what constitutes Australian content continues to blur."[45] Is a film "Australian" because of the writer's or director's or actors' nationalities, or because of the actors' accents? Or is it Australian because of where it is shot? Or because of where the funding comes from? When Australian filmmakers James Wan and Leigh Whannell could not secure funding for their horror film, they took it to the U.S. Subsequently, *Saw* (2004) and its sequels became one of the most successful horror franchises ever.[46] But does it still count as Australian?

On this note, one more film ought to be mentioned. *Daybreakers* (2009) is a big-budget film ($20 million, according to IMDb); it is written and directed by Australians (Peter and Michael Spierig); it is filmed in Australia with a largely Australian/New Zealander cast; and it secured funding from both Film Finance Corporation Australia and the Queensland state government. But it is set in the United States and Americans Ethan Hawke and Willem Dafoe are its leads; Australians Claudia Karvan and Isabel Lucas also feature, along with New Zealanders Sam Neill, Michael Dorman, and Jay Laga'aia, among others, but all of them play Americans. Is it, then, an Australian film? If the purpose here were to celebrate Australian filmmaking talent, I would argue that it is. But my purpose has been to examine *culturally* Australian vampire films, and this film erases too much of its cultural identity to be considered in that regard. Even so, one aspect of it warrants attention.

In the world of *Daybreakers*, a plague has seen almost everyone turned into a vampire. Supplies of human blood are dwindling and corporations rush to develop a substitute. Vampires who go too long without blood degenerate into hideous bat-like creatures known as "subsiders." Scientist Edward Dalton, who is sympathetic to the plight of humans, joins with a group of them and discovers that there is a cure for vampirism. Once a person has been cured, it turns out, other vampires will also be cured when they drink from them. The film concludes with the commencement of a chain reaction: as the vampires are now desperately hungry for human blood, those who are turned back into humans are soon fallen upon, producing in effect a snowballing reverse vampirism.

Though its Australianness has been almost entirely expunged, one distinctively Australian feature remains. Much of the action takes place outside of the grim, desaturated city, at the various locations where Dalton holes up with renegade humans, and we find ourselves once more among eucalyptus and under the golden light of the Australian countryside. Sunlight matters to this story not only because a whole society has had to learn to live in shelter from it but also because it is the origin and source of the cure: a vampire's humanity is restored if they burn briefly in the light and are quickly doused with water. "The sun?" Edward asks Lionel "Elvis" Cormac, who discovered the cure by accident. "You're human because of the sun?" It may be the most Australian moment in all the films discussed here.[47]

NOTES

1. Drake Douglas, *Horror!*, Macmillan, 1966, page 10.
2. Nina Auerbach, *Our Vampires, Ourselves*, University of Chicago Press, 1995, page 130.
3. Bram Stoker, *Dracula*, Wordsworth, 1999, page 118. The mad Renfield in *Dracula* is led away "repeating over and over again: 'The blood is the life! the blood is the life!'" For a discussion of the urbanization of vampires in film, see Stacey Abbott, *Celluloid Vampires: Life After Death in the Modern World*, University of Texas Press, 2007, pages 141–94.
4. Dorothea Mackellar, "My Country," *The Witch-Maid and Other Verses*, 1908, J.M. Dent, 1914, page 29.
5. The poem can also be understood as implicating Australians who, deferring to England, disavow their Australian identity.
6. Australians are generally more familiar with the poem's second verse, in which the implied English reader, like their beloved English countryside, fades into the background, making room for those who might comprehend and share the speaker's sentiments.
7. Stoker's own Dracula would not have been particularly put out, though depictions of vampires since Murnau's *Nosferatu* (1922) have overwhelmingly embraced the "killed by sunlight" convention.
8. "Capital is dead labour, that, vampire-like, only lives by sucking living labour, and lives the more, the more labour it sucks," said Karl Marx, employing a symbolism not lost on a culture that has long revered the dignity of labor.
9. Six by my count. I am not classing *Pandemonium* (1987) as a vampire film, though it does includes a vampire character (along with a Dingo Girl, a voodoo zombie, and the genetically engineered sons of Hitler). Nor am I counting the ultra-low-budget *Bloodspit* (2008) which is replete with vampires but which is better read as a film written in the international language of schlock horror. None of this is intended as a judgment of these films, which are in some ways more inventive, entertaining, and capable than certain others discussed here.
10. Geoff Stanton, "Dead Heart: Australian Horror Cinema," *FilmInk*, 31 October 2018.
11. Celeste Lipow MacLeod, *Multiethnic Australia: Its History and Future*, McFarland, 2006, page 59.
12. Richard Brennan, interview, *Not Quite Hollywood: The Wild, Untold Story of Ozploitation*, directed by Mark Hartley, City Films Worldwide, 2008.
13. Quoted in John Barnes, *The Writer in Australia: A Collection of Literary Documents 1856–1964*, Oxford University Press, 1969, page xii.
14. A.A. Phillips, "The Cultural Cringe," *Meanjin*, volume 9, number 4, Summer, 1950, page 302.
15. Stoker, page 17.
16. I am using American terminology here. Note that in Australia, the party actually called the "Liberal Party" corresponds most closely to American conservatism.
17. Anne Pender, "The Mythical Australian: Barry Humphries, Gough Whitlam and 'New Nationalism,'" *Australian Journal of Politics and History*, volume 51, number 1, March 2005, page 72.
18. Ozploitation: a term "denoting 1970s and 1980s commercial genre films including action, road movies, sexploitation, and horror films" made in Australia (Ryan 2). They sometimes (not always) exploit Australianness, amplifying whatever might strike and Australian or an outsider as peculiar.
19. Pender, page 69.
20. Pender, page 134, and Tony Moore, "'What Route Are You Taking?' The Transnational Experience of the Barrie McKenzie Movies," *Continuum: Journal of Media & Cultural Studies*, volume 28, number 5, 2014, page 632.

21. Your author, an Australian living in Texas, is often asked which part of England he is from.

22. Moore quotes Anne Pender, *One Man Show: The Stages of Barry Humphries*, ABC-HarperCollins, 2010, page 123.

23. Pender, *One Man Show*, page 123.

24. Pender, *One Man Show*, page 72.

25. Tim Kane, *The Changing Vampire of Film and Television: A Critical Study of the Growth of a Genre*, McFarland, 2006, page 43.

26. Pender, "Mythical Australian" page 68.

27. The line is from "Clancy of the Overflow."

28. Bill Bryson, *In a Sunburned Country*, Broadway 2001, page 127.

29. Paul Theroux, *The Happy Isles of Oceania: Paddling the Pacific*, Mariner, 2006, page 44.

30. Pender, "Mythical Australian," page 75.

31. Robert Hughes, *The Fatal Shore*, Knopf, 1987, page 158.

32. Babette Smith, *Australia's Birthstain: The Startling Legacy of the Convict Era*, Allen and Unwin, 2008, 6.

33. Hughes, page 195.

34. Smith, page 4.

35. This sequence was created in response to producer Antony I. Ginnane's advice to the director: "I want you to know, right up front, this is being made for the drive-in set" (Hardy).

36. Stoker, page 97.

37. Theroux, page 36.

38. Uri Windt, interview, *Not Quite Hollywood: The Wild, Untold Story of OZploitation!*, directed by Mark Hartley (City Films Worldwide, 2008).

39. Vincent Monton, interview, *Not Quite Hollywood: The Wild, Untold Story of OZploitation!*, directed by Mark Hartley, City Films Worldwide, 2008.

40. Actor Colin MacPherson is Canadian, but the filmmakers were likely counting on Australian audiences to read him as American.

41. Mark David Ryan, "Whither Culture? Australian Horror Films and the Limitations of Cultural Policy," *Media International Australia*, volume 133, number 1, 2009, page 5.

42. Ryan, page 5.

43. Ryan, page 4.

44. Ryan, page 5.

45. Ryan, page 5.

46. *Saw* is the second most successful horror franchise, after *Alien* (IMDb).

47. A new film, *In the Blood*, has been in the works for some years, but has been held up by financing issues (Cocks). It is set in "a remote farmstead" in "a post-apocalyptic 'world'" and will film in the desert regions of northern South Australia (Bawden).

A Monstrous Showing

Movement and Deformed Discourse in Guy Maddin's Vampire Ballet Film Dracula: Pages from a Virgin's Diary

Lorna Hutchison

"...and did you see with my eyes and know with my knowledge, you would perhaps better understand."
—Count Dracula to Jonathan Harker[1]

"Monsters are used as a necessary corrective to the vanity of human intellect, to critique human institutions, ideas and reality. They remind us that our truth is not necessarily the truth."
—David Williams[2]

"Bad Dreams" is the screen title of the first scene, set in 1897 on the east coast of England, in cult favorite director Guy Maddin's *Dracula: Pages from a Virgin's Diary* (2002).[3] In Maddin's typical silent film-evoking style (black and white with the exception of tinted color, no audible dialogue, intertitles, a particular fetishized, weighty *pathos*), Lucy Westenra is indeed having what she believes is a very bad dream. Hovering above the tides of England's east coast, Lucy appears to fly while yet still asleep. On her back, her arms thrown above her head, she is the gothic victim, prostrate and vulnerable. Her throat, arms, and upper chest rise, pale and bare, above the edge of her Hellenistically-draped gown; sacrifice incarnate, all for the purposes of nourishing the monster's appetite and dastardly schemes. Suddenly, Lucy's eyes spring open: she is awake and aware of the nightmarish net in which she has been caught. Dracula's face appears, visible through the missing slats of the coffin that holds him, there, on the cursed ship that has brought him to England's fertile

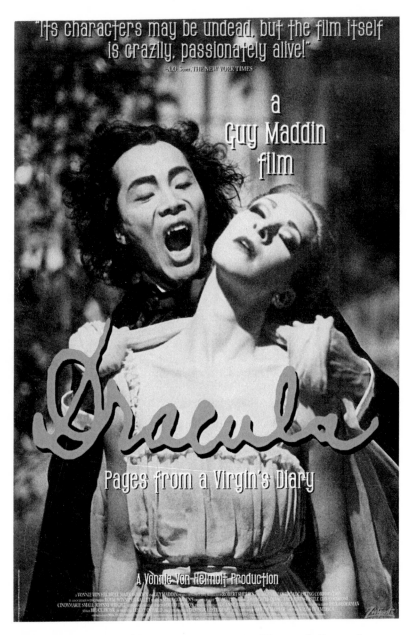

Dracula: Pages from a Virgin's Diary (2003). The film is a ballet performance-adaptation of the novel, choreographed for the screen, silent but for the music, with intertitles like an old movie in black and white—except for the blood, which is, of course, red. The opening credits show the word "Immigrants!!" while blood seeps westward across a map of Europe.

Dracula: Pages from a Virgin's Diary (2003). In this scene from the silent ballet film version of *Dracula*, Lucy (danced by Tara Birtwhistle) expresses delirious pleasure over just having been bitten by Dracula (Zhang Wei-Qiang), who is behind her, leaving her to her three outmatched suitors.

shores. Hemp ropes and the shadow of a thick chain crisscross the image of Dracula's ethereally-perfect face, shapes mimicked a moment later when we see Lucy's twisted sheets. She writhes in her bed, unable to escape the doom that awaits her.

From Renfield's cockroaches, their swollen abdomens wriggling in a bid for freedom, to the wispy tendrils of Lucy's bed canopy that, blowing in the wind, taunt and beckon her to open the door to the monster, all of the movement in this, the film's dreamscape opening, leads the narrative to the unique form and language Maddin's cinematic *Dracula* expresses through the sign of the monster and dance. *Dracula: Pages from a Virgin's Diary* is a film of a ballet. It's a *ballet-film*, and thus is its own particular composite creature. One has only to compare an image from the ballet of *Dracula* with a still from the feature film to see that, while each is artistically elegant, Maddin's style, which is like looking at the world through a bewitched kaleidoscope, is its own thing. Performed by Canada's Royal Winnipeg Ballet, the dancer-actors simulate flight and depict monstrous shape-shifting, sexual cannibalism, and infinite duality through movement.[4] The film becomes wonderfully gruesome, playful, in motion and unfixed, deformed discourse about film and dance and the monstrous act of *showing* in all its confounding glory.

Dracula: Pages from a Virgin's Diary (2003). Zhang Wei-Qiang, the Chinese-Canadian dancer playing Dracula, enters unfazed by the image of Jesus. Opposition of the divine with the profane, sacred with the unconsecrated, *et voilà*, the grotesque. But there is nothing simplistic about Maddin's monstrous. His is a sophisticated and appropriately confounding *tour de force* of monstrous iconography in motion (Photofest).

Before the age of cinema, depictions of monsters appearing in literature and visual art were almost always marked by motion. Grünewald's *The Temptation of St. Anthony* (1512–1516), a favorite among theorists of the grotesque, or the 16th-century drawing of *A Group of Figures Taking Part in a Bacchanal, or a Witches' Sabbath,* and the vivid *A Triton Blowing on a Conch*—all create discomfort in viewers not just for the fantastical creatures featured there, but because of the implied movement that is a part of their pictorial enterprise. Even Henry Fuseli's well-known painting *The Nightmare* is no still depiction of a slumbering woman. Rather, the drama of the sleeper's arched form, the draping of her gown, and the white-eyed madness of the black horse emerging from the shadows render a sense of movement akin to the angst-laden reverberations of the nightmares that, presumably, haunt us all. Animation, even its suggestion, elevates our response in primordial ways. As motion pictures were just gaining their legs, Stoker fashioned a monster whose movement aesthetically transcends the written word. Consider, for example, Jonathan Harker's first sighting of Count Dracula not as the human he feigns to be but, rather, the unnatural monster whose locomotion resembles that of a lizard:

What I saw was the Count's head coming out from the window. I did not see the face, but I knew the man by the neck and the movement of his back and arms. In any case I could not mistake the hands which I had had some many opportunities of studying. I was at first interested and somewhat amused, for it is wonderful how small a matter will interest and amuse a man when he is a prisoner. But my very feelings changed to repulsion and terror when I saw the whole man slowly emerge from the window and begin to crawl down the castle wall over the dreadful abyss, *face down* with his cloak spreading around him like great wings. At first I could not believe my eyes. I thought it was some trick of the moonlight, some weird effect of shadow, but I kept looking, and it could be no delusion. I saw the fingers and toes grasp the corners of the stones, worn clear of the mortar by the stress of years, and by thus using every projection and inequality move downwards with considerable speed, just as a lizard moves along a wall.[5]

In part, Stoker's genius with the monstrous and its function of *showing* is in opposition to the mundane, the fixed, here the study of Dracula's hand juxtaposed with the chillingly unfamiliar: the same hands now in motion in decidedly non-human ways.

On celluloid, the medium of moving images, the vampire first appears in 1922, with F.W. Murnau's *Nosferatu: Eine Symphonie des Grauens (Nosferatu: A Symphony of Horror)*. But with director Guy Maddin's 2002 film of Mark Godden's Royal Winnipeg Ballet production, the undertaking assumes new profundity in the way Maddin renders the monstrous (the extraordinary, the marvelous), already preoccupied with its role in the symbolic *showing* of the limitations of human understanding, through dance. Maddin's "aesthetic production" of the monster is not just a ballet of Dracula, it's a *film* of a ballet of Dracula. Part of my task, therefore, becomes the unpacking of the sign of the monster in a medium—a monster-ballet-motion picture—that is also a strangely misshapen being.

Maddin does not just depict duality through the monster, Dracula, who is, of course, a hybrid being. Rather, his is a film that is *also* a ballet: the film becomes, therefore, in and of itself, a composite creature. It's a curious blend for the medium of film, perhaps especially because it is so clearly connected and faithful to Bram Stoker's 1897 novel and its storyline, and firmly establishes itself within the tradition of *Dracula's* numerous cinematic offspring. Even as Maddin tries its mutability and pliability, there's an evident preoccupation with roots. In fact, my argument lies in the *deformation* of the genre Maddin involves himself in and, equally, the illuminating ties that this new language of the monstrous enjoys with a rich repertoire of medieval monsters and teratology, their study.

The medievalist and historian-critic David Williams shows us the medieval function of the monster and the manner by which it reveals the inadequacy of human signifying processes meant to communicate meaning. In his study, *Deformed Discourse: The Function of the Monster in Mediaeval*

Thought and Literature, Williams outlines how human perception of form (such as the body) limits understanding of substance.[6] Williams's taxonomy provides a model through which to read Maddin's combination of film (medium 1) with dance (medium 2) and, equally important, the director's depiction and employment of the *monstrous through* these combined media.

The monstrous is already a composite sign. Dracula stands in a long line of monsters that have, in their medieval origins, the dual function of conveying the human desire to probe form, substance, and existence, as well as a symbolic function of "deformation necessary for human understanding."[7] Maddin probes the limits of the form of film and, like his dancers, to whom Maddin's creation gives particular license, and like the creature at the center of his story, the film takes flight. It transcends, or at least gives its audience an acute awareness of an artistic attempt to ascend, to lift, to *move* and break free from, both literally and figuratively, the confines of the body and its insufficiencies as sign.

Deformed Discourse, Williams's *magnum opus*, reveals how the monstrous has existed at the heart of philosophical and theological inquiry (into knowledge, being, sign and discourse) since the Middle Ages. Williams, who was a mentor of this writer, and for whom this study stands in part as a kind of love letter to a person whose ethics, guidance, and sublime class of intellectual pursuit exist much less commonly today, posits the notion of aesthetic speculation in his study of "the basic concept of nonbeing" and "symbolic representation in the monsters and misshapen fantasies of medieval art and poetry."[8] I have posited elements of this work to serve as a model for this study of the vampire in film. Williams's research on the monstrous symbolic sheds light on Dracula's lineage and the *showing forth* that Guy Maddin's particular treatment of the monster reveals. Rather than representing, the monster *shows forth*. In addition to the definition of "prodigy" and "marvel" that the term comprises, this sense of the inherent possibilities of the visual sign of the monster comes from the word's origins, to show. As Williams writes:

> a critique is created through a certain dismantling of rational and logical concepts in which conventional signs of these concepts are deformed in ways intolerable to logic so as to "show forth" (*monstrare*, as distinguished from *[re]praesentare*).[9]

New to the cinematic canon of the vampire, Maddin's aesthetic speculation on the monstrous is one in which he pairs film with dance: an act if not "intolerable to logic," than intriguing and perplexing, and one that prompts the mind to seek further, maybe somewhere up there in the heights where the dancers appear to fly. While ballets of *Dracula* have been filmed before, there is no other film of a ballet of Stoker's novel; therein lies the distinction.

Now, obviously vampires are not medieval creatures. They also post-date the entry of the term and category of the grotesque (to which the oppositional sign of the monstrous belongs) in the lexicon of critical theory. However, vampires do belong to the ancient tradition of monsters and the intricate and fascinating association between the monstrous and language, which so often reveals, as it does in a study of a monstrous ballet, the ontological.

Taxonomy of the Body Monstrous in Movement

Maddin combines the figure of the monster with a second form of narrative discourse: movement. Dracula shows us what the limits of human rationality cannot, if through his excess (stronger, infinite "life," endless hunger) and embodied paradox (immaterial *and* more solid than any human, walking dead, a male procreator) he defies the wretched limitations of human language. The film's dance brings to us the monster's oppositional aesthetic in a parallel form, and one that is inventive in the vampire film canon. Dancers of the premier company, the Royal Winnipeg Ballet, create tension through movement that seems to defy gravity and the physical limitations of the body. In their excess, their prodigiousness, the bodies of dancers become a kind of deformed symbol.

To demonstrate, we can apply the "aesthetic production"[10] of the monstrous to the scene where Mina Murray (played by Royal Winnipeg Ballet dancer CindyMarie Small) dances with her fiancé Jonathan Harker (Royal Winnipeg Ballet dancer Johnny Wright) at the convent to which Harker has just escaped from the vampiresses at the Count's castle. His recovery leads to a meeting with his fiancée in the convent's idyllic garden in what very much resembles a courting ritual. Conventions abound: trees, flowers (are those actually pussywillows?) frame the couple in their pastoral environment via Maddin's clever cinematographic style. White stone benches and a hedge in the background provide the atmosphere of a medieval bower.

Viewers of this surreal spectacle—human bodies seemingly superhuman, weightless, in flight—cannot but "call into question the adequacy of the intellectual concept of the thing in relation to its ontological reality."[11] Is Mina what she appears to be by virtue of what is signified by her appearance alone? There is a discomfiting duality to the dance that flies in the face of societal convention and civilized restraint. Virtuous Mina's prim white dress, hair brushed and pulled into conformity, the austere and chaste convent environment: these elements are "deformed" by her dance and thus transcend their symbolic meaning. The function of the monstrous sign—the monstrous showing of seemingly preternatural bodies in movement—has been accomplished.

Ballet, moreover, is a form of contradiction. In *Apollo's Angels: A History of Ballet*, dancer and ballet historian Jennifer Homans describes the art as both rigidly confined to the most extreme rules of law and precision, and also a realm of emotion. "Above all," she writes, "there was the exhilarating sense of liberation that came when everything worked. If the coordination and musicality, muscular impulse and timing were exactly right, the body would take over. I could let go. But with dancing, letting go meant everything: mind, body, soul. This is why, I think, so many dancers describe ballet, for all its rules and limits, as an escape from the self. Being free."[12] Ballet, therefore, is akin to the doubled forms (paradox, contradiction) of the monstrous and the grotesque. Through the tight control of the body, the body transcends its own form and meaning arises.

In the convent garden, Mina makes an appeal to Jonathan's loyalty and love; he allows her to read his diary chronicling his misadventures with the vampiresses. Mina reads the scandalous narrative, is conciliatory toward her fiancé. Together, they glide across the courtyard in perfect unison, balanced, light-footed, and elegant. Their timing and precision evokes four hundred years of ballet, of civilized art and reason. All is movement in the name of order. But traditional ballet positions easily recognizable are suddenly juxtaposed with sexual movements that break from the classic (ballet) lexicon and conjure the presence of the monster. Their dance narrates a story rife with norms put to the test.

Cannibalism and the Vagina Dentata

Dracula has contaminated order. Mina's impulse, now that she has read about her fiancé's sexual urges awakened by the vampiresses, is to shift to meet those urges. *Look,* look, she seems to say, pointing to her love's diary, *you've written forthrightly about what you conceal in the light of day.* An inversion takes place between the site of the head (governance by reason, where the mouth reigns, which separates humans from beasts, and self from other), and the lower body. Mina first places her hands on the fabric covering her breasts, offering herself to Jonathan, but the inversion is underway and will soon be complete. They dance, and Maddin interposes a beautiful bird's eye view of the couple as Jonathan lifts Mina to the skies, as though we are a divine presence looking down on the sanctified couple.

Now Mina goes farther, or rather, perhaps, the contamination spreads. Spurred on by what she has just read, Mina flouts convention and, in middle of their courtship, kneels in front of Harker. With a nod toward his diary, she begins to unbuckle his pants. Jonathan writhes, losing momentary control to the sexual movements that overtake him, movements that this author can say with certainty she's never seen in a classical ballet. It is a fascinating transgression and one certainly suggestive of the medieval sign of the *vagina dentata*, the "devouring female sex."[13] In this iconography, mouth and vagina are equated, and a sexual cannibalism[14] evoked: "The figure of the *vagina dentata* is the most overt identification of sex with eating, eating with sex, in which both acts, fundamental to life itself, become life's destruction."[15] Sexual cannibalism is most à propos for the movie's monster, Dracula, and the consistent—in Maddin's film but also throughout the oeuvre of the vampire—amalgamation of the vampire's bite with sex. And it is the more so as it advances the notion of the vampire's profane procreative design, which I discuss further below with its relationship to the historical, shapeshifting monster. If we return to the agitated couple, they stand near a looming doorway that leads to the interior of the convent. Maddin replicates this O'Keeffean-shaped entranceway, an avocado-form resembling that of a vagina, inside the convent. Moments from now, it will become the site of Dracula's apparition and portal to the monster's replacement of Jonathan.

And, of course, Maddin's ballet is not on stage; it's on film. Thus, just as we see the aerial view of the lift toward the sky's heights in the young couple's *pas de deux*, a lift that would not be visible from the same perspective were we in the audience sitting horizontal to the stage, we are treated to the elastic narrative limits of Maddin's film. Mina and Jonathan's movement become the monstrous sign: their dance contradicts and confounds the conventions of civilized society and pre-marriage rules that are otherwise on display everywhere (for example, through the couple's physical attire and in the convent's garden). The conventions and rules are static, limited; the pair, in movement, are therefore greater than their physical embodiment. Mina's movements, evocative of the *vagina dentata* symbolism and what she will do to Jonathan if her role as potential vampire is completed, given the ambivalence of human existence. Maddin's film *shows forth* Mina in her monster-tainted and thus liminal state, her conflicted movements, the betrayal of her human body's needs in contrast to the austerity imposed by social oppression. In this scene with Jonathan there is no speech, no standard movements by actors, only sublime dance.

Here, as elsewhere the dancers moving through Maddin's composite medium generate, I believe, an acute sense of our limitations of understanding with conventional signifiers. In this dance-film that centers on the monstrous sign exists something lofty; in and through it occur the strange, marvelous, and bizarre. Perhaps the difference between representation (to display in a secondary manner, to stand in place of, mimesis) and *showing forth* become clear: we are put in touch with the very nature of being despite the unfamiliarity of this particular moving "aesthetic production" and its monstrous apparition.

Shape-Shifters

In the scene where Mina and Jonathan dance in the garden and, simi-larly, Lucy's dance (wherein she shows she is neither in control of herself or her newly bold sexuality), Dracula operates through his targeted victims. In each, something of the *inadequacy* of the representation of the characters' being—that which is portrayed through appearance and location—becomes visible. Typically a form of movement, that of displacement, occurs with the threat of the monster in historical narratives. For example, in the oft pictorially-represented story of St. George, as a young woman is displaced to the monster's lair, offered in sacrifice by the town's officials in order to appease the dragon, as the hero commissioned with its slaying is subsequently dis-placed. But Maddin employs another form of movement, one in line with both the vampire and the taxonomy of the monster: shape-shifting.

Shape-shifters, Williams outlines, are "human beings who, by their own power or that of another, change their entire appearance by adopting the body of a foreign creature...."[16] The medieval scholar traces the phenomenon of shape-shifting, called lycanthropy, to Apollo Lycaeus[17] and Augustine's account in *City of God*,[18] wherein Apollo Lycaeus relates to the metamorphosis of men into wolves.[19] Furthermore, there is a connection between Apollo Lycaeus and cannibalism.[20] Maddin's film depicts Lucy biting one of her suit-ors. And Dracula, of course, once human as was Lucy, feeds on members of his former human race.

The association between the origins of lycanthropy in the figure of Apollo Lycaeus[21] and the popular vampire, Dracula, become clear through research of the literature, Roman and Greek sculpture, as well as Stoker's por-trayal of Dracula as a kind of lord of the wolves. In the novel, Jonathan Harker describes his terrifying arrival at the edges of the Count's realm with nothing but the flimsy walls of the calèche between him and the riotous creatures of the night:

> All at once the wolves began to howl as though the moonlight had had some peculiar effect on them. The horses jumped about and reared, and looked helplessly round with eyes that rolled in a way painful to see. But the living ring of terror encom-passed them on every side, and they had perforce to remain within it. I called to the coachman [Count Dracula] to come....
> How he came there, I know not, but I heard his voice raised in a tone of imperious command, and looking towards the sound, saw him stand in the roadway. As he swept his long arms, as though brushing aside some impalpable obstacle, the wolves fell back and back further still.[22]

Dracula becomes aligned with the wolf-god worship associated with Apollo Lycaeus. In Maddin's version, another link to the wolf, lycanthropy, and the ballet dancers comes to light if we examine the early beliefs concerning "wind-wolves" and Apollo Lycaeus, which Daniel E. Gershenson outlines in *Apollo the Wolf-God*.[23] While a closer look at this subject supersedes the scope of this essay, the intriguing parallels between wind-wolves, Dracula as wolf-god, the concept of wind as *inspiration*,[24] and the airborne dancers in Maddin's film—a film that has a central conceit of flight and weightlessness—merits mention, nevertheless.

Maddin's combination of flight and shape-shifting, and the aesthetic and metaphorical duality of each in the director's hands, confounds the audience and its ability to read and decipher sign. As we watch Dracula (Zhang Wei-Qiang) shape-shift into a bat, the unreliability of form, so meticulously recorded in the taxonomy of the monster in the Middle Ages, materializes and warns us of danger. Behold the treacherous trickery of form (signifier) that the film seems to proclaim, lest we be so foolish as to equate it with identity and find there some reassurance: "The monstrosity of the shape-shifter is inherent in the very concept of metamorphosis and transformation. It suggests, terrifyingly, that the boundaries of natural form are insecure, that it is somehow possible for a self to slip out of the protective clothing that declares its identity and become trapped in a shape that misidentifies and misrepresents it."[25]

Maddin's Dracula heralds anew the conundrum of Stoker's figure. We cannot reconcile the philosophical suggestion that a man's "advanced" learning, a life commitment to knowledge and *raising* of oneself—a kind of metaphor for human flight—could result in the weighty darkness and extinction of life that Dracula represents. But this is so in Stoker's novel, where Dracula's existence as a human being was marked with his consistent efforts to attain, in the span of his human lifetime, the heights of knowledge and science. Professor Van Helsing tells Dr. Seward (as recorded in Dr. Seward's diary) that Dracula reached uncommon heights of human accomplishment, thereby raising himself above the majority of his peers: "Soldier, statesman, and alchemist—which latter was the highest development of the science knowledge of his time. He had a mighty brain, a learning beyond compare, and a heart that knew no fear and no remorse."[26] In Maddin's version of the story, the first of lycanthropic transformations—shape-shifting—is that of a (former) human, Count Dracula, into a bat.[27] Lucy has just been bitten a third and final time by Dracula. Too late, Professor Van Helsing (David Moroni) enters the room; spying movement from the bed, he watches in horror as Dracula rises from next to Lucy's unconscious form. The Count is formidable: he wears a large black cape the lining of which has been tinted in brilliant red. Dracula moves swiftly in a half circle around the doctor and, transforming suddenly into a bat, takes flight.

Both the shape-shifting and almost superhuman agility of dancer Wei-Qiang's accentuate a feeling that faith in our "literacy" to "read" in any way conventional the signs that make up this scene will only lead to deception. We're in the realm of the monstrous where muddled perception could lead to both invention and insight. And as if the uncanniness of lycanthropy and Dracula's (Wei-Qiang's) movement isn't enough to enlighten, the history of the monster tells us that shape-shifters reproduce. In the theory of the grotesque, repetition beyond what the mind can make sense of engenders the uncanny, the monstrous. If we consider the concept of human reproduction as an act or achievement that typically lies within the "natural" domain of the human female species including, of course, human females, and thereby exists in the positive domain of legitimate creation, Dracula's reproductive enterprise stands as a grotesque deviance of a natural order. His is a blasphemous act. It brings into existence even as it destroys. In a *pas de deux*, Dracula holds Mina in an extended pose, groin to groin. He dominates her, both by carrying Mina's weight in this position, and by the physical display of their bodies: he stands straight, she arches backward, allowing him to reign over her abdomen, which houses her reproductive organs. Dracula lays her on the top of a wooden coffin, a clear expression of the sexual act that is about to take place, and the monstrous inversion of mouth and genitalia (biting as an act akin to sexual union) is established.

There is another element of the monstrous here, however: procreation through death. Their bed is a coffin. In Mina, Dracula has chosen his queen. Again, if we return to the novel and the roots of the Dracula figure, we see a continuous line between medieval iconography and Stoker's wondrous addition, all leading in a lineage worthy of the Count's noble ancestry to Maddin's own *showing forth*. The novel's Dr. Seward relates Van Helsing's discoveries and deductions concerning Dracula, the vampire who will reproduce, colonize, engender a new order: "But he is growing, and some things that were childish at the first are now of man's stature. He is experimenting, and doing it well. And if it had not been that we have crossed his path he would be yet— he may be yet if we fail—the father or furtherer of a new order of beings, whose road must lead through Death, not Life."[28] The goal of the vampire's procreative abilities and colonizing schemes is to dominate and annihilate human existence. Each of these plural concepts around flight and reproduction seem, through the dancers, to sprout wings and visually take flight. Throughout Maddin's filmed ballet, the audience sees actors—not special effects, but actors—who seem to defy gravity. Solely through their prowess as artists and athletes, they sustain the tension of the monstrous aesthetic through their flight-simulating acrobatic performance. "Today this Vampire is limit to the powers of man, and till sunset he may not change," says Van Helsing to Dr. Seward.[29] But as Dracula sets his sight on seducing Mina, and the dancers, in Maddin's vision, establish their associations with the historical monstrous, the audience can find no reassurance in the possibility of Dracula's limitations. Aesthetic speculation cannot but occur in the audience as Maddin drives movement and film toward a new arrangement.

Mina and the Monster

When Dracula seduces Mina in a *pas de deux*, it clinches the opposition fundamental to the grotesque and the monstrous. It's truly a denouement in doubled motion because of the plot's action that brings the story to a head, and as a result of the dance (its own language) that carries it forward. At the convent, when Mina says goodbye to Jonathan, her courter, a group of nuns— the *corps de ballet*—dance to keep intact a chaste barrier of safety between Mina and the departing Harker. From beneath a large, horizontal sculpture of Jesus Christ, Harker sends a parting look toward his beloved Mina. At this moment, eight nuns position themselves in the form of an arrowhead pointed at Harker. He'll have to get through them to reach Mina in the event that he changes his mind and goes to her, in every sense. Arranged thus, Harker is blocked from our view by the nuns, there where he stands at the nunnery door. Just as Mina seems to succumb to the pull of her courter and runs toward the door, which, like Jonathan, is still screened by the nuns, the *corps de ballet* suddenly moves away and—cue the crash of cymbals—Dracula appears. The Count walks, unfettered by the nuns (who have suddenly disappeared) and unaffected by the icon of the Savior under which he passes. Dracula has come for Mina. Unstoppable, he approaches with assurance godlike and powerful, willing to take every risk to *claim* Mina. Their dance begins and, through it, Maddin's Dracula diverges from other cinematic versions of the story. The high art of classical ballet becomes the vehicle for the grotesque.

Dracula transports Mina to his castle lair. Vampiresses (Sarah Murphy-Dyson, Gail Stefanek, Kerrie Souster) have replaced the nuns. In satiric mockery, they're dressed in saloon-girl versions of white wedding gowns. Opposition remains between what we once saw (black-clad nuns) and the sudden presence, in their absence, of white-clad vampiresses. Contrary to Jonathan's frigid ascetic, Dracula invites, encourages, coaxes the release of Mina's sexuality. Nothing in the film marks more the tension of the paralysis of language that dichotomy creates than the unbridled dance Dracula shares with Mina.

This scene is filmed beautifully; the dancing hypnotic. Each frame of the couple's *pas de deux*, like much of the film, is exquisite, haunting, like an enchanted and elusive silvery fish. These dancers are also actors: their expressiveness filtered through Maddin's vision brings to the fore an element of the grotesque that is in and of itself magical: that of the mundane transposed with the extraordinary. The depiction of this particular juxtaposition almost always brings with it a twofold response in the viewer, a high, as we behold such seemingly unearthly beauty, and a sense of unease, loss, even. Maddin's camera focuses on Mina at the beginning of her *pas de deux* with Dracula; it is a dramatic image. Mina's raven hair and large, dark eyes are fixed on us, on Dracula, her seducer, against a cloud-white background. Only her head and neck appear in this momentary portrait. Though she faces the Count with remarkable presence, awareness, and strength, it is a moment of loss for Mina. Loss of her innocence, and of the simplicity of her view of the world and future. And moments from now, when the vampire claims her with his bite, she will experience a loss of form.

Monstrous Oeuvre

The late David Williams, who I'd like to think would get a kick out of the application of aspects of his oeuvre on the monstrous to Guy Maddin's dancing vampires, despite his pronouncements against the dilution of the monster's power in its overly-prolific use in popular culture.[30] Williams would have appreciated Maddin's beautiful film and would probably have discussed the importance of "locus and position" of the human body in its deviance from natural to monstrous. The particular enactment of dancer Wei-Qiang's monstrous character through movement. Williams states,

> The Antipodes, first mentioned by Cicero, are humans whose monstrosity is consti-tuted by their inverted repetition of our every move and action in a place, the Antipodes, where inversion is the norm. They are our mirror images, functioning only as a kind of pantomime of human existence—exact duplicates of every human body in existence, transported to a realm "below" where, foot to foot, they reenact each human gesture upside down. The monstrosity of the Antipode is that of parody, the location of the human body in a place that is the sphere of travesty itself.[31]

The monstrosity of Wei-Qiang's vampire is, in part, his parodic repetition of the Dracula story.

In *The Vampire Film: Undead Cinema*, Jeffrey Weinstock attributes the longevity of interest in vampires and their proliferation in cinematic genre to two of the figure's principal features: "First, the allure of the vampire is related to his or her power over life and death. Second, the vampire is always already a metaphor.... It is the thing that has died and come back, that has defied humankind's greatest fear. In addition, the vampire in both literature and cinema has come to symbolize power over the lives of others."[32] But while the film critic names metaphor as part of the hold the vampire has over us from version to version in film, he only goes so far as to connect the power of its metaphorical function to the vampire's ability to both attract and repulse its audience, as though Dracula does not belong to a long line of monstrous incarnations in thought, religion, and philosophy. For Weinstock, our fascination can be explained in part because of blood and the symbol of life it stands for:

> [B]lood is never just blood: it is life itself. Thus the vampire's draining of blood symbolizes the exertion of its control over the lives of others. The combination of the two—the powerful force or entity that defies death through draining the life of others—yields a terrifically potent and endlessly malleable combination. The vampire thus is always already a sort of dictator and obsession and addiction that both seduces and repels in equal measure. And when this power dynamic is inserted into a particular cultural context and sexualised, technologised and othered, what emerges is a supercharged, overdetermined surplus of meaning—a symbolic supertext operating on multiple levels simultaneously.[33]

The dynamic Weinstock refers to, where we are simultaneously drawn to and repulsed by the monstrous is, in fact, the grotesque aesthetic. The presence of opposition is a central component to the grotesque and a feature of the push-and-pull reaction it creates in audiences. This may occur as conflicting sentiments, for example, in the beholder's ambivalent response to the gruesome and simultaneously fascinating monster-figure of Dracula, or in the tension and paralysis created when we *partially recognize* a composite creature—for example, the human aspects of the witches in a 16th-century drawing—but are at a loss to reconcile the *unfamiliar* components of the winged, unnatural creatures. And as Weinstock adds, to resolve that binary tension is to collapse the effect of the grotesque. In the longer quotation above, Weinstock aptly describes the duality and its metaphorical power of the vampiric act of defying death and sucking blood. "The combination of the two," he writes, "yields a terrifically potent and endlessly malleable combination."[34] However, although Weinstock recognizes the "endless fascination the vampire exerts"[35] over audiences of the cinema of the vampire, and while he aptly outlines the liminality of Dracula, he does not relate Stoker's monster to its historical predecessors, including in his exploration of vampire as metaphor. And I think that in the very word *monster*, in all its original senses of "marvel," and "prodigy," and "to show forth," lies the important historical connections that hold and *show* something of the depth and originality of Guy Maddin's cinematic incarnation of Stoker's story and central figure.

Moreover, how Dracula stands as metaphor and symbol in Maddin's vampire film-ballet belongs to a long tradition, even as it tests—with its crossing of genres—the boundaries of that tradition. To overlook this, to view Dracula as some impossibly independent creation whose monstrous existence begins in 1897, is to conceal, I believe, Dracula's teratological past, chronicles, and poetics. And as Maddin's film conveys, the monstrous *showing* of these through his own particular composite creation is at once revealing and marvelously confounding.

NOTES

1. Bram Stoker, *Dracula*, 1897, Canterbury Classics, 2012, page 22.
2. Sylvain-Jacques Desjardins, "A Monstrous Task," *McGill Reporter*, interview with David Williams (McGill University, Montréal, 5 Nov. 1998), reporter-archive.mcgill.ca/Rep/r3105/williams.html.
3. Guy Maddin, director, *Dracula: Pages from a Virgin's Diary*, A Vonnie Von Helmolt, Mark Godden and Guy Maddin Production, based on Marc Godden's *Dracula*, adapted and choreographed for Canada's Royal Winnipeg Ballet, Domino Films, 2002.
4. Marc Godden, choreographer, 1998 Royal Winnipeg Ballet Dracula production, staged again in Winnipeg in 2016 for the company's 77th season. This is not the only Dracula ballet, of course. Bram Stoker's story has been the source of inspiration for over twenty ballet interpretations, from the Royal Ballet of Flanders (Antwerp, Belgium, 1991), to Corpus Christi Ballet's recent 2019 version in New Zealand. But Maddin's is the only Dracula ballet film.
5. Stoker, pages 34–35.
6. David Williams, *Deformed Discourse: The Function of the Monster in Mediaeval Thought and Literature*, University of Exeter Press, 1996. I dedicate this essay to Dr. Williams (1939–2015), professor emeritus, mentor, and quite simply the most profound thinker I have had the privilege and pleasure of knowing.
7. Williams, page 3.
8. Williams, page 4.
9. Williams, page 4.
10. Williams, page 5.
11. Williams, page 5.
12. Jennifer Homans, *Apollo's Angels: A History of Ballet* (Random House, 2010), pages xv–xvi.
13. Williams, page 164.
14. Williams, page 165.
15. Williams, page 165.
16. Williams, page 121.
17. Note the various spellings: Apollo Lycaeus, but also, Apollo Lykeios, the latter the more common form for titles of ancient Greek and Roman sculptures of the God.
18. Williams, page 121. There appears to be a typo in Williams's text, which references 17:17 in Augustine's *City of God*. The section referenced refers to, rather, 18:17. Saint Augustine's account is derived from Varro.
19. Saint Augustine, *City of God*, circa 413–426 CE, Random House, 1950, 18:17, page 623.
20. Williams, page 121, and Augustine, 18:17, cited above.
21. "In his name and essence," writes Walter Donlan in his review of Daniel E. Gershenson's monograph, "Apollo Lykeios is the 'wolf-god'" in Walter Donlan, review of *Apollo the Wolf-god* by Daniel E. Gershenson, *JSTOR*, DOI: 10.2307/4351508, page 321. Gershenson illustrates that Apollo, derived from (Indo-European) *apelo-, aplo-, meaning* 'strength" and "power," leads to the configuration of Apollo Lykeios as the powerful master of the wolf (*lukos*) in Gershenson, *Apollo the Wolf-god, Journal of Indo-European Studies*, Monograph No. 8. Institute for the Study of Man (1991).
22. Stoker, pages 14–15.
23. Gershenson, cited above.
24. Inspiration, defined as "the action of blowing on or into; a breathing or infusion into the mind or soul." "Inspiration, n." *OED Online*, Oxford University Press, June 2019.
25. Williams, pages 123–24.
26. Stoker, page 291.
27. In Bram Stoker's *Dracula*, the Count was indeed once human, and an accomplished human at that. "I have studied, over and over again since they came into my hands," writes Professor Van Helsing, "all the papers relating to this monster.... All through there are signs of his advance." Van Helsing concludes that "he was in life a most wonderful man." Already, even in his human existence, Dracula inspired wonder. It is in this passage that Stoker leads

his readers to the origins of Dracula's transformation from human to monster, and thus the Count's ability to shift shape. "Well," Van Helsing relays to Dr. Seward, "in him the brain powers survived the physical death" (291). And ... *voila!* Man becomes monster.

28. Stoker, page 292.
29. Stoker, page 293
30. Desjardins, cited above.
31. Williams, page 119.
32. Jeffrey Weinstock, *The Vampire Film: Undead Cinema*, Wallflower, 2012, pages 128–29.
33. Weinstock, page 129.
34. Weinstock, page 129.
35. Weinstock, page 128.

The Hong Kong Vampire Returns

Nostalgia, Pastiche and Politics in Rigor Mortis

FONTAINE LIEN

When Juno Mak's *Rigor Mortis* (2013) arrived in cinemas, marketing materials and press releases hailed the film as a revival of the Hong Kong *geong si* (hopping vampire) film popular in the 1980s and 1990s.[1] The film tells the familiar supernatural story of a *geong si*, usually created inadvertently by improper burials, but here created deliberately through the use of Taoist dark magic, arising to terrorize a group of unsuspecting victims. As events unfold, the film presents stock characters and familiar tropes from popular *geong si* films, but remixed and adapted for a new millennium.

Instead of rising from a coffin temporarily housed in a traditional Chinese residence during the mourning period, this *geong si* gains its second unnatural life in the cramped confines of a Hong Kong widow's public housing apartment. Auntie Mui (Nina Paw) seems to be the unofficial caretaker of the building's inhabitants, but when her husband (Richard Ng) dies, she is unable to accept the loss, and enlists the occultist Gau's (Chung Fat) help in bringing him back to life. The result is, of course, not quite what she imagined. The stock "Taoist master" character in this film is a street food vendor named Yau (Antony Chan) who seems to spend most of his time shuffling about in a dressing robe, reminiscing about his father's trade as an actual vampire hunter. Chin Siu-ho, star of several vintage vampire films, plays a fictionalized, down-on-his-luck version of himself, who eventually fights and defeats the *geong si* with Yau's help.[2] When Chin moves into the sinister housing complex, apparently to commit suicide, he becomes entangled in the series of events that eventually results in the creation of the *geong si*. A familiar

Rigor Mortis (2013). This Chinese publicity poster features a mask of coins that will help occultist Gau (Chung Fat) to resurrect the dead husband of Auntie Mui (Nina Paw) as a *geong si*, or hopping vampire. The results are not pretty (Photofest).

struggle between the living and the dead, between the natural order of things and supernatural transgression, embroils the entire complex and ushers the characters toward the film's brutal conclusion.

Like the 2014 update to the Wong Fei-hung series *Rise of the Legend*, *Rigor Mortis* capitalizes on nostalgia for an earlier time, but repackages the final product for contemporary sensibilities. Fans of the 1990s Tsui Hark Wong Fei-hung series *Once Upon a Time in China* (starring Jet Li and Vincent Zhao) and the series of horror-comedy films inspired by the success of *Mr. Vampire* (1985) will recall middling production values, choreographed kung fu action at breakneck speed, and plenty of physical comedy, comedic dialogue, and comic misunderstandings. And just as *Rise of the Legend* has updated the legendary martial artist's story with slick production values, a darker visual palette, earnest and grim character interactions, and dramatically heightened and CGI–augmented violence, Mak's film follows in much the same vein. A common observation was that *Ju-on: The Grudge* (2002) director Takashi Shimizu's involvement as a producer influenced the film's emulation of Japanese horror film aesthetics. However, even as *Rigor Mortis* incorporates a slew of tropes from the earlier vampire films, it goes above and beyond to reference (and update) that genre's traditions. In its amalgamation of globalized style with local culture, and in its commitment to a frustratingly ambiguous ending, *Rigor Mortis* is a true hybrid product that is the perfect *geong si* revival for Hong Kong in the twenty-first century.

Rigor Mortis: *Nostalgia Remixed*

Rigor Mortis places itself confidently within the continuity of Hong Kong vampire films, most obviously through its usage of familiar tropes and wholesale citation from the original films. In addition, it reinforces that notion through its casting and its paratextual elements. While the film references the past, it does not do so slavishly, but invents playful new frames for the genre's familiar elements and allegorical scenes that comment on the current status of the vampire film.

In Chinese, *geong si* literally means "stiff corpse," and though film marketers used the term "hopping vampire" to appeal to anglophone audiences,[3] this iconic cinematic creature shares characteristics of both the vampire and the zombie: it rises from a state of death and decay to pursue the living relentlessly, and has sharp fangs with which it can puncture victims' necks. It then either sucks their blood or absorbs their *qi* (life energy), depending on the film. Though the *geong si* became globally recognized through Hong Kong films, Tang Wenyu shows how it is a particularly significant horror symbol for wider Chinese culture by tracing its appearance to the *Classic of Mountains*

Rigor Mortis (2013). **Twin sisters, having been killed during a rape, return as ghosts with long hair, white dresses, spider-like movements, surrounded by a cloud of blood-red tendrils that resemble externalized veins. They are creepier than the film's vampire.**

and Seas (*Shanhaijing*), a folkloric and mythological text with origins as early as the Warring States Period (475–221 BC). The creature was then further popularized by the Qing Dynasty works *What the Master Would Not Discuss* (*Zibuyu*) by Yuan Mei, and *Strange Tales from a Chinese Studio* (*Liaozhai zhiyi*) by Pu Songling, both highly popular and influential collections of strange and fantastic tales.

In addition, Tang highlights the possible folkloric origins of the *geong si* via the alleged Hmong practice of carrying corpses home for burial on poles. In order for the carriers to transport several corpses at once, the corpses are stood upright, both arms stretched out in front and tied parallel to long poles. One carrier shoulders the two poles at the front of the line, while another does so at the back: thus two men are able to transport several corpses together in single file. Because the dead were buried with traditional clothing featuring long billowing sleeves, the poles would be obscured, thus creating an especially frightening and easily misinterpreted scene at night. The conveyance traveling over rough terrain might have caused the corpses to appear as if they were hopping up and down, creating the "hopping vampire" legend. Another theory holds that some corpse-bearers carried their freight on their backs, and would thus be obscured by the corpses' burial gowns. In either case, Tang speculates that these practices might have been the origins of *geong si* lore, which has had enduring relevance in Chinese folklore, literature, and cinema.

In a nod toward *geong si* lore and Chinese cultural tradition, then, *Rigor Mortis* establishes itself within a cinematic genre that caters to local tastes by including a wealth of props, references, and tropes that would be familiar to fans. Yau makes a living selling bowls of glutinous rice, a type of rice that in previous films has been customarily used to inhibit vampirism. Other familiar tools of combat against *geong si* also make an appearance here: the chalk line (used to confine *geong si* or ghosts to a certain area or inside an enclosed space), the peach wood sword (possesses magical powers), yellow paper inscribed with arcane symbols (inhibits *geong si* movement or calls forth other magical powers), the bell (used to control or even command *geong si*), copper coins (inhibit a *geong si*'s power), and the Taoist eight-trigrams board (contains powerful magic).

As with previous films, the vampire is not the only supernatural entity that the protagonists must reckon with—the housing estate is also populated with numerous spirits of children, phantoms from a bygone era that wander the hallways, as well as with the vengeful ghosts of twin sisters who died under tragic circumstances. The twin spirits in this film are a much more malevolent version of the beautiful female ghosts that customarily seduce male protagonists in Chinese supernatural films; here, they bear a greater resemblance to the long-haired wraiths of recent Japanese horror. This adaptation of a popular Chinese ghost film trope will be discussed in the next section of this essay.

The film also references the past in other significant ways. At the very beginning of the film, a melancholy and haunting tune sung by children plays over the film's opening credits. The song comes from a sequence in *Mr. Vampire* where a ghostly bride notices and follows one of the film's protagonists (played by *Rigor Mortis*'s Chin Siu-ho), with plans to seduce him. In minor key, the tune sounds appropriately haunting, especially as it is sung by a children's choir and accompanies grim visual imagery that anticipates death and destruction to come in the film; however, if one listens closely to the lyrics, it becomes apparent that they are simply a poetic description of the original "ghost bride" scene in Mr. Vampire, and entirely unrelated to the events in *Rigor Mortis*.[4] Therefore, this is an act of citation for citation's sake, to proclaim the film's relationship with its predecessors right at the outset of the film.

In its casting as well, the film bears a continuity with the past. Actors Chin Siu-ho, Antony Chan, Chung Fat, and Richard Ng are all veterans of the genre. In fact, director Juno Mak went out of his way to recruit these actors for his film. It was a difficult task given that the actors were either retired, or in physical conditions that did not allow for the usual long shooting hours, a deliberate way to preemptively establish the film's genre authenticity for the first-time director.[5] Before the end credits, the film also acknowledges two pillars of the genre who recently passed away: Lam Ching Ying and Ricky Hui, who both co-starred with Chin in *Mr. Vampire*.

While some of the aforementioned references are straightforward or earnest, *Rigor Mortis* does contain instances where its usage of tropes is more playful than serious. This type of self-referential humor largely replaces the physical and situational slapstick humor that characterize older *geong si* films. This signals that this film, while referencing the past, wishes to establish an identity of its own. Its primary locus of playful reminiscence is Yau, who is the descendant of vampire hunters. As none of his family is alive during the events of the film, all of his inherited tools-in-trade are gathering dust in his cramped apartment. When the time comes for Yau to spring into action, in addition to removing his eight-trigrams board from its decorative place on the wall, he fashions a sword by sharpening his wooden back-scratcher, exchanging a tool associated with elderly men for one associated with Taoist masters. What he does not change, however, is his wardrobe—he battles the *geong si* dressed in a slovenly costume that, by the third act of the film, has become permanently associated with the character: undershirt, boxer shorts, and dressing robe. And yet, when Yau heroically leaps to his near-certain death in order to subdue the *geong si*, his billowing robe does temporarily function as a suitable stand-in for a Taoist master's robes.

In terms of this character's appurtenances, they can be read as collective stand-ins for the *geong si* film's place in popular culture: the tools of the trade were allowed to sit unused and gather dust, but Yau (and the film) gathers them up once more as objects of great significance both for his battle against the *geong si* in the film, and for the revival of the genre in film audiences' consciousness. Though in some of the substitutions the film clearly has a sense of humor, it never uses the tools for outright physical comedy as previous films might have done.

Chin Siu-ho's out-of-work actor character (a version of himself) moves into the dilapidated public housing complex with only a single suitcase and a wooden crate of his belongings. Referencing once again the current status of the vampire film, the suitcase is filled with only a few pieces of clothing packed in haphazard fashion, but also contains three sets of film costumes that are actually from—or referencing explicitly—the real-life Chin's previous films, *Mr. Vampire* and *The Tai-Chi Master* (1993). While Chin the character has very few belongings, these pieces are wrapped delicately in plastic and handled with careful attention. He treats them with reverence as he hangs them up on the wall, but they play no further role in his current life, as the next action he takes is his attempt to commit suicide by hanging himself. This can be read as a particularly acerbic and morbid take on the current status of the *geong si* film, which has lost much of its luster compared to its 1980s and 1990s heyday.

Rigor Mortis *and Recent Japanese Horror*

While *Rigor Mortis* does highlight its own unmistakable connections to previous vampire films, it also differentiates itself tonally and stylistically in significant ways. For instance, its primary locus of comedy is its playful yet subdued references to vampire film tropes, rather than outright mimicry of their slapstick. Director Juno Mak has stated that the filmmakers were "revisiting the genre, not remaking it."[6] This implies that his film returns to the themes, storylines, and tropes of the original films, but diverges elsewhere. This is a self-aware and succinct overview of the film, because it does seem to combine essential elements of *geong si* films with the superficial trappings of recent Asian horror cinema, particularly Japanese horror.[7] In an interview, Mak acknowledges Takashi Shimizu's stylistic influence: "He helped me with the sound effects and the overall colour tone. But he didn't change my script or ask me to shoot or edit the film in any particular way."[8] *Rigor Mortis's* resemblance to Japanese horror films, then, could be explained by a combination of direct influence and subconscious borrowing.

Certainly Mak and other producers of Chinese horror cinema would have a financial incentive to imitate recent trends. After the success of Hideo Nakata's *Ringu* (1998), Adam Knee identifies a regional trend in Asia toward "glossy, highly stylized, intertextually self-conscious horror films which often feature (among other elements) the vengeful ghost of a young woman and the revelation of grim secrets from the past, in a context emphasizing the technologically mediated unsettling of traditional Asian culture."[9] In describing such overall traits of profitable Asian horror, one distributor gave the following summary of the genre he calls "Asia Extreme": "slick and glossy with fast, MTV–style editing … [sequences] over-the-top grotesque to the point of being surreal."[10] As Choi and Wada-Marciano observe, this description elides many of the differences between and within national markets of Asia, but it is true that many of the horror films produced by Asian countries have tried to capitalize on the popularity of Japanese horror films such as *Ringu*, *Ju-on*, and *Dark Water* (2002). *Rigor Mortis* certainly fits this categorization in terms of its style: compared to older *geong si* films, Mak focuses more on gory creation and develops the grotesque appearance of his film's *geong si* to an unprecedented degree. Similarly, the fight scenes between the film's protagonists and supernatural creatures feature stylized kung fu, dramatic slow motion, polished digital effects, and over-the-top violence and destruction.

In terms of setting, Mitsuyo Wada-Marciano points out that J-horror films often use the "dense topography" of Tokyo to "represent a uniquely urban sense of fear attached to the possibilities of the megalopolis and its mythos." The city, with its hidden "derelict spaces" both "dysfunctional and archaic," "ordinary and familiar, and yet isolated, neglected, and dreadful" provides a moody and unsettling backdrop for frightening events.[11] Mak takes this one step further in *Rigor Mortis* and confines his characters to one towering apartment building within Hong Kong's famously congested urban geography. The film takes advantage of its setting to emphasize its uncanny elements. For instance, any multi-unit public housing estate like the one depicted in the film would have been teeming with residents, yet most of the time only the characters involved with the film's events are shown on screen. Otherwise, the dark hallways seem unnaturally deserted, occupied by more ghosts than actual human beings. The supernatural beings provide the dilapidated building with a sense of history, while also being highly suggestive of its unpleasantness and the desperate circumstances one needs to be in to find oneself living there. As Chin muses at the beginning of the film, "I was once very successful. But if you ask me again, I did it all just to get by. I never imagined I would end up in this shit hole at this point in my life."

Despite the relative lack of human presence in the building, the characters still seem to bump into each other at remarkably opportune moments, providing the chance encounters necessary to spur the action forward. Unlike the seemingly abandoned hallways, whenever the camera glimpses one of the occupants' apartment homes, we see that they are packed with the eccentric artifacts of their lives, as such spaces in high-occupancy Hong Kong are expected to be. The building is thus a liminal space with no future and a haunted past, both deserted and teeming with life, both homely and *unheimlich*.

Beyond these formal similarities, one can undoubtedly draw additional parallels between the way the story is told here with producer Shimizu's film, *Ju-on: The Grudge*. *Rigor Mortis* borrows more than just style: while it is primarily a *geong si* film, it also includes many tropes and sequences from Japanese horror for seemingly purely referential purposes. For example, the mop-headed little boy running around the estate, who may or may not be a ghost, is clearly a borrowing of *Ju-on*'s Toshio; the boy's childish yet disturbing crayon drawings may be a reference to *Ringu*'s American remake, *The Ring* (2002). Given Mak's ready acknowledgment of Shimizu's stylistic influence, there is no evidence that *Rigor Mortis* is consciously borrowing content as well from those films, but a subconscious influence is certainly possible given *Ringu*'s tremendous success and the many Hong Kong imitations in the early 2000s, during Mak's formative years.[12]

Colette Balmain points out that the opening scenes of *Ju-on* are less narrative than impressionistic and tone-setting in nature, specifically highlighting "[the] sepia tones of the opening sequence, the panning down deserted streets, the high-angled disorienting shot of the outside of the [Saeki] house."[13] These shots are intercut with close-up shots in the Saeki household that hint at the murders committed by the originator of the film's curse, Takeo. Balmain explains that rather than explicitly narrating an event, the opening sequence "maps out visually, within the *mise-en-scène*, the dominant motifs of emptiness and alienation which lead to the eruption of male violence within the home."[14]

Likewise, *Rigor Mortis* opens with the camera circling over bloodied bodies in a vacant courtyard either dead or in the process of dying. Viewers familiar with the *geong si* genre will recognize various accouterments associated with *geong si* encounters: a broken wooden sword and an unspooled chalk line lie strewn about on the floor haphazardly amid debris and rubble, as burning pieces of ritual paper flutter about in the air. At this point, the accustomed viewer recognizes that an act of great violence involving the supernatural has taken place, but does not yet know the details of the story. A man who seems to be barely alive reclines against a destroyed wall, smoking; his posture and seemingly nonchalant act indicate a sense of resignation. The muted color palette, with only blood red highlighted, as well as the mournful tune from *Mr. Vampire* described in the previous section, hint at the film's tonal composition and final outcome. It is only after this sequence that the film begins to tell its story.

Another parallel with *Ju-on* is the theme of male violence destroying women's lives. Wronged women that turn into vengeful ghosts are common fixtures of both Japanese and South Korean horror.[15] In *Ju-on*, Takeo's murder of his wife Kayako creates the curse that takes over the lives of the film's characters and eventually kills them. Balmain writes that "the murderous Takeo can be best understood as a representation of Japanese masculinity in the aftermath of the so-called economic bubble" during which cases of domestic violence, for the first time recognized as such, rose in number and the courts issued a landmark ruling with respect to sexual harassment in the workplace.[16] This ruling, and the fact that domestic violence was acknowledged as a problem at all, was a qualified improvement for women's rights in Japan, which remains nonetheless androcentric and patriarchal. The theme of male violence as catalyst for the creation of vengeful female ghosts is thus a well-worn cinematic trope in Japan, and is recreated in *Rigor Mortis*, where a male tutor's rape of one of his twin students spurs them to murder the tutor and commit suicide, thus becoming malevolent spirits. The tutor's wife Feng (Kara Wai) happens upon all three of their bodies and, heavily traumatized, thereafter refuses to re-enter their home; instead, she and her young son Pak (Morris Ho) wander the estate's hallways scrounging for food, and live in a makeshift tent provided by the building's kindhearted security officer.

In appearance and movement, the twin girls also bear a strong resemblance to the long-haired female ghost garbed in white made popular in Japanese films like *Ringu* and *Ju-on*. Classic examples from Chinese cinema include the female ghost in *Mr. Vampire*, or Siu-sin from *A Chinese Ghost Story* (1987), which tend to be graceful, with period clothing and artfully arranged hairstyles, rather than the disheveled appearance, unnatural bodily contortions, and crawling movement of Sadako (from *Ringu*) or Kayako (from *Ju-on*). In earlier Chinese cinema, the primary signifiers of the supernatural are a pale face, a vaguely melancholy affect, and an introduction accompanied by fog and haunting music. However, for both the Japanese female ghost and the ghosts in *Rigor Mortis*, the common characteristics are long hair that obscures the face, loose white clothing, animalistic or insectile physicality, and a wrongful death. As it does elsewhere with its version of the *geong si* and other supernatural phenomena, *Rigor Mortis* adds its own macabre stylistic flourishes: in the case of the twins, vein-like red tendrils surround the girls as they move, but also seem to twist and grow of their own accord, adding to the ghosts' otherworldly appearance. Though the twins are related to the central *geong si* story only in that their malevolent souls inadvertently cause the vampire to become murderous, it is significant that their vengeful nature is emphasized to such a degree in the film, whereas in previous films the female ghosts were merely an additional supernatural obstacle for the male protagonists.

These stylistic, tonal, and thematic elements of *Rigor Mortis* indicate that the film was heavily influenced by Japanese horror; however, these characteristics merely seem to exist to add visual or dramatic interest in the film, or to enhance the setting and the viewer's sense of the uncanny. There is no serious investigation, for example, into how perhaps societal neglect created the spaces and conditions that allowed the twins (and the tutor's wife) to be victimized by such a horrific crime. This is in contrast to how, for example, seeing the curse propagated through multiple character sets in *Ju-on* lends weight to the idea that neglected and victimized women (and children) are a recurring problem in Japanese society. *Rigor Mortis* does not seem to seriously comment on social issues, except perhaps to suggest that transgressing the boundary between life and death is inadvisable.

The (Ir)resolution of Rigor Mortis and the Fate of Hong Kong

It is clear thus far that *Rigor Mortis* is an intriguing amalgamation of the *geong si* film with more contemporary Asian horror. Yet ultimately, a film like this risks becoming simply a checklist of tropes for consumption, carefully designed to satisfy both nostalgic viewers and those looking for the latest *Ju-on*.

While the film was successful overall in terms of box office and critical reception, its ending was polarizing because it seemed to invalidate most of the events that had transpired during the film.[17] I argue that far from being its greatest weakness, the ending is a fine encapsulation of what a *geong si* film can signify in 2010's Hong Kong. Its ambiguity, while frustrating to some, is the grace note for a film that is, intentionally or unintentionally, a representative hybrid of its time.

What, then, is *Rigor Mortis*'s true *raison d'être*, other than an excuse to repackage the *geong si* film? With approximately five minutes remaining in the film, the narrative seems to have come to a satisfying if tragic conclusion. Both the evil vampire that threatened the building's inhabitants, and the mourning wife who inadvertently summoned it into existence, lie dead and broken in the destroyed courtyard. However, Chin and Yau have evidently also sacrificed their lives to defeat the *geong si*: Chin is clearly on the verge of death; Yau has lost a forearm and is bleeding heavily. Chin wearily rolls onto his back, and looks up at the night sky as ashes from the battle drift down towards him: the scene is elegiac, even beautiful. The viewer realizes that this sequence echoes the one at the very beginning of the film, and understands that Chin's opening narration was his reflection on the final days of his life; the film has come full circle. It is a bittersweet ending of the type seen more frequently in Chinese films than in mainstream American ones.

What happens next, however, seemed to some viewers an unnecessarily confusing addition, or to others a complete betrayal of the bleak but heroic narrative that came before. From Chin's point of view of the drifting ashes, the shot dissolves into a visual effect of a swirling, shifting halo. The camera then zooms out—giving viewers the impression that they are traveling backwards through a light tunnel—until Chin's lifeless eye is revealed in an extreme close-up. In his eye, we can still see a reflection of the ashes. This "crossing over" sequence, from Chin's dying point of view to the close-up on his eye, effectively results in a reversed perspective. It is suggestive of a transition between life and death, a transition between alternate histories or even alternate universes, or perhaps a glimpse into Chin's dying thoughts.

The ensuing sequence mirrors the beginning of the film, where Chin moves into the housing estate and attempts to commit suicide, but this coda differs in significant ways. The first set of scenes shows two characters that Chin encountered at the beginning of the film: the security guard Yin (Lo Hoi-pang) and Pak, Feng's young son. Both characters died gruesome deaths in the film's previous course of events. The film suggests that now perhaps their fates have changed, or will change. Chin walks past Yin, sleeping soundly and peacefully in his office. In the elevator, instead of a brief encounter with Pak, Chin shares the ride with both mother and son, their hands clasped together as Feng suggests pork chops for dinner in an amiable tone. She even turns around to smile warmly at Chin. No longer wandering the halls in a tattered nightgown, she is dressed neatly, even fashionably. Gone is the trauma that seemed to tinge her previous existence.

As he walks into the building carrying his worldly belongings, Chin also encounters characters who were not present at the beginning of the film. The first one is Yau, who is clipping his toenails next to his food stall. His physical appearance in this scene has been cleverly modified to make him seem more lively and less world-weary: he has fewer white hairs, is sporting a more youthful haircut, and his disheveled "dressing robe priest" costume has been exchanged for a casual short-sleeve shirt and shorts. Chin nods at Yau in greeting, and Yau's glance at Chin lingers just long enough to be suggestive of prior acquaintance. The film's diegetic soundtrack in this moment noticeably differs from when Chin conversed with Yau in the food hall after his suicide attempt. Whereas then it seemed silent and haunted, now it is alive with the sounds of many people eating and chatting.

As Chin approaches his designated apartment, he walks past the open door of Auntie Mui. She pauses to look at Chin, then turns toward a photograph of her husband on an altar. It seems that she has accepted her husband's death and is no longer seeking to revive him. The scene then transitions into Chin's suicide attempt. As before, Yau rushes in to save Chin, but this time he does not need to struggle with the twin girls' malevolent spirits. The next shot shows Gau working as a coroner. In this existence, he is apparently someone who presides over death in a clinical manner. A voice off-screen announces that someone is here to identify a body, and Gau pulls out a storage rack with a body bag on it, and unzips the bag. A cut to Chin's lifeless staring eye *inside* the bag connects this scene with Chin's previous death scene. The next shot is a close-up of a toe tag, inscribed with Chin's name, date of death, and cause of death ("suicide"). In this version of events, the suicide attempt was apparently successful.

Tony Rayns's interpretation of this ending sequence is thus: "[Juno Mak] cruelly caps the fantasy [of becoming a vampire-slaying hero] by rationalising it as Chin's dying-moment dream; Chin actually does hang himself." A quick search of internet commentary reveals that many viewers found the ending to be either confusing or unsatisfying, and they are basically in agreement with Rayns that this final sequence seems to invalidate everything that transpired in the film. This is the most straightforward interpretation of the ending, because many films actually do opt for this kind of conclusion in order to portray the supernatural without situating their stories in outright fantasy. It is possible that the filmmakers added this final ambiguous sequence with the mainland Chinese market in mind, because Chinese censors frown upon depictions of the supernatural that cannot eventually be explained away rationally.[18] Literature and cinema have also been fond of the "dying hallucination" storytelling device, in which a subject imagines an extended sequence of events, even an entire lifetime, in the short moments before death.[19]

A second interpretive possibility is understanding the final scene as a metaphor and the entire film as an allegory. Szeto and Chen, for example, argue that *Rigor Mortis* is an example of the "cinema of anxiety," forcefully reminding Hong Kong audiences of the exploitation, poverty, and disappearing ways of life swept under the table in recent decades. The inhabitants of the public housing estate represent "five generations of Hong Kong poor," and the *geong si* that has come to life represents globalist and neoliberalist exploitation of those poor. Citing the elderly Auntie Mui's selfish desire turning her husband into a *geong si*, a process that required Pak to be sacrificed, they argue that the film is "a horrifying statement about the older generation devouring the young and the specters of China crowding out the space of quotidian Hong Kong."[20] Regrettably, Szeto and Chen do not mention the ending twist in their analysis, but it is reasonable to assume that the film's denial of its own events could represent the citizens of Hong Kong choosing once again to deny the specters in their own lives.

If the majority of the film takes place within Chin's dying fantasy, then another interpretation might be that the fantasy is symbolic of the vampire film itself. Thus Mak's outlook is not an optimistic one: his own film is recast as the last-gasp fantasy of a misguided enthusiast (with Chin standing in for the director himself), which ultimately proves to be ephemeral and false. This interpretation is supported by the presence of artifacts from Chin's films and the casting of previous stars of the genre, in which case these signifiers are not gratuitous references or homages but clues to an overall outlook. Within this interpretation, Chin's actual life and death are a glimpse at the sad state of affairs now that vampire films are no longer in vogue: the Taoist master character Yau has been reduced to a street food vendor, who can only demonstrate his flair for the martial arts when he tosses the food in his wok with a flourish; the occultist Gau no longer has the dubious ability to reanimate corpses, but instead has to watch them remain lifeless in the morgue. Significantly, a *geong si*-free existence is still not entirely a happy one, as Chin is still haunted by the failures in his life and takes them to his grave.

Another data point from the film that supports this interpretation is director Juno Mak's self-insertion at the end of the film. This shot, which appears approximately fourteen seconds into the closing credits, is less than a second long, and was probably easily missed in theaters. It shows Mak apparently seated in the audience section of an empty movie theater, his left forefinger placed in front of his mouth in a contemplative pose. Given its placement during the credits, the most obvious interpretation of this shot is that the director is considering the film that came before, his completed work, giving it added significance. Mak has stated regarding his self-insertion: "The film represents me, and I want a record of myself in each film from the time I make it."[21] Therefore, it is reasonable to read what transpires in the film as representative of the director's personal perspective.

None of these interpretations, however, takes into account the eerie and deliberate parallels where the "crossing over" visual effect is used. As mentioned earlier, the effect appears as Chin, having defeated the *geong si*, is lying on the ground observing the falling ashes. However, the first time this visual is employed is during Chin's first suicide attempt at the beginning of the film. There, the effect is intercut with shots from Chin's old films, as well as images meant to evoke decay and disgust, such as wilting flowers, rotting strawberries, and wriggling worms. The effect appears a final time as Gau the coroner pulls out Chin's body for identification, after the shot of Chin's eye. To summarize in chronological order, the "crossing over" visual effect appears when Chin first commits suicide by hanging (and apparently does not succeed), when Chin dies as a result of fighting the *geong si*, and when Chin seems to be truly dead, his body deposited in a morgue's cold storage.

Based on when the effect is employed and its associated imagery—the movement through light indicating passage, the images of decay—it is clear that it is meant to represent the transition between life and death. What is not so obvious is whether these moments give any clear indication about the (un)reality of events in each section of the film. I propose a reading as follows: the first use of the effect suggests a transition between Chin's actual life and a second, different ontological status through which most of the film's events are narrated (the vampire-fighting, as well as all the tragedies and human errors that lead up to it). The second "crossing over" represents an attempt by Chin to disengage from those events, but he does not fully do so until he is truly dead in the morgue. That is, *both* his battle with the *geong si* and what we witness after his supposed death post-battle are of *equally* uncertain status. Either the supernatural and mundane realities are both true in some way, or they are both false in some way.

The reading that grants the film the most narrative richness is one that interprets both as being true.[22] The *geong si* fight actually occurred, but the events post-fight are also true in the sense that they are part of Chin's dying dream or fantasy. As Chin lies dying after having vanquished the *geong si*, he wishes that all the horrific events that followed his first attempted suicide could be undone. The only scene that follows the final "crossing over" visual effect is the shot of Chin's toe tag, with the background in soft focus. There the coroner is apparently greeting Chin's adult son, who has come to identify the body. Since the coroner's image is not in focus, it is unclear whether he is actually Gau, or whether the identity of Gau was one imposed upon him by Chin's dying wish-dream. This leaves open the possibility that Gau is still an occultist who creates unnatural life from death in this reality, but a no-nonsense coroner who oversees death in clinical fashion in Chin's fantasy. Since Gau is the only character whose essence undergoes a major change before and after the *geong si* storyline, discovering the coroner's actual identity in the final scene would be key to interpreting most of the film's events. The fact that the film deliberately withholds this information is significant.

I would thus propose a third interpretation of the film's controversial ending: that it is deliberately ambiguous and an apt representation of the status of Hong Kong, which seems to always be in flux, particularly in this fraught historical moment. In an interview, Mak stated that he has heard at least fifteen different interpretations of the ending, but does not give a definitive one himself.[23] Combined with his fleeting self-insert as a philosophical thinker in the film's credits, this is evidence that there is not meant to be a definitive reading of the film's final moments.

Many films, of course, have ambiguous endings. What makes the *geong si* film particularly well-suited to convey Hong Kong's political anxiety and complexity? First, the tension between East and West has been a frequent topic of exploration in Hong Kong cinema, and the *geong si* film is no exception, as I shall demonstrate. Secondly, recent mainstream Chinese cinema has steadfastly shied away from overtly political topics, instead choosing to focus on ancient history or hiding its topicality under a veneer of harmless fantasy. Therefore, the *geong si* film has always been more than a combination of silly effects and slapstick humor; having been the site of Hong Kong's coming to terms with colonial power, it now necessarily takes on a different kind of threat, given Hong Kong's political status in the early twenty-first century, and the lack of other more direct cinematic means of expression.

In film criticism, the link between Hong Kong's conflicted identity and its cinematic output is often a foregone conclusion, especially after the publication of Ackbar Abbas's influential and oft-cited article on the *déjà disparu* concept, where he explores how 1990s Hong Kong cinema was "being used to explore and negotiate a problematic and paradoxical cultural space without abandoning its role as popular entertainment."[24] That Hong Kong and the Pearl River Delta area should be culturally "paradoxical" is not surprising, given Guangdong Province's many treaty ports in the nineteenth century, and more recently Hong Kong's status as international financial hub and former colony of the British Empire. Many Hong Kong films interrogate or display this cultural tension as explicit subject matter, as in the *Once Upon a Time in China* series or *Rouge* (1987). Even when the subject matter is local or parochial, however, foreign influence is nonetheless always on display in Hong Kong cinema, as a result of Great Britain's physical and cultural transformations of the city itself in the last century.

Stephanie Lam, for example, argues that the real conflict in *Mr. Vampire* "is not between humans and cadavers, but between an abstracted Chineseness and a British colonial presence." For her, the *geong si* "signifies an unstable middle ground in that its body, always in transit toward a final resting place, is neither here nor there, neither dead nor truly alive."[25] Thus cultural identity is at stake when the police officer, bearing the authority of an institution imported from the West, cannot subdue the *geong si* with guns and bravado, and it comes down to Lam Ching Ying's Taoist priest, using traditional knowledge from China, to vanquish the *geong si* once and for all. The film is thus an affirmation of traditional Chinese heritage and its usefulness in an age of rationality.[26]

While many fans of the older *geong si* films may simply enjoy them for their humor and fight sequences, the *geong si* itself as a creature that is neither dead nor alive is no doubt a particularly apt representation of Hong Kong. Its in-between status is a perfect encapsulation of a former colony caught between East and West, between the past and the present. As discussed earlier, Tang Wenyu traces the origins of *geong si* in Chinese myth and literature in order to show why it has particular resonance in Chinese culture to this day. More significantly, Tang argues that the *geong si* that appeared in earlier films tended to be dressed as Qing Dynasty officials, which reflects the Cantonese peoples' resentment at submitting to foreign (Manchurian) rule, as well as their anger at being surrendered to Great Britain by that same outsider authority. Dressing the traditional cinematic *geong si* in Manchurian officials' robes and *guan mao* (officials' caps) was an easy way to evoke the authoritarianism and corruption of late imperial China. Thus from its very cinematic origins, the *geong si* was appropriated as a political symbol.

To continue along this line of conjecture, it is not surprising that a significant number of *geong si* films were produced in the 1980s and 1990s, as Hong Kong approached its return to mainland China in 1997 and would presumably face a different kind of authoritarianism and "outsider" influence. Once the genre reached a certain level of popularity and maturity, its films increasingly incorporated Hong Kong's cosmopolitan outlook as well; titles such as *Legend of the Seven Golden Vampires* (1974), *Robo Vampire* (1988), *Vampire vs Vampire* (1989), and *Crazy Safari* (1991) reflect the genre's ability to irreverently absorb outside influences.[27] The year 1992 marked the appearance of the last film in the *Mr. Vampire* series, uncreatively titled *Mr. Vampire 1992* in English (the Chinese title, *New Mr. Vampire,* was not much better). *The Era of Vampires* (2002), unprecedented in the genre due to its lack of comedy, was the last significant *geong si* film to appear prior to *Rigor Mortis.*

What kind of political climate welcomed the arrival of Juno Mak's film? Significantly, Hong Kong has experienced significant turmoil over the past few years. Post-handover, the Basic Law of the Hong Kong Special Administrative Region ostensibly guarantees that Hong Kong and mainland China will remain "one country, two systems" until 2047. The Basic Law also states that the people of Hong Kong shall be granted "a high degree of autonomy" and that they have the right to administer themselves.[28] In practice, Hong Kong has seen its freedoms gradually eroded by Mainland influence. The Umbrella Movement of 2014 erupted in response to Beijing's interference in local elections, the culmination of many years of discontent and growing localist sentiment—that is, the people of Hong Kong increasingly identify as

Hongkongers rather than as Chinese citizens.[29] Many of the Umbrella Movement's leaders have since been indicted or jailed.[30] To add insult to injury, in 2015 the Chinese national police arranged a series of ultra-secretive and extra-judicial kidnappings of prominent Hong Kong booksellers and members of the publishing industry, a shocking move because the Hong Kong publishing industry had thus far remained relatively free of restrictions compared to their mainland counterpart. These and many other incidents in the past decade are contributing to the sense that personal freedoms and democracy are slowly being extinguished in Hong Kong, many years prior to the 2047 expiry of the Basic Law.[31]

Conclusion

At a time when Hong Kong is trying to protect its last vestiges of democratic self-determination, *Rigor Mortis* harkens back to a time of similar uncertainty, but with a postmodern twist. Dale Hudson reminds us that the older *geong si* films generally enforced the conservative status quo, because the forces of traditional Chinese culture (kung fu and Taoist rituals) were always able to subdue the *geong si* eventually[32] *Rigor Mortis*'s ending, while indeed reminiscent of other ambiguous endings of twenty-first century Asian horror, endorses a different, more open-ended kind of truth. If Chin and Yau's fight against the *geong si* was indeed a fantasy, then one possible interpretation is that it represents Hong Kong's desire to revive authentic local traditions and nostalgia for a heroic past.[33] If Chin's vision of a relatively uneventful death and his neighbors' lives untainted by the supernatural is a fantasy, one possible interpretation is that it is a wish for normalcy and for one person's sacrifice to have meaning. What is certain is the film's refusal to provide closure and its intention to leave the ending open to interpretation.

The Hong Kong publishers and booksellers recently harassed and kidnapped by Chinese authorities see themselves as purveyors of a different kind of truth, one that should be allowed to exist alongside the official version promulgated by the Chinese Communist Party. They published anything from memoirs where Mao Zedong is portrayed in an unflattering light, to compilations of online gossip; both types of books are condemned by party officials. But those condemned believe that having multiple truths is better than having only one version disseminated through official channels. As bookseller Bao Pu states: "In their rumor-mongering, [the books] share glimpses of truth."[34] Therefore in *Rigor Mortis*'s non-committal ending lies the true spirit of Hong Kong.

It is fitting that even while following the increasingly transnational trends of Asian horror cinema, *Rigor Mortis* is also a film that commits steadfastly to its Hong Kong *geong si* roots. This potentially irreconcilable contradiction is congruous with the film's deliberately ambiguous ending that can be read multiple ways, as the viewer desires. Chin is both dead and not dead, just as the vampire/*geong si* is both alive and not alive. At this important political moment for Hong Kong, one cannot imagine a metaphor that is more apt.

NOTES

1. *Rigor Mortis*, directed by Juno Mak, Kudos Films Limited, 2013. *Geong si* is *jiang shi* in Mandarin; I prefer to use the Cantonese term *geong si* in this essay, out of respect for the Hong Kong origins of the genre.

2. Chan is also playing a version of himself, as the actor's Chinese name is Chan Yau.

3. Dale Hudson, "Vampires and Transnational Horror," *A Companion to the Horror Film*, edited by Harry M. Benshoff, Wiley-Blackwell, 2014, page 476.

4. The original lyrics to what has become known as "the ghost bride song" were composed by Kwok-kong Cheng for *Mr. Vampire*, directed by Ricky Lau, Bo Ho Film Company, 1985.

5. Boon Chan Media Correspondent, "New Life in Death; Rigor Mortis' Juno Mak Has Given Himself a New Image as a Critically Acclaimed Film-Maker," *The Straits Times* (Singapore), 27 November 2013, *Nexis Uni*, advance-lexis-com.ezproxy.valpo.edu/api/permalink/01e6a475-b20e-4fc9-9201-e8bea7bff89b/?context=1516831; Karen Chu, "Hong Kong Filmart: Vampire Genre Gets Chinese Spin," *The Hollywood Reporter*, 19 March 2013, www.hollywoodreporter.com/news/hong-kong-filmart-vampire-genre-429815.

6. Boon Chan, cited above.

7. Film scholars make a distinction between "Japanese horror" and "J-horror." Takashi Shimizu's *Ju-on* series, particularly the earlier direct-to-video installments, belongs in the latter category. Chika Kinoshita explains that J-horror is a "local movement from the late 1990s that comprised films, TV series, and film theory and criticism written by filmmakers, with particular emphasis on everyday life and media" (103), while the former presumably encompasses all Japanese films aimed to frighten, which are often but not always supernatural. For my purposes, I use "Japanese horror" to refer to the specific late 90s genre of J-horror as well as to horror and supernatural films made after the J-horror boom, as both were influential in other parts of Asia.

8. Edmund Lee, "Juno Mak Resurrects His Career in Rigor Mortis," *South China Morning Post*, 23 Oct. 2013, www.scmp.com/magazines/48hrs/article/1334595/juno-mak-resurrects-his-career-rigor-mortis.

9. Adam Knee, "The Pan-Asian Outlook of *The Eye*," Choi and Wada-Marciano, page 71.

10. Jinhee Choi and Mitsuyo Wada-Marciano, editors, *Horror to the Extreme: Changing Boundaries in Asian Cinema*, Hong Kong University Press, 2009.

11. Knee, pages 18–19.

12. Robert Hyland, "A Politics of Excess: Violence and Violation in Miike Takashi's *Audition*," Choi and Wada-Marciano, pages 201–02. Mak was born in 1984.

13. Colette Balmain, *Introduction to Japanese Horror Film*, Edinburgh University Press, 2008, page 143.

14. Balmain, 143.

15. See for example Colette Balmain ("East Asian Gothic") and James Byrne.

16. Balmain, page 145.

17. Szeto and Chen, page 97.

18. Tsui. Szeto and Chen claim that the film was never intended to be screened in China, but do not provide a source in their reference list (97). Their essay lists box office data for the film from Hong Kong, Taiwan, and Southeast Asia, but not from China (97). Whether the exclusion of mainland China was pre-determined or not, a large market like China's is difficult for Hong Kong filmmakers to ignore completely, particularly since films not receiving a theatrical release can still potentially be released in other formats.

19. The best-known work which employs this device is the 1890 short story "An Occurrence at Owl Creek Bridge" by Ambrose Bierce.

20. Szeto and Chen, pages 96, 101.

21. Lee.

22. Of course, the alternate possibility is that both the *geong si* storyline and the version of events imagined after that are false—that is, Chin could have simply committed suicide and hallucinated the terrifying supernatural events, as well as the better versions of his neighbors' lives, as he lost consciousness. This is the reading that grants the least narrative interest.

23. Boon Chan.

24. Ackbar Abbas, "The New Hong Kong Cinema and the 'Déjà Disparu,'" *Discourse*, volume 16, number 3, spring 1994, pages 65–77. Abbas explains *déjà disparu* as "the feeling that what is new and unique about the situation is always already gone, and we are left holding a handful of clichés" (67). Though an important component of Abbas's article, this aspect of Hong Kong cinema is not under discussion here.

25. Stephanie Lam, "Hop on Pop: *Jiangshi* Films in a Transnational Context," *Cineaction*, no. 78, 2009, pages 46–51.

26. Other scholars who analyze *geong si* films in the context of identity conflict and political anxiety include Lin Chunyan, Mandy Yee Man Liu, and Szeto and Chen.

27. *Legend* is a Hammer co-production that features both Count Dracula and Van Helsing (played by Peter Cushing); *Robo Vampire* features a knock-off of *RoboCop*; *Vampire vs Vampire* tells the story of a Taoist priest and his tame *geong si* apprentice, and their battle against European vampires. It also stars Chin Siu-ho of *Rigor Mortis*. *Crazy Safari* is an unofficial sequel of sorts to *The Gods Must Be Crazy* (1980), in which Xixo the Bushman from the South African film crosses paths with a *geong si*.

28. "Some Facts About the Basic Law," *Basic Law Homepage*, 17 Mar. 2008, www.basiclaw.gov.hk/en/facts/index.html.

29. Sebastian Veg, "Hong Kong's Enduring Identity Crisis." *The Atlantic*, 16 Oct. 2013, www.theatlantic.com/china/archive/2013/10/hong-kongs-enduring-identity-crisis/280622/.

30. Tiffany May, "Hong Kong Umbrella Movement Leaders Are Sentenced to Prison," *The New York Times*, 23 Apr. 2019, www.nytimes.com/2019/04/23/world/asia/hong-kong-umbrella-movement.html.

31. Alex Palmer, "The Case of Hong Kong's Missing Booksellers," *The New York Times Magazine*, 3 April 2018, www.nytimes.com/2018/04/03/magazine/the-case-of-hong-kongs-missing-booksellers.html.

32. Hudson, page 476.

33. On this point, the film's casting of Chin Siu-ho as himself is particularly apt, as the popular '80s and '90s actor's career was derailed by scandal in the early 2000s—*Rigor Mortis* has also revived Chin's career (Xu).

34. Alex Palmer, "The Case of Hong Kong's Missing Booksellers."

Nosferatu's Daughters

*Radical Feminism, Lesbo-Vampirism
and Fluid Identities in Dennis Gansel's*
Wir sind die Nacht *(We Are the Night)*

KAI-UWE WERBECK

Introduction: Nosferatu's Daughters

When Dracula, played by Klaus Kinski, welcomes Jonathan Harker to his castle in Werner Herzog's 1979 *Nosferatu—Phantom der Nacht* (*Nosferatu the Vampyre*), the pale count revives Germany's cinematic past.[1] Some differences notwithstanding, he is the *doppelgänger* of Max Schreck's Count Orlok from F.W. Murnau's 1922 seminal silent film *Nosferatu—Symphonie des Grauens* (*Nosferatu: A Symphony of Horror*).[2] These two prominent undead aristocrats—one the poster child of Weimar Expressionism, the other representing the auteur revolution of the New German cinema—have entered the collective imaginary of critics and audiences alike, yet they belong to a rare phenotype. In an already marginalized genre—post–1945 West German horror—the vampire himself is an outcast.[3] It would be too simple, however, to attribute the vampire's absence merely to the general dearth of domestic horror productions after the end of the Third Reich.[4] After all, serial killers, succubae, and cannibals—among other staples of modern monstrosity—have appeared in postwar German cinema on a relatively regular basis. Yet, even when vampires once more became hot commodities in cross-medial juggernauts such as the *Twilight* series during the first decade of the twenty-first century, German filmmakers were hesitant to bring back their native Nosferatus. This rejection is not only noteworthy given their famous predecessors, but also with regard to a global economy in which "the horror film traditions of other national and regional cinemas are engaged in a process of cross-

We Are the Night (*Wir sind die Nacht*, 2010). A German publicity poster features three of the female vampires walking on the ceiling while their male victims lie strewn on the floor above their heads. Lena (Karoline Herfurth, center) is being groomed by alpha female Louise (Nina Hoss, right) to join her and the glamourous Nora (Anna Fischer, left) in a lethal vampire posse. The poster, with its upside-down title, is scarce—probably pulled from distribution as too clever to be effective, or perhaps because of the hole in Lena's stocking.

cultural exchange with American mainstream, independent, and underground horror alike."[5]

When the vampire finally did return to the nation's multiplexes in Dennis Gansel's big-budget genre update *We Are the Night* (*Wir sind die Nacht*, 2010), the creature looked nothing like the ones of yore. Gansel's film features female, urbane vampires and thus constitutes an anomaly within postwar German cinema on multiple levels. As academic lore has it, Weimar horror—like the supernatural creatures that populated its nightmarish worlds—had crumpled to dust during the Second World War and remained "undead" until the dawn of the twenty-first century. To be sure, Weimar's expressionist *Haunted Screen* had suffered under the media politics of National Socialism—who considered it degenerate art—and after the end of the Third Reich the horror genre found itself in a difficult position.[6] Yet, while National Socialism clearly affected the genre negatively, many scholarly accounts have incorrectly treated (West) German horror cinema as virtually non-existent. Steffen Hantke criticizes this oversight, pointing out that "if there was a German horror film before 1933, there is little reason to assume that the twelve years of the Third Reich would have killed it off once and for all."[7] While a detailed account of the challenges—from a strict media regulation system to escapist desires that excluded anything horrific in the years immediately following the Second World War—that (West) German horror faced in the second half of the twentieth century goes beyond the scope of this essay, two things are important to note. One, while the number of releases are indeed lower than in many other national cinemas, there have always been (West) German postwar horror films from the 1960s onward; two, since the beginning of the twenty-first century the overall output of professionally made genre titles has increased which in turn resulted in a diversified portfolio.[8]

This said, both the lesbo-vampiric subject matter and the relatively high production values set Gansel's *We Are the Night* apart from most other 21st-century German horror films. With its polished presentation—replete with a pumping soundtrack and well-choreographed action sequences—Gansel's film evokes Stefan Ruzowitzky's stylish slasher *Anatomie* (*Anatomy*, 1999) rather than the cinema of Murnau or Herzog. The unexpected box-office success of *Anatomie* resulted in a short-lived renaissance of German mainstream horror that lasted approximately five years and produced a number of similar films such as Ruzowitzky's own *Anatomie 2* (2003), Michael Karen's *Flashback* (2000), or Robert Schwentke's *Tattoo* (2002).[9] However, these films emulate U.S. slashers—from Sean S. Cunningham's *Friday the 13th* (1980) to Wes Craven's *Scream* (1996)—and feature human killers. Attempting to replicate *Anatomie*'s commercial and cultural impact within the vampire sub-genre, however, Gansel's contribution failed as audiences largely rejected *We Are the Night*.[10] Yet, the film nonetheless provides a "counterprogram to what we might call the *Normalisierung* aesthetic of both the 'cinema of consensus' films of the early to mid–1990s and post-'cinema of consensus' historical films such as Oliver Hirschbiegel's *Der Untergang* [or] Florian Henckel von Donnersmarck's *Das Leben der Anderen*" (*The Lives of Others*, 2006). Rather than to rely on a filmic realism that forces audiences "to resee that with which they assumed sufficient familiarity: Germany itself," *We Are the Night* retrains the viewer's perceptive habits through the distorting lens of the explicitly fantastic.[11] Eschewing the explicitly political, Gansel populates post–Wall Berlin with female vampires who are every bit as "unreal" as the elusive *Berlin Geist* that has shaped the capital's self-image as a sub-cultural melting pot and liberal safe-haven that—as the story goes—openly welcomes and accommodates non-normative lifestyles and worldviews.

As Berlin features prominently in Gansel's film, one final remark about *We Are the Night*'s spatial and temporal coordinates is in order. While this essay does not necessitate an in-depth history of Berlin in the decades that follow the fall of the Wall, a couple of words on key discourses are helpful to ground my reading of gender and class. After the country's reunification in 1990, Germany's parliament finally moved from its "provisional" headquarters in Bonn to Berlin in 1999, completing the long transition of the city into the country's capital on the level of government. Caught in a whirlwind of reconstruction—politically, socially, and culturally, but also with regard to infrastructure—Berlin had become a postmodern city in which architecture "reveals the past traumas whose traces are still lodged in the spaces of everyday life."[12] As the spatial center of these post-reunification growing pains, the city experienced the broader problems associated with reunification, but also became a sub-cultural playground due to its unregulated condition and influx of people from all over the world. This essay acknowledges these discourses, such as gentrification, culture-clashes, and the capital's hipster charm. Subtending my analysis of class and gender is thus the city's alleged libertine utopia, the much-debated *Berlin Geist*, which denotes the legacy and update of the city's *Golden Twenties*, whose entertainment culture "in Berlin […] in der Rückschau einen beinahe mystischen Glanz angenommen [hat]" ["in retrospect has assumed an almost mystic sheen"].[13] In this light, Berlin should for all intents and purposes be the one place that can accommodate "queer" vampires. Yet, Gansel includes a subtle critique of the *Berlin Geist* in *We Are the Night*; ultimately, the city cannot accommodate all forms of deviancy. Twenty years after the fall of the Wall, it has changed to a point where the aforementioned elusive cool has been relegated to the realm of the mythical.

Before I begin with my analysis, let me offer a brief synopsis as my reading at times disregards the chronology of the events. When the centuries-old vampire Louise (Nina Hoss) meets Lena (Karoline Herfurth), an androgynous working class girl and part-time pickpocket, she believes to have found her soul mate once again. Even though the elder vampire already entertains a harem that includes Charlotte (Jennifer Ulrich) and Nora (Anna Fischer), Louise bites and turns Lena. From this point on, the narrative chronicles Lena's coming to terms with her new existence as a vampire. After a short period of adjustment, she learns to enjoy the benefits of being a supernatural creature in an exhilarating, ever-changing city that never sleeps. Lena eats at the most expensive restaurants, goes after-hour shopping in luxurious department stores, and disregards the constraints of daytime society. Soon, however, the situation spins out control when Lena realizes that she has to kill people to sustain her own existence and falls in love with Tom (Max Riemelt), a local cop. Louise further aggravates the situation when, in her jealous rage, she begins to threaten Tom's life. Things take another turn from bad to the worse when the police picks up the trail of the vampires and Nora and Charlotte end up destroyed by daylight and bullets alike. Ultimately, Lena challenges and kills Louise before leaving Berlin with Tom, the ending suggesting that she may have turned Tom into a male vampire, the first—as the narrative establishes early on—in a very long time. Where exactly the couple go, *We Are the Night* leaves unanswered, setting the stage for a sequel that has never materialized.

Radical Feminism, Lesbo-Vampirism and Fluid Identities

True to the vampire genre as a whole, the subtexts in *We Are the Night* are complex and multi-faceted. As Judith Halberstam cautions about the figure of the vampire, "an analysis of the vampire as perverse sexuality runs the risk of mere stabilizing the identity of perversity."[14] Following her advice, my reading takes into account "the historically specific contours of race, class, gender, and sexuality" that the female vampires in *We Are the Night* have absorbed and remixed into symbiotic yet distinguishable updates of the bloodsucker.[15] Traditional cinematic vampires such as Dracula, Count Orlok, and their many, mostly male successors are often threats because of their origin, with the pre-modern East usually marked as Other. However, such xenophobic interpretations of vampirism do not apply to the homegrown threat of Louise, Charlotte, and Nora, as all four are white, modern, and fashionable women of German nationality. While the National Socialist blood-and-soil metaphor may seem more productive here—after all, Louise is a charismatic leader who creates and controls her minions—it is noteworthy that none of them turned during the Third Reich. National Socialism is thus conspicuously absent from the narrative. Along these lines, the vampires in *We Are the Night* also do not represent a counter-concept to modernity. Gansel's protagonists—

whose music is not the howling of the wolves but the staccato beats of electronic dance music—are children of an urban night that is firmly rooted in the localized experience of Berlin as a place where nature has long been replaced by neon lights and Techno culture. Their "unnatural" state is completely in tune with a digitized environment that has left nature behind a long time ago. Finally, religious reasons also do not play a role. *We Are the Night* does not explicitly address religion beyond a single, potentially useless crucifix in the hands of a frightened Russian criminal, suggesting that Berlin is not a sacred space to begin with. What remains as a distinguishing characteristic is thus the four vampires' sexuality, gender, and class as well as the ways in which they cross borders, physical and otherwise. In a sense, Louise and her group subvert the motif of vampires having to be invited to enter private—in this case, late capitalist and consumerist—places. In fact, they have long been allowed into these environments.

Since *We Are the Night*'s four female protagonists are the nexus where these categories are negotiated, it is necessary to briefly illustrate their backgrounds and characteristics. Louise, Charlotte, Nora, and Lena mirror the various stages of Germany as a nation state, from Empire to reunified Germany. In a montage during the film's opening credits, the viewer learns that Louise—likely an aristocrat—dates back at least to the founding of modern Germany in 1871. The film portrays her as a sophisticated product of the Wilhelmine era, yet ruthless in her search for power and love. Before her transformation, Charlotte was a famous, bourgeoise actress in the Weimar Republic, married to a man and mother of a young daughter. Even though she, like Louise, is a woman of good taste, impeccable manners, and intellectual curiosity, Charlotte is much more at odds with the ennui and decadence that the vampire life brings with it. She repeatedly flirts with suicide, a death wish to which she succumbs toward the end of the narrative. Nora, finally, is middle-class, and the text represents her as less sophisticated. Nora was turned during one of the early *Love Parade* techno festivals, the first one of which took place in 1989. She grew up in one of the separated Germanys, but became a vampire amidst Berlin's reshaping in the decade after reunification. Nora makes full use of the options granted to her as an undead party queen of Berlin.

In addition, the narrative assigns all three vampires ostensible weaknesses that justify their eventual demise toward the end of the narrative. Louise's flaw is her serial homosexual monogamy, the egotistic urge to turn her love interests into vampires with no regard for their well-being. What is more, she forces her sexuality on heterosexual women, turning them, quite literally, into something that goes against their nature. Charlotte, on the other hand, has rejected her role as mother and wife. She abandons both her daughter and her husband when she joins Louise's group. Not fulfilling her role as caregiver leads to severe depression, the eventual reason for Charlotte's suicide after she visits her aged daughter on her deathbed. Nora, finally, suffers from her aggressive, self-determined sexuality. She promises sexual pleasures to men, only to either withhold them completely or kill her mates after the act. Yet, their community implodes only when Lena tips the delicate balance. Thus, the main transgression in *We Are the Night* is neither that of lesbianism *per se* nor that of rejecting heteronormative gender roles—even though these aspects do play a role—but ultimately Lena's refusal to accept established power relations.

We Are the Night is concerned with the threat that powerful, independent, and potentially homosexual women pose to patriarchal structures, primarily embodied in the text as police officers, gangsters, and night guards. After she is bitten, Lena is gradually initiated into the circle of wealthy women, a group that came into existence because of Louise's search for a soul mate. This romantic notion is ridiculed by the fact that Lena is already her—at least—third attempt at eternal love. Louise grows bored with her lovers after a while, condemning them to an undead life for her own selfish pleasure. Yet, while *We Are the Night* never shows Charlotte and Nora having sex with Louise, the latter tries to seduce Lena. Before this can happen, however, Lena's appearance has to change from relatively androgynous and boyish to blond *femme*. When Louise reshapes Lena to her own liking, she also creates a male fantasy that she then refuses to share with the man in Lena's life. Interestingly, Tom's wooing markedly intensifies after she becomes a pseudo lesbo-vampire. Developing a taste for the things that her social standing has denied her so far, Lena at first rejects Tom's advances. She thus threatens to withdraw from the patriarchal paradigm despite her upcharge in desirability, a decision that, as *We Are the Night* suggests, can only be the result of a supernatural sickness. By taking on supposedly masculine behavior patterns that contrast starkly with her new feminine appearance, Lena aggressively pushes the self-confident and attractive cop to the margins, rendering obsolete what he has to offer both as a man and as an agent of state authority.

As the narrative progresses, however, Lena switches her loyalties and saves Tom from Louise, possibly making him a vampire, too. Lena's dismissal of reversed gender inequalities eventually leads to the demise of the group—they have to disappear before balance can be restored. At a cursory glance, the central relation between Louise, Charlotte, Nora, and eventually Lena, invokes the category of the lesbian vampire in horror cinema such as Jesus Franco's infamous *Vampyros Lesbos* (1971).[16] Other genres invoked would include the Techno-infused action film *Blade* (1998) and the neon-drenched coming-of-age story *The Lost Boys* (1986). However, the fact that only Louise is a lesbian is a departure from lesbo-vampiric conventions. Nor does Louise's bite infect her victims with homosexual desires, as with the newcomer in many entries to the subgenre: "once bitten the victim is never shy. She happily joins her female seducer"—albeit with the possible intention of replacing her one night.[17] Lena, however, is not interested in succeeding Louise, even though she does wield her supernatural powers if pushed. While Louise's interest initially flatters her, Lena quickly rejects her sexual advances. She does kill Louise, but only to save Tom rather than to take her maker's elevated position of power. Thus Lena establishes herself as non-binary while seeking to flatten the off-kilter power relations in place in the secretive, centuries old, exclusively female vampire society. *We Are the Night* thus equates lesbianism with vampirism—a traditional linkage between the supernatural predator and sexual desire and potency—yet recalibrates both paradigms in the process. Ultimately, the film's final act argues for a "moderate" feminism that (a) rejects a more radical one and (b) identifies the supernatural as the only tool to level the playing field from within the group of overly powerful women.

As a strong, supernatural woman Lena is able to turn the tables. When Lena defeats and kills Louise at the end of *We Are the Night*, she creates a "balanced" feminism that contrasts Louise, Charlotte, and Louise's version bordering on misandry. Louise's behavior in particular goes way beyond the utopian equilibrium in which men and women have equal rights. Gansel's text thus suggests that women, equipped with the same powers as men or even surpassing those, will act exactly the same or even worse, turning cruel and power hungry in their (lesbo-)vampirism. As soon as Lena has overcome this temptation, the film delegates her back to a heteronormative relationship, but only after Louise succeeded in reshaping Lena's look and boosting her self-confidence, giving Tom the best of both worlds. While sexuality and the related "threat" of virulent lesbianism play a critical role in *We Are the Night*, the question remains why Lena has to leave Berlin even after she succeeded in resetting the power imbalances. The answer, the text repeatedly suggests, lies in Lena's ability to switch effortlessly between identities—including but not limited to that of (homo-) sexual object—which so far she has utilized for her illegal actions and which now grants her supernatural access to parts of Berlin that have been hitherto off-limits. *We Are the Night* ultimately implies that the excessive crossing and blurring of class and gender lines renders Lena unacceptable. Despite their vampiric condition, Louise, Charlotte, and Nora exist within fixed parameters. Their identities remain clearly defined, whereas Lena oscillates between them. To illustrate this point, Gansel repeatedly includes the motif of border crossings into the narrative.

The border crossings in *We Are the Night* include physical barriers as well as intangible ones, be they psychological or social.[18] After she is turned, for example, Lena's return to her old life proves to be a painful one. Following Louise's bite at an illegal rave in the abandoned *Spreepark*—itself a moment of border crossing as Lena is allowed to enter the exclusive club only because Louise instructs the bouncer to grant her passage—Lena flees from the venue in shock. Instinctively, she returns to her apartment located in one of Berlin's poorer neighborhoods. In her messy room—far away from the strobe light-filled wonderland of the vampires on the other side of town—Lena realizes that something is off and that the bite was not merely a case of sexual harassment on Louise's part. Visibly confused, Lena reacts violently to the sunlight filtering through her blinds, and, when trying to eat, she realizes that she is unable to keep regular food down. Instead, she feels drawn to the raw meat in the fridge that she devours, also drinking some of the meat juices at the bottom of the Styrofoam container. This short scene set in Berlin's bleak projects—literally a broken home—suggests that Lena does not belong to this particular part of the city anymore. Having turned into a vampire, she cannot inhabit the social strata of the lower middle and working classes anymore, yet she also is not truly like the financially independent and socially transgressive vampire that created her. She is a liminal creature without a "room of her own," albeit one that quickly learns to blend in. Becoming increasingly aware of her heightened sense of displacement, Lena successfully adapts to her new position in society and crosses lines with great ease. This ability ultimately marks Lena as dangerous, forcing her to leave the allegedly hyper-liberal capital at the end—a sweeping critique of Berlin's self-understanding as a place where anything goes.

In contrast, the group's earlier transgressions were ostensibly not severe enough to result in noteworthy repercussions or even expulsion. As long as they stay in their lines, the vampires go largely unnoticed despite their murderous behavior. For example, the women own a vehicle fleet of luxury brands, in which they race the streets of Berlin ignoring any traffic rules and speed limits. Yet, this breaking of the rules still operates within Berlin's acceptable parameters, a city notorious for reckless drivers. When they go shopping in a luxury department store after it is closed, they never disrupt the flow of capitalist transactions. Bribing the night guard, the vampires engage in a money spending competition that remains well within the limits of the tolerable. As it were, financial transactions allow these urban bloodsuckers to be invited into the city's consumerist temples. When Louise and the others take Lena to an exclusive restaurant, Nora tells her how they do not have to eat—with the exception of blood, that is, often served in shot glasses in the film—but can do so just for the satisfaction this brings. However, the most important aspect, as far as Nora is concerned, is that they will not gain weight. In addition, Nora explains, female vampires cannot become pregnant, which in turn allows them to have unprotected sex without having to worry about the consequences, a supernatural trait that increases male desire. Even when Charlotte begins smoking inside the restaurant and a toxic male patron reprimands her, ordering her to stub out the cigarette, she doesn't refuse to comply even though the vampires' status might allow them their inconsiderate actions. Charlotte seemingly obliges, only to push the burning embers of the cigarette into her eye, the burn wound on her eyeball healing immediately. Shocked both by Charlotte's preternatural powers *and* her insolent refusal of his barked request, the man calls for the check and leaves immediately, an instance of (male) power trumped by an unexpectedly even more powerful entity. However, like the Russian gangsters earlier in the film, the toxic male gets what he has coming to him, even as Charlotte complies with social norms and the vampire women don't get asked to leave.

Shortly afterwards, however, the vampires do cross a line when the four women break-and-enter into a large, tropical indoor water park, even though it is not the act of trespassing *per se* that triggers the backlash. Wearing bikinis, they relax on sunbeds and in the pool. The water park offers an artificial sunrise, allowing the vampires to see the "sun." When two security guards—blue-collar exponents of male authority and gatekeeping—discover the women, Louise, Charlotte, and Nora begin toying with them. They flirt and make sexual advances, only to mercilessly kill the two men before it comes to sexual intercourse. This time, their violent behavior leads to severe repercussions, in equal parts triggered by their own carelessness and Lena's interference from within the group. In the narrative, the killing of the two innocent—if easily seduced—guards constitutes the tipping-point for Lena, who now realizes where the blood she drinks from shot glasses is coming from. The narrative's treatment of the vampires' escapades changes suddenly at this point, a remarkable choice given that the vampires enter Berlin by crashing a passenger plane at the beginning of the film and go unpunished. It is not primarily the immoral and emotionless killing of their unsuspecting victims that renders the female vampires unacceptable at this particular point—after all, they have killed people, men and women, before—but rather their audacity to refuse these two men the reward that has been promised to them. Yet, because three out of the four women are presented as heterosexual—and thus double as potentially available sex partners to the male characters—this rejection cannot be solely justified by the vampiric curse of lesbianism spread by Louise, the seeming ground zero of female dominance and insubordination. With daylight approaching, Lena runs away from the others in a remarkable long shot, a scene that visually underscores her exit from the world of the vampires.

Lena cannot stay in Berlin because she aggressively fluctuates between categories via performative acts. Her identity becomes too fluid, which in turn allows Lena to cross borders on a whim, going back and forth rather than settling into a stable position. *We Are the Night* foreshadows her chameleon-like talent early on. When Lena runs into trouble with the police at the beginning of the film, her escape strategy includes stealing a summer dress and changing clothes, shedding her dark, baggy clothes for a more "feminine" and less "class-revealing" dress code. Yet, when finding her sitting on a bridge, Tom—chasing her in his function as a policeman—sees through Lena's disguise and quickly realizes that she is in fact the elusive pickpocket he is after—her short, dark hair and the piercing having revealed her true identity. When trying to arrest her, however, Lena breaks character and kicks Tom in the groin. Reverting to her former rebellious, lower-class self, she then jumps onto a passing tourist boat, evading apprehension by the authorities. This moment of impromptu cross-dressing not only sets in motion the romance between Lena and Tom, it also mirrors Lena's physical transformation into an ostensibly more "feminine" and "bourgeoise" character. After a violent run-in with the Russian mafia, Louise brings Lena to one of the vampires' lavish safe houses. In a central scene, Louise places her into a baroque bathtub, where Lena undergoes an act of baptism and rebirth—a paradigm— as in many a horror film—for re-thinking identity formation.[19] Submerged, her wounds heal, while her body also rejects Lena's tattoos and her piercing. Yet, the cleansing does not stop with these ornamental markers of the Other, as the bath also turns her short, black-dyed stubble into long, blond curls. Afterwards, Louise dresses her in an elegant gown, adding signifiers of upper class luxury to Lena's already reshaped body. Draped in fine clothing, Lena becomes an imposter. She pretends to be something that she is not and does it all-too well, which in turn renders her problematic primarily due to her lower class background.

Class and social standing have historically been central themes of vampire cinema. As Tony Magistrale notes, vampire films have traditionally brought to the fore not only the sexual undercurrent of vampire cinema but also link "the vampire to consumer culture and capitalist imperialism" which turns the former "Old-World Count" into a "world citizen."[20] As discussed above, *We Are the Night* honors this tradition in Louise and Charlotte, but also challenges it when Lena can never truly be such a "world citizen," no matter how much she indulges in consumerist practices and the pastimes of the über-wealthy. While Lena's outward appearance may change, her class background ultimately marks such a physical transformation as pointless, leaving her no other option but to leave the city for good with her boyfriend. Lena has to exit Berlin not because she is queer—after all, she yearns for a monogamous, heterosexual relationship—but because she plays with shifting identities, becoming a changeling that threatens to give Berlin's social repressed access to the world of the upper-classes. This said, Lena is not truly gender fluid nor a queer activist, rather she knows how to put these categories on display to her own advantage. Even though Lena's sexual preferences are clear, her imitation skills pose a threat to the community in the context of her class affiliation. Her quite conservative wish to form a nuclear family—with the caveat that getting pregnant may be an impossibility and Tom may or may not become the first male vampire in centuries—has thus to be transferred to a different place and a different time. Post-wall Berlin, it seems, cannot tolerate and accommodate a monster like her, despite the city's "valorization of its many liberatory practices" in the face of "a new constellation of illiberal social conditions (consumerism, gentrification, and xenophobia) [that] might actually neutralize these very practices."[21] Ultimately, Lena defies categorization, blurring too many lines by leaving behind her designated social strata. In this regard, it does not matter that her life-goals are ultimately quite normative. The fact alone that she is capable of temporarily recalibrating her sexuality, gender, and most critically, her economic position as needed renders her uncanny—as scary a creature as the lesbo-vampire herself.

Conclusion

In *We Are the Night*, Dennis Gansel updates the famous German Nosferatus, portraying his four female vampires as a threat to the deeply flawed but ultimately preferable (male) power matrix already in place.[22] The German high-budget genre film, as I have shown, is as much about crossing borders—those of class, gender, and sexuality—as it is about the fear of non-binary identities. What begins as a story of female empowerment soon evolves into a rather conservative tale of heteronormativity and conformity. After all, Lena survives because she deflects the "threat" of blood-borne lesbianism and by association radical feminism, before returning to a heterosexual relationship and reestablishing a more balanced relation between the sexes. Yet, because she has to leave Berlin in the end, the text ultimately remains ambiguous about its message. While Gansel partly equates lesbianism and vampirism, the latter does not produce homosexuality in *We Are the Night*. Clearly, Charlotte, Nora, and Lena retain their heterosexuality, yet they use their supernatural state to change skewed power-relations in their favor. Only when Lena's identity, at least temporarily, becomes non-binary, does the group meet its fate while Lena has to go into exile. Whereas the other vampires occupy binary identity patterns, Lena's parameters are constantly transitioning. She does not settle into stable identity positions, refuses to be either man or woman, lower class or bourgeoisie, exclusively heterosexual or homosexual. Lena is queer only in the sense that she takes recourse to performativity, while her preferences and desires seem ultimately heterosexual and monogamous. Lena's supernatural power helps her to accentuate and fortify her essentially straight sexuality, but she no longer belongs to Berlin due to her uncanny ability to cross over into social spaces and psychosexual positions that are not her own. At the end, she and Louise—along with the *Berlin Geist*—have all vanished into the night, albeit in different ways and for altogether different reasons.

NOTES

1. *Nosferatu: Phantom der Nacht (Nosferatu the Vampyre*, directed by Werner Herzog (1979), Herzog's remake of *Nosferatu: Eine Symphonie des Grauens* (1922, directed by F.W. Murnau). Kevin L. Stoehr notes, is "really an amplification of many of the moods and images that were evoked by Murnau's earlier movie" (253).

2. As John Coulthart writes, Kinski's "appearance—modelled on Max Schreck's original—is shockingly bloodless and inhuman, […] a reinvention of the Dracula role" (213).

3. See for example Harald Reinl's 1967 *Die Schlangengrube und das Pendel* (*The Snake Pit and the Pendulum*; released as *The Torture Chamber of Dr. Sadism* in the U.S.) featuring Christopher Lee as Count Regula. I disregard films that assign the moniker "vampire" to human killers.

4. Steffen Hantke, editor, "Postwar German Cinema and the Horror Film: Thoughts on Historical Continuity and Genre Consolidation," *Caligari's Heirs: The German Cinema of Fear After 1945*, The Scarecrow Press, 2007, page vii. Hantke convincingly identifies and then challenges "the prevailing critical opinion that there is no such thing as German horror cinema after 1945" (vii).

5. Steven Jay Schneider and Tony Williams, Introduction to *Horror International*, Wayne State University Press, 2005, page 2. Schneider and Williams argue that cinema's "situation […] has changed drastically due to the effects of the new global economy, the decline of rigid national boundaries, and the transcultural phenomenon affecting virtually all sectors of cinema" (3).

6. Ursula Vossen, *Filmgenres: Horrorfilm*, Stuttgart: Reclam, 200), pages 20–21. Vossen claims that "Während des Zweiten Weltkriegs erlebte der Horrorfilm einen deutageslichen Einbruch, galt er doch angesichts des realen Schreckens und Leides als unangemessen" ("During the Second World War, the horror film experienced a significant drop, as the genre was considered inappropriate in light of the real terror and suffering").

7. Hantke, page 67. As Hantke further reminds us, "the economic and cultural postmodernization of Germany in the mid-1990s has reabsorbed traces of its own prehistory, reproducing them today just like any other commodity," allowing also for a return to Germany's gothic tradition (2005, page 67).

8. Kris Vander Lugt, "From Siodmak to Schlingensief: The Return of Horror as History," *Generic Histories of German Cinema—Genre and Its Deviations*, edited by Jaimey Fisher, Camden House, 2013, page 161. As Vander Lugt points out, "recent scholarship suggests that horror film "reemerged' in the period surrounding reunification, but this is not the whole story" (161). Indeed, as I have argued elsewhere, the genre's return to the big screen happens about 10 years after the fall of the Berlin Wall.

9. Marco Abel, "22 January 2007: Film Establishment Attacks 'Berlin School' as Wrong Kind of National Cinema," *A New History of German Cinema*, edited by Jennifer Kapczynski, and Michael D. Richardson, Camden House, 2012, page 603. The return of commercial German horror films in the new millennium coincides with "the emergence of a larger self-confident cultural discourse in Germany expressing a desire for *Normalisierung*" after reunification, a desire that also found expression in the German film industry's "unexpected renaissance" in the first decade of the 21st century.

10. Heiko Rosner, "Toni Erdmanns Erben," *Cinema*, November 2016, page 119. As Rosner, a writer for Germany's largest movie magazine, *Cinema*, bemoans in one of his opinion pieces, "gute Genrefilme trauen die Deutschen den Deutschen erst recht nicht zu […], man denke an den Flop von Dennis Gansels eleganter Vampir-Modernisierung 'Wir sind die Nacht'"(["the Germans do not believe that their own directors can make good genre films, […], one only has to take a look at Dennis Gansel's elegant vampire-modernization 'We are the Night,' which bombed at the box office").

11. Marco Abel, "22 January 2007: Film Establishment Attacks 'Berlin School' as Wrong Kind of National Cinema," *A New History of German Cinema*, edited by Jennifer Kaperczynski and Michael D. Richardson, Camden House, 2012, page 606.

12. Dimendberg, page 954.

13. Daniel Morat, *Weltstadtvergnügen. Berlin 1880–1930*, edited by Daniel Morat, et al., Gottingen, Vandenhoeck & Rupprecht, page 21.

14. Judith Halberstam, *Skin Shows: Gothic Horror and the Technology of Monsters*, Duke University Press, 1995, page 88.

15. Halberstam, page 89.

16. Tony Magistrale, *Abject Terrors: Surveying the Modern and Postmodern Horror Film*, Peter Lang, 2005, page 38. Magistrale writes that the lesbian vampire film "constitutes a rather extensive subgenre of the vampiric cinematic history," whose most prominent examples include the revenants in Harry Kümel's *Daughters of Darkness* and Tony Scott's *The Hunger* (38).

17. Barbara Creed, *Phallic Panic: Film, Horror, and the Primal Uncanny*, Melbourne University Press, 2005, page 61.

18. Interestingly, the most obvious German "barrier" is missing from the film: *We Are the Night* never addresses the Berlin Wall and its aftereffects on the city.

19. Anna Powell, *Deleuze and Horror Film*, Edinburgh University Press, 2005, page 75.

20. Magistrale, page 38.

21. Mirko M. Hall, "Review of Berlin Calling and Cityscapes: Berlin," *German Studies Review*, Volume 41, Number 2, 2018, pages 441–42.

22. Stefan Schwenk's fantasy-horror-hybrid *Montrak* (2017) is another recent German vampire film. *Montrak*, while not quite as polished as *We Are the Night* or its North American inspirations, evokes the successful *Underworld* franchise in which Kate Beckinsale plays the vampire Selene, a so-called death-dealer who wages war against werewolves as well as traitors among her own kind in a modern, often urban setting.

Chutney Vampires

Contextualizing Bollywood's Undead Cinema

ANURAG CHAUHAN

Bollywood cinema has its own long tradition of horror movies, from the time of black and white movies like *The Palace* (*Mahal*, 1949) to the recent *Silence* (*Khamoshi*, 2019). However, this tradition includes borrowing and other derivations from the West and especially from Hollywood, with and without reservation or acknowledgment. The debts are complex. In his book *Filming Horror: Hindi Cinema, Ghosts and Ideologies*, Meraj Ahmed Mubarki says about the Hindi horror genre: "If it has borrowed its aesthetics from the German Expressionism early on, it has also maintained a faithful contiguity with the generic formulations of Hollywood, the Italian Giallow and lately, the Thai, Japanese, and Korean horror" and "has used Hollywood horror as an extensive point of derivation."[1] With reference to Dracula films in particular, one might ask, how is Indian borrowing from Hollywood different from Hollywood borrowing from Europe? Given such cultural exchanges it is fair to say, with Stacey Abbott, "The modern vampire has gone global."[2]

The word Bollywood, a conflation of Bombay and Hollywood, was coined in the 1990s, but India's vampire movies go back at least to 1978 with *The Door* (*Darwaza*), which shows ghouls and glimpses of vampiric killings but not full-fledged vampires. *That Terrible Night* (*Wohi Bhayanak Raat*, 1989) is an Indianization—some would say a rip-off—of the Hollywood movie, *Fright Night* (1985). Directed by Vinod Talwar, *That Terrible Night* has a young man, Vikki (Rohan Kapoor), who finds out about his vampire neighbor, Kumar (Kiran Kumar). Kumar, who seduces and kills young women, is the nephew of a king 300 years ago and seeks revenge for a wrong done to him at that time. He is killed by the combined powers of a *sadhu* (sage), prayers, and a holy *trishul* (trident). *The Closed Door* (*Bandh Darwaza*, 1990) is from a line of horror movies by the Ramsay brothers. In it the vampire, Nevla

(Anirudh Agarwal), who is a seducer and has a strong army of followers, is finally destroyed when the repository of his evil existence, a bat-faced voodoo-doll statue and its lair in the Black Hill (*Kali Pahadi*), is burnt down and a romantic pair is reunited. Another Bollywood vampire movie *Bloody Dracula* (*Khooni Dracula*, 1992) has a Dracula figure (Harinam Singh) who, revived by a rich man, obeys his orders to kill people, mostly women. He is finally killed with a trident. The movie, too, has a love angle and a couple of other subplots with many characters. The Hindi movie *Dracula* was released in 1999. A nobleman is seduced and murdered and comes back as Dracula, who one by one kills those who killed him as they search for a fabled *nagmani*, a rare gem believed to be borne by a she-snake One of them manages to obtain help from a *tantric* (shaman), and the vampire is killed with a trident. In 2013 *One More Dracula* (*Aur Ek Dracula*, originally *Dracula 2012*) was released in Malayalam, the language of India's southwesternmost state. A man, Roy (Sudheer Sukumaran), revives Dracula at Bran Castle in Romania, has his body overtaken by Dracula, comes back as William D'Souza and he goes on a spree of killings and finally, his pursuers manage to bring him out so that the rays of the sun disintegrate him. A love story marks this vampire movie as well, with the Dracula falling in love with the girl, Mina (Monal Gajjar)—not unlike the first vampire film, *Nosferatu*, in 1922. Most recently *Neighbours: They Are Vampires* (no Hindi title, 2014), is another horror-vampire movie by the Ramsay brothers. It resembles *That Terrible Night* in that it also has a character, Sanam Chopra (Hritu), who discovers that her neighbors are vampires (Arbaaz Ali Khan, Roushika Reikhi). Although these vampires kill many, with the help of a professor, an expert on vampires, Sanam and her boyfriend are able to finish off the vampires at the opportune time of a moon eclipse. The parallels with *Fright Night* (1985) are conspicuous in this movie, too.

None of these movies was a big banner production. Those of the twentieth century especially were low-budget movies produced by small production houses. Cost-cutting measures pervade every aspect of these movies and in case of most of them, it is not uncommon to see the director donning the caps of producer and screenplay writer as well. As a result, these movies—more often than not—produce broad effects and suffer in terms of aesthetics. The sets are crude, and so is the cinematography, the editing is slipshod, with anomalies and discrepancies. The acting is also wanting at times, even by the Bollywood standard of "heightened" acting. The twenty-first century vampire movies are "less crude"; they don't show the vampire in close-up shots with exaggerated and grotesque expressions; they do not show tridents or other religious insignia threatening the vampire.

The influence of western movies is very conspicuous, not only in terms of plots but also in things like use of color and lighting in the style of Mario

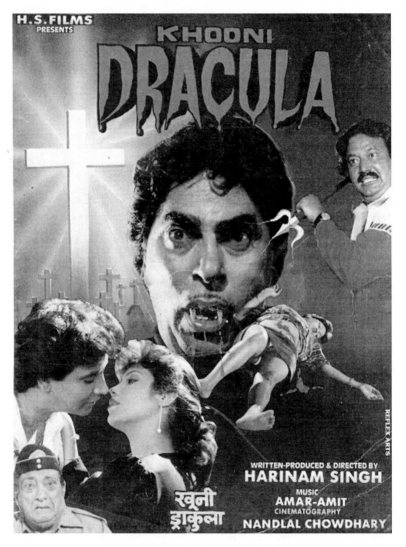

Bloody Dracula (*Khooni Dracula*, 1992). A dead criminal returns as a vampire when the blood of a murdered girl seeps into his grave and revives him. The vampire having been buried is implicitly a former Muslim, since burial of the dead is Islamic, whereas Hindus cremate the dead (Photofest).

Bava, for example, or musical scores like those of James Michael Bernard. *One More Dracula* and *Neighbours: They Are Vampires*, both of the twenty-first century, show improvement in these terms. Another reason why a "mature" vampire movie has not been produced by Bollywood is because the West has already offered a plethora of quality vampire movies. The young from India would rather see those and the old generation might prefer the Indianized versions.

There are other similarities and differences among these movies, too. In all of them, the vampire can be overpowered or controlled by sacred objects and religious icons such as holy water, tridents, crosses, garlic, or sunlight. While a romance is a part of *Neighbours: They Are Vampires*, in *Dracula* there is no romantic sub-plot. Revenge is the important motif, with the vampire holding a certain moral ground in killing the evil and greedy persons who murdered and turned him into Dracula. The vampire in *That Terrible Night* is also motivated by revenge, but he himself is evil. On the other hand the vampire in *Bloody Dracula* looks tame and works as a henchman of a person who had accidentally revived him when the blood of a girl he was murdering reached the dormant vampire in a graveyard. In *One More Dracula* the vampire does not obey the man who revives him but overtakes his body and uses it and with that body proves to be quite verbal and suave. In *The Closed Door* the vampire hardly speaks and is anthromorphic but, unlike the vampire in *Bloody Dracula*, he makes his presence known dominantly and intimidatingly.

The vampire cinema of Bollywood is more dominated by horror and sensationalism and not so much by a cinematic tradition of representing a "pure" vampire. The vampire comes from the West. The vampire figure in Indian cinema cannot be a Dracula; it can only be a hybrid, a quasi-Dracula or proxy Dracula. The Indian vampires are handicapped by a lack of historicity, mythical and cinematic both. They are challenged entities, displaced, without the backing of an indigenous tradition and have to create their own space in the diegesis of a movie, an exclusive unit in some ways. No doubt the tradition of horror movies or the component of horror—for example, demons shown in mythological movies adding to the horror component in Indian cinema—provides a background to the vampire and s/he can adopt it and adapt to it and rely on audience's foregrounding in horror and in the western concept of the vampire or Dracula. Thanks to Bram Stoker, the Indian audience is aware of Dracula as a blood-sucking vampire, even if they do not have knowledge of other associated details. In the 1999 movie *Dracula* one character simply informs the other, "Thakur has died and he has become a Dracula." The audience can use the foregrounding outside the diegesis of the movie to be prepared for the ensuing acts of the vampire. The vampire then has the more challenging task of accommodating and gaining acceptance by creating its identity in social, moral, psychological aspects. The vampire is also a secular construct to some extent because the Christian and the heathen principles and ideologies do not govern it entirely but are used for their performative potential rather than constitutive potential in that the vampire is not limited by them; his disruptive potential results in a strife which is not one-sided in favor of the vampire-destroyers in the movie's opening scene. Moreover, in the Indian context the vampire has the advantage that he will not be governed by conventional and predictable tools all the time. This places Bollywood vampires on a certain virgin land of suspense where he is an alien and free—like Stoker's Dracula or other western vampires, at least in racial and geographical terms.

Although the vampire bypasses the Hindu social hierarchy, he cannot escape it; he is not able to defeat the system based on Hinduism. In *That Terrible Night*, an ages old story is told in which a king favors his daughter over his undeserving nephew in the matter of accession so the nephew takes the help of a *tantric* (shaman) to get special powers, and becomes a vampire. He gets killed but is reborn after 300 years and his mission is also to take revenge on the king's reborn daughter. Here, the vampire is born out of a questionable ritual which is not of the mainstream faith and religious practice. He is evil too. Thus, his end through the powers of sanctioned religion and god is inevitable. J.M. Tyree analyzes Dracula as a threat to England "with a new model of life-draining efficiency but this terrifying vehicle of exploitation is itself destroyed by restorative forces of reaction, tradition, and religious superstition."[3] In *The Closed Door*, for example, not only does the vampire, Nevla, impregnate the wife of Thakur, thereby transgressing the moral codes of the society, he also stands as a threat to conventional power, represented by Thakur Pratap Singh (Vijayendra Ghatge). Even the Dracula from Romania in *One More Dracula* does not come with a white European body but occupying the body of an Indian man, the Dracula occupying the body showing at times as an animated demonic figure. Within the schema of the movie the vampire would look out of place or ludicrous if represented by a white man. This Dracula does not show a western sensibility and is governed by the personality of the man whose body he has occupied in social interactions—it becomes a metaphor for a Dracula who has adapted itself culturally. A vampire who has tamed its raw impulses that it cannot help exercising is kind of self-defeating, expressible jocularly as in the movie *Hotel Transylvania*. The vampire in Bollywood is emancipated from both the West and the East; paradoxically, it is doubly trapped—by Indian as well as western traditions.

The popular cinema of India relies on spectacle, and Indian vampire movies certainly belong to this fold because of their potential for performativity and spectacular events. The backdrop of India culture is used but with the complexities of class, caste, region, etc., reduced. For example, Thakur in *The Closed Door*, and the Thakur in *Dracula* belong to an upper class in the caste system, but the realities and tensions of caste system are not shown. In popular cinema, the cobwebs of difference and uncomfortable social realities are generally removed to make a clearing where all the spectators can converge with their expectations, the movie having taken away the baggage of the discordant elements and having presented them in an oblique, minimal and palatable way in order to end up being complicit with the status quo and the hegemonies that perpetuate harsh social realities.

Yet, the social realities are not totally ignored. In *The Closed Door* Lajo, the wife of Thakur, is called "banjh" (a sterile woman) and, under pressure to conceive, since her husband is being pressured by a relative to remarry, she approaches Nevla, the vampire and servant of a bat-like demon god. This is not unlike many cases in India of childless women seeking the help of "gurus" and getting deceived or disillusioned by them later on. Here the vampire is servant to a bat-winged demon god-idol who does produce a child, but the child is female and, lacking agency, must be given up to Nevla when she reaches the ages of sixteen. She is finally saved for marriage by Thakur, the family patriarch. Social hierarchies and gender roles are maintained in Indian vampire movies.

Representing a "pure" vampire in a Hindu film would entail a difficult task in terms of willing suspension of disbelief. It is a different thing when an Indian audience is watching a western movie—even if dubbed—as they are prepared to recognize, if not appreciate, the dynamics of it. In case of an Indian movie with a vampire, a foreign element gets introduced, which has to be handled artistically so that it leads to acceptance of the vampire and appreciation of the movie. On the other hand, this tralatitious character of Bollywood or Hindi cinema has roots in Hindu mythology and folk beliefs too. The vampire gains acceptance in India because "he" fits the paradigm of epics showing the contest between good and evil, where poetic justice is found and evil is punished or destroyed. Vampires are susceptible to Hindu demonizing. In this, Bollywood follows the epic tradition of the *Ramayana*, in which the antagonist's subjective world—at least in the abridged version which lives in the public memory—is not shown and remains invisible.

There is an ideological tradition which can be traced in horror movies of India. First, in terms of horror movies, Bollywood has drawn more on Indian beliefs, mostly Hindu beliefs in supernatural *atmans* (spirits), *bhoots* (ghosts), *dayans* (witches), and demons such as *pishachas, rakshasas, vaitals*, and *asuras*, etc. Tulsi Ramsay, from the movie house of Ramsays, who have made around 30 horror movies, assents: "The atma (spirit) is more common to Indian films."[4] Of these, the *pishachas* are the nearest to vampires as they are flesh-eating creatures. As for the concept of vampires, it is possible that the Hindu burial rites discourage belief in vampire narratives, vampires being from the West, where burial practices allow for revenants from the grave. Hindu cremation would seem to discourage belief in reanimated corpses. On the other hand, vampires lend themselves to full exploitation in terms of sensationalism and implied sex in the potpourri of "masala" cinema, with its romances, songs and dances, etc. In *Dracula* there is even a *nagin* (she-snake) and her snake dance, an often-enough used motif in Bollywood cinema to have earned it a parody in Gurinder Chadha's diasporic Indian film *Bride and Prejudice.*

In India, the journey of the mind did not have an Enlightenment phase as there was none for a large portion of the masses. However, the mythological *Ramayana* and *Mahabharata* on one hand and popular beliefs in ghosts and other non-human forms on the other hand were ingrained on the public consciousness. This was a mass inception wherein instead of deeper issues, simple, uncomplicated, and objective views of phenomena and explanations thereof reached and developed the common consciousness. Indian popular cinema derives from, and in turn, feeds this common consciousness. Bollywood movies show clear-cut, conspicuous polarities of good and evil, and Indian vampire cinema relies on that. This clarity is not simply an ideological stance; it gets expressed in the presentation too. Meraj Ahmed Mubarki, talking about the horror cinema of the Ramsay Brothers, underlines "their explicitness as part of the self-avowed aesthetics of supererogatory gore and sex." He would be describing *The Closed Door* when he goes on to say, "The monster/ghost in a generic Ramsay production is a fully constituted ontological presence brought forth not by any suicide or murder or unperformed last rites. It commands a prior existence. Visual blatancy leaves no room for cognitive uncertainty and with no delayed collective social confirmation in the denouement, the camera does not shy away from the monster, it fetishizes it. The monster's all too physical presence is there for all to see and acknowledge."[5]

With reference to these polarities, in many vampire movies under discussion, the vampire is referred to as "Satanic." The word seems to refer to the obvious physical act of sucking blood and killing people but also to a mythologized, metaphysical concept of evil, presenting a contrast with good and with associated things like religion, morality, and god.

The vampire does work indirectly to expose certain realities of the society. Women certainly work as touchstones of this morality and when they don't live up to the social expectations or codes of conduct, they are punished. Again in *The Closed Door*, we see this worked out clearly. Lajo, the wife of Thakur, agrees to their child. Their daughter, Kamya, has grown up to be willful, capricious, sexually expressive, and inclined to evil. Even her father, Thakur, says at one point that she should be shot dead. She turns to vampiric ways and does get killed, as does the vampire's procuress, a witch. Thus all the women who are associated with the vampire do not survive.

At the same time, the vampire, as an ambivalent signifier, also stands for resistance. The capers of the vampire are an exercise of power and resistance. His elation, killings, and demonic conduct are carnivalesque, disturbing the status quo of society, cutting through the hierarchies of caste, class, region, and religion—all strongly present in India. This is one reason that the vampire has been adopted by filmmakers because the vampire is embraced by the simplest groups in the population, the poor and the lower middle class, for whom the verbal vampire resonates. The vampire in Bollywood embodies a paradox, wielding and inspiring power before he is destroyed, an agent provocateur, an anti-establishment power whose presence is enjoyed at a certain subconscious level by this class of movie goers for whom any change is welcome. It is a matter of common belief in the twentieth century that it was "rickshaw wallahs" (rickshaw pullers)—a collective, albeit condescending and partly figurative term for those on the lowest rung of society—who watch such second grade or third rate movies with sensationalism and sex. If in the darkness of the cinema hall all are equal, the rickshaw puller is more than equal, enjoying the satisfaction of impulses that the socio-cultural setup of the society will never allow him to have. The liminal and border existence of the vampire parallels that of his fellow spectators in the cheaper, lower-level seats, the poor and the oppressed, drowned by the narratives of caste, class and even of nation. The umbrellas of nation and society attempt to be their representatives and promise them cinematic pleasures provided that they maintain the status quo. The vampire hates status quo, but the vampire is always destroyed. According to Stacey Abbott, the vampire is a force of movement and change and is always in a state of "disintegration and renewal."[6] This might be one reason why the masses in small towns or a certain section of the society in bigger cities whose literacy level is low and financial status poor, those worst affected by caste divisions, throng to watch such vampire movies because they strike a chord with them at a certain level. At the same time, this audience, conditioned by the ideological hegemony of morality and religion, endorses the defeat of the vampire. Sangita Gopal notes, "immediately after the [1990s liberalization of the film industry] Hindi horror suddenly went upscale, recasting itself as a metropolitan product addressed to India's globalizing middle classes."[7] The twenty-first century vampire cinema of Bollywood has become more chic and invites the attention of all sections of society. This became possible because of the changes to the film industry toward the end of the last century.

The vampire entered the Hindi cinema somewhat late, in the second half of the twentieth century. In a strict sense, there have not been many vampire movies in Hindi. This does not mean that they are an exclusive entity, unrelated to the society, the times, and to Bollywood. The melodrama of "masala" movies of Bollywood carries over to the horror movies and vampire movies too. In the final moments of the horror movie *The Maneater Beauty* (*Aadamkhor Haseena*, 2002) the predator and her assistant spirit are killed by a combination of religious insignia that include not only the Hindu trident and the Christian cross but also words representing the power of other monotheistic religions like Islam and Sikhism that chase and kill them—endorsing for one thing, the idea of post-independence secular India where all religions are held in regard. I endorse Harold Bloom when he says, "in some sense *all* movies are vampire films, so that those explicitly vampiric merely expose all the implications of the medium."[8] Vampire movies are extended or amplified versions of the conscious or subconscious desires, even perverse sexuality, Oedipal dynamics, and early developmental issues that get diluted or hidden behind other manifestations. Vampire movies bring them out more clearly in many ways.[9] Indeed, Connolly contends that horror presents a "royal road" to the understanding of the "shadow side" of our culture and to the possibility of an increase in consciousness.[10]

A tradition of consciousness affects the vampire movie, too. T. Zeddies posits that a specific historical context provides an experiential and interpretive template and it conditions the dividing line between the conscious and unconscious.[11] Yoshitaka Inoue explains this, saying, "The relationship between inside and outside, which are strongly connected to the vampire image, go deep into the heart of the historical change of consciousness. In this context, 'inside' and 'outside' are not used literally, but as psychological concepts."[12] Add to this the historical developments and we get an insight into the construction of consciousness as it has evolved with socio-cultural changes. The Western historicity of consciousness had a paradigm of this change with Enlightenment and other changes. In the context of India, however, it did not work the same way because a different dynamic was at work there: the caste system prevented knowledge or enlightenment from reaching many. Furthermore, colonial invasions and the resulting cultural changes were unique in their impact in India. Cultural consciousness was not really a collective "cultural" and, yet, it was cultural because a certain base of Hinduism remained dominantly present, at least, among the majority of population. The broad dissemination of Hinduism and social conditions that included poverty and illiteracy among the masses resulted in polarities of good-evil being presented in art forms that have persisted.

That Bram Stoker's Dracula found his way from Transylvania to India is not an accident. Its appropriation by the commercial machinery of western cinema and in turn, by Bollywood, is a phenomenon of economic forces of the market. The appropriation was by the second grade movies at the lower rung of the cinema industry, with an aim to make a fast buck with a low budget. At the same time, it is a process that mimicked colonialism. The "exotic" East grabbed the Dracula of the West, a modern construct of urban nature, fit to be adapted on the home ground for the Indian masses. The mimicry can be puerile, distorting the original as in most vampire movies of Bollywood, whether in part or whole. The Bollywood vampire, then, has become a postcolonial subject, marked by ambivalence.

Also, the vampire of Bollywood is textually an orphan, no Stoker having fathered it, and so lacks any textual foregrounding. Attempts are made, however, to put on it the seal of history and the word, for example in *The Closed Door*, when a red book with skull on the cover is shown as belonging to the disciples of the vampire, Nevla; further, the book plays a function in the plot too: Kamya (Kunickaa Sadanand Lal), fathered by the vampire, turns to vampiric practices after reading the book. In *One More Dracula*, Stoker and Dracula are acknowledged as influences in a voiceover right at the start of the movie. In the discussions in *Neighbours: They Are Vampires* (2014) Professor Indernath Malhotra (Shakti Kapoor), a writer of books on vampires, convinces skeptical young people about the presence of vampires. In the same movie, a book titled *Black Magic* is shown in the house in which the vampires live. In India, where illiteracy is still high, the book as a source of knowledge elicits a subconscious regard. In general, the Bollywood vampire's oral existence lacks the legacy of textuality and its stamp of tradition and antiquity, or even a link to Hindu religion and mythology, those being linked with the West and Christianity. Indian vampire cinema is like the anonymous oral and performing art forms of a colonized nation whose origins have been lost because they lacked a textuality. The application of Freudian and other theories that can be related to the origin, growth, perception, and reception of the vampire is frustrated somewhat because the Indian vampire lacks its subjectivity. It parallels the postcolonial nation which cannot return to its precolonial identity. Its infusion in the present times caused by globalization and its identity residing in hybridity and mimicry, in the oeuvre of Bollywood cinema, still not given a subjectivity.

In vampire movies from India, the vampire is born out of a subsystem unsanctioned by mainstream religion, or challenging the mainstream sociocultural system, or contending with people who have the access to and use the tools of mainstream religion to end it. He occupies a subaltern status not quite unlike that of people who have been at the lowest rung of caste system in India. The voices of the marginalized people get subsumed or drowned by the metanarratives of nation, caste, class, religion, etc., but the voice and subjectivity of the vampire also gets drowned by them and by the Bollywood machinery which caters to and carries the mainstream voice with itself.

Where the vampire lives speaks about his marginalized status too: Neola, the vampire in *The Closed Door* lives on Black Mountain, or Black Hill (*kali pahadi*), outside the village; the vampires of *Bloody Dracula* and *Dracula* of 1999 live in graveyards, and those of *One More Dracula* and of *Neighbours: They Are Vampires* live in gothic houses, not in normal abodes. Unlike its western counterpart who has enjoyed "geographic and often transnational mobility," the Bollywood vampire lacks circulation and adaptation as compared to the Western vampire.[13] This remote or morbid character's abode is as much congenitally attached to the vampire as is its blood sucking habit, without which the vampire would not be a vampire. So, in these fixed localities there may not be something exclusive to the Bollywood vampire but yet, some local color has been added. Also, while the vampire in earlier Bollywood movies was present as repulsive and ugly on most occasions, as in *The Closed Door, Bloody Dracula*, and *Dracula* of 1999, in the more recent vampire movies—*Neighbours: They Are Vampires* and *One More Dracula*—the vampires come in the shape of attractive human beings.

Like a subaltern, the Bollywood vampire does not enjoy a proper nomenclature. The Dracula of Bollywood is denied the coveted title of Dracula or the description as a vampire. In *The Closed Door*, the vampire is named Neola, which means mongoose (considered an uncanny creature); when the vampire appears in the human shape in other Bollywood vampire movies, it has normal human names but when it appears as vampire, the words "vampire" and "Dracula" are not used—except for the movie *Dracula*, where the title makes the connection; whereas in *Neighbours: They Are Vampires* and *One More Dracula*, being twenty-first century movies, they do not avoid the words. In *One More Dracula* the word "Dracula" is not used as a synonym for "vampire" but as the name of the Romanian character who has come to India. In *Neighbours: They Are Vampires* the word "vampire" is used as the generic term. Both of these words indicate the Indian audience's familiarity with vampire movies of the West, especially with the *Twilight* series. That familiarity indicates a growing literacy and a younger urban audience being the target audience, for whom earlier terms for vampire such as like *shaitan* (Satan), *haivan* (demon), *rakshas* (demon), and *darinda* (animal/beast) would now seem linguistically backward. Even on posters of the earlier movies such as *Bloody Dracula* the English word "Dracula" was used to promote a Bollywood vampire movie. This was a kind of exoticization of the vampire in an Indian context—English and knowledge of it being held in high regard—to attract an audience. Ironically, it also was an exoticization of the West by the erstwhile exoticized East.

The Ramsay Brothers, makers of many horror movies including vampire movies, do not get a mention in most books about Indian cinema. The vampire movies of India rarely have been shown at premium cinema halls. This vampire is like a diasporic subject, too, uprooted and hybridized, neither totally linked with the non-human or sub-human constructs like *chudail* or *pishach*, etc., nor is it like the Western Dracula or vampires it is trying to mimic. Relegated to second-rate movies and a lower-class viewership, the vampire itself is a marginalized entity that fails to find a place in the mainstream Bollywood cinema. On the other hand, the vampire survives because it does not shirk from the dingy quarters of the cinema halls or their lower-class viewership, indifferent to the high regard of the elite. The Indian, "chutnified" vampire is a paradoxical entity at times, kitschy, corny, rough around the edges. In *Bloody Dracula* the vampire looks like a black bear putting on a mask or draping on a furry dress. The Bollywood vampire trudges its own path and so is anti-canonical, but it is canonical as well, mimicking the western vampire, and so, very much fit to be called a postcolonial subject. Add to it the fact that in the Bollywood vampire movies being discussed, it often appears as a decorated marionette, muted, with exaggerated gestures, and melodramatic, a two-dimensional entity. This verbal limitation is especially prominent in pre-twenty-first century Bollywood vampire movies. Generally speaking, the Bollywood vampire is unable to express interiority. In the recent *One More Dracula* and *Neighbours: They Are Vampires,* however, the vampires exhibit some character and seem to be more lively. Transported from Romania to India, Dracula says at one point in a soliloquy, "Nobody in this country is my own, and I have come to know the cause of my loneliness now—the princess, my princess in Transylvania." This interior glimpse, however, is more to create a conflict in the romance space in the movie. Generally, the interiority, the inner space, and subjectivity of the Bollywood vampire is hardly seen. The vampire is, in this, like the colonized subject, objectified, seen from the outside and a judgment passed on it. The vampire's situation can be compared, ironically, to the female situation and to the marginalized, having been excluded and othered. It does not leave a trail, has never become part of the master narratives or motifs of Bollywood cinema, and stops at being a subgenre of horror cinema.

Despite this outsider status, the vampire in India reflects the mainstream patriarchal ideology largely working within the Indian society. The woman becomes an *objet de désir* and the vampire her seducer, lover, master, torturer. Scenes of women getting slapped by a lover or a father are not uncommon in Bollywood movies, and *Bloody Dracula* is no exception. In the more recent, twenty-first century vampire movies *One More Dracula* and *Neighbours: They Are Vampires,* this kind of casual violence is not seen, but slapping is conspicuously present in *That Terrible Night, The Closed Door, Bloody Dracula,* and *Dracula*—all of the twentieth century. In the twenty-first century movies the aspect of seduction, sex, and body exposing is also less, but not absent. In *One More Dracula* of 2013, there is a seductive dance, a part of prayers before the Goddess Kali to remove an impending negative power—presumably the Dracula. In *Neighbours: They Are Vampires* of 2014, there is a seductive dance by the female vampire. The vampire thus satisfies male desires by proxy, so it is not a surprise that the audience of these movies is largely male. Females may tend to avoid them because of mainstream, reserved attitudes about sex.

The sexuality of the vampire is always a threat. In *The Closed Door* the vampire, Neola, is called a "seducer" and, given the Indian sense of morality, is killed as much for his sexual transgression as for his vampirism. In *One More Dracula* the vampire falls in love with the same girl being loved by the hero of the movie. The vampire is a threatening force not only because it challenges the "right" or morally sanctioned sexuality of the hero, but also because its desires are arbitrary, unsanctioned, and carnivalesque. To give females a choice of partner would be to subvert patriarchal authority.

In fact, the sexuality of the vampire has a double character: while it intensifies his villainous nature, particularly in the context of conservative Indian society, it leads to the display of the sex on screen, thereby titillating and fulfilling the expectations of sex from the audience. While the vampire is committing the sexual act, the audience knows the culmination of it will be a killing, yet the feelings of fear (for the victim) and desire (for sexual gratification) both contend. In one long scene in the 1999 *Dracula*, a girl is shown in her last moments, pursued by the vampire, dragging herself on the ground, her cleavage showing, and from the camera angle it is obviously not her struggle that the audience will notice but her body. Interestingly, this movie's prurience serves to remind us that Dracula himself was the one seduced in his pre-vampire, human form.

In the West, vampires of different kinds appear with different racial and sexual identities, and with several layers and shades of personality. In India, the vampire will always be associated with the Indian undead forms. As vampire or Dracula, it has already been inscribed, from etymology to evolution. Should Indians worry that their vampire is not true to the original or is diverting from the western models? Writer Mukul Sharma, whose short story "Mobius Trips" was the basis for a supernatural thriller movie *Once there was a Witch* (*Ek Thi Daayan*, 2013), asks, "If Hollywood does not miss the *ulte pair wali chudhail* (the witch with inverted feet), why should we in India worry about the lack of iconic vampire characters?"[14] However, India is opening up to vampires in more ways now. There have been vampire writings like the novel *The Company Red,* by Shantanu Dhar, television serials featuring vampires like *This Story of Love* (*Pyar Ki Ye Ek Kahani*, 2010). The vampire is not dead.

Poetic justice seals the fate of the vampire in a way and makes the vampire movie closed ended. The tragic impact brought about by the vampire gets diluted, too, due to the poetic justice in the end. The pair of lovers usually survives too, but that cannot be taken as a rule since many horror movies have shown lovers getting killed. Many other horror movies have shown evil forces triumph in the end, so future vampire movies from Bollywood may not always go for poetic justice and may give the vampire a screen life recognizing that the modern audience, more literate, more skeptical and more disillusioned with religion and morality may accept or even welcome a vampire of a different kind or with a different end.

Overall, however, Indian vampire cinema has not progressed much. Mainstream Bollywood cinema has progressed more in comparison to it, mainly because vampires have been relegated to horror cinema with simple, straight effects without making use of or morphing into the new-age settings and issues. Indian vampire movies so far have remained transmogrifications of the western vampire movies. Perhaps the cultural and moral metanarratives and involvement with simplistic binaries have restricted its growth. At the same time, it is a truth that the Western vampire has been adopted by the cinema of India.

NOTES

1. Meraj Ahmed Mubarki, *Filming Horror: Hindi Cinema, Ghosts and Ideologies*, Sage Publications, 2016, page 31.
2. Stacey Abbott, *Celluloid Vampires: Life After Death in the Modern* World, University of Texas Press, 2007, page 215.
3. J.M. Tyree, *Warm-Blooded:* "True Blood and *Let the Right One In.*" *Film Quarterly*, Volume 63, Number 2, Winter 2009, pages 31–37.
4. Quoted in Poulomi Banerjee, "Why Dracula fails to get a bite of India but atmas, dayans make us shiver," *Hindustan Times*, 12 November 2017, www.hindustantimes.com/art-and-culture/dracula-didn-t-come-to-india-why-atmas-and-dayans-have-us-spooked/story-TNYKHxXVtsjDEOO6TcrwsK.html.
5. Meraj Ahmed Mubarki, *Filming Horror: Hindi Cinema, Ghosts and Ideologies*, Sage Publications, 2016, pages 146–47.
6. Stacey Abbott, *Celluloid Vampires: Life After Death in the Modern World*, University of Texas Press, 2007, page 5.
7. Sangita Gopal, *Conjugations: Marriage and Form in New Bollywood Cinema*, University of Chicago Press, 2011, page 91.
8. Harold Bloom, Introduction, *Viva Modern Critical Interpretations of Bram Stoker's Dracula*, New Delhi: Viva Books, 2010, page 1.
9. Barbara R. Almond, "Monstrous Infants and Vampyric Mothers," *International Journal of Psychoanalysis*, Volume 88, 2007, pages 219–35.
10. A. Connolly, "Psychoanalytic Theory in Times of Terror," *Journal of Analytical Psychology*, Volume 48, 2003, pages 407–31.
11. T. Zeddies, "Behind, Beneath, Above and Beyond: The Historical Unconscious," *Journal of the American Academy of Psychoanalysis*, volume 30, number 2, 2002, page 211.
12. Yoshitaka Inoue, *Jung Journal: Culture & Psyche*, volume 5, number 4, fall 2011, page 86.
13. Jeffrey Weinstock, *The Vampire Film: Undead Cinema*, Columbia University Press, 2012, pages 12–13.
14. Quoted by Banerjee, cited above.

Reclaiming the Marginalized Female Body in Ana Lily Amirpour's *A Girl Walks Home Alone at Night*

U. MELISSA ANYIWO

> I am your dark secret. I am a girl who walks home alone at night.
>
> —Ana Lily Amirpour

The last decade has seen the slow but steady acceptance of female-driven narratives that reflect, or attempt to reflect, the ever-elusive female gaze. Most evident in the horror genre concept of "the last girl," horror narratives have garnered a confusing, yet necessary critique of female protagonists who ultimately reflect an embedded male gaze for a seemingly predominantly young male audience. Yet the desperately yearned for return of feminist icon *Wonder Woman* and the massive success of her Disney counterpart *Captain Marvel* (who arguably solves many of the critiques of the old fashioned, scantily clad Wonder Woman) exemplifies the transitional aspect of today's audience in a world where females make up more than 50 percent of humanity.[1] Women on screen can now save themselves and the men around them without making romance a primary requirement. Nor can movie producers convincingly argue that an audience won't accept a female protagonist outside of a romantic comedy, or without a love interest by her side. But do any of these elements create true equality in the cinematic gaze based on a Western, patriarchal worldview? After all, the vast majority of domestic releases are still written, directed, and star men in male-driven stories. The same question can be asked of images of race in twenty-first-century film. The runaway success of the Marvel/Disney properties like *Black Panther* (2018) and *Luke Cage* (2015–

17) or the horror films of Jordan Peele provide examples of such change. The core element that allows for a post-colonial, post-patriarchal gaze is the ability of marginalized filmmakers like Jordan Peele or Ava DuVernay to finance their projects through non-major studios and distribute them through non-traditional means like Netflix or Amazon. As more writers, directors, and producers of color are allowed to distribute their work, their financial successes provide different views and types of experiences as well as crack the cinematic glass ceiling.

However, a core problem with creating cinema outside the traditional gaze is that audiences and critics impose a dizzying, crushing weight of expectation on the product to solve all the inequities in cinema and to be an explicit attempt to destroy white colonial patriarchal messages. This issue is particularly salient in the work of African American filmmaker Jordan Peele, vilified by the press for not making every film he directs an explicit challenge to contemporary racism. Audiences desperately in need of films that present their experience thus interpret films through their own gaze and often add what is not there. Lily Amirpour's 2015 film *A Girl Walks Home Alone at Night* illustrates many of these complexities as audiences starved of non-racist views of the Middle East, and images of strong female protagonists have attempted to read into the film an intent that is perhaps, at best, not shared by a writer who simply wanted to make a contemporary Western-Iranian fairytale.

The Muslim gendered body has become one of the most contested sites, or battlegrounds highlighting the problems of the Western post–9/11 feminist gaze. As Western Caucasian women are increasingly presented in complex ways, the Muslim woman remains excluded, demonized, and politicized. Conversely the Western feminist gaze appears to pity the ways in which the Muslim dress obscures the female form, using its existence as an example of religious and gendered oppression. The saliency of this historic moment opens and exposes the colonial white feminist gaze that has historically demonized and patronized the cultural choices of non-normative females, illustrating a consistent paternalistic/maternalistic perspective that assumes females can only make free choices if those choices match those of Caucasian, Western, middle-class feminists.

Amirpour's version of the contemporary Muslim body thus becomes feminist because of her non–Western vision of the marginalized, serving as both a celebration and a scathing critique of the visual treatment of the non–Western female body, while her work exposes the complexities of contemporary nationalism and the context of culture. *A Girl Walks Home Alone at Night* becomes another example of the problems of the contradicting forces at play in contemporary cinema where the audience sees far more than the filmmaker, who is thus "forced" to backwards engineer their intent. Amirpour's black-and-white movie and graphic novel series *A Girl Walks Home*

A Girl Walks Home Alone at Night (2014). Indie film director Ana Lily Amirpour pictures an avenging female vampire in a chador rather than a cape. Although shot in the USA, in black and white, the location could be anywhere and the Farsi (Persian) language helps to create a convincing Iran (Photofest).

Alone at Night, features an Iranian landscape in literal shades of gray, peopled with men who enforce female invisibility and weakness while simultaneously engaging in the very behaviors they claim the chador protects against. By making her unnamed girl-heroine a vampire Amirpour doubles down on her critique of the modern world where women's bodies remain not their own. This essay unpacks the girl's narrative, illustrating the ways in which female directors have consistently challenged the limits of the female body while simultaneously attempting to create simple, fun, superficial, fairytale-like stories accessible to all.

The Complexities of Culture

> Amirpour presents a film that challenges not simply the center or the fixed concept of the Western nation-state, but also the margins or the constant fluctuating borderlands of the diaspora paradigm by creating a private world outside these dichotomous communally defined spaces.
> —Emily Edwards

A Girl Walks Home Alone at Night is most often described as the first Iranian or Persian vampire movie. This is a complex claim to make primarily because of the cultural positioning of the writer-director. Ana Lily Amirpour is a product of globalism, born in the coastal town of Margate in the United Kingdom to atheist Iranian parents in exile, then growing up in and around the United States from Miami, Florida, to Bakersfield and San Francisco, California. Her early years in Margate were isolated and devoid of other Iranians, while her formative years were spent in the U.S. where she grew up speaking Farsi but completely immersed in U.S. culture. For those who do not exist in a cross-cultural space, these elements might seem unimportant since immigrant bodies, and their offspring, are characterized as separate cultural beings, a fact emphasized by the very U.S. practice of double-barreled, hyphenated ethnic identities such as Irish-American. Thus, Amirpour becomes Iranian-American because her parents were Iranian. The fact of her parents' atheism is central to her upbringing, creating a very different worldview filtered through the experiences of dissidents who fled Iran during its brutal 1979 Revolution. Amirpour thus grew up in a home that was indeed culturally Iranian, but on the fringes of the religiously centered culture. In the U.S. from the age of eight she, like other children of the 80s, enthusiastically absorbed all elements of the newly visual pop-culture typified by horror movies, with her "most treasured" possession being a VHS tape of Michael Jackson's "Thriller."[2] There were no Iranian movies or other cultural prompts beyond her mother's cooking, so her film becomes Iranian/Persian from an outsider's perspective, albeit one closer than others with no such connections at all.

Danny Leigh's 2015 interview with Amirpour opens with a recounting of her first trip to Iran in 2003. "A young American woman in Tehran with an eccentric haircut and a nose piercing, Amirpour was advised to wear the chador, a full-length robe that leaves only the face exposed. She still stood out; she was heckled and spat on by older women." In her ancestral home her Americanness stood out like a sore for "they knew right away I was western—I keep my head up and I look you in the eye." The desire to return to her roots thus exemplified the problems of hybridized culture; she might have been born to Iranian parents but she is culturally American and sees the world through U.S. eyes making her a cultural outsider where she might be expected to be on the Iranian-inside. It would be most honest to refer to Amirpour as an American-Iranian or a British-born American-Iranian. Even Amirpour balks at the label Iranian-American when referring to her childhood, and thus sees herself as merely American.

Much of this would be moot if it weren't for the fact that Amirpour herself describes this film as an Iranian fairytale, which thus garners the title of First Iranian Vampire Film. In reality this is the first vampire movie shot in Farsi, *but* the location for the film, Bad City, could be any decaying oil town, anywhere. Moreover, Bad City is peopled with characters desperate to be American, from the James Dean–esque Arash (Arash Marandi), to the spoiled rich girl, Shaydah (Rome Shadanloo), who wants to find America via the latest hedonistic experience. Our über-cool heavily kohl eyelinered protagonist is a record-loving vampire who wears Breton stripes and a fluttering, inky chador, cruising around a tumbleweed town on a stolen skateboard, her bedroom papered with images of eighties pop stars. Every recognizable pop culture reference is American. Even the style is a mashup, Amirpour says, "inspired by pop icons I love from the 50s all the way through the 90s, like James Dean, Sophia Loren."[3] Yet Guy Lodge argues that these "Western design intrusions are significant in a film that repeatedly shows Iranian cultural tradition—not least the status of women in Muslim society—to be in a state of flux."[4] The film operates as a cultural mashup of her experiences on the fringes of culture, and her characters exist in a space where they dream of a different culture than the one imposed on them. Ultimately, the labels imposed on this film are more distracting than accurate, pulling the audience away from its inherent originality to force it into cultural boxes that don't really fit, just like the auteur herself.

Yet the cultural positioning of a film like *A Girl Walks Home Alone at Night* is important chiefly because of the limited representations available to an audience of marginalized identities. Just as for Amirpour in Iran it "was a rush to hear Farsi spoken everywhere, being surrounded by people who looked like her,"[5] so too will any audience starved of realistic images of themselves flock to a film ostensibly about their world. But the gaze here is that of an American, not an Iranian, thus she would be hard-pressed to authentically fulfill her desires to make an Iranian film; an Iranian fairytale is perhaps the best way to describe it, a critique of a romanticized and imagined space. But as an example of a non–Western text, its cultural position becomes important, even central to the ideas that she attempts to expound. Even more apparent than the world created by Marjane Satrapi in *Persepolis* (2000),[6] *A Girl Walks Home Alone at Night* is a film that reflects a hyper-critical gaze from someone whose experiences of Iran are tainted by her parents' dissident experiences, her limited insider cultural contacts, and her failure to be accepted on her only visit. Ultimately, we can look to the author's own grappling with the problems of the hybridized cultural eye: "I wanted to make an Iranian film, but the question was how? Since I obviously can't shoot in Iran, the solution became the invention of the entire film; I found a desolate, vacant oil-town in the desert of California which became the fictitious Iranian ghost-town Bad City, and suddenly there were no rules. I created my own universe, and made the rules."[7] Unable to create a world she had never known, she created an entirely imagined space but one built on a negative critique. As a result, the film cannot lay claim to a non–Western perspective without acknowledging the limits of her outsider's eye. Creating a fairytale from negative memories can only add to the prejudiced colonial views of a decayed Middle East, lost in time and space. A cultural hybrid, then, *A Girl Walks Home Alone at Night* reflects more the mashup of contemporary cultures than a clear national vision of a real place and time.

An Iranian Vampire?

> The vampire functions as a convenient catch-all figuration for social otherness, …as the overdetermined condensation of a constellation of cultural anxieties and desires.
> —Jeffrey Weinstock

> I definitely have loved vampires for a very very long time.
> —Ana Lily Amirpour

The unnamed protagonist—in the credits The Girl (Sheila Vand)—is a vampire who exists in a Westernized space, rather like the author. While her chador wearing, skateboarding, silent voyeurism reflects a cross-cultural image, she is definitely NOT an Iranian version of the vampire myth. Strangely, though not surprisingly, The Girl is clearly a descendent of the Slavic (Dracula) vampiric tradition. In an interview with *New Republic* journalist Esther Breger, Amirpour supports this normative view by explaining her cultural references. "I got into Anne Rice when I was a kid. I fell in love with Lestat…. I've seen all the vampire movies, everything from *Lost Boys* to *Once Bitten* to Coppola's *Dracula*, Kathryn Bigelow's [*Near Dark*]. I love *Only Lovers Left Alive*."[8] Thus her image of the vampire is in the tradition of Rice's sympathetic outsiders. In the first of her two graphic prequels, Amirpour even pays homage to Rice's vampires when she has The Girl think the words "I came here to die," reminiscent of Louis's opening narration.[9] Like Rice's vampires or Jarmusch's in *Only Lovers Left Alive*, The Girl is achingly cool, sympathetic, and monstrous. Her existence reflects the experiences of the marginalized, rather than serve as a cautionary tale. As noted earlier, Amirpour's personal positioning as an American-Iranian complicates her cultural positioning, her understanding of historical Persian culture, and her desire to create an Iranian fairytale. Indeed, it complicates the inclusion of this film into the idea of a non–Western narrative since this is truly a U.S. production from the mind of an American. The European version of the vampire presented here underscores the challenges of hybridized culture and becomes one of the core problems in its laying claim to be the first Persian vampire film.

The oldest known vampires actually hail from Mesopotamia, now essentially the nations of the Middle East, almost 3,000 years before the Slavs found their *strzyga* or the Romanians their *strigoi*. From Persian artifacts we know that there were strong beliefs in blood-drinking demons who can retroactively be deemed vampires. We have tales of the ancient Babylonian Lilitu, arguably the template for the Hebrew Lilith, a broken-hearted monster who fed on the

A Girl Walks Home Alone at Night (2014). The unnamed "Girl" (Ana Lily Amirpour as stand-in for Sheila Vand) steals a skateboard and rides through the desolate Bad City of Iran. Her open chador sails behind her creating a cape-like effect.

blood of babies. The Babylonian goddess Lamashtu was another monster with vampiric tendencies. In Labartu texts she is described: "Wherever she comes, wherever she appears, she brings evil and destruction. Men, beasts, trees, rivers, roads, buildings, she brings harm to them all. A flesh-eating, bloodsucking monster is she."[10] Then there was the Hebrew Estrie, a shape-shifting female vampire who fed on blood to survive. Finally, myth tells of the Ekimmu (Edimmu), the most feared demons in Assyrian and Babylonian myth who can be traced back to 4000 BCE. The first blood-drinking and psychic vampires, these demons were said to be the souls of the restless dead, wronged in life and unable to find peace. Ekimmu focused their rage by preying on any living being, sucking both their blood and energy, and causing as much discord as they could.

Thus, the vampires born in the original Persia are horrifying, vengeful monsters who consume and destroy those around them. The unending search for vengeance and their penchant for attacking small children make them unsympathetic characters antithetical to the beliefs of their age. For example, the Hebrew Lilith, cast out of Eden for refusing to submit to Adam, is irredeemably monstrous, not just because she refuses to accept her subordinated place, but also because she consumes the blood and flesh of children—the worst crime according to Jewish beliefs. She, along with Estrie, focuses her attacks on the innocent *because* they are innocent, those who suffer under the presumption that life was fair or just. We are supposed to be terrified of monsters and do everything we can in life not to become them or become their victims. These are not the self-hating, emo, Byronic creatures intended to "grapple with their own kind of killer instinct" in ways that mirror our own identity crises.[11] The Middle-Eastern vampire, like their Asian counterparts, are terrifying creatures to avoid or destroy not befriend or fall in love with. There is little complexity to these ancient vampires. They were there to explain the unexplainable: sudden infant death syndrome, disease, infidelity, and unexplained deaths. Today we have scientific explanations for most things and human nature explains the rest. Moreover, humanity has proven to be far more monstrous than vampires could ever be, both in the ways we treat each other and the ways we treat our natural environments. With humanity the true source of the monstrous, our mythological monsters have become somewhat moot or defanged, their problems simplified and humanized. In short, ancient Middle Eastern cultures are overflowing with primarily female blood-drinking monsters that Amirpour has ignored for her Iranian fairytale.

Rather than being a descendant of any of these culturally relevant monsters, The Girl descends from the Slavic narrative or, perhaps more correctly, the Anne Rice tradition of the sympathetic monster suffering from guilt and ennui. Even though the comic begins with The Girl in the desert, the prequel comics give us a glimpse of how she found her way to Bad City, through Tehran, Marrakesh, Beirut, Paris, Prague, Moscow, and Istanbul over an indeterminate amount of time that, given the nation choices, must have spanned centuries. "Places I never belonged," she thinks. Each place has cultural relevance to those of Persian descent, and they are listed as spaces where The Girl has left a swath of dead bodies behind her. "Death," she thinks "belongs in a graveyard, not a metropolis full of beating hearts."[12] Like the author, this vampire is disconnected from both nation and time, existing in a future-past where she does not fit, because the world from which she hailed no longer exists. Her search becomes one for acceptance, but only in a space where she believes her monstrosity belongs.

As a reflection of this body out of time, we are never told how old this "girl" is, thus exacerbating her monstrosity by juxtaposing her visual youth with her essential immortality. We meet her in the prequel comics, at the end of fifteen years in the desert, and it seems clear that she is old, old enough to have seen civilizations rise and fall, old enough to have given up on life. Yet Sheila Vand's cinematic performance gives her a sense of childlike naiveté, dressed as a teenager who skateboards and who lives in a place with walls covered in pop music posters of eighties icons like Michael Jackson and Madonna, items usually associated with young adults. Amirpour describes the vampires in a way that reflects her positioning as Western observer admitting to liking "the more existential emo vampires" such as Jim Jarmusch's Adam and Eve or Anne Rice's Louis and Lestat, figures that reflect an Americanized self-absorption. Such vampires, intentionally or otherwise, provide a mirror on society creating a body one can empathize with. Director Amirpour also tells Breger that they're "like eternal observers of all this stuff .... They're very romantic and eternally lonely and extremely powerful."[13] These characteristics do not reflect the Persian vampire myth, nor do they reflect the Iranian world she claims to create. Her vampire, seemingly the only one in her universe, is much like Anne Rice's Maharet or *True Blood*'s Lilith, an ancient non-western vampire imagined by a Western mind and dropped into a non-western landscape.[14] Like Amirpour, The Girl is Iranian only outwardly, dressed in a façade of that culture.

The American "Girl" thus exists in a liminal space in which she both mirrors and contradicts the world and humanity around her. We are perhaps supposed to empathize with her, to pity her loneliness and root for the success of her relationship with Arash. She's seemingly guileless and innocent, while underneath she is a perfectly evolved predator who uses her sexuality to draw in her victims before destroying them in vicious attacks that splash more blood than she manages to consume. The graphic prequel *Who Am I* perhaps complicates the movie character of The Girl by presenting her as a pre–Bad City vampire who "came to the desert looking for death," spending fifteen years trying fruitlessly to kill herself out of guilt for her years as a killer of anyone who could fill her thirst. "I kill because I must," she tells us, in a frame where we see the vicious brutality of her murdering of a pair of lovers mid-coitus, decapitated with their guts ripped out, the Eiffel Tower in the background. "It is my design" she tells the reader.[15] She is not Lestat, a vampire who revels in his place as apex predator; instead she is closer to Louis, whose guilt forces him to despise his nature and abstain from the one thing he needs to survive. She believes others will hate her for what she did, and thus she hates herself. But like emo vampires such as *Twilight's* Edward Cullen or Stefan of *The Vampire Diaries*, she has waded through oceans of blood before she is ready to face her ambivalent guilt and wallow in her ennui. Girl is a very contemporary vampire, reflective of the writer's experiences of marginalization and loneliness and this historical moment in which all identities have a right to acceptance. Perhaps then the Persian vampire myths have lost their relevance in today's world of tolerance. As Amirpour says, all "people underneath have strange weird secrets inside and when you get to those things it makes you re-evaluate the outside and re-evaluate your assumptions."[16] We don't know why The Girl is a vampire, but we can see that Amirpour wants the audience to empathize with her "addiction," an identity marker that is outside of her control. Just as Hossein's heroin addiction is the result of his inability to cope with his wife's death, The Girl's reasons have become irrelevant and all that matters is their cost, which through her vigilantism she has seemingly found a way to pay. The Girl's vampirism is used to prove that "everyone has a secret. Something that keeps you alone … something people won't understand," a world in which we are all marginalized, if unevenly, by the choices we make and those made for us.[17] Perhaps in this way Amirpour's vampire offers more richness than the Persian monsters whose desire for vengeance is more akin to the ghost who can only replay its final trauma. Girl's isolating coolness is a more effective reflection of today's self-absorbed world where "far from the vampire frightening us into rejecting its difference (and thus all the differences that it symbolizes), the vampire has become an image [for] emulation, a glamorous outsider, a figure whose otherness we find versions of (sometimes ambivalently) in ourselves."[18] Like Adam and Eve, The Girl is simply too cool in her monstrosity to be despised by the audience. Instead she becomes one of the über cool kids, dark, gothic, and misunderstood, whose deeper understanding of the banality of life excludes her from it, making her a truly modern vampire whose strength now comes from not fitting in and who exists as just one more of society's rejects.

The Chador as Symbol of Oppression and Freedom

> As a vampire, and an allegorical outcast in society, the girl in the chador represents Amirpour's conception and criticism of identity. She is the ultimate social exile. To reject society's norms, accordingly, one can only exist in the shadows, in the margins.
>
> —Emily Edwards, 2017

Deniz Çakir notes that "there is not a single mention of Islam or Muslims in *A Girl Walks Home Alone at Night*, but it is still a movie that is important in the examination of Orientalism and conservatism. It is a messy issue."[19] Amirpour's use of the chador is the core element that separates this film from all other vampire tales because the unfamiliar, exotic and hidden fit the concept of the monstrous outsider well. The film was born from Amirpour's experiences with the chador (apparently a film prop) "and I put it on," she tells Esther Breger, "and I felt like a creature. I felt like a bat or a stingray, and I just instantly saw that this was an Iranian vampire."[20] For her, as for Western Feminists, the chador is a sign of the oppressive regimes and a religion that treats the female body as something to fear. When she visited Tehran in 2003, her first experience embedded in her familial culture, she found that even the dress did not hide her Americanness. "It's a mess. Medieval. Suffocating … like if I put my hand around your neck."[21] Thus, like other Westerners, she views this traditional form of dress as the most visible sign of the backwardness of Islamic cultures and their oppression of women. This very Western perspective assumes a woman's right to dress how they want reflects Westernized freedoms—as long as the West approves of the outfit. Once again, her place as diasporic observer complicates her ability to create an authentic experience while freeing her to use the chador as both evidence of disempowerment and source of power.

Amirpour recollects that the first time she wore the chador it made her feel alien, like a bat and she certainly plays on that bat-like imagery to bring home her point. Each time Girl attacks, she does so by stretching her arms up and out in a bat-like gesture reminiscent of Dracula. Amirpour even goes so far as to explicitly shape the edges of Girl's chador to resemble a vampire bat as she skates toward the camera until the chador fills the entire frame. The Girl becomes a literal creature of the night, covering the world (the frame) in darkness, leaving nothing but her starkly white face with fangs. The chador thus becomes an image of horror intended to signal fear and death like Dracula's—or Batman's—cape.

Amirpour's perspective was not simply born of personal experiences.

Rather, her experiences confirmed the images of the Middle East produced by Western eyes. In "I am a Hijabi Feminist" Sidra Binte exposed this "messy issue" when she made the decision to wear a hijab out of "an intense desire to obey Allah." Despite being a successful and engaged student, her choice was met with outright hostility and disdain by those in authority including her teachers. One teacher called her an "illiterate who needed to be educated" while her best friend admitted that if she had not known Binte she would have assumed she was "Restricted in all the worst possible ways. To put it short, oppressed." To Binte and millions of others, the hijab/chador is a symbol of empowerment, primarily because it levels an unfair playing field where women are judged only by their looks. She quotes Wendy Shalit's TED Talk "A Return to Modesty, Discovering the Lost Virtue": "Hijab is a symbol of empowerment and feminism wherein the woman not only accords herself respect but also demands it from others."[22] Thus, the ability to cover oneself, to display modesty in dress, is a free choice that releases the Islamic female from the types of disorders such as body dysmorphia, anorexia, bulimia, and the endless dieting that imprisons Western women in a cycle of shame. The female form is thus protected behind a sea of black until she chooses to reveal herself.

The use of the chador as the vampire cape offers multiple issues to discuss, primarily in terms of post–9/11 Islamophobia and the rights of women. Thus The Girl's dress is not just an iconic symbol, it "also starts to carry more meaning within its contextualization as a symbol of the clear and dangerous othering of Middle Eastern people in Hollywood, especially after 9/11." In short, the chador can only have two meanings to Western eyes: you "can only be in need of help, because you're made into a submissive servant by your own culture, or you can be dangerous, because you look different and remind me of terrorism."[23] Amirpour plays with both of these ideals by presenting a monster wolf in sheep's clothing. The chador makes The Girl appear vulnerable while providing the audience with visual proof that all Muslims are to be feared and the chador/burqa is there for the terrorist to hide behind before they kill us all. Amirpour plays with several cultural assumptions, not least of which are the ways the chador is used as a symbol of oppression. Bad City is filled with the dregs of humanity, even the "good" people do bad things such as when Arash steals a pair of diamond earrings from Shaydah (Rome Shadanloo), his wealthy employer's daughter. In the graphic prequels The Girl is searching for "something different ... a place that reeks of death and loneliness. A place like me." This is followed with a frame of the billboard welcoming people to town that reads "Founded: What difference does it make? Population Who Cares"[24] Bad City—like Jarmusch's Detroit—is a metaphor for spiritual and physical decay. Here the females covered by the chador are the most marginalized, as exemplified by sex worker Atti. Her

modesty is presented as a fetishized image, a fantasy figure for her male customers who can purchase the sexual services of a woman presented as modest.
Like light-skinned sex workers who might appeal to white men, a woman in
a chador represents both the modesty and unfettered sexuality of all women.
That she is also transgendered (and the first victim in the prequel comics)
only underscores the hypocritical nature of this covering. In contrast, the
men in this tale are variations of moral and physical weakness, contradicting
the belief in male superiority. From the heroin addicted father to the sexually
aggressive pimp, these men are the only representations of the Muslim male.
Amirpour argues that it is their natures that need to be covered up, their
crimes that the chador exposes, and their crimes that the chador cannot protect women from. The only female we see without a chador is ironically the
spoilt, rich Shaydah, whose youthful hedonism thus illustrates the problems
of Islamic femininity and the corrupting nature of Western popular culture.
Thus, the chador becomes a visual critique of the hypocrisy that keeps women
oppressed.

Bad City is peopled with prostitutes, drug addicts, pimps, and bullies;
thus, the Girl fits right in and, to a certain extent, is accepted by this community at the end of the world, or at least is ignored. Like Jarmusch, Amirpour
sees the world as a space of hopelessness: we are all rotting corpses with death
our only destination, and no one cares. This is a story about the reality that
"all people underneath have strange weird secrets inside and when you get
to those things it makes you re-evaluate the outside and re-evaluate your
assumptions."[25] Yet she simultaneously offers moments of hope such as the
existence of one innocent little boy that The Girl spares.

But as Amirpour tells Breger, "But then I'm American. I'm very American" and thus sees through eyes informed by white colonialism and its
imposed belief that all other cultures are non-normative and thus inferior.
As Attiya Latif states, "Western feminists tell Muslim women that they can't
conceptualize their own feminism, and instead adhere to theirs. In reality,
feminism is a diverse movement where women of various cultures and religions can determine equality for themselves." Feminism is about equality to
be sure, but that equality comes with the freedom to make informed choices
about what women are allowed to do with their bodies. Thus, the use of the
chador to highlight the visual inferiority of women actually adds to the negative post–9/11 image of Islam, a series of cultures represented as dangerous,
backward, and oppressive. As with Marjane Satrapi's protagonist in *Persepolis*,
The Girl is a character achingly obsessed with the romanticized image of the
United States as the land of free will. Girl and Marjane wear traditional dress
to provide visual evidence of their conformity. But underneath their clothes
they are as Western/American as can be. Amirpour's use of such Western
clothing is even more apparent than Satrapi's because of the nature of the

uniform; the hijab goes over the head to completely cover the female form, while her chador is more akin to a cape, left open at the front, making it harder to hide female dissent.

A Feminist Project?

> When women write about violence against women, it will almost inevitably be more terrifying because women grow up knowing that to be female is to be at risk of attack. We write about violence from the inside. Men, on the other hand, write about it from the outside.
>
> —Val McDermid

Is Amirpour's film feminist? Does it reclaim the female body by reframing the audience's gaze? We've already explored the ways it's not about Iranian or Persian vampires. But negations highlight the fact that filmmakers like Amirpour are not documentarians; instead they are auteurs who create films as reflections of themselves. "I want to explore my own brain," she tells interviewer Danny Leigh: "I think I make films because I'm lonely ... and it's a way to try to tell the world who I am."[26] This personal desire also highlights the difference between the desires of the filmmaker and those of their viewer. We see what we need to see or as Deniz Çakır puts it, this film "needs to be a feminist movie to exist." Asked the question with great frequency, Amirpour sighs "That probably says more about you than it does about me. A film is like a mirror. What I connect with in a movie is my own stuff. So consciously, no."[27] However, by positioning the characters the way she does, by having a marginalized female body as the protagonist and creating a product written and directed by a woman, she is inevitably creating a feminist product. The financing of the film, cobbled together by individual donors including Margaret Atwood through the crowdsourcing platform Indiegogo, reflects the non-normative fundraising inherent in feminist filmmaking. Even the title is an indictment of toxic patriarchy where the idea of a girl walking home alone at night inevitably conjures the sexual vulnerability of all women.

Denis Çakır, who chose this film to start their Women in Horror Month, writes that *A Girl Walks Home Alone at Night* is "a movie that creates space for important conversations on issues such as conservatism, patriarchy, female rage, sexuality and cultural isolation." This highlights the fact that it is the conversation of the film that matters more than the director's intent. After all, *A Girl Walks Home Alone at Night* would be unable to pass the low bar of the Bechdel Test, which requires only that two women in a movie have a conversation about something other than a man. It ends with the male and female protagonists riding off into an uncertain future, but together. "It is also weird in the sense that it is a movie that fits the portrayal of what [we], as consumers of [the] twenty-first century, think of as feminist media, but it is not a feminist movie."[28]

Amirpour is quick to dispute the moniker of "feminist" for her film, perhaps recognizing the limits such a label places on a film. When asked whether the film is explicitly about sexual politics Amirpour replies, "Am I saying something about women? Yes, and men, and children, and cats. If the film is feminist just because it's about a girl who kills men, then maybe I am [a feminist]."[29] As a filmmaker who creates stories that feature versions of herself (actress Sheila Vand could be her little sister), and a story with a strong, independent, female protagonist she is a feminist and her work is feminist. Indeed, her feminism is more apparent than her claims that this is an Iranian fairytale. The movie is about female empowerment, about women finding and using their power. Yes, The Girl is looking for a connection to make her a part of the world, and ultimately she finds one, even falling in love, but that in no way undermines that feminist nature of her journey, where time and again she proves she can save herself (even if she chooses men to help her navigate and connect to this world).

This film "like all other movies, is destined to be perceived and examined within the socio-political implications of its audience." This particular historical moment of effective critiques against rape culture makes this aspect of the film stand out even more, as a revenge fantasy. This is "a movie about a female vampire who hunts men that are guilty of gender-based violence, that is written and directed in a patriarchal time and society, and is not shy of symbolisms that carry a lot of meaning in that very society."[30] It's also a film about power reversal, with The Girl becoming the predator and the men her prey. While in reality a woman's sexuality is presented as a weakness that leaves them vulnerable to male sexual demands, The Girl uses that same vulnerability to draw her victims to their violent ends. For example, in her first premeditated attack again the drug dealer Saeed (Dominic Rains), a bully with the word Sex tattooed on his neck, she is completely silent. From the moment he first eyes her and invites her to his apartment, she simply watches and waits, accepting each of his expected gender-based moves based on his sexual arrogance. He fails to see any threat inherent in this diminutive silent girl in an open chador, even turning his back on her to snort a line of cocaine while showing off his monetary hoard. We have already seen Saeed attack the prostitute Atti (Mozhan Marnò) including striking her and forcing her to perform fellatio; thus he is deserving of his ultimate punishment. His fate is doubly signaled as a role reversal through the tigers emblazoned on his walls and furniture. Here he thinks he is the predator, safe at the top of the food chain, unsuspecting of the female who observes and then destroys. This girl who walks home alone is to be feared, not the thing to be afraid for. That is very much an example of contemporary feminism, a space in which female voices are amplified, and women can protect one another from those who say they are there to protect.

Much has been made of the construct in which The Girl preys exclusively on men. However, the accompanying graphic prequels show a very different pre–Bad City Girl who has gone from city to city courting death. Indeed, the first victims we see are a couple gutted and beheaded in Paris in an attack that seems more about rage than feeding. There is no sense that this is a case of vengeance or that the Parisian woman was being raped. Instead Girl was hungry, and they were food. We might be able to use conjecture to suggest that the prequels are intended to show The Girl's guilt over her years of indiscriminate killing. After all the first issue is about her attempts to commit suicide. Perhaps, like other Byronic vampires she has simply had enough of needing to take life to live. Her first victim in Bad City is thus a man engaging in gendered violence, striking a transgendered prostitute and calling them a homophobic slur. Yet there is no inner dialogue to suggest The Girl gained any pleasure from rescuing the prostitute or committing this act of vengeance. Instead we are provided with a frame that shows a pit of decomposing bodies, presumably her burial site, with all the victims appearing to be male. Still, there is nothing in either the graphic prequels or movie that explains why men are her victims, no triggering incident or memory that highlights some incident of sexual violence. That is perhaps a need of the audience, to find a reason or a cause. She kills because, as she says, it is her nature. Lest we get carried away with The Girl's unstated goal, not only does she dump the bodies contemptuously in the open, she also steals from her victims. In the film we watch her ignore Saeed's suitcase of money, but in the second graphic prequel we see her steal the ring of her last victim and drop it into a pile of such jewels in a bowl next to her bath (in a frame reminiscent of the Countess Elizabeth Bathory, a woman who bathed in the blood of her virgin victims). Thus, Girl's actions become feminist because a girl does them. If this were Anne Rice's Lestat, who does similar things to make a living, or Louis who stands in judgment as he can choose "bad men" the conversation would be very different, despite *Interview with the Vampire* also having been written by a woman. But the protagonist and the writer/director storylines coincide to open the doorway to feminist discussion essentially by allowing us to look beyond the surface of filmic images. Or, as Lilith Saintcrow argues, violence "in our culture is a man's game. Women are supposed to be weaker and more passive—the recipients of violence or protection, instead of active agents dishing it out."[31]

It really doesn't matter if Amirpour sees her film as making some form of feminist or ethnic statement. It only matters that *we* think she is.

NOTES

1. Emily Edwards, "Searching for a Room of One's Own: Rethinking the Iranian Diaspora in 'Persepolis,' 'Shahs of sunset' and 'A Girl Walks Home Alone at Night,'" *Glocalism: Journal of Culture, Politics and Innovation*, volume 3, no page.

2. Danny Leigh, "The Skateboarding Iranian Vampire Diaries: Director Ana Lily Amirpour Talks about Feminism, Porn and her Eerie 'Fairy Tale' *A Girl Walks Home Alone at Night*," *The Guardian* (London), 11 May 2015.

3. Press Kit. *A Girl Walks Home Alone at Night*, directed by Ana Lily Amirpour, Say Aah Productions, 2015.

4. Guy Lodge, "Sundance Film Review: 'A Girl Walks Home Alone at Night,'" *Variety*, 24 January 2014, variety.com/2014/film/reviews/sundance-film-review-a-girl-walks-home-alone-at-night-1201069599/.

5. Lodge, cited above.

6. Marjane Satrapi, *Persepolis* (Pantheon, 2000).

7. Press Kit, cited above.

8. Esther Breger, "'We Like Vampires Because We Hate Death': An Interview with the Director of *A Girl Walks Home Alone at Night*," *The New Republic Daily*, 24 November 2014, newrepublic.com/article/120376/interview-ana-lily-amirpour-director-iranian-vampire-movie. Brackets in original.

9. Ana Lily Amirpour, "Death Is the Answer" [prequel 1], *A Girl Walks Home Alone at Night: Essays and Graphic Novels* [included with DVD], Radio Comics, 2014, no page.

10. Sabrina Boyer, "Thou Shalt Not Crave Thy Neighbour: *True Blood*, Abjection, and Otherness," *Studies in Popular Culture*, volume 33, Number 2 (Spring 2011), no page.

11. Lodge interview, cited above.

12. Ana Lily Amirpour, "Who Am I" [prequel 2], *A Girl Walks Home Alone at Night: Essay and Graphic Novels* [with DVD], Radio Comics, 2014, pages 51–54.

13. Lodge interview, cited above.

14. Anne Rice, *Queen of the Damned*, Warner Books, 1988; *True Blood*, showrunner Alan Ball, HBO, 2008–14.

15. Amirpour, "Who Am I," cited above, pages 52–54.

16. Breger, cited above.

17. Amirpour, "Death Is the Answer," cited above, pages 21–22.

18. Boyer, cited above, page 22.

19. Deniz Çakir, "A Girl Walks Home Alone at Night is the Feminist Horror Movie of our Dreams. Literally," medium.com, 25 February 2015, page 3.

20. Lodge, cited above.

21. Breger, cited above.

22. Sidra Binte, "I Am a Hijabi Feminist: Hibjab Is a Symbol of Empowerment," huffingtonpost.com, page 4.

23. Çakir, cited above, page 4.

24. Amirpour, cited above, pages 63–68.

25. Breger, cited above, page 3.

26. Leigh, cited above.

27. Çakir, cited above, page 2.

28. Çakir, cited above, page 2.

29. Leigh, cited above.

30. Çakir, cited above, page 3.

31. Lilith Saintcrow, "Angry Chicks in Leather," *Pat's Fantasy Hotlist*, 2009.

Creating an Irish Neomyth

Byzantium's *Feminist Vampires*

JAMES AUBREY

Ireland famously has no snakes and, less famously, no vampires. Or so I thought, as did screenwriter Moira Buffini, who skeptically asked Irish director Neil Jordan how she could plausibly move the seminal event in her 2008 stage play *A Vampire Story* from Turkey to Ireland, which has no vampire tradition, for the movie they were developing as *Byzantium*.[1] Jordan assured her that Irish traditions include placing stones on burial sites to prevent undead corpses from returning from the grave—thus revenants such as vampires would have a history in Ireland. My similarly skeptical reaction to hearing of this tradition was to recall my long ago climb up Maeve's Mount to place a stone on top in order, I then believed, to honor the mythical warrior—not to keep her buried. Then I realized that Jordan might be thinking of the bog people, whose preserved corpses have been discovered across northern Europe, sometimes under burial stones that I had assumed were to keep bloated bodies from surfacing—not to pin down revenants. Only later did I discover that the Irish folklore Jordan had in mind was probably the story of Abhartach, a tyrannical wizard from Ulster who returned from his grave twice, each time vampirically demanding a bowl of blood from the veins of his people. He was prevented from returning a third time by Druidical intervention and re-burial, this time upside down and beneath a large stone.[2] So Ireland does have a vampire tradition—one of the oldest.

Partly due to its misleading title, *Byzantium* is not widely recognized as a film set in Ireland and England, let alone as a vampire film about female empowerment. I will examine how these features relate to the underlying story of a mother-daughter pair of 200-year-old vampires being pursued by a society of male vampires who call themselves The Brotherhood, who want to exterminate these only two females. Clara (Gemma Arterton) appears to be about thirty while her apparently sixteen-year-old daughter, Eleanor (Saoirse Ronan), poses as Clara's younger sister. As the film begins, a ruthlessly pragmatic Clara is working in a nightclub as a lap-dancer who also prostitutes herself for a living. The thoughtful and sensitive Eleanor spends her time writing in a journal and then destroying the pages that would reveal what they are and where they are living. For blood Clara sometimes kills her clients, whereas Eleanor kills only elderly people who feel ready to die. When one of the vampire brothers finds Clara and she kills him with a garotte, the pair flee and find themselves in the same English seaside town where they grew up 200 years before. They are taken in by a lonely local man named Noel (Daniel Mays), who has just inherited his mother's hotel, named Byzantium. Clara sets up a brothel there, to the dismay of the morally conscious Eleanor, who meanwhile makes friends with a local boy, Frank (Caleb Landry Jones) and reveals her secret self in a writing class they are both taking at a local college. In flashbacks to the early nineteenth century, we learn that Clara was originally recruited into child prostitution by a British naval captain named Ruthven (Jonny Lee Miller). Clara subsequently gives birth to Eleanor and leaves her with a local orphanage, but surreptitiously watches her grow up in what is recognizably the same building as a modern college. Some years later Ruthven visits Clara again and meets with a former midshipman named Darvell (Sam Riley), who is now a vampire. Darvell offers Ruthven a map to a rocky island with a mysterious cave where he, likewise, can become a vampire and gain eternal life. However, Clara steals the map and turns herself into a vampire. Ruthven takes revenge by raping Eleanor, hoping to infect her with venereal disease. Clara retaliates by killing him and taking Eleanor to the island to turn her teenage daughter, like herself, into a vampire. After two subsequent centuries of pursuit, Darvell and the head of the Brotherhood, Savella (Uri Gavriel), manage to track down Eleanor through her writing tutors and kidnap her in order to lure her protective mother to where they can execute her; however, Darvell intervenes and beheads Savella, instead. Clara is grateful but, valuing her independence, declines Darvell's offer of a future partnership. Clara further decides to emancipate Eleanor, whose relationship with Frank has turned romantic, and in the last scene Eleanor is taking Frank to the island to turn him into her own vampire partner.

Perhaps to help give the story a mythic aspect, the film never names the places where its events are supposed to be taking place, but the town is evidently in England and the island where vampires originate is evidently Ireland. Some evidence is in the dialogue. When Darvell and Ruthven meet in a flashback on the beach of a town, wearing English naval uniforms from the Napoleonic wars of the early nineteenth century, Ruthven mentions that he has been away "putting down a rebellion in Ireland"; so the town is not in Ireland. That it is England is implied by Frank's explanation to Eleanor that

Byzantium (2013). A publicity poster features the mother-daughter vampire pair, Clara (Gemma Arterton) and Eleanor (Saoirse Ronan), who are being pursued by an all-male vampire Brotherhood. Instead of fangs, these vampires drain victims' blood with a talon on the right thumb—an innovation of director Neil Jordan, whose Lestat (Tom Cruise) used a similar, artificial claw-device in Jordan's 1994 film *Interview with the Vampire*.

he has a disease that requires him to be on a blood thinner, so he and his mother have moved to the town "because the health care over here is free"; his father commutes, evidently from over there—Ireland. The seaside town with its abandoned pier would be recognizable to English audiences as Hastings, the famous site of the French (human) invasion of 1066, from across the English Channel. When Clara steals the map, she must ride overland from there to some distant location indicated on the map and then take a boat to get to a steep rock island with a hemispherical stone hut and a mysterious cave beneath. The island is recognizably Skellig Michael, with its natural bridge and dome-shaped monks' cells and cemetery—the site of an abandoned medieval monastery some twenty miles off the shore of County Cork, in southwest Ireland.[3] In the film an Irish mainland waterfall is graphically interfaced with the cave to provide a visual sign of transformation as its waters turn blood-red whenever a human is turned to a vampire in the cave below. The extremity of the site follows in the vampire tradition of exotic locations for vampires to come from, always from elsewhere to threaten home. In the vampire classic *Dracula*, the threat comes from Transylvania, then considered an eastern outpost of European civilization, as the vampire invades London.[4] In *Byzantium* the vampires come from the remote West; however, these vampires are sympathetic, and it is the vampire hunters who are evil misogynists. The Hastings that serves as the setting for most of the film is a decaying town with a decrepit waterfront, inhabited mostly by drug addled women, sex-deprived men, misguided teachers and the elderly. Neil Jordan's England seems a grim place.

Byzantium (2013). The vampires in this film come from Ireland, where they originate on the island of Skellig Michael, off the southwest coast, in a mysterious cave beneath one of the monastic stone huts there. When a human is transformed to a vampire, CGI birds noisily fly out of the cave, and the water of a nearby waterfall turns blood red.

Byzantium is loosely based on a 2008 stage play that has nothing to do with Ireland. The play is titled *A Vampire Story*, written by Moira Buffini, who also wrote the screenplay for the film.[5] As with Anne Rice's development of the 1994 screenplay from her own 1976 novel *Interview with the Vampire*, Jordan was involved in the development of each script but gave full screen credit for the adaptation to the author. Buffini's play takes place mostly in a comprehensive high school "somewhere in Britain." The main character, Eleanor, is a troubled sixteen-year-old student who thinks she is a vampire. In one scene Eleanor horrifies her biology class by drinking pig's blood from a bowl in the laboratory. She may have killed a classmate. In the last scene of the play Eleanor's blood lust is revealed to be the appetite of a deluded, hungry, anorexic teenager who has been sent by her mother, Claire, to a mental facility named Byzantium.[6] The play can be challenging to follow, with realistic and delusional scenes mixed.

Buffini's Eleanor has evidently acquired the vampire fantasy from having read two early nineteenth-century vampire stories with characters named Darvell and Ruthwen. One story is George Gordon, Lord Byron's 1816 "Fragment" which tells of an Englishman named Darvell, dying near Smyrna, in what is today northwest Turkey, who instructs a companion to perform a pagan ritual upon his death.[7] Having visited Greece and Turkey in 1809–10, Byron wrote this unfinished story during the cold summer of 1816 that kept him and his doctor, John Polidori, with neighbors Percy Shelley and Mary Godwin (soon to be Mary Shelley), all confined indoors at the Villa Diodati, on Lake Geneva.[8] While Mary wrote the first draft of *Frankenstein*, Byron wrote a fragment of what might have become a vampire story. The other story that Eleanor knows is Polidori's *The Vampyre: A Tale*, a work in which a character named Lord Ruthven dies, and his companion performs a burial ritual at a mysterious location near Constantinople, formerly Byzantium, today Istanbul. Ruthven returns from the grave, kills a local victim with a special blade (like Savella's), then turns up in London, where he murders the sister of his former companion by draining her blood on their wedding night. Polidori's story was inspired by—some would say stolen from—Byron's fragment and published in 1819.[9] Buffini pays tribute to these early vampire stories by naming her nineteenth-century characters Darvell and Ruthven. Instead of Darvell having buried Ruthven, in Buffini's play Darvell tells of having buried a friend at a ruined Greek temple, only to encounter him later, alive in Constantinople.[10] Buffini's use of the two male characters' names serves to alert playgoers that Eleanor's vampire fantasies are linked to vampire traditions which she has learned about, like anyone in the audience, from cultural lore. Eleanor's reading of obscure texts from British Romanticism is unusual, to be sure, but her having done so would be consistent with her obsessive identification with vampires. Frank, like most of us, has learned vampire lore from the movies.[11] Buffini reminds us of the fact that Romantic literature still affects today's culture by having Frank's classmates laugh at the Mary Shelley allusion when Frank reluctantly admits that his full name is Franklin Stein.[12] Even the name Byzantium in Buffini's play may be a sign of Eleanor's fantasizing. Buffini's Darvell twice insists on calling Constantinople by its pre-Christian name, Byzantium, for no evident reason. When the last scene of the play reveals Byzantium to be the name of the "nuthouse" where the deluded Eleanor is told by her doctor that her sister—not her mother—has come to visit,[13] we can surmise that Eleanor in her imagination has connected the name of her mental institution with the vampire materials that Byron once called "Turkish" to weave her elaborate fantasy.

Moira Buffini was lucky to be invited to develop the screenplay for the film. In 2008 her stage play *A Vampire Story* was being performed by high school students near Bath. In attendance was Stephen Woolley, who had produced several previous films directed by Neil Jordan, including his highly successful *The Crying Game*. Woolley happened to be at the play in the company of his daughter, who was a good friend of one of the student players. He thought that the play had cinematic possibilities and encouraged Buffini to develop a script, which he then sent to Jordan. The director was enthusiastic and the project was soon underway, with Buffini attached as screenwriter.[14]

From other interviews, it is evident that the idea to make the vampires Irish was Neil Jordan's. He has said that an early version was to be filmed in Morocco. Perhaps he was planning to situate the flashbacks there, in what might have substituted for Turkey. Jordan has added, without explanation, that "it didn't work out." Jordan must then have proposed Ireland, instead, for he mentions that Buffini was initially skeptical of his proposed location because Ireland had no history of vampires. Jordan assured her by email that there were Irish burials in history with rocks on corpses that were obviously meant to keep them from returning from the dead. Further justifying the change of setting to Ireland, Jordan has since remarked that he considers vampires to be like faeries, from an alternate reality.[15] Jordan's reference to *burials* in the plural suggests that, besides the case of Abhartach, he is probably referring to the corpses that have been found preserved in peat bogs across northern Europe, including nineteen in Ireland as of 1965, according to P.V. Glob's pioneering study *The Bog People*. Glob uses the word *ghosts* rather than *vampires* to describe the creatures that the burial stones or stakes through their bodies were meant to prevent corpses from "climbing out of the bog" after they had been ritually sacrificed to some local fertility goddess.[16] Although Buffini receives sole credit for the screenplay of *Byzantium*, director Jordan clearly influenced the production in this and other collaborative ways characteristic of *auteurist* film making. In this instance, Jordan turned an English story into an Irish one, with mythic aspects, to be discussed below.

First, however, another example of another contribution that must have been Jordan's idea is the thumbnail device, which, like conventional vampire fangs, is shown to grow into a curved, pointed talon when it is needed. In the film Eleanor uses her talon delicately to puncture an artery in the wrist and then suck the blood of an old man who wishes to die and, likewise, later, of an old woman in a hospital bed who welcomes her as an angel of death. Clara, by contrast, uses her talon as a slashing weapon, aggressively cutting the throat of Ruthven for having raped her daughter and, later, to kill a random male who has picked her up for sex on the beach. A similar fingernail device is used in Jordan's earlier film *Interview with a Vampire* (1994) when the eighteenth-century gentleman-vampire Lestat wears a silver claw-like extension on his index finger, like a pointed thimble, and uses it to puncture the neck artery of a lady admirer. This artificial fingernail-device is not mentioned in the Anne Rice novel the film is based on, so it probably was Jordan's innovation, which he later would make natural—that is, supernatural—in *Byzantium.*

This use of a fingernail instead of fangs to puncture victims may have been new to the vampire film genre, but the idea was not wholly original with Jordan. Indeed, like many vampire conventions, it derives from the novel *Dracula.* In a scene from Chapter 21, Mina Harker, married to one of Dracula's male pursuers, relates having been assaulted by Dracula, who has just used his fangs on her neck to extract blood, which he turns to wine in a metaphoric reversal of the Christian sacrament, quoted below. Dracula then uses his fingernails on his chest, to draw his own blood that he can then force Mina Harker to swallow in a symbolic act that consummates their mock-marriage:

> And you, their best beloved one, are now to me, flesh of my flesh, blood of my blood: kin of my kin; my bountiful wine-press for a while; and shall be later on my companion and my helper. [...] With that he pulled open his shirt, and with his long sharp nails opened a vein in his breast. When the blood began to spurt out, he took my hands in one of his, holding them tight, and with the other seized my neck and pressed my mouth to the wound, so that I must either suffocate or swallow some of the—Oh my God! my God! what have I done?[17]

What she has done is exchange bodily fluids with a vampire. The 1965 Hammer film *Dracula Prince of Darkness* replicates this scene, as Dracula opens a vein in his chest with an elongated, pointed nail on his small finger; in what Jordan may have meant as an homage, a vampire-staking scene from that same film is showing on the television that Noel and Eleanor happen to be watching one evening at hotel Byzantium. And for the same episode in Francis Coppola's 1992 film *Bram Stoker's Dracula,* the Count uses his thumbnail to cut open his own chest. In vampire lore in general, however, a vampiric mouth on the neck is customary—and more erotically charged than a vampiric fingernail—and has become the standard, even the clichéd form of vampire assault. Eleanor's unromantic use of her talon in *Byzantium* seems almost clinical in comparison to neck biting, so it is understandable that this alternative form of skin puncture has not caught on as a vampire film convention.[18] In *Byzantium*, however, it serves fittingly.

Other than adhering to the conventions of blood draining and vampire longevity, Jordan and Buffini do not adopt most of the Dracula traditions. For example, the vampires of *Byzantium* are not afraid of sunlight, mirrors, or garlic. However, one vampire convention is observed in the film, without explanation: the idea that a vampire cannot cross a domestic threshold without an invitation. Perhaps Jordan did not want to ignore this belief in the aftermath of Sweden's widely-admired 2008 film *Let the Right One In*, whose title refers to a unforgettable scene in which a twelve-year-old vampire begins to bleed from her pores when she steps uninvited into a boy's apartment.[19] In *Byzantium* Clara and Eleanor wait politely outside until Noel first invites them into his home at the hotel. Later, about to kill Frank for having found out that they are vampires, Clara confronts him at the door of his house. Frank asks, "Do I have to invite you in?" She nods, but he demurs. Clara declares, "Well, you're just going to have to come out then." The conversation is interrupted by a phone call from Eleanor, but the access issue resonates with many vampire stories including, of course, *Dracula*. Regarding the scene in Chapter 2 where Count Dracula ceremoniously invites Jonathan Harker into Castle Dracula, commentators have noted that this idea of requiring invitation may be invoking the belief in the middle ages that one must be willing or even complicit in order to be seduced by Satan, that a victim cannot plead that "the devil made me do it."[20] It is ironic that the famous scene from the novel has the vampire inviting the victim in, not the prospective victim inviting the vampire in.

In addition to the *Dracula* story, Jordan draws on Celtic mythology to make this into an Irish vampire story. In *Byzantium*, when a vampire candidate travels to the mysterious Irish island, he or she must be willing to be killed and replaced by a vampire double in the magical cave. At the moment of transfiguration, the waterfall outside turns blood red and hundreds of black birds fly noisily upward out of the cave entrance. The waterfall sign may be derived from the Irish myth of the sea god Mannanán; when he travels by chariot, the ocean is "churned to the colour of blood."[21] The significance or symbolism of the birds may similarly be derived from Irish mythology, where blackbirds can be "a sign of eternal life, bridging the gap between heaven and earth."[22] The idea of including them may have come to Buffini from a detail in Byron's "Fragment of a Novel," where the dying Darvell instructs his companion to bury him where a stork has repeatedly been perching on a particular tombstone; the moment Darvell dies, the stork flies away. Thus *Byzantium's* bird flights are similarly linked to the place and time of death of a corpse that will return. Alternatively, the bird motif may have been an inspiration of Jordan's, incorporating the legend of Óengus, who lives in the holes of rocks and has a flight of birds that wheel and sing in a kind of halo above his head.[23] The birds of the film might even be associated with the apotheosis of Midir and Étain, who leave the sinful world for "an unfallen and eternal life" in the world of the divine *sid* by changing into a pair of wild swans, rising "up through the skylight" and flying off like the birds from the cave in *Byzantium.*[24] There is even a Celtic tradition that gods can be killed by beheading, like the vampires of *Byzantium*, but decapitation of monsters is hardly unique to this story.[25] In any case the film's vampires not only originate in Ireland, they seem to be associated iconographically with immortals of Irish mythology.

Jordan visually introduces another European mythical creature to the film by including in the *mise en scène* a bas-relief sculpture of a melusine over the entrance of the North Haven orphanage where Clara once deposited the newborn Eleanor on the steps in one of the flashbacks to the early 1800s. A melusine is a two-tailed, fresh water mermaid of the type that has been made familiar by the Starbucks logo. Later in *Byzantium* the same sculpture is visible above the door of the same building in the present day, now the Northhaven School of Adult Education.[26] Eleanor meets Frank in front of the building, and they enroll there in a writing course, whose classroom has the same skylight that once illuminated the orphanage when Eleanor was growing up—and through which Clara would surreptitiously observe her daughter.[27] Complementing the old melusine over the entrance, the North-haven School's logo on the glass door is of a more traditional mermaid, with one tail. Evidently fascinated with mermaids, Jordan in his previous, 2009 film *Ondine*, refers in its title to the name of a character that seems at first to be the type of mermaid known as a selkie, or seal-woman, a shape-shifting mermaid-woman that Jordan teases his audience to imagine that an Irish fisherman has chanced to catch in his net. Jordan's earlier werewolf film *In the Company of Wolves* (1984) or his *Interview with the Vampire* (1994) indicate that Jordan has had a career-long fascination with strange, half-human, hybrid creatures—a fascination that might further extend to his transgender character Dil (Jaye Davidson) in *The Crying Game* (1992), who presents as female in the first half of the film and as male in the second half. It is perhaps significant that mermaids, like vampires, are traditionally a threat to humans, luring sailors to their death in manifestations as far back as Homer's *The Odyssey.*[28] Continuing in this mode, the visual references in *Byzantium* to melusines and mermaids, along with the verbal references to Irish *neamh-mhairb* (undead) and Jamaican *sucrients* (blood suckers) are personal contributions of Jordan's to the film, elements that make the story mythical and Irish at its core.

Byzantium's other visual and verbal connections to Irish folklore are complemented on the sound track by its occasional use of folk songs credited as "traditional." One is "The Unquiet Grave," sung by Clara in the background of the first scene inside Noel's former hotel. The other song is a lullaby, "A Mother's Lament," this time sung by Clara to Eleanor while they are traveling, singing about a skellington (modern Irish slang for skeleton). The scene is a tender display of mother-daughter affection—as long as the spectator is not put off by the idea of calling a thin baby "a skellington wrapped up in skin."

Another connection to Irish traditional culture is the film's odd, even misleading title, *Byzantium*, the old name for a Greek city that would become Constantinople in the fourth century and is today Istanbul, Turkey. The city itself is neither mentioned nor used as a location in the movie, nor does the title *Byzantium* give any indication that the film is a vampire movie, let alone a horror-thriller with a feminist angle, so Jordan must have liked the title for some reason having nothing to do with plot or marketability. Within the film, the name BYZANTIUM appears on a neon sign outside the former hotel that Noel has inherited from his mother, which provides a kind of asylum for Clara and Eleanor, perhaps derived from Buffini's calling the mental asylum in her play Byzantium, which inmate Eleanor probably associates with Romantic literature. Buffini's play also contains two verbal references to the Turkish city, when Ruthven tries correct Darvell for calling Constantinople by the anachronistic name Byzantium.[29] Perhaps Buffini proposed the film title as an homage to the Romantic writers who once traveled there, admiring its pre–Christian past, associating it with vampire folklore, and providing her with the names Darvell and Ruthven. Buffini may have been further attracted to the obsolete name for Istanbul by the fact that Ruthven in Polidori's *The Vampyre* dies and returns from the dead as the result of a transformation ritual that is supposed to be Greek; the Brotherhood leader, Savella, reminds nineteenth-century Clara that "our gods are much older than yours." So the sixth-century BCE name Byzantion—later Latinized to Byzantium—nicely invokes the pre–Christian mysteries of ancient Greece. But these connections are remote. As a movie title, the aptness of *Byzantium* is dubious.

The film's title does, however, in another, less remote way invite association of The Brotherhood with the Roman Catholic church, whose Eastern Orthodox branch was known for many centuries as the Byzantine empire. Viewers are told that the men's ritual sword, a large curved blade, is named after its place of origin, "from Byzantium, my souvenir of the Crusades," says Savella, where it evidently was appropriated in the name of Jesus. Savella orders Darvell to fetch the sword from their car, in order to properly execute Clara for having usurped the male prerogative of creativity in having created a vampire of her daughter. Savella explains, "our code does not permit women to create."[30] Earlier in the film he has told her that the Brotherhood represents "the nails of justice" and that women have "no part in our order." Clara declares that she intends to "curb the power of men"; thus she is not just trying to survive and to protect her daughter but also to oppose the Brotherhood on feminist principle that justice should be egalitarian. Thus the sword Byzantium, besides establishing that vampires have existed long before the nineteenth century, becomes a symbol of patriarchal authority, employed ritualistically to eliminate the female vampires and reestablish The Brotherhood's male exclusivity. Near the climax of the story, Savella reaffirms his anti-feminist feelings by exclaiming, "I hate these crying females" just before murdering the woman next to him in a car, by violently twisting her head around. His is such an extreme case of misogyny that it prompts the more progressive-minded Darvell to behead him instead of Clara. Viewers who know the history of Catholicism in Ireland can hardly fail to notice The Brotherhood's similarity to the highly patriarchal organization of the Catholic church, with its exclusively male priesthood and authoritative male hierarchy—not to mention its elite male society, the Jesuits. The male vampires against the oppressed female vampires provides for a suspenseful plot in *Byzantium*, and by making the villains of the story a men's group with a religious history, the narrative implicitly critiques church politics, which have been particularly fraught in Ireland since the 1980s, when the church went from a national political authority to political near irrelevance—a change alluded to on National Public Radio with reference to the boycott of the Pope's visit to Ireland in 2018 as "unimaginable a generation ago."[31] Reform of church politics is a part of the larger women's liberation movement, and both can be attributed to screenwriter Moira Buffini, whose screenplay for the 2010 film *Tamara Drewe* was also a study of an independent woman in a man's world. In *Byzantium*, Clara is her feminist representative.

Language further heightens the religious overtones of The Brotherhood's philosophy. In the film's opening monologue, in a voiceover, Eleanor calls Clara her "savior." Eleanor's first interlocutor, the old man who knows Gaelic, tells Eleanor that he knows about vampires from the "stories that priests used to tell to frighten the children." The vampire cave on Skellig Michael is called "a shrine" with "healing power," and the immortal inside the cave is referred to at one point as "a nameless saint." Even Morag (Maria Doyle Kennedy), the skeptical educator at Northfield, uses religious language to express her doubts about vampires, referring to the unlikelihood of their existence as something that would constitute a modern day "miracle" if they were found to exist. In *Byzantium*, as in many vampire movies, vampires are the enemy of the church.

Perhaps most significantly, the title *Byzantium* may also be meant to invoke a famous poem with the same title by Ireland's national poet, William Butler Yeats. A poet always interested in Irish cultural traditions, Yeats considered Constantinople in the seventh century CE to be an important moment in history, when politics and art enjoyed a harmonious relationship at the court of the emperor Justinian, and he idealized the setting using the older name Byzantium in two of his best known poems, "Sailing to Byzantium" (1927) and "Byzantium" (1930). In "Byzantium" Yeats employs images of living bodies aspiring to the status of living-dead "shades" that transcend "the fury and the mire of human veins," whereas the soul is more permanent, like an artistic "Miracle, bird or golden handiwork" that scorns "complexities of mire or blood." In between the real and the ideal is what Yeats terms "the superhuman / I call it death-in-life and life-in death." From this vampiric-sounding description Yeats goes on to imagine a human, death-defying transformation to a superhuman, bloodless state:

> Where blood-begotten spirits come
> And all complexities of fury leave,
> Dying into a dance,
> An agony of trance,
> An agony of flame that cannot singe a sleeve.[32]

Ultimately Yeats seems ambivalent about making this transformation

Byzantium (2013). Before Clara (Gemma Arterton) became a vampire, around 1805, she had been forced into prostitution and placed her child, Eleanor, into an orphanage. Two centuries later, when both are now vampires, Eleanor (Saoirse Ronan) takes a writing class in an unnamed English town, at Northhaven college, whose logo on the door is a mermaid, another mythical creature that traditionally preys on humans, one of whose versions is the two-tailed melusine, seen above the school entrance on a bas-relief of the creature that inspired the Starbucks logo.

from human to post-human, but he was evidently fascinated by the idea of immortality and associated it with the city of Byzantium, where he wrote that he aspired to be gathered there "into the artifice of eternity."[33] In 1939 Yeats was buried at his own suggestion in Sligo, near Ben Bulben and also within sight of the legendary burial mount of Queen Maeve.[34] Having himself been born in Sligo eleven years later, Neal Jordan must feel some connection to Yeats, and Yeats's feeling of connection to Byzantium could further help account for Jordan's liking of the name *Byzantium* for his film.

As the old Irishman tells Eleanor at the beginning of the film, after having collected and saved the discarded pages of her writing, "There's a story here." That is equally true of the film *Byzantium*, whose narrative could serve as a neo-myth for the new Ireland.[35] Film making is a collaborative undertaking, but Neil Jordan seems to deserve much of the credit for adding so many Irish elements to Moira Buffini's British vampire story that it became an Irish vampire story, whose vampires, like most vampires in recent decades, are not evil but, rather, sympathetic, even heroic. Jordan's casting of Saoirse Ronan and Caleb Landry Jones, with their Irish and Welsh names and faces, adds to the film's Celtishness. In the final scene Eleanor and Frank set out for Ireland and a new beginning, for a new race. Frank is to be transformed there to a vampire, not as a monstrous creature of the night or as a misogynistic brother of the church, but, like Eleanor or Clara or Darvell, an ethically evolved, super-human in a newly just, gender-inclusive society, like Yeats's mythic "rough beast [slouching] toward Bethlehem to be born" or like the newly reborn astronaut-baby at the end of *2001: A Space Odyssey*.[36] All four characters represent newly empowered, post-masculinist, post-humanist, mythic heroes of a reconceived, egalitarian Irish society.

NOTES

1. Neal Jordan, director. *Byzantium*, Demarest Films, 2012.

2. Moira Buffini, interview on *Byzantium* Blu-ray DVD, IFC Films, 2013; Neal Jordan, interview on *Byzantium* Blu-ray DVD, IFC Films, 2013; P.V. Glob, *The Bog People*, Faber and Faber, 1969; on Abhertach (400–500 CE), see Gallagher, *The Irish Vampire: From Folklore to the Imaginations of Charles Robert Maturin, Joseph Sheridan Le Fanu and Bram Stoker*, McFarland, 2017, page 26.

3. Skellig Michael will look familiar to some as the site of Luke Skywalker's cave-refuge in the film *Star Wars: The Last Jedi* (2017).

4. Bram Stoker, *Dracula*, 1897, Broadview, 1998. In the same year, 1897, Joseph Conrad reversed the terms of alien invasion in "An Outpost of Progress," which presents the British as the invaders of colonial Africa. The most extreme cinematic example of "elsewhere" is *Queen of Blood* (1966), whose vampire comes to earth from a planet outside the solar system.

5. Moira Buffini, *A Vampire Story*, Samuel French, 2008.

6. Buffini, pages 4, 55, 64.

7. George Gordon, Lord Byron, "Fragment of a Novel," 1819 (titled "A Fragment," dated 1816, on knarf.english.upenn.edu/Byron/fragment.html, no page. Retrieved on 18 January 2017.

8. Fiona MacCarthy, *Byron: Life and Legend*, Farrar, Straus and Giroux, 2002, pages 109–24.

9. John William Polidori, *The Vampyre: A Tale*, 181, Cavalier Classics, 2016.

10. Buffini, page 25.

11. Buffini, page 28.

12. Buffini, page 7.

13. Buffini, pages 25–26, 49, 64; the half-title of Byron's 1814 poem *The Giaour* calls it *A Turkish Tale*, and it contains a curse upon a character, that he should become a vampire. Stephen Wooley, interview, Blu-ray DVD of *Byzantium* (IFC Films, 2013).

14. Buffini and Jordan, interviews cited above. The alternate reality in which Irish faeries are said to exist is traditionally called the *sidhe* or *sid* (pronounced shee).

15. Buffini and Jordan, cited above.

16. P.V. Glob, *The Bog People*, Faber and Faber, 1969, pages 66, 74–77, 101, 105, 114, 149, 190–92.

17. Stoker, page 328 (ellipsis added).

18. There are two exceptions, probably borrowed from Jordan's *Interview with the Vampire*: in the 2003 film *Eternal*, Elizabeth Bathory puts a silver claw on her finger to kill her young female victims, and in the 2009 film *Cirque de Freak: The Vampire's Assistant*, a novice vampire is trained to slash with his elongated fingernails.

19. Thomas Alfredson, director, *Let the Right One In*, EFTI, 2008.

20. Leslie S. Klinger, editor. *The New Annotated Dracula*, Norton, 2008, page 43, note 9. Klinger's explanation is tentative, based on speculations by previous commentators. In chapter 18 of *Dracula*, Dr. Van Helsing describes the invitation as merely one of many limitations on vampires: "He may not enter anywhere at the first, unless there be some one of the household who bid him to come; though afterwards he can come as he please" (Broadview edition, cited above, page 279).

21. Mark Williams, *Ireland's Immortals: A History of the Gods of Irish Myth*, Princeton University Press, 2016, page xiii.

22. Carla-Rosa Manfredino, review of *Blackbird, Bye Bye* in the *Times Literary Supplement*, 14 December 2018, page 25.

23. Williams, page 430 and Figure 11.4. Óengus is often spelled Angus.

24. Williams, pages 86, 89.

25. Williams, page viii.

26. The school name is discernible on a poster in the background, inside.

27. Frank and Eleanor meet in front of the school, when he has a bicycle accident and starts bleeding profusely. After he is safe, she tastes the blood on his discarded handkerchief in a scene that recalls classic moments of disgust as characters desperately lap up blood from the floor, including Renfield in the novel *Dracula* (1897), Dracula in *Blood for Dracula* (1974), Jesus Gris in *Cronos* (1993), and Eli in *Let the Right One In* (2008).

28. Homer, *The Odyssey*, translated by Robert Fagles, Viking Penguin, 1996, Book 12, lines 198–204. Homer's Sirens were singers rather than swimmers with fishtails.

29. Buffini, page 25.

30. The medieval belief, from Galen and Aristotle, held that in animal generation, the male seed actively shapes the raw material provided by the female, a concept traced in Thomas Laquer's history of *Making Sex: Body and Gender from the Greeks to Freud* (Harvard University Press, 1990). In the 1971 Hammer film *Twins of Evil*, a similar, all-male group of Puritans in seventeenth-century England also refer to themselves as a "brotherhood" and justify their extreme hostility toward women in religious terms. Unlike *Byzantium*'s Brotherhood, however, theirs is to be seen as a lesser evil than the local vampires they fight against.

31. Sylvia Poggioli, "2018 Puts Pope Francis to the Test," *All Things Considered*, 27 December 2018.

32. William Butler Yeats, "Byzantium," *The Poems* (Dent, 1994), pages 289–99, lines 8, 13–14, 17, 29–32. I am grateful to Carol Samson for pointing out the resonant, identical names of the film and the poem.

33. Yeats, "Sailing to Byzantium," line 8.

34. Yeats, "Under Ben Bulben," part 6, lines 1–2.

35. Williams, page 380, explains the term *neomyth* as a mythic narrative of a modern writer's own devising.

36. Yeats, "The Second Coming," lines 21–22; Stanley Kubrick, director, *2001: A Space Odyssey*, MGM, 1968.

Dario Argento's *Dracula 3D*

History, Genre and the Politics of Camp

Vincent Piturro

Dario Argento, one of the most famous and most lauded of all Italian directors, has worked across and among genres throughout his long and diverse career. He cut his teeth on Westerns, moved to Thrillers, and then worked in Horror and Zombie films. Along the way, he gained success, notoriety, prestige, and acclaim from filmmakers and audiences alike. In 2012, some 50 years after breaking into the film business, he decided to dip into another genre—the vampire film—with an adaptation of Bram Stoker's novel *Dracula*. Unfortunately, he may done more to diminish his reputation rather than burnish it. *Dracula 3D*, which was screened out-of-competition at Cannes, is a thin, campy, over-sexed and over-acted, unintended parody of a serious vampire film. Rather than have Dracula transform into a bat, he turns into a large, ridiculous, CGI, green praying mantis that stalks and kills. The film was panned by critics and even laughed at during the Cannes screening, which portended a possible life as a cult favorite in the camp/horror/vampire genre. Thankfully for everyone involved, that has not panned out. When the film was eventually released, critics were even a bit kind, in the mind of many. As David Rooney notes in his review (at the Cannes screening) of the film,

> This is a tired rehash that adds little to the canon aside from such *outré* touches as having Drac shapeshift into a swarm of flies or a giant grasshopper in one howler of a scene. The film sits awkwardly between the 1958 Hammer Horror version with Christopher Lee and the campy 1974 Andy Warhol-Paul Morrissey *Blood for Dracula*. Sadly, there's nothing even remotely as fun here as Udo Kier sinking his fangs into the scenery and the "wirgins."[1]

Rob Nelson, writing for *Variety*, notes, "Director Argento half-heartedly mixes schlocky 3D f/x with one-dimensional characters for a near-two-hour joke that ought to have been funnier."[2] Mercifully succinctly, Neil Genzingler states in his *New York Times* review, "When insects are the best thing in your movie, it's probably time to retire."[3] And finally, in his review of the film for *Indiewire*, Gabe Toro states, "With 'Dracula 3D,' we finally know which of the great '70s genre filmmakers have fallen the hardest, and the answer is Dario Argento." After panning the film, he finishes the review with perhaps the best advice one can give if someone needs to watch it: "Bring alcohol."[4] If only I had read that before seeing the film.

So why does a venerated director, in the autumn of his career, take a stab (intended!) at a well-worn and well-established genre? First, as a matter of definition, I will use the term "genre" to discuss vampire films (and other would-be-genres or sub-genres such as zombie films or thrillers), understanding the stickiness of the term and how it has been used or not used in the course of film history. I find Argento to be a genre director in the classic sense, and why he chose to work in yet another genre is important to the current discourse. Peter Sobczinski, in his review of the film, gives us a clue as to Argento's purpose:

> "Dracula" is a story that has been told so many times on film over the years that anyone daring to do it again needs to bring something new to the party—a fresh take to the narrative or a striking visual approach—if it is to have any hope of standing out from the rest. This is what filmmakers as diverse as Werner Herzog, Francis Ford Coppola and Guy Maddin did with their respective versions (*Nosferatu*, *Bram Stoker's Dracula* and *Dracula: Pages from a Virgin's Diary*) and the results were among the finest vampire-related movies of our time.[5]

I would add to Sobczinski's list of venerated directors tackling the vampire genre: Neil Jordan's *Interview with the Vampire* (1995) as well as his (much more interesting) *Byzantium* (2013) and Jim Jarmusch's *Only Lovers Left Alive* (2014). The last two films are excellent examples of smaller, independent films made by two of the most talented directors of the past 30 years. The international and independent streak in recent vampire films gives us different types of vampires and vampire stories—from hipster vamps to feminist vamps to vigilante female vamps to vampire parodies. All of these recent films have enriched and expanded the genre in new and interesting ways. Enter Argento, and his desire to break new ground in what seems to be a fully-formed area.

Great directors wishing to make genre films is nothing new. The same dynamic swept through Europe in the 60s in the Science Fiction genre: Jean-Luc Godard made *Alphaville*, François Truffaut made *Fahrenheit 451*, and even the great Federico Fellini wished to make an artistic science fiction film (Remember that the premise of the film-within-the-film of *8½* was a science-fiction film!). Fellini later said that after seeing *2001: A Space Odyssey* that he was "cured" and no longer needed to make a science fiction film. The great directors always want to show their versatility and step out of their comfort

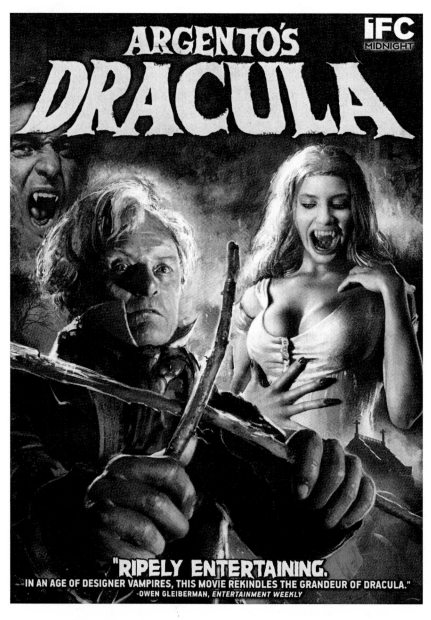

Dracula 3D (2012). In this Italian production directed by Dario Argento, Count Dracula (Thomas Kretschmann) runs his medieval village like a corrupt Mafia don (modern political implications are intended). Rutger Hauer plays Doctor Van Helsing, who doesn't appear until midway through the film.

zone to engage with genre: John Ford wished to make more than westerns, Vincent Minelli wanted to make more than musicals, and Martin Scorsese always yearned to make more than gangster films. The lure of showing your versatility has always been a staple of the great director, especially after the classic Hollywood cinema days. Dario Argento is no different, and his road to *Dracula* helps us understand the film and his desire to step outside of his comfort zone.

Argento started his career as a writer—initially as a film critic, followed by his first big break as a co-writer, along with Bernardo Bertolucci, on Sergio Leone's *Once Upon a Time in the West* (1968). His plunge into film involved a deep dive into the greatest genre in film history, the Western, with a director who re-defined that genre and arguably brought it back from the dead in the early 60s: Sergio Leone. So Argento would learn from a master who learned from a master. Leone started his career working as an assistant to Vittorio De Sica on *Bicycle Thieves* (1948), one of the greatest Italian films of all time and one of the greatest Italian directors of all time. Leone also worked as a screenwriter and assistant director on many of the epic productions at Rome's famous *Cinecittá* studio during the '50s and early '60s. The studio itself was a paean to the studio era, where many of the great international "sword and sandal" epics were produced; the entire era would be canonized in Fellini's *La Dolce Vita*. Italian cinema has a wonderful history of the greats schooling the next generation of greats: Federico Fellini began his career working for Roberto Rossellini (who many consider the father of Italian cinema) and then, in turn, tutored the likes of Giuseppe Tornatore (*Cinema Paradiso*) and Roberto Begnini (*Life Is Beautiful*). Bernardo Bertolucci (*The Conformist, The Last Tango in Paris*) learned from the great poet/director Pier Paolo Pasolini (*Accattone*), who also learned from Fellini, before Bertolucci began his own magnificent career. The great lineage of Italian directors going back to Rossellini and the Neorealists remains intact today, and Argento is a product of that lineage.

After several other screenplays, Argento secured his directorial debut in 1970 with *The Bird with the Crystal Plumage*. The film was a critical and box-office success, and it launched his career into the stratosphere. It also defined him as a director of thrillers, in particular, the *giallo*. *Giallo* is a uniquely Italian movement in literature and film that began in the Mussolini era, named for the book jacket color (*giallo* in Italian is translated as "yellow") of crime and mystery novels re-published in Italy in the 1950s. The books of such authors as Agatha Christie and Raymond Chandler, formerly banned during the Fascist-era, were edited and published with the distinctive yellow covers so they would be easily recognized as morally dubious. Italian *giallo* was born. The movie version of *giallo* came into existence in the next decade and hit its stride in the late '60s and early '70s as a thriller/horror/shock-genre that was popular with audiences and critics alike. And while there are no simple definitions of the type, *giallo* films usually have several qualities, according to Hossein Eidi Zadeh: "Movies with annoying shocking music, disguised and masked murderers, sharp knives and sex maniacs in the shadows."[6] For Bondanella and Pacchioni, *giallo* is really a subset of gothic horror with its own specific twists and a movement they saw as injecting life into the Italian horror scene of the '70s:

> The Italian horror film seemed to have run out of steam until Dario Argento (1940–) turned from producing films in the thriller or *giallo* tradition (characterized by graphic violence, serial murderers, and psychoanalytical plots that almost always remained in the realm of everyday reality) to films that treated the supernatural or the occult—the horror genre proper.[7]

By the end of the '70s, *giallo* seemed to have run its course as Argento moved to horror "proper." His most famous film, *Suspiria* (1977) is one of the most influential horror films in history and inspired a whole generation of filmmakers in many different genres. As Bondanella and Pacchioni note, "The extraordinary visual qualities of *Suspiria* make it a horror classic worthy of art film status. Films from German expressionism and images from psychoanalytical classics provided inspiration for Argento's masterpiece. The striking, sumptuous sets remain impressive and perhaps unsurpassed in any contemporary horror film."[8] But Argento's legend does not begin and end with his groundbreaking work in *giallo* and horror. He also extended his reach beyond his own work to follow in the footsteps of the great Italian directors before him and those who taught him: "Argento became an important mentor and sometime producer to young horror directors, thus making significant contributions to the genre by producing a number of important horror films."[9] The lineage of great Italian directors thus continues on through Argento. He also moved beyond horror to help elevate yet another genre: "Argento's most ambitious and important task as a producer was to support the making of the American horror film director George A. Romero's *Dawn of the Dead* (*Zombi*, a.k.a. *Zombies* 1978), a seminal work that, along with Romero's *Night of the Living Dead* (1968), launched the worldwide craze for zombie-themed horror films."[10] Argento would continue to work with Romero on various projects and churn out projects on his own, even contributing episodes to the Showtime series *Masters of Horror* as late as 2006. His own work, as well as his work in producing for others, has kept him relevant and important across genres: "Argento's reputation remains quite high among such directors in Hollywood, including John Landis (who gave Argento a cameo role as a paramedic in *Innocent Blood* [1992], an amusing story of a French vampire preying on Italian American gangsters in Pittsburgh), Joe Dante, John Carpenter, Wes Craven, and Quentin Tarantino."[11] Yet the output and the quality of Argento's films started to decline as he continued to make films into his 60s and 70s, and the reviews became more wistful and nostalgic with sub-par films such as *Mother of Tears* (2007) and *Giallo* (2009), both of which were attempts to bring him back to his *giallo* roots. So after 70 years and working across several genres—the western, thrillers, *giallo*, horror, and zombie films—Argento turned his attention to the vampire film, a path on which he had not traveled. He would attempt to re-invigorate his once stellar reputation within a genre that was experiencing a renaissance. That film would be *Dracula 3D*.

The narrative stays somewhat close to Stoker's novel but is limited in its scope. After a sex- and violence-goosed opening in the woods around the Count Dracula's castle, the Count (Thomas Kretschmann) turns the busty vamp Tanja (Miriam Giovanelli) into a literal vamp as his sycophant Reinfield (Giovanni Franzone) looks on in delight. It is right from the beginning, then, that we get a sense for the "knowing deal" the townspeople have made with the Count. Tania's mother even implores her to bolt the garlic-infused windows before Tanja sneaks off to meet her paramour. Next, we meet the meek and boyish Jonathan Harker (the fantastically-named Unex Ugalde) who has arrived in the nearby village to work as the Count's librarian. When he stops at the inn for a meal and a room, he notices a preponderance of garlic hanging from every exposed part of inn. He pays no mind. After making his way to the Count's castle, he is soon turned by the charmless Count; the poor schlemiel is reduced to nothing more than a prop for the remainder of the film before being killed in a poof of elementary-school-rendered CGI. Meanwhile, his wife Mina (Marta Gastini) arrives in the town to stay with her best friend Lucy (Asia Argento). After her father tells us that the town owes the Count for its prosperity, we get more gratuitous nudity in a gratuitous bath scene with gratuitous dialogue. Lucy, who shows bite marks on her thigh rather than her neck, turns into one of the Count's minions and soon meets her death, unceremoniously. Mina, we find out, is the focal point of the whole yarn, "summoned" by the Count to live with him after the Count believes she is the incarnation of his long-dead love. Along the way, we get ample amounts of gore and nudity, including both at the start of the film. The Count later gets to dispense of several ingrates in the tavern in an extremely violent, bloody scene worthy of a B-*giallo* film with stop-motion effects barely worthy of Mèliés. The film pivots when the Count's nemesis, Van Helsing (Rutger Hauer), arrives and quickly eliminates the minions before vanquishing the Count as he is about to turn Mina. Hauer's turn as Van Helsing is the actor equivalent of Argento's turn as director: Hauer is a glimmer of his former self and while it is supposed to be a serious performance, it comes across as pure camp (once again, drawing laughs at Cannes). The ending comes in the same forest where the film started. The film thus begins and ends in and around the town, and here lies the biggest omission from the book: the lack of any action in England (or wherever home is for Jonathan and Mina in this version) which would seem to absolve the film of any in-depth value as an allegorical story of invasion from elsewhere—one of the most important aspects of the vampire novel or film since Stoker. As Jeffrey Weinstock notes in *The Vampire Film: Undead Cinema*: "The Vampire, I conclude, is a sort of ready-made metaphoric vehicle waiting for its tenor. Its potency, however, derives from its intrinsic connections to science and social constructions of difference"[12] (19). Stoker's novel began the wonderfully metaphorically diverse run for the vampire and it has continued unabated since, with contemporaneous issues of fascinating relevance, including the repressiveness of the Victorian era in Stoker, the post–German malaise and xenophobia in *Nosferatu* (1922), the AIDS-era concerns in Kathryn Bigelow's *Near Dark* (1987), the coming-of-age struggles in *Let the Right One In* (2008), and the feminism in *Byzantium* (2013) and Ana Lily Amirpour's *A Girl Walks Home Alone at Night* (2014)—not to mention all manner of styles, subjects, and themes. Considering the thin campiness of Argento's film, one might seem to be hard pressed to find allegorical value, or any value, considering how equally panned and even mocked the film has been. However, there is an interesting twist in the film that saves it from utter and complete embarrassment—a take on history and politics that saves the film from ruinous absurdity.

The political twist in this film is that the townspeople of the village surrounding the Count's castle seem to be working in concert with him, as Pete Sobcyzinski notes in his review of the film: "As it turns out, Dracula has had a long-standing agreement with the townspeople in which he helps the village

Dracula 3D (2013). Argento's vampire doesn't always bite the victim's neck. Here Mina Harker (Marta Gastini) notices strange marks on the thigh of her friend Lucy Kisslinger (Asia Argento), who insists that they must be insect bites (Photofest).

prosper in exchange for unlimited snacking privileges, a deal that the locals are finally beginning to realize may not have been such a smart bargain after all."[13] This idea that the townspeople have made a deal with the devil to keep them safe raises issues ranging from government corruption to animal rights. It turns out that the seemingly thin, campy film has a lot to say.

In Argento's version, Dracula lets the town prosper so that they are allowed to live in relative safety from outsiders. Yet Dracula still picks off some of the townspeople at will ("snacking privileges"), so they live in fear of being the next sacrifice. Eventually, one assumes, Dracula will need to feed on all, if not most, of them. And as Dracula turns others—such as Tanja, Lucy, and Jonathan—they will need to feed on the townspeople as well. The cycle will continue, just as cycles do with overpopulation on our own planet and the human need to be fed. In his famous book on our current eating habits, *The Omnivore's Dilemma*, Michael Pollan defines this "deal" animals have made with humans. In discussing animal domestication throughout history, and how humans penned animals for eventual slaughter, he states:

> domestication took place when a handful of especially opportunistic species discovered, through Darwinian trial and error, that they were more likely to survive and prosper in an alliance with humans than on their own. Humans provided the animals with food and protection in exchange for which the animals provided the humans their milk, eggs, and—yes—their flesh. Both parties were transformed by their new relationship....[14]

Pollan continues on to note that this relationship, forged thousands of years ago, changed during the industrial age and the rise of factory farms. At the risk of reaching for academic hyperbole about a really bad movie, there is evidence for this reading in Stoker's novel and in *Nosferatu* as well. The practice of eating animals and using animal blood as sustenance has been around since the first humans invented weapons, but Stoker invests an inherent evilness and unholiness into the practice of feeding off another animal's blood. The practice of large-scale animal slaughter for food began in the Victorian era, coinciding with the era of industrialization and thus informing Stoker's novel (and meshing with Pollan's more recent argument about the history of the human-animal "deal"). As animal-killing for food moved from small family farms into factories, the relationship between humans and other animals changed as fewer people had to kill for food. People increased their dominance over nature and over animals in this era, and England in particular, with its relentless policies of imperialism and colonialism, now extended those policies toward animals as well.[15] Stoker's madman, Renfield, eats spiders and chants "The blood is the life" in a satirical exaggeration of human carnivorousness. Stoker's characterization of Dracula, however, is less easily dismissed: "This vampire which is amongst us ... can command all the meaner things, the rat, and the owl, and the bat, the moth, and the fox, and

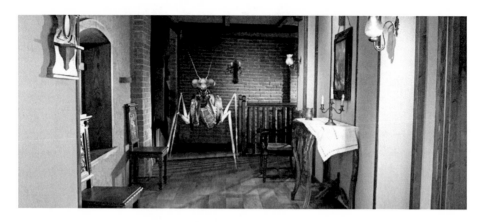

Dracula 3D (2013) Dracula can shift his shape in unusual ways. He attacks his first victim, Tanja (Miriam Giovanelli), as an owl; he saves Mina (Marta Gastini) as a wolf. He materializes in a town council meeting from a swarm of flies. Here Dracula attacks Lucy's father in the form of a giant praying mantis. Why not? (Photofest).

the wolf, he can grow and become small, and he can at times vanish and come unknown," says Van Helsing.[16] Dracula, the animal, eats us. He is the reverse imperialist who colonizes the English colonizers. Considering his predilection for turning into an animal and then feeding on humans, he highlights the dangers and horrors of the relationship between people and other animals. Dracula is literally made animal as a praying mantis that stalks and kills Lucy's dad in a particularly bloody scene. Oh, the horror, when the colonized turn on the colonizer.

F.W. Murnau's *Nosferatu* (1922) also addresses this dynamic. When Hutter meets Count Orlok and eats at his table, he is slicing bread when he cuts himself and draws Orlok's attention. Orlok is physically portrayed as rat-like and pestilential, and when his bloodthirsty urges take over and lead to Hutter's demise, Murnau is highlighting the horror of one animal feeding off another. The ease with which Orlok lives off the blood of his prey is thus analogous to the practice of eating other creatures for sustenance—be they plant, animal, or "other" humans. Professor Bulwer reinforces this idea later in the film, as he talks to his students about vampires. An intertitle card tells us: "I should note that, in those days, Professor Bulwer was teaching his students about the dreadful methods of carnivorous plants. One viewed with horror the mysterious workings of nature." We then see a Venus Flytrap ensnare a bug, after which Bulwer (John Gottowt) states, "Just like a vampire, no?" The next card refers to Orlok as "the predator," and then we see successive scenes of Knock (Alexander Granach) and a spider (another "predator") and then Bulwer again with another natural predator. The juxtaposed sequences of events together indicate that predator animals (or worse, plants!) capturing, torturing, and eating other animals is horrible business, especially when we can see it, as Bulwer demonstrates and the viewer sees. The relationship between humans and the animals we are eating by the billions can thus be seen as unholy and evil, just as Dracula is viewed.

That horror then, extends to the allegory of imperialism and beyond. Despite the absence of literal, geographical conquest, Dracula is a metaphorical imperialist—promising safety and prosperity to the townspeople who then allow him to rule them, rape them, and kill them. The villagers, some reluctant and scared, others sycophantic, pay the price like chickens in an industrial henhouse for that relative safety, security, and prosperity. The common ground for such obedience is fear: fear of reprisal, fear of death, fear of outsiders, and fear of losing their place—fears that lead to a yearning for safety and the comfortable.

Again, as Weinstock has noted, the vampire film is almost a blank canvas onto which we can project contemporaneous issues as well as subconscious yearnings or fears. Through this lens can be seen the topical: we can read former Italian Prime Minister Silvio Berlusconi as a metaphorical stand-in for the Count. Berlusconi held the position in four different governments between 1994 and 2011. He was also a business tycoon—the majority shareholder and co-founder of the Italian media company Mediaset as well as owner of the popular football club A.C. Milan from 1986 to 2017. He was involved in various scandals throughout his tenure as the leader of various Center-Right governments, but he somehow kept coming back, even after serious legal issues including tax evasion and allegations of underage sex. His hold over the Italian people is almost inexplicable—he kept making promises of prosperity, safety, and security, akin to the Count's hold over the townspeople. Catherine Edwards notes in *The Local*:

> Berlusconi, the ex-media magnate turned four-time PM, resigned from office in 2011 after losing his parliamentary majority, as the country was engulfed by an economic crisis from which it has barely recovered. One year later, he was banned from holding public office due to a tax fraud conviction. It was the first to stick in two decades of investigations for accusations ranging from mafia association to bribery. Many political observers declared his long stint in politics over, but he has somehow engineered a remarkable comeback.[17]

This was the Italian political mindset in 2011 as Argento's film was being produced; Berlusconi had dominated the country's politics for so long that the Italian people had become somewhat dependent on him, regardless of specific economic conditions, failed policies, or all manner of scandal—sexual, financial, or otherwise. For many, especially the older generation, he evinced a sense of safety, security, and at least the outward face of a successful Italy. And as the U.S., Britain, and his own country swung further to the right (especially on immigration policy), Berlusconi once again became the political opportunist. Speaking to *The Local* magazine about the 2018 elections, Professor Francesco Riccati discusses Berlusconi's move to the far-right in the recent elections: "The coalition with the extreme right is one that can better represent anxious Italians who have been losing ground due to the economic and political crisis and who manifest their frustration against other social groups who are even weaker, especially migrants and refugees," he says. "It also serves the purpose of those many Italians who continue to make money by not always transparent or honest means."[18] The parallel to Count Dracula in Argento's version is obvious: Count Dracula rules by fear, keeping up the specter of prosperity and safety as a carrot, and never failing to be an opportunist when it comes to the shifting fears of the populace. One of these shifting fears has been an increasing intolerance and disregard for immigrants and outsiders. The train station attendant in the film makes this explicit to Harker when he first arrives in the town, warning him of becoming too comfortable as an outsider: "These woods can be dangerous for anyone who doesn't know them." And while the fear of outsiders such as immigrants can make effective policy when used as a scare tactic, they are perfectly acceptable as workers (or concubines) when they silently do the work asked for by the master, as Harker does for the Count in his library or when the remainder of the townspeople pay a blind eye to the Count's deviances. And it is always interesting how political exigencies can dissolve when personal profit or pleasure is at stake; as Nick Squires of *The Telegraph* reported in 2010, Berlusconi had no reluctance to joke about the issue:

> The Italian prime minister, who is renowned for making jokes of questionable taste, was speaking to journalists after holding talks with the prime minister of Albania, Sali Berisha. Mr Berlusconi, 73, said an accord between Italy and Albania had successfully clamped down on the trafficking of illegal immigrants across the Adriatic Sea by people smugglers. He then joked: "I said to Sali—we'd make exceptions for anyone bringing over beautiful girls." Mr Berlusconi, whose wife is divorcing him for his alleged philandering, also joked with female Albanian journalists: "You know I'm single now."[19]

Put together Berlusconi's strange hold over Italian politics and the Italian people that includes the fear of the outsider, along with his appetite for women and philandering (noting as well that the Count in the film turns the beautiful, young, and bustiful Tanja and Lucy before trying to conscript Mina), topped off with his promises of prosperity, the comparison of Berlusconi to the Count in Argento's film is quite on the nose.

The xenophobia of Stoker's novel and *Nosferatu* in particular also show up in the film as a fear of outsiders coming into the town to break up the reign of terror with prosperity. One woman, caught as she is trying to leave town to alert others of the scourge, is unceremoniously killed before she can sound the alarm. The town has a metaphorical, nationalist urge that relates to contemporary Italy's—and Europe's writ large—an increasing intolerance, even hostility toward immigrants. Italy has had a particular problem with African immigrants coming across the Mediterranean from Tunisia and Libya, with the Italian island of Lampedusa as a particular point of contention; its location, equidistant between Africa and Sicily has landed it in the middle of the immigration/refugee debate (and has made it the subject of films such as the stirring documentary *Fire at Sea* or the fictional *Lampedusa*). As Angela Giuffrida notes in *The Guardian*, "Italy is a favoured landing point on Europe's southern coastline for people making the perilous journey across the Mediterranean, often on board unseaworthy boats, to enter the continent."[20] The issue festered throughout the whole of Berlusconi's tenure but came to head in the years just before and after the release of *Dracula 3D*. With the passage of Brexit in 2017 and the election of Donald Trump in the U.S. in 2016, a right-wing anti-immigration movement was materializing on both sides of the Atlantic. Ever the opportunist, Berlusconi used the same fear tactics in the Italian elections of 2018. As Giuffrida points reported in article from 5 February 2018:

> Silvio Berlusconi has pledged to deport 600,000 illegal immigrants from Italy should his centre-right coalition enter government after elections on 4 March [2018], as tensions simmer over the shooting of six Africans by a far-right extremist on Saturday. The 81-year-old rightwing former prime minister said in a TV interview that immigration was a "social bomb ready to explode in Italy" and that the shooting in Macerata posed a security problem.[21]

Again, the comparison between Berlusconi and the Count is striking. The Count's business interests seem to be self-serving and self-perpetuating, as his hiring of Harker as a librarian in order to lure Mina displays. Throughout his own tenure in politics, Berlusconi has maintained his business interests and has refused to divest himself from any of his companies or to place them in blind trusts. Critics have accused him of self-interest by enriching himself at the public trough while keeping himself inoculated from criticism and scrutiny by means of his media ownership. As David Hine notes in his article "Silvio Berlusconi, The Media, and the Conflict of Interest Issue," "From the moment Silvio Berlusconi entered politics in 1994, the conflict of interest issue has rarely been off the political agenda."[22] Berlusconi's ability to control the message has helped to keep him in the good graces of the Italian people (or some, anyway), much the way the Count's ability to portray himself as the town savior has kept the townspeople feeling indebted to him. The allegory, it seems, is also secure.

What seems, then, to be a seemingly thin, campy, over-sexed and over-acted, unintended unsuspecting parody of a serious vampire film is actually quite a bit more, following in the great tradition of the vampire film as a conduit for contemporaneous issues. Dario Argento, the progeny of the studio-era genre directors of the past, made his bones in genre filmmaking and continued to work in that realm throughout his career. Much like Hitchcock, Argento's most prolific work was in thrillers, a genre which was never taken as seriously—certainly by critics or academics—as other genres such as the Western. Of course, critics and academics now look back upon Hitchcock's work as much more than "simple genre work," and see him for the singular genius that he was. Argento's career may some day be similarly reviewed. Zombie films, for example, are now seen as critiques of hyper-capitalism, and Argento's work with Romero alone buttresses the case for more serious Argento retrospection. With *Dracula 3D* his foray into vampire films may likewise be seen as a work with more allegorical, and therefore, academic value. Perhaps further study of his career will reveal more such depth and acuity toward contemporaneous issues. And at the same time, it could be just great fun.

NOTES

1. David Rooney, "Dario Argento's Dracula 3D: Cannes Review," *The Hollywood Reporter* 5 May 2012, www.hollywoodreporter.com/review/dario-argento-dracula-3d-cannes-326991. 2. Rob Nelson, "Dario Argento's Dracula," *Variety* 21 May 2012, variety.com/2012/film/reviews/dario-argento-s-dracula-1117947598/.

3. Neil Genzingler, review of *Dracula 3D*, *New York Times* 3 October 2013, www.nytimes.com/.../argentos-dracula-3d-is-the-latest-entry-about-the-count.html

4. Gabe Toro, "Review: Dario Argento's Dracula 30D," Indiewire 3 October 2013, www.indiewire.com/2013/10/review-dario-argentos-dracula-3d-93078/.

5. Peter Sobcyzinski, "Dracula 3-D" RogerEbert.com 4 October 2013, www.rogerebert.com/reviews/dracula-3d-2013.

6. Hossein Eidi Zadeh, "15 Essential Films for an Introduction to Italian *Giallo* Movies," *Taste of Cinema* 14 October 2014, www.tasteofcinema.com/2014/15-essential-films-for-an-introduction-to-italian-giallo-movies/.

7. Peter Bondanella and Federico Pachioni, *A History of Italian Cinema*, 2nd edition, Bloomsbury Academic, 2017, page 379.

8. Bondanella and Pachioni, page 381.

9. Bondanella and Pachioni, page 379.

10. Bondanella and Pachioni, page 379.

11. Bondanella and Pachioni, pages 379–80.

12. Jeffrey Weinstock, *The Vampire Film: Undead Cinema*, Columbia University Press, 2012, page 19.

13. Peter Sobczinski, "Dracula 3-D" RogerEbert.com 4 October 2013, www.rogerebert.com/reviews/dracula-3d-2013.

14. Michael Pollan, *The Omnivore's Dilemma*, Penguin, 2006, page 320.

15. Paul Young, "The Victorians Created Our Meat-Eating Crisis: Can they also teach us how to escape it," *The Independent* 16 February 2019, www.independent.co.uk/life-style/food-and-drink/meat-eating-vegetarian-victorians-factory-farming-a8741136.html.

16. Bram Stoker, *Dracula*, Dover, 2000, page 203.

17. Catherine Edwards, "Berlusconi's back: Understanding the enduring popularity of Italy's 'immoral' former PM" 31 January 2018, www.thelocal.it/20180131/silvio-berlusconi-back-italy-election-forza-italia.

18. Edwards, cited above.

19. Nick Squires, "Silvio Berlusconi says immigrants not welcome but 'beautiful girls'

can stay," *The Telegraph* 13 February, 2010, https://www.telegraph.co.uk/news/worldnews/europe/italy/7223365/Silvio-Berlusconi-says-immigrants-not-welcome-but-beautiful-girls-can-stay.html.

20. Angela Giuffrida, "Berlusconi pledges to deport 600,000 illegal immigrants from Italy" 5 February 2018, https://www.theguardian.com/world/2018/feb/05/berlusconi-pledges-to-deport-600000-illegal-immigrants-italy-election. Accessed 20 May 2019.

21. Giuffrida, cited above.

22. David Hine, "Silvio Berlusconi, the Media and the Conflict of Interest Issue" *Italian Politics*, volume 17, 2001, pages. 261–75, *JSTOR*, www.jstor.org/stable/43041922.

The Intertextuality
of *Moon Child*

*How Japanese Popular Culture Molds
and Interprets Gender and the Vampire*

JADE LUM

It is the twenty-first century, and Japan has collapsed due to the burst of its economic bubble. Within the melting-pot society located in fictional "Mallepa," one can find children struggling in the slums, violent gang battles, stand-offs, and even a powerful vampire or two. The Japanese film *Moon Child*, released in 2003, tells the story of a human named Shō and his male vampire companion named Kei. The men attempt to survive in the gang-scape, question their own identities, and navigate personal relationships within their close circle and with one another. Though *Moon Child* utilizes an amalgamation of filmic genres and has been labeled in varying ways, from a melodrama to an action movie, it especially employs generic aspects of science fiction and the fantastic through its focus on the vampire. Through the elements of the fantastic vampire and the science fiction dystopian setting of Mallepa, *Moon Child*'s world opens audiences to explore gender, as well as offers insight on popular culture and intertextuality within Japan. By adapting the vampire together with recognizable features of Japanese communities and popular culture, *Moon Child* is able to question and reflect on gender dynamics within Japan and Japan's mass culture scene, especially in consideration of how masculinity is constructed, how male relationships function, and to whom exactly this film is attempting to appeal through its narrative and visual choices. Within this essay, I plan to question how through the lens of Japan's popular culture, genres, and structures, *Moon Child* expands and reshapes certain vampire motifs, allowing spaces to explore and approach

Moon Child (2003). This film is in part a vehicle for two J-pop stars Hyde and Gackt, who portray Kei and Sho in a dystopic future Japan. Kei (Hyde) is a vampire, but the story is more of friendship and a bit of romance than of vampiric blood killings.

figures and narratives that may push against hegemonic images of masculinity and male relationships.

The Adaptation, Vision and World of the Vampire in Japanese Popular Media

Before surveying *Moon Child*, it is first important to briefly review and acquire a greater understanding of the vampire within Japanese culture. Japan, in the course of multiple texts, has produced vampires that retain globally recognized concepts of the vampire, while also forming a local image and idea of the vampire, which then could open discussions of culture and gender. While considering *Moon Child* as a vampire text, it should be noted that Japan's relationship with the vampire is a very contemporary one.

Japan only started creating vampire media and literature less than a century ago. According to *The Vampire Encyclopedia*, Japan has never needed the classical vampire due to its own extensive list of tales and legends about mystical beasts and specters.[1] *Yokai*, for example, are Japanese supernatural beings, creatures, and spirits who are part of traditional folklore but are still heavily present in Japanese media today. While there are no traditional tales relating to the classic Western vampire, there are *yokai* that are known to suck blood from creatures to gain energy, such as the *Yamamba* or *Yamauba*, a mountain witch, or the *Kappa* or *Kawataro*, a water creature that grabs victims and then "[sucks] blood out of their rumps."[2] Thus Japanese traditions may have *yokai* with similar traits, but it was not until 1956 that the idea of the vampire was first mentioned in Japanese popular media, with *Kyuketsuga (Vampire Moth)*.[3] Later, in 1979, due to a high interest in integrating more Western-like products, the first European conception of the vampire was present in *Lake of Dracula*.[4] From then, the image of the vampire in Japan grew and evolved from the classic Western vampire into more locally identifiable conceptions through different types of media.

There have been a wide variety of interpretations of vampires in Japanese media in films, animations, comics, and games, which have helped to create a vampire quite different from the classic Western stereotype. There are Japanese *manga* (comics) and *anime* (animation) with vampires that are sadistic, deadly beings whose main purpose is to kill, as in *Hellsing* (1997–2008), or vampires with wide eyes, cutesy natures, and school uniforms, as in *Karin* (2003–2008), or vampires who would rather just watch *anime* and be homebodies, as in *Blood Lad* (2009–2016). There are also Japanese mobile games, like *Sengoku Night Blood*, that turn historical figures such as Oda Nobunaga, into illustrated pretty boy vampires with long flowing hair, pointed ears, and dangerously wielding a sword while at the same time romancing the player. As Yoshitaka Inoue states in "Contemporary Consciousness as Reflected in Images of the Vampire," "The images of vampires not only are universal but also have characteristics that change throughout history and cultures, corresponding to time and place."[5] Over time, as Japan's culture, media, and target audiences changed, so did their vampires. While keeping certain conventional aspects of the vampire that make it a recognizable figure, Japan's vision of the vampire within media is overall very diverse and does not seem to have much of a limit to what the vampire should or should not be or look like, which does make it easier to explore aspects outside of hegemonic value or mundane experiences, especially in comparison to what people may consider the "universal" vampire.

Considering Japan's use of the vampire within multiple, different media in contemporary times, though Japan's modern society and "norms" are often looked upon as dominant and strictly heteronormative, many of Japan's products of popular culture do open avenues to discuss or break heteronormative images of men, or reconsider how the "ideal" man should dress, act, or look. It should be mentioned, though, that a large portion of these media products are aimed toward a female audience. By experiencing both the fantastic elements of the vampire and the science fiction aspects of the setting in *Moon Child*, a general audience may find it easier to reflect and push different gender dynamics within an overall heteronormative society. In his chapter "On the Poetics of the Science Fiction Genre" Darko Suvin describes Bertold Brecht's ideas of "estrangement" as a portrayal of a subject that is recognizable, but still made to be new and unfamiliar.[6] A world of vampires can create an unfamiliar space and, in so doing, could estrange or distance the audience from the real world, which may allow for exploration, or even normalization and acceptance of aspects that are present in reality that may be difficult for certain audiences to confront outside of fiction. Through the vampire, as well as the relatable yet still unfamiliar dystopian setting of Mallepa, *Moon Child* is able to reflect in imaginative ways on gender, masculinity, and relationships of men within Japan and its popular culture.

Blurring Lines of Masculinity Through Visual-Kei and the Vampire

One can also find estrangement within Japan's music culture; understanding how genres are culturally coded and utilized within the music in Japan can allow further reflection into how *Moon Child* sets up the vampire within the film, while opening up a world to approach gender dynamics more openly. While media such as *manga, anime,* and games have helped to generate a variety of vampire figures, popular music scenes, particularly J-Rock and *Visual-Kei,* helped to adapt the figure into mainstream popular culture. At the time, idol musicians often portrayed and adapted vampires or Gothic wear, and then, under the guise of the vampire or in over the top costumes, could more comfortably push boundaries of gender and masculinity. For example, in his J-Rock solo debut music video "Mizérable" (1999), Gackt, who plays Shō in *Moon Child,* dresses up in high leather boots, a white ruffled shirt, and an extravagantly adorned black jacket with a high vampiric collar. With his face done up in pale makeup, dark kohl eyeliner, and his reddish hair messily falling into his eyes, Gackt holds himself, conveying pain through facial expressions and body motions, while singing about loneliness and lost love. Since Gackt is associated with the *Visual-Kei* genre, a "musical movement that centers much attention in the appearance of the musicians" and extends from J-Rock, he is able to play with theatrics and performance more freely within his music and then later *Moon Child.*[7] As explained in Ken McLeod's *Visual Kei: Hybridity and Gender in Japanese Popular Culture,* "The most pronounced aspect of visual-kei is the elaborate gender-crossing cosplay [or costume play] of band members, typically inspired by the visual and thematic elements of Goth Punk and Glam Rock as well as by Japanese manga, anime and computer games."[8] It is understood that within this genre that gender is much more fluid and there is an expectation of gender crossing within visuals and mannerisms. J-Rock and *Visual-Kei,* which have also adopted aspects of the vampire, are Japanese music genres that really push boundaries of gender through choice in clothing, performance, and music styles; elements of these two genres are heavily interwoven into *Moon Child* in its icons, fashion, melodrama, and emotions that are conveyed through both song and body language.

Visual and Coded Influences on the Vampire and Masculinity in Moon Child

Moon Child's image of the vampire is molded from Japan's *Visual-Kei*, but especially reflects Gackt and Hyde, who play Shō and Kei respectively. These leading actors are culturally coded and, as a result of their popularity at the time, were highly recognizable from their personas as fantastic or estranged figures, which helped to build the vampire narrative. In the early 2000s, both leading actors of the film were already very well-known, particularly for their presence in the music industry and J-Rock genre. In particular Gackt, who is also a writer of *Moon Child*, had previously assumed the role of a vampire multiple times within his solo music, and as part of the group Malice Mizer, he would perform as a dark, mysterious, yet ethereal figure. Though the other lead actor, Hyde, and the J-rock group he was a part of, L'Arc~en~Ciel, were not completely associated with the *Visual-Kei* movement, Hyde often sported longer wild hair, dark black eyeliner, and clothing that would erotically expose parts of his body. Hyde would also dress androgynously, comfortably gender-crossing on and off stage. By choosing actors with very established images, who are already coded and associated with the vampiric images, allure, and gender fluidity, there is an expectation for the movie to contain these elements as well. Many who sought out the movie were familiar with the genres and knew the two famous musicians playing across from each other in the movie. Both Hyde and Gackt's images had already created an expectation for how the vampire would be portrayed and what one might anticipate in terms of the film's visual features, relates to how Japan uses other texts to help to inform new ones.

Looking back at the costuming and design of the movie in 2003, but particularly at Kei as the vampire figure, and Shō, since he is the lead character and becomes a vampire at the end of the movie, one can see how the intertextuality of J-Rock, *Visual-Kei*, and Gackt and Hyde themselves were adapted into the visual appearances that would build the gendered vampire images. The two characters wear a variety of flashy clothes throughout the movie. Set in "2025 Mallepa West Ward," when an older Shō and Kei are first shown together in the movie after the introduction, Shō is donned in tight leather pants and a flashy white jacket, contrasting with the gray dilapidated setting.

His dyed hair consists of several long rattails, which flashily whip around as he dodges bullets from his enemies. Kei is lounging on a shipping crate, watching Shō shoot his enemies, while wearing a form-fitting tank top and red jacket that suggestively slips off his shoulders. Much like this early scene, throughout the movie both men continue to wear very stylized hair and tight leather clothing that shows off some skin or is very gaudy, a variety of jewelry items, and eye make-up reflecting the punk-like style of J-Rock. For Shō, there are a few scenes where more apparent cosplay and the exaggerations of Visual-Kei come out, such as long billowing coats and multiple leather straps, which reflect Gackt's over-the-top styles he usually sports. The costuming choices push against what is "normal" or heteronormative clothing at the time, but also displays how close of a relationship the film has with contemporary musical texts and genres. From the moment the audiences first see Shō and Kei together, the film is already setting up the world's estrangement while also using these culturally coded actors to create a space where their colorful and elaborate fashion choices are modeled and accepted within the movie.

As pointed out, both Kei and Shō noticeably set off the dystopian environment with their flashy outfits, but they also contrast physically with the rest of the cast as well. Besides the costuming aspects that allow for Kei and Shō to stand out and step out against hegemonic images of masculinity, both Gackt and Hyde themselves are both considered beautiful or pretty men, especially during *Moon Child* when they were in their early 30s, which allows them to stand out from other characters and the rest of the cast. In Japanese popular culture texts, a male who is on the prettier side is called a *bishōnen*. *Bishōnen* or 美少年 literally means "beautiful youth" and is often translated as "handsome youth (male)" or "pretty boy."[9] *Bishōnen*, a common character type, are often main characters in *manga*, *anime*, games, and of course films. Many vampire figures within Japanese media are portrayed as *bishōnen*. Frequently *bishōnen* are portrayed both visually and characteristically as more gender-fluid and not as heteronormatively masculine in certain respects, which is how both Shō and Kei are portrayed within *Moon Child*. Where Shō and Kei are coded as *bishōnen* characters with leaner body types, most of the other characters, men in particular, are on the burly or muscular side and more hegemonically "manly." Male side characters have more facial hair or are on the older side making the two main characters look younger in comparison. Shō's friend Toshi, played by Taro Yamamoto, rather than lean or pretty, is more muscular. And while Son, played by Wan Lehom, is a handsome presence in the cast, his image, from body type to facial features, to his more natural make-up, as well as being dressed in standard white shirts and black suits, fits much more into the ideal of heteronormative masculinity. He is portrayed as much more human than the two *bishōnen* characters, who either are, or become, the fantastic vampire. Interestingly, Son, who is an antagonist later in the movie, can be juxtaposed with both main protagonists in both visual aspects and moral aspects. This reflects how within Japanese popular culture, men who are pretty *bishōnen*, and may not fit within stereotypical manly images, are idolized and are reflected in a positive light within texts. *Moon Child* uses the Japanese role and image of the *bishōnen* and sets up comparisons so that both Shō and Kei especially stand out from the rest of the cast as elevated figures, while also inviting the audience to question how gender and men are portrayed in the film in comparison to hegemonic and heteronormative cultural standards.

Noticeably, these choices of fashion and the physical attributes for the two main men of the film also meet up with conventions of the vampire as well. In the Introduction of *Blood Read*, Joan Gordon and Veronica Hollinger explain that the vampire is "an ambiguously coded figure, a source of both erotic anxiety and corrupt desire," which could also be stated for many outfits, concepts, and images coming out of the J-Rock and *Visual-Kei* genres as well as *Moon Child*.[10] In *Moon Child*, the film seems to take these ideas of the vampire being "ambiguously coded" and to bring them to life by using actors who are already ambiguously coded through their outside work and image in music, while also possibly evoking erotic anxiety by pushing against hegemonic images of men by using *bishōnen* men as protagonists, creating sensual male figures that contrast with others in the narrative. These examples also fit within the ideas of "corrupt desire," since what is worn throughout the movie by Kei and Shō clearly contrasts with the hegemonic and heteronormative "everyday" man at that time. These visual costuming choices and how the two main characters present themselves not only reflect *Visual-Kei* and J-Rock but also really play into how the film adapts key attributes of the vampire. Within *Moon Child*'s visual choices, it is clear how the image of the vampire, while still retaining its key characteristics, is definitely adapted in correlation to Japan's popular culture scene at the time, which includes how there is a desire to explore gender images and boundaries, or the lack thereof.

Utilizing Music to Create an Emotion-Filled Vampire Relationship

Besides paratextual components and visual elements of the movie, there is one more aspect of the movie that is connected to the Japanese Music industry and helps to construct *Moon Child*'s vampire, which is the theme song of the film, オレンジの太陽 ("*Orenji no Taiyou*"), or "The Orange Sun." "*Orenji no Taiyou*" is a soft rock song, written and composed by both Gackt and Hyde. The song appears not only on the film soundtrack, but plays an important role in the film, as it is a central point to Kei and the vampire narrative. The song first appears when Kei has a traumatic flashback dream of Luka, Kei's vampire companion and mentor, singing it on the beach, as he is burning alive in the sun after deciding to end his life. From then, the song is coded and narratively functions as a melancholy suicide song for the vampire. It also works as exposition to help the audience to understand how the vampire works within the estranged world of *Moon Child*. The film adopts vampire conventions and makes the sun dangerous and fatal, which raises the stakes on Kei's life and his bond with Shō. In connection with the song, Kei questions mortality and whether it is worth living as a vampire. When he has doubts, he finds meaning in life through Shō, and it is only when Shō is also ready to pass on, that Kei takes his own life, which creates some poignant and dramatic scenes. As shown in the final scene of the movie, Shō (who was turned into a vampire by Kei) and Kei sing the song in a melancholy fashion together as they drive to the beach to watch the sunrise and die in the sun. The studio version of the song, a duet between Gackt and Hyde, then plays, as the film flashes through a montage of Shō, Kei, and their close friends in the possible afterlife, happily together again, without strife. The music is used to continue to draw sentiment from the audience since the characters are together now for eternity. "*Orenji no Taiyou*," though part of the film, also ends up on Gackt's solo album, *Crescent*, separate from the film. Hence, the film and the emotional ties to the story, helped to market Gackt's own work, which reflects the further intertextual connection that the movie had with Gackt's musical career. Having the studio version as a duet between the two musicians also reflects the men's emotional connection and bond within the film, which can be further analyzed by looking at the song's lyrics.

Through analyzing key lyrics of "*Orenji no Taiyou*," one can consider how through using the music medium, the film can also explore male relationships that may seem to step outside of contemporary heteronormative male friendships and sentiments, while also estranging it through the vampire narrative. The studio version of the song is actually over nine minutes, and one verse and phrase is noticeably repeated over and over again. The repeated verse relates the singer watching the sunrise together with someone, as both cry in an "eternal" good-bye. The repeated lyrics reflect *Moon Child*'s vampire narrative and how Kei and Shō do make their eternal good-byes as the sun rises, so the estrangement is still working within context. However, out of context, the song could be read in multiple ways, from a song about intimate and lasting friendships to even a song about loss of love and farewells, which breaks heteronormative conventions of male friendships and relationships with each other. One can see the same happening with other lyrics that reflect closeness and longing within the relationship in this song. For example, another line from the song relates how both the singer and the person they are with in the past would dream of the eternity they had together, while embracing and laughing. The line goes on to express that their embrace was as if they would never separate. Through these lyrics, there is a clear closeness shared, along with sentiments such as embracing and never letting go. Also, throughout the song, the use of the repeated word *eien*, which means forever or eternity (Jisho.org), continues to reiterate how this song pushes forward these eternal bonds and vows. While the repetition of eternity can be read through the estranging lens of the vampire, it can also be read from the perspective of blood brothers with sworn loyalty or other oaths like marriage. Through the use of music within the narrative, *Moon Child* adds layers and exposition to the vampire in the movie, while also exploring and perpetuating male relationships that go beyond simple friendships. Though music is one way that Kei and Shō's relationship is explored, there are further ways that the vampire movie is adapted into Japanese popular culture to further investigate male bonds and relationships.

Considering Male Relations Through Nanshoku and Shounen Ai

Though music is one way that Kei and Shō's relationship is explored, there are further ways that the vampire aspect of the movie is adapted into Japanese popular culture to further investigate male bonds and relationships. Much like how the song, "*Orenji no Taiyo*" reflects intimate eternal bonds and is able to be read in a way that steps away from what many may perceive as a heteronormative bond between men, *Moon Child* also has many scenes, especially between Kei and Shō, that reflect a deeply intimate and even homoerotic dimension to their relationship. The film takes this, and concepts of Japanese culture, and parts of the vampire genre, to explore male relationships and homoeroticism. Nina Auerbach states in her chapter "My Vampire, My Friend: The Intimacy Dracula Destroyed" that the vampire genre "simultaneously expressed and inhibited its century's dream of homoerotic friendship"; Auerbach reflects that the male focused vampire stories tend to promise the intimacy of friendship, but at the end the homoerotic feelings are "aroused and denied."[11] In *Moon Child*, Kei and Shō also play with "the intimacy of friendship," as audiences see them often holding one another, staring intimately at each other, and dramatically protecting one another. The homoerotic feelings between them are not fully realized in the sense that the two men become boyfriends or engage in a sexual relationship. However, by adapting genres and concepts from Japanese culture, such as "brotherhood" relationships and the popular related concept of *shounen-ai*, Kei and Shō's bond goes beyond being simply an aroused attempt of homoeroticism that is then denied, but one that can be read in more complex ways. While reading Kei and Shō's actions and scenes through Japanese concepts and texts, Kei and Shō's relationship can be seen as not only the teased homoerotic friendship that Auerbach sees in vampire narratives but also as an exploration of Japanese popular culture outside of heteronormative bonds through intertextuality of genres.

Within Japanese culture, there have been many instances where the bonds between men go beyond just simple friendship. In literature, art, popular culture, and even history, Japan has substantially explored male relationships beyond Western heteronormative friendships. In Gary Leupp's *Male Colors: The Construction of Homosexuality in Tokugawa Japan* he discusses how within during the Tokugawa period (1603–1867) there were many socially structured male relationships, often between those of samurai status or monks, that were homosexual and homoerotic, while still fitting within hegemonic culture for its time. Leupp states that the concept of *nanshoku* is "role-structured male homosexuality" involving "brotherly bonds," "finger cutting, and violent rivalries." Leupp also relates these "brotherly bonds" to "Lord-retainer bonds," where protégés, "younger brothers," or vassals would become loyal within battle and in the bedroom.[12] So while there may have been sexual and intimate relationships between men, there is still an overtone of shared hyper-masculine bonding through violence, fighting, and intense rivalries, which are also apparent in the gang violence in *Moon Child*.

In *Moon Child* one can see similarities to the *nanshoku* relationship dynamics with Shō and Kei. In the midst of gun battles with their backs against each other as they kill their enemies, Shō and Kei playfully banter with friendly rivalry, but are loyal and protective of one another in battle, particularly Kei using his vampiric abilities to constantly protect and assist Shō. Hyper-masculinity is retained through the movie's violent over-the-top gang scenes. Much like *nanshoku*, the bonds and friendship within the movie are mostly formed through the violence within Mallepa. The main five characters meet and have connections with each other only through their rough situation. It is only Shō and Kei who are shown very intimately beyond the battles within private spaces. Through fictional gang-filled Mallepa, which creates that estrangement from reality, these "lord-retainer" types of relationships are easily accepted and seem natural within the space, as they were during the Tokugawa period. The way violence forms the male bond is only one way that reading the vampire narrative through Japanese culture and *nanshoku* opens up more possibilities of male relationships.

Besides the male bonds and relationships still being hyper-masculine through the battles within *Moon Child*, Shō and Kei also seem to have the structured relationship of a lord-retainer bond in the manner in which they care for and watch out for one another, with Kei seeming to have a more loyal, retainer-type role to Shō. At the beginning of the movie after Luka tells Kei he is going to kill himself, Kei asks, "What will I do without you?" to which Luka replies, "Find another 'friend.'" While Luka does stress the word *tomodachi* (friend), interestingly, in the DVD's English translation, friend is in quotation marks, perhaps implying more meaning behind the term. After that scene, it is Shō as a child who then finds a suffering and injured Kei, waiting for the sun to take him. Smiling Shō, unafraid of Kei, helps him and tends to him, while his brother sees Kei as a monster. From then on, Kei finds his "friend," and in a sense, his "lord" in Shō, as Kei loyally stays by Shō's side. As a vampire, Kei is a never-aging companion to Shō, taking care of him as he grows up. As adults, Kei still comforts and assists Shō. In one scene, Kei is sick and weakened, since he hasn't been drinking blood, and Shō breaks down in tears, scared of losing Kei. Kei, in his weakened state, still goes up to Shō, huddled on the floor and holds him, caresses his face, and wipes his tears away saying, "Just like when you were a kid," and comforts him. Kei is loyal and affectionate to Shō even as an adult, and Shō is shown being quite reliant on Kei as well. The emotion and the way the men treat each other in this scene and others also allows for a consideration of men showing emotion and consoling one another in ways that may not fit within contemporary and heteronormative ideas of masculinity. From watching his back in battle to supporting him emotionally, the film depicts Shō holding a dear place in Kei's heart, and vice versa. While reading Shō and Kei's relationship in the lens of a lord-retainer relationship, and beyond the vampire genre's homoerotic friendship, one can see in *Moon Child* how the homoerotic friendship is not denied, but explored throughout the narrative, especially in the men's more personal and emotional moments.

While homosexual relationships between men in Japan existed in Japan's hegemonic social structures and texts in the past, which Gary Leupp explains culturally shifted due to Western influence and colonization in Japan,[13] in Japan's contemporary heteronormative culture, a popular genre and texts where these homosexual relationships between men can still be explored is *shounen-ai*. Shonen-ai or *shounen-ai* means "boy love," and "emphasizes relationships and romance over sex."[14] The emphasis of relationships and the love beyond just friends can be seen in *Moon Child* as the narrative revolves around the relationship between Kei and Shō. Though there is no sex, there are multiple scenes where body language and actions between the two characters really seem to evoke sexual imagery and images from the *shounen-ai* genre. For example, after Kei wakes up from the dream about Luka dying, he is sweaty, panting, and groaning hard, which is when Shō comes in and comforts him, declaring he always wants to be with Kei. In the scene, not only are there small teases of sexuality, but there is also the focus on the deep love between the two men, which reflects the *shounen-ai* genre. There are also times where the two share a single cigarette in a couple-like fashion, and there are times when the two hold each other close, with arms flung around each other's shoulders. Kei even once sensually asks Shō, "Should I drink your [blood]?" using the vampire genre and its estrangement to play with their relationship as well. Small body language and action is key to indicating relationships in the movie and in *shounen ai*, though these actions do fall more into Auerbach's ideas of how the vampire genre often "arouses" homoeroticism, rather than fulfilling homosexuality. *Moon Child* seems to be drawing from ideas of "boy love" and applying it to a vampire film, especially in how Kei and Shō's bond is depicted.

While homoeroticism is teased through Shō and Kei's actions and body language within the film, their overall relationship is reflected in ways much like a marriage vow, especially through the use of the vampire narrative. Like "*Orenji no Taiyo*," the movie reflects their bond as eternal and dear, which is also seen in certain *shounen-ai*, where men are bonded in such a way like marriage, though they are not explicitly stated to be in a relationship. Kei and Shō are shown together "in sickness" and "in health," and often tell each other how they could not live without one another, as in the scenes previously mentioned. Even within the vampire narrative, while Kei refuses to turn Chi, Shō's wife, into a vampire after she becomes terminally ill, he cannot bear to lose Shō and live without him, so he turns him before he dies. And while Chi marrying Shō in the narrative may seem to go against what an audience would desire to see in *shounen-ai*, it is also important to point out that Chi, who does not have much autonomy within the story, is often used as a plot device to push forward Shō and Kei's relationship. Having a female plot device that pushes the relationship between the men in some way is actually a common trope within *shounen-ai* as well. Where Shō seems disconnected from Chi, and their relationship is not shown in depth or does not seem to have much complexity, the movie focuses on the male bonds and relationships, much like a *shounen-ai* text would. *Moon Child* seems to adapt the estranged vampire narrative along with *shounen-ai* to create a space that allows for a depiction of homoerotic male relationships within contemporary culture. Also, by applying *shounen-ai* tropes, the vampire is morphed into one that is more recognizable and understood in Japan. While *Moon Child* perpetuates hypermasculinity through violence and by considering a traditional *nashoku* relationship amid the gang-filled Mallepa, there are also many undertones relating the film to *shounen-ai*, which opens up the male relationship into more sensual and romantic territories. By adapting and coding the film in these ways, not only does the film allow for a reflection of male relationships, bonds, and homoeroticism in Japanese culture, but it also depicts the vampire as one that does not completely deny homoeroticism and male relationships within the genre.

Conclusion: Setting Up an Intertextual World to Explore Gender in Japan

As discussed throughout the essay, there are many texts and genres within Japanese popular culture that are adapted and integrated within the vampire narrative in *Moon Child*. From *Visual-Kei* and J-Rock to other genre tropes that are apparent in literature and manga like the *nanshoku, bishōnen,* and *shounen-ai, Moon Child* is able to integrate Japan's pop culture world into its story to allow an exploration of gender and male relationships that go outside of contemporary heteronormative constructs. Through adapting local genres, using culturally coded images, and reflecting other texts, Japanese popular culture is able to estrange stories to allow exploration of non-hegemonic or heteronormative spaces in refreshing ways. As stated by Salvador Murguia in *The Encyclopedia of Japanese Horror Films,* "Many Japanese vampire films can be satisfying for Western viewers, primarily because their creators are either unaware of or uninterested in the various aspects of the Western vampire lore … this unorthodox approach can sometimes be refreshing, bringing in welcome changes to the traditional-bound world of vampire legends."[15] Since Japan loosely adapts the vampire and molds the vampire within its culture, as Murguia states, Japanese vampire films and texts bring refreshing and new changes to the genre, which can also be said for *Moon Child. Moon Child* utilizes universal motifs of the vampire, while also heavily incorporating *Visual-Kei* and J-Rock's gender crossing and theatrics, allowing for imaginative engagement with gender and masculinity. It also adapts aspects of historical social structures and contemporary genres within Japanese popular culture to explore male relationships. The estranged space the vampire genre and other Japanese genres create, allows exploration of male representation outside of what may be "normal" within Japan's heteronormative society, while molding the vampire. *Moon Child* is one text that has helped to establish the vampire within Japan, and as vampires have become a constant figure within popular culture, I am sure we will continue to see the vampire being redefined and evolving in new, imaginative ways.

NOTES

1. Matthew Bunson, *The Vampire Encyclopedia,* Crown, 1993, page 138.
2. Michael Dylan Foster, *The Book of Yokai: Mysterious Creatures of Japanese Folklore,* University of California Press, 2015, page 174.
3. Salvador Murguia, "Bloodthirsty Films," *The Encyclopedia of Japanese Horror Films,* Rowman and Littlefield, 2016, page 26.
4. Bunson, cited above, page 138.
5. Yoshitaka Inoue, "Contemporary Consciousness as Reflected in Images of the Vampire," *Jung Journal: Culture and Psyche,* volume 5, number 4, 2011, page 83.
6. Darko Suvin, "On the Poetics of the Science Fiction Genre," *Science Fiction Criticism: An Anthology of Essential Writings,* edited by Rob Latham, Bloomsbury, 2017, page 118.

7. Venâncio Monteiro and Núria Augusta, "Gender Bending in Anime, Manga, Visual Kei and Lolita Fashion: Representations from Portugal," *Prisma Social: Revista de Ciencias Sociales*, number 7 (2011), page 4.

8. Ken McLeod, "Visual Kei: Hybridity and Gender in Japanese Popular Culture," *Young*, volume 21, number 4, 2013, page 1.

9. *Jisho* dictionary, jisho.org/.

10. Joan Gordon and Veronica Hollinger, "Introduction: The Shape of Vampires," *Blood Read: The Vampire as Metaphor in Contemporary Culture*," University of Pennsylvania Press, 1997, page 1.

11. Nina Auerbach, "My Vampire, My Friend: The Intimacy Dracula Destroyed," *Blood Read: The Vampire as Metaphor in Contemporary Culture*, University of Pennsylvania Press, 1997, pages 11–12.

12. Gary P. Leupp, *Male Colors: The Construction of Homosexuality in Tokugawa Japan*, University of California Press, 1995, page 203.

13. Leupp, cited above, page 203.

14. Cathy Camper, "Essay: 'Yaoi' 101: Girls Love 'Boys' Love,'" *The Women's Review of Books*, volume 23, number 3, 2006, page 24.

15. Murguia, cited above, page 27.

Blood, Dust and the Black Universe

From Asia Extreme to the Vampire World-Image in Thirst, The Wailing, and the New Korean Vampire Horror Cinema

DAVID JOHN BOYD

Introduction

This essay is a critical reevaluation of two South Korean horror films—Park Chan-wook's *Thirst* (*Bak-jwi*, 2009) and Na Hong-jin's *The Wailing* (*Gokseong*, 2016)—as existentially engaging texts that pose intent film-philosophical questions about the ontological nature of an extreme *existence*, rather than films that simply adhere to the logic of the brand of Asia Extreme. This essay examines both Park and Na's films through the ontic and optic lenses of Gilles Deleuze's *Cinema* books and François Laruelle's *The Concept of Non-Photography*. By doing so, I hope to reveal the non-human impulses of each film in their stylistic and technical deployments of color and framing, as well as each film's narrative inversions and refractions of vampire and horror genre templates. Through Park and Na's nonhuman film-philosophies of the cinematographic image, this essay recontextualizes both films as ciphers for what I call the *vampire world-image*, or what might be described as a philosophical image of the world that reexamines how the extreme deterritorialization of the human perspective in cinema—expressed by a nonhuman film that focalizes on becoming-undead (vampire, ghost, zombie, etc.)—can be mobilized against the world of the living to articulate an extreme existentialism articulated by furious posthuman becomings and the fractal unbecomings of the nonhuman. While Park's *Thirst* asks if we can save humanity in the wake of

Thirst (2009). The publicity poster indicates the erotic aspect of this Korean film, directed by Park Chan-wook (previously director of *Old Boy*), which is as much about the sexual needs of a Catholic priest turned vampire as it is about his thirst for blood (Photofest).

finitude by overcoming the human, Na's *The Wailing* answers back with a violent, incomprehensible utterance, a whispering negation that echoes throughout the black universe.

Orientalizing the "Extreme" in East Asian Cinema

The brand *Asia Extreme* as applied to East Asian extreme cinema, is defined by Jinhee Choi and Mitsuyo Wada-Marciano as "the moral and visceral extremes manifest in recent Asian horror" popularized by global cult films like Miike Takashi's *Audition* (*Odishon*, 1999) Park Chan-wook's *Oldboy* (*Oldeuboi*, 2003), and Fruit Chan's *Dumpling* (*Gaau ji*, 2004), as well as a penultimate short film horror compilation of the Asia Extreme brand *Three ... Extremes* (Lionsgate Films, 2004) that includes three shorts from Miike, Park, and Fruit Chan. The cinematic genre popularly defined as Asia Extreme throughout Anglophone commercial and academic circles must necessarily be denaturalized in any critical evaluation of the rise of globally distributed East Asian genre cinema, and therefore, I treat such a task as a jumping off point for traversing the nuances of the global non-vampire film. The term is more accurately a marketing brand rather than a genre or an ideological/aesthetic category, and it must continually be viewed and described with intent skepticism. As Chi-Yun Shin artfully explains in her essay "The Art of Branding: Tartan 'Asia Extreme' Films," the term was not introduced by East Asian auteurs, commercial film critics, or academic film theorists while out on the local or international film festival circuit during the rise of South Korean cinema in the early millennium. Rather, the term Asia Extreme was invented by Hamish McAlpine, a London-based Scottish film-boss, provocateur, and founder of the international distributor Tartan Films.[1] Problematically for effective global film criticism, however, McAlpine did not classify Asia Extreme in terms of the cinematic theorization of the extreme on stage or screen. Choi and Wada-Marciano explain that Tartan Films developed a brand for youth counterculture in North America and Europe, writing that in his assessment of Asia Extreme, "McAlpine compares such youth audiences, who endorse films imbued with extreme sensibilities, with the art theatre audience of the 1960s, who visited theatres to relish foreign films for their explicit sexual content."[2] While Asia Extreme is a brand designed to appear as a countercultural assault against American moral puritanism and European bourgeois sensibilities, McAlpine's everyday orientalism impoverishes the philosophical and cultural value of said cinematic texts, regardless of the taboo content and subject matter. In other words, the branding of Asia Extreme ignores the political and ideological battles that cinema was engaged in, with, and against state censorship and state-founded propaganda networks, the rise and expansion of authoritarianism, the strains of compressed and accelerated modernity, and the scars of colonial wars, civil wars, two world wars, and the persistent threat of nuclear war.

And yet, even if McAlpine did establish some sort of "continuity between European art cinema of the 1960s (and even the contemporary) and the Extreme cinema of the 1990s onward" as Choi and Wada-Marciano note, the films that shocked McAlpine should not be immediately genrefied as art house cinema of the 1960s, simply because of the perceived trendy anime-esque editing style and the depiction of transgressive sexual and violent content (6). The cinema of Miike, Park, and Chan that McAlpine and many critics view as equally cool and abject should not be read in earnest as an effective strategy of categorizing contemporary trends in East Asian cinema; Tartan Film's branding is nothing more than a commercial exoticization that hinges on the commodification of "subject matters that are not easily permissible within Hollywood, such as sex, gore, and violence" within an orientalist context.[3] Hence, it is no surprise that McAlpine ditched global cinematic history, aesthetic histories of transgressive or experimental art, or even curious readings of exploitative or pulp cinema as a style or cinematic legacy. Instead, McAlpine sought to capitalize on the sense of a handful of titles that he found intense, and in keeping with North American and European youth culture of the early millennium, "borrowed the term 'extreme' from extreme sports [...] referring to activities such a skateboarding, snowboarding, and BMX racing that are associated with youth subculture and inducing an adrenaline rush in participants, even though they are not necessarily more inherently dangerous or generate more adrenaline compared to 'conventional' sports." The crass marketing strategies of McAlpine's brand should not surprise scholars of cinema or media for that matter, but it should inform the ways in which we challenge what Shin calls the "genrification [sic] of East Asian cinema," by which "the output of the label, and the name of the label itself, invoke and in part rely on the Western audiences' perception of the East as weird and wonderful, sublime and grotesque [...] operating within the discourse of Orientalism." As Shin affirms, McAlpine's branding of Asia Extreme is entirely framed by the "discourses of difference and excess," forcing the image of a globalized version of East Asia to "fit comfortably into the widespread notion about the East" that has consistently framed East-West relations for centuries.[4]

With McAlpine's banal consumer orientalism established, we must also interrogate the problem of genrefying a region of diverse cultures. In selling an entire image of the culturally, linguistically, historically pluralistic region of East Asia to European and North American consumers as an authentic, niche vision of the new, hip Orient, Tartan Films deploys tactics similar to

"Hollywood studios practice that strategically avoids specific generic terms. In fact, Tartan's promotional material seldom employs generic vocabulary prevalent in film reviews [...] it evokes shocking and dark nature that 'unites' the films."[5] Tartan Films' misguided marketing campaigns of Asia Extreme has contributed to the development of an East Asian cinema canon and stylistic category as mere exotica, as Shin reminds us:

> McAlpine has referred the label to be a "brand [and]—a genre in itself," and Tartan's promotional booklet claims to provide "the story of the origin and development of the most exciting and unique of all contemporary genres" [....] This is problematic in the sense that the label in effect lumps together distinct and different genres of horror, action, and thriller films from Japan, South Korea, Hong Kong as well as Thailand under the banner of Asia Extreme.[6]

Importantly, McAlpine not only confuses cultural, national, or regional cinema for genre, but his company excludes dozens of other contemporary East Asian filmmakers that do not fit their brand, like Hong Sang-soo, Lee Chang-dong, Bong Joon-ho, Wong Kar-wai, Lee Kyoung-mi, Iwai Shunji, and Zhang Lü. Therefore, it is safe to claim that Asia Extreme is no mere brand, as Choi and Wada-Marciano claim: "it carries a set of cultural assumptions and implications that guides—and sometimes misguides—the viewer in assessing the political and ideological significance of the film."[7] Asia Extreme is an imperial *world-image* of East Asian cinema which promotes an illusory projection of the weirdness, otherness, monstrosity, and excessively embodied onto East Asia, once again rooting an aesthetic category or movement (*japonisme* in nineteenth and twentieth century French painting, for example) in the very real hegemonic history of Western colonialism, imperialism, and commercial exoticization of East Asia. Regarding the dangers of orientalizing and genrefying the entirety of millennial East Asian cinema, Shin concludes that such genrefication of certain East Asian films "should be understood as an integral part of providing illusions of discovery, that is, a way of knowing and classifying East Asian cinema," whereby we must challenge Asia Extreme not only as "a marketing strategy that fronts certain films to sell all other titles," but also an emphatic reminder "that no one in East Asia would set out to make an 'extreme' film" in the manner Tartan Films describes.[8]

Shin's conclusion is exceptionally well stated, as is Choi and Wada-Marciano's entire reframing effort of the East Asian horror renaissance of the millennial period against Asia Extreme in the introduction to their critical essay collection *Horror to the Extreme: Changing Boundaries in Asian Cinema*. Thus, following Choi, Wada-Marciano, and Shin, it should be known that the problem with current academic criticism of *Thirst* and *The Wailing* is that it relies on the tautology of the traits of Asia Extreme, which perpetuates the same regressive cultural readings of East Asian horror cinema. The problem of the Asia Extreme brand beckons media and film scholars to readdress these films in alternative ways, deterritorializing previous positions and perspectives on the *extreme* in East Asian horror cinema as an aesthetic and philosophical project rather than a mere cultural, national, or commercial one. Therefore, this essay argues that filmmakers like Park Chan-wook and Na Hong-jin are more playful, experimental, self-aware, and philosophical in their expression and understanding of the *extreme*, seemingly challenging the notion that extreme (intense, affective, speculative, experimental) cinema should not be categorized as a stylistic label for marketing sensational content, which many viewers are becoming more and more attuned to in contemporary screen culture. Park and Na's films expose an extreme cinema of the inhuman (posthuman and nonhuman), a non-anthropocentric way of seeing the world (or world cinema) in explosive affects and fracturing percepts, hence resulting in the production of the vampire world-image.

What Is the Vampire World-Image? A Global Jiangshi Cinema

The concept of the *world-image* is a philosophical concept informed by Gilles Deleuze's comprehensive history of cinema in *Cinema I: The Movement-Image* and *Cinema II: The Time-Image*. As David Martin-Jones warns in the introduction of *Deleuze and World Cinemas*, "[a]pproaching world cinemas, using Deleuze, requires care. To attempt to validate Deleuze's ideas through their application to films from around the world would run the risk of imposing already Eurocentric conclusions onto cinemas that belong to very different, context-specific cultures and aesthetic traditions." Indeed, Martin-Jones suggests that to avoid this imperial-ideological pitfall of essentialized categorization (*à la* Asia Extreme), we must examine world cinema to describe "the plurality of cinemas that exist globally," which in turn reveals the difference of many diverse cinematic histories and aesthetic visions. By observing each cinema of difference (in genre, form, mode, narrative, etc.), Martin-Jones explores how world cinemas contribute to a transcultural and transnational web that reflects the social and ideological concerns of a globalized world and the rise of "the global rhizome of world cinemas."[9]

Like many emergent globalized visions of vampire cinema, vampire horror cinema is difficult to pin down as a specific genre in East Asian cinema, primarily because it is largely a borrowing from Western cinematic and literary traditions, inherently bound by questions of postcoloniality, modernity, and a contradictory (and at times, antagonistic) relationship with Westernization. In this context, the vampire world-image of East Asia is widely diverse and incredibly dynamic, revealing the ways in which the genre can be rewritten, reincorporated, or recontextualized for both localized and globalized East Asian contexts, often pitting the vampire genre against the West as a vehicle to challenge its religious, political, and economic domination of East Asia. Unlike in most North American or European vampire cinema, East Asian vampire cinema is often used in conjunction with other genre elements like comedy, romance, or martial arts, and they manifest in both animated and live-action film. Moreover, many East Asian vampire films conflate blood sucking vampires with other undead figures like body-possessing spirits and soul-sucking ghouls, as well as dozens of other ghastly variations that haunt the imaginaries of East Asia, including the tradition of *jiangshi* (hopping cadaver) of continental China, Hong Kong and Taiwan, the *yeogwi* (female ghost) tradition of Korea, and the *yōkai* (strange spirit) visual and literary tradition of Japan. While these folklores of East Asian burial rites and the afterlife were originally informed by indigenous spiritualism and organized religious beliefs of Shintoism, Sindoism, Taoism, Confucianism, and Buddhism, many other East Asian vampire films have also adapted the Western image of the vampire, like in Park's *Thirst* or Na's *The Wailing*, to reveal the cultural and spiritual alienation expressed in East Asian spiritual life, a result of an arduous and painful history of Western colonization and Christian conversion.

Specifically, Lisa Odham Stokes writes that while the "earliest vampire movie made in Hong Kong was Yeung Kung-Leung's *Midnight Vampire* (1936)"—three years after the first Filipino talkie, *The Vampire* (*Ang Aswang*, George Musser, 1933)—the vampire genre was not revisited regularly in East Asian cinema until the 1970s (448). The same can be said about Japanese vampire film: Japan's first vampire film was Nakagawa Nobuo's *The Vampire Moth* (*Kyuketsuga*, 1956), but vampire cinema did not become widely popular until the release of Yamamoto Michio's "Bloodthirsty Trilogy": *The Vampire Doll* (*Chi o suu ningyo*, 1970), *The Lake of Dracula* (*Noroi no yakata: Chi o su me*, 1971), and *Evil of Dracula* (*Chi o suu bara*, 1974). Hence, while many East Asian markets began testing the Western genre of vampire cinema in local and global film distribution, Stokes writes that "the vampire became a popular Hong Kong movie staple from the mid–1980s to the early 1990s, with 24 films made between 1986 and 1990," largely leading the popularity of the genre throughout East Asia.[10] Not only was the Hong Kong rise of *jiangshi* cinema influential in East Asia, but as Jeffrey Weinstock explains, this "series of vampire/kung fu hybrid films" like Hammer Films and Shaw Studios' joint venture *The Legend of Seven Golden Vampires* (1974), Sammo Hung's *Encounters of the Spooky Kind* (*Gui dagui*, 1980), Ricky Lau's *Mr. Vampire* (*Jianshi Xiansheng*, 1985), and Billy Chan's *Crazy Safari* (*Fei zhou he shang*, 1991) were the first of their kind to successfully "incorporate choreographed martial arts sequences" into the genre, influencing the American vampire film franchise

Blade (1998) as well as many other video games and comic books.[11] The significance of the rise of *jiangshi* throughout East Asia might be contextualized in the context of world cinema by the rising anxieties about postcolonial identities in a global context. For Stephanie Lam, these comedy kung-fu vampire cult films are an essential world film vehicle for East Asian diasporic communities, working against the notions, sensibilities, and philosophies of the traditional Western vampire film.[12]

In South Korean cinema, however, the vampire film is relatively recent in its emergence, and is not as relatively popular. Excluding Park's internationally popular *Thirst* (2009), other K-vampire films include the *jiangshi*-flavored *Vampire Cop Ricky* (*Heuphyeol Hyeongsa Nadoyeol*, 2006), the teen romance *You Are My Vampire* (*Geudaen Naui Baempaieo*, 2014) and the vengeful *yeogwi* film *Beautiful Vampire* (*Byutipul Baempaieo*, 2018) have been received with mediocre critical and commercial success locally and abroad. Like the categorical conundrum of the hybridized *jiangshi* film, South Korean horror also mixes and matches its images of undead together, which makes many other subgenres like the supernatural thriller and zombie apocalypse coalesce into vampiric shapes, as we see in K-horror classics like Bong Joon-ho's *The Host* (*Gwoemul*, 2006) or more recent para-vampire films including Na Hong-jin's *The Wailing* and Yeon Sang-ho's *Train to Busan* (*Busanhaeng*, 2016). Like many *jiangshi* films, it is often difficult in Korean horror to differentiate vampire from zombie from a spiritually possessed body or a body overcome by an external virus, and as in *Thirst* and *The Wailing*, the questions of exorcism (Catholic or indigenous) are encoded critiques of Western (and Japanese) colonization, occupation, and religious conversion. As Kyu Hyun Kim writes, the protagonist's battle against the undead in Korean horror is often revealed as "an ironic statement about the impotence of the religious authorities," who more specifically manifest as powerless priests in *Thirst* and sham shamans in *The Wailing*, challenging "the authenticity of religious faith, philosophical reflections on the meaning of evil or other such issues that are usually engaged in highbrow commercial horror films."[13]

While the first conceptualization of the vampire world-image of East Asia reflects the *jiangshi* renaissance as an equally global commercial success as well as a nuanced postcolonial and antireligious critique of East-West relations, a second way of conceptualizing the vampire world-image in East Asia is not only understanding the world film histories that depict vampires in geopolitical or commercial contexts, but rather, as a philosophical cosmology of the ontology of human-ness and its extreme existential limits in undead cinema. When thinking about why world vampire cinema is so important in understanding global perception, we must first understand that global cinemas are not only a material collection of culturally, linguistically, or geographically specific histories or experiences created by filmmakers, and then

Thirst (2009). A Catholic priest who has been turned into a vampire by a blood experiment gone wrong, Sang-hyeon (Kang-ho Song, right), visits a family to play mah-jongg but falls in love with Tae-ju (Ok-bin Kim), who is unhappily married to the doltish Kang-woo (Ha-kyun Shin). Ensuing events include adultery, murder, and suicide (Photofest).

distributed abroad by corporations and consumed by either film connoisseurs at local theaters, film reviewers at festivals, or average consumers viewing world cinema on multiple platforms and devices. World cinema in its simplest terms for Deleuze is a philosophical schema that adds dimensions, textures, and layers to an image, or a percept, of the world that might at one point appear as homogenous, contiguous, or striated. A world-image, then, or the imaging-of-the-world, describes a fractal or sliced perception of the world, as Christopher Vitale writes: "The universe is nothing but a crystal of images, reflecting and refracting each other. Each entity, by slicing the universe up in its own way, produces its own cinema, framing and cutting, slicing and imaging."[14] Therefore, the vampire world-image, accordingly in this context, is a way of viewing the highly affective and anomalous slices of nonhuman existence, whereby the world-image is split optically and ontologically between infinite visions of reanimation, consumption, and the transformation of the human to the nonhuman. This is the position this essay will be examining in more detail with *Thirst* and *The Wailing*, two slices of the vampire world-image that designate the ontology of the cinematic vampire as a vehicle for intense affective becomings and unknowable perceptual unbecomings, or put another way, as a philosophy of *seeing-red* in the *affection-image* (i.e., the expressions of rage, fury, and bloodlust as becoming-animal) and a philosophy of *seeing-ghosts* in *the photographic-image* (i.e., the impressions of darkened shadows, obscure fractals, and illusory mirrors).

"It's not blood, it's red": Seeing-Red and Becoming-Intense in Thirst

If the second conceptual embodiment of the world-image is equally ontic and optic, then the Korean vampire world-image is mobilized in two ways, cinematographically speaking: (1) as an intensified cinema of affect (excess of) and (2) an anomalous cinema of perceptual lacking. Put another way, this essay examines how Park and Na explore a cinema of the inhuman intensities of what Gilles Deleuze and Félix Guattari refer to as "becoming-animal, becoming-intense and becoming-anomalous" as introduced in *A Thousand Plateaus: Capitalism and Schizophrenia* (262). In their chapter on becoming-animal, Deleuze and Guattari explain that inhuman becomings are historical, biological, and philosophical solutions to the failures of the State, its institutional forces, and ideological extensions. Thus, let us begin with the first example: becoming-animal and becoming-intense in *Thirst*.

Park Chan-wook's *Thirst* is a curious outlier in the internationally and commercially successful genre of vampire cinema. Park's film weaves together a witty adaptation of Émile Zola's bourgeois, domestic, love-affair drama, *Thérèse Raquin*, with a Scorsese-esque, Catholic-flavored vampire action film that explores the destruction of the familial institution, the impotence of the Church, the paradoxes of redemption, the limitations of faith, and the (im)possibility of transcendence. The film tells the tale of Sang-hyun (Song Kang-ho), a mild-mannered Catholic priest from Busan who is sent to West Africa by the Church to help aid victims of a mysterious virus, called the Emmanuel Virus (EV). To help administer the possibility of a cure, medical researchers inject Sang-hyun with the virus, and within what seems like days, the priest is afflicted by the virus that produces large blood boils across his limbs and within his organs. Sang-hyun, already having accepted his own death, is overcome by the virus and dies choking on his own blood while playing his beloved recorder. In an attempt to save the priest, the doctors in the facility give Sang-hyun a standard blood transfusion. After Sang-hyun's time of death is marked by the head physician, he is miraculously reborn, brought back from the grave as a vampire from the blood transfusion.

Believing he was saved by the grace of God, Sang-hyun returns to South Korea as a living Lazarus. Sang-hyun blesses his congregation and returns assisting the infirmed at the hospital that he volunteered at previously. The priest is convinced to pray for his old childhood friend, Kang-woo (Shin Ha-kyun), by his frantic mother, Mrs. Ra (Kim Hae-sook). The priest prays for Kang-woo—a compulsive hypochondriac—who is afflicted by esophagus cancer. After praying for Kang-woo, he is miraculously healed, and is invited by his old childhood friend and her mother to spend each Wednesday evening with them at their house to play *mahjong* with the family and their friends. Over time, Sang-hyun sparks a passionate love affair with Kang-woo's wife, Tae-ju (Kim Ok-bin), and in the adaptative portion of *Thérèse Raquin*, the first half of the film concerns the affair as a symptom of Sang-hyun's vampirism. Furthermore, Sang-hyun plots against Kang-woo after Tae-ju lyingly explains that he has been abusing her, and following Zola, the lovers kill Kang-woo by drowning him in a reservoir. Kang-woo's death leads to Mrs. Ra having a stroke, leaving her cogent, yet paralyzed, immobile, and mute. The second half of the film explores the guilt and resentment that bubbles up in their relationship—represented by Kang-woo's ghost who humorously appears to haunt the lovers during intimate moments—and the two succumb to Kang-woo's haunting and struggle to maintain their romance. Sang-hyun later learns that Tae-ju lied about Kang-woo abusing her, and in a guilt-ridden rage, kills Tae-ju. Regretting his first kill, the priest decides to bring Tae-ju back to life by feeding her his vampiric blood. The remainder of the film depicts the duel between Sang-hyun and Tae-ju as they vie for dominance as vampiric opposites (Sang-hyun does not kill for blood, yet Tae-ju does). The duel is doomed, however: Sang-hyun concedes to Tae-ju, concluding that no matter how hard he tries, he is unable to stop her from killing and feeding on her victims, which she refers to as "prey" and "the weaker species." In the end, Sang-hyun, to stop Tae-ju's killing spree, tricks her by luring her to a deserted seaside cliff in the early morning to kill her by sunlight. The film ends with the couple dissolving into ash in the blinding light of a dawning sun as they view the blue ocean transform into a crimson sea of blood, a trademark effect Park uses throughout the entire film.

The film's seemingly disparate conceptual threads of Zola's tragic literary treatise on desire and revenge, Park's own Catholic education of "ecclesiastic discourses on soteriology and eschatology,"[15] and the biomedical logic of a modern vampire thriller blend together beautifully to produce an engaging, heady, and darkly humorous tableau of the quintessential global vampire art film, similar in tone and style to other recent art-house vampire films, including Jim Jarmusch's *Only Lovers Left Alive* (2013) and Ana Lily Amirpour's *A Girl Walks Home Alone at Night* (2014). Moreover, the film's formal virtuosity and intellectual complexity made *Thirst* an unexpected cinematic gem, earning the 2009 Cannes Film Festival Jury Prize and dozens of other Korean and international awards, nominations, and accolades. *Thirst's* critical appeal

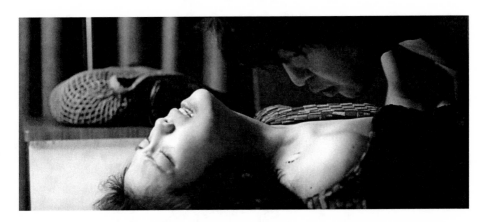

Thirst (2009). The combined sexual pleasure and pain of a vampire bite is evident from the visible pain accompanied by pleasurable dialogue in this first experience of sex together by Tae-ju (Kim Ok-bin) and Sang-hyeon (Song Kang-ho). The fangless bite marks on her collarbone signal the unconventional nature of this vampire story.

is perhaps also in part because Park invests an aesthetic and philosophical seriousness in the globally popular vampire cinema genre that has garnered the attention of New Korean Cinema scholars Kyu Hyun Kim and Steve Choe. As Kim explains in his groundbreaking essay, "Park Chan-wook's *Thirst*: Body, Guilt and Exsanguination," the film can be read as a historical materialist interrogation of Catholic history from the 1790s to the present in Korean society, as well as a critique of "quasi-Gnostic yearning for transcendence" of the human body, and also "a multi-layered work of art that deals seriously with the corporeal and spiritual realities of our lives, which we would rather sweep under the carpet, expertly marking use of the seemingly irreconcilable vocabularies and idioms of more than one cinematic genre."[16] Following Kim's reading, Steve Choe argues that *Thirst* could be read as a posthuman addition to the Vengeance Trilogy, which might best be described as a triptych of New Korean Cinema that explores Park's critiques of ethics, violence, and subjectivity in a post-dictatorial, post-globalized, overdeveloped millennial South Korea with three mysterious revenge and crime thrillers. Choe views "the aesthetic and ethical problems [of Park's oeuvre] through the syncretic nature of the film medium, which grounds the many allegories that the film inspires, including the liminal status between life and death, human life and technology, and the particular and the universal," concluding that the film produces "a new non-human politics, one that operates as a means without any teleological ends."[17]

Building upon both Kim and Choe, I argue *Thirst* is a film that explores transformative posthuman becomings in form and philosophy. As Kim reminds Anglophone readers, "the Korean title is *Bakjwi*, literally meaning 'The Bat,'" which like other early vampire films including the German Expressionist film *The Cat and the Canary* (1927) and the first Japanese vampire film, *The Vampire Moth*, blends together a cinema of becoming-animal with the vampiric cinematic tradition.[18] What we might refer to as "a cinema of becoming-animal" is first described by Deleuze and Guattari through a reading of the American B-horror film *Willard* (1971). In a critical assessment of *Willard*, Deleuze and Guattari explain that becoming-animal is an expansive disanthropocentric discourse of swarming and furious animal becomings (non-fixed subjectivities) that simulate the experience of bodies in intensely affective flux, cinematic bodies that are overdetermined by their relationships with "a pack, a band, a population, a peopling, in short, a multiplicity" and "modes of expansion, propagation, occupation, contagion, peopling."[19] For Deleuze and Guattari, an ideal film of becoming-animal seeks to unravel the centralized ideologically-steered state institutions (family, work, education, medicine, etc.) by ravaging the anthropocentric framework of the human subject, the subject's body, and the human's subjectivity through intensified animal pack affects.

Park's *Thirst* is perfectly attuned to these necessary traits of intense expression that Deleuze and Guattari identify in *Willard* because it formally and philosophically reveals that "the vampire and werewolf are becomings of man, in other words, proximities between molecules in composition, relations of movement and rest, speed and slowness between emitted particles," spectacularly shaping Sang-hyun and Tae-ju by the EV virus and its molecular mutations (303). Additionally, the infectious nature of Park's vampire is not merely molecular or biological, but rather, affective, whereby the rising animal affects of Sang-hyun and Tae-ju are exercised with "enough feeling, with enough necessity and composition" in the film that viewers quickly become aware that a cinema of becoming-intense is simply a cinema of "becoming-animal in action, the production of the molecular animal."[20] Such a cinema of becoming-animal fulfills the characteristics of what McKenzie Wark calls a "furious media," or as he writes, a swarming cinema of "a plethora of protocols, an everyday poetics, a materialist attitude to life which does not foreclose or claim to command its mysteries" which can manifest in a multiplicity of mediations: aurally, optically, kinesthetically, viscerally, etc.[21]

As fans of Park's films may note, the prime aesthetic force of his films is the deployment of intensified affect through rapid movement of characters, frames, camera, and perception. Park's intensified use of movement (spatial replications and simulations of affect) is mediated often through uniquely extreme ways. One way that is often misrepresented in critical readings of Park's work is the way he uses the colors of intensity, especially red, ranging from the Pollock-esque blood paintings of the Vengeance Trilogy to the crimson-tinted camera lens that frames the process of becoming-vampire throughout *Thirst*. If Deleuze and Guattari are correct in writing that affect is not merely an extreme feeling (i.e., that of immediate sensory-motory reaction like fear, disgust, or desire) and that it "is not a personal feeling, nor is it a characteristic; it is the effectuation of a power of the pack that throws the self into upheaval and makes it reel," then Park's most *extreme* elements of *Thirst* are not driven by the narrative or the sensational content that even Kim seems to attribute to the film.[22] Rather, I argue that Park specifically deploys reddened cinematographic elements throughout *Thirst* to illustrate his fascination with what Deleuze calls "the affection-image" in his extreme filmmaking style.[23] More specifically, Deleuze explains the affection-image is a mode of actualizing the ontological power of a trait of expression in the cinematic image:

> The pure affect, the pure expressed of the state of things in fact relates to a face which expresses it (or to several faces, or to equivalents, or to propositions). It is in the face—or the equivalent—which gathers and expresses the affect as a complex entity, and secures the virtual conjunctions between singular points of this entity (the brightness, the blade, the terror, the compassionate look...). Affects are not individuated like people or things, but nevertheless they do not blend into the indifference of the world. They have singularities which enter into virtual conjunction each time constitute a complex entity. It is like points of melting, of boiling, of condensation, of coagulation, etc.[24]

Throughout *Thirst*, then, Park frames posthuman becomings through the affection-image so that viewers may begin to simulate and feel the expressive rise of raging, swarming becomings, or of the individuated affects of the non-human world like "a climate, a wind, a fog, a swarm, a pack (regardless of its regularity)," or like a fluttering of bats, a leaping gam of whales, a "cloud of locusts carried by the wind," as Deleuze and Guattari poetically wax.[25]

Therefore, if furious or extreme cinema is a cinema of becoming-animal and becoming-intense, then Park's vampire horror film fits this categorization as a film-philosophical text that tinkers and plays with intensified posthuman existential experiences. In the first montage of the film, Park exposes the undoing of the human subject and its anthropocentric centrality of sovereignty, subjectivity, and autonomy by framing Sang-hyun's vampiric transformation in a fit and start of raging, swarming, bestial engagements with intensified affect. After his resurrection and his subsequent return home, Sang-hyun realizes that he has in fact become undead. In this becoming-vampire scene, Sang-hyun is overwhelmed by intense affects and sensations from a previous scene in which he realizes his ravenous lust for Tae-ju. Alone in his room, he responds to this furious desire in a quintessential Catholic method: self-harm as penance. After flogging himself a dozen time on the thighs and genitals (a scene that is further intensified by a soundtrack of Tae-ju's intense, bestial breathing and moaning that enunciates the sounds of furious sexual intercourse and/or an unending marathon sprint), the scene ends with the camera panning up to the moon, a nocturnal and cosmic sign that serves as an activator in the process of becoming-animal, transforming the priest into "a vampire who goes out at night, a werewolf at full moon," as Deleuze and Guattari describe.[26] As Sang-hyun begins to cough up blood, he is thrown into a dizzyingly embodied transformation, undermining the previous scene of his denial of the body and his animal affects.

The montage following unearths Sang-hyun's becoming-vampire as an eruption of repressed animal affects that explode on the surface in a furious, kaleidoscopic, and cacophonous way. The scene opens with an overhead close-up of a pearly white sink containing bloodied water; framed by contrasting the lyrically pure white with the ruby whirlpool, the primary affection-image of the sink mutates rapidly and furiously, conjoining the red traits with a flurry of other affection-images that show a slice of the quotidian at Sang-hyun's monastery: (1) a monk moving office chairs; (2) jeering priests watching television; (3) a knife chopping onions; (4) a radio playing nostalgic Korean love songs; (5) a bandaged figure crucified; (6) priests jogging on a treadmill; (7) a tree blowing in a strong breeze; (8) a cat meowing at the sky; (9) a reddened cigar burning brightly; (10) a priest smelling red wine; (11) parishioners praying; (12) a smiley, masturbating monk; (13) a flushed pearly-white toilet, etc. With these close-up affection-images conjoined together in a rapid sequence, once each image seems to diverge from Sang-hyun's perception, it is quickly threaded together through the color red. After the first four images, Park reddens a medium shot of Sang-hyun holding his ears, overwhelmed by his incredibly powerful hearing ability gained by vampirism. The frame is not only red; it is as if a distorted, wavy, flow has invaded the eye, coalescing into a whirling, ebbing, throbbing red sea of sight and sound: a red color-image. For Park, becoming-vampire is a necessary process of *seeing-red*. Even further, Park does not only excessively overwhelm the viewer (and Sang-hyun) by seeing-red and becoming-animal: the red is an expressive lens that anchors these affection-images and furious rapid cuts in a vortex of "a single *Furor*," in a cinematic "complex aggregate" of a "becoming-animal of men, packs of animals, elephants and rats, winds and tempests, bacteria sowing contagion," as Deleuze and Guattari explain.[27] Park caps off the becoming-vampire montage in spectacular fashion; his final shot in the short sequence depicts a shot-reverse-shot of Sang-hyun's horrified face and his elbow. The conjunctive close-ups transform into a penetrative long shot into his epidermis; the camera dives into Sang-hyun's skin to reveal a previously unviewable biological, molecular, and microscopic landscape swarmed by blood-sucking mites that he can hear and see feasting on him. This expressive montage of becoming-vampire gives the film "a new rhythm: an endless succession of catatonic episodes or fainting spells, and flashes or rushes," as Deleuze and Guattari describe, leaving the viewer and Sang-hyun overloaded (393). Within a flash, Sang-hyun falls to the floor and passes out, confirming Deleuze and Guattari's description of furious media's most extreme and affective potentiality: catatonia. And thus, while catatonia says "'This affect is too strong for me,'" the circuit-breaking flash of detonated affects enunciates the Deleuzo-Guattarian maxim: "The power of this affect sweeps me away."[28]

This montage is important in the film for a number of narrative reasons: it shapes Sang-hyun's new identity as a superhuman vigilante, as a passionate libertine like Laurent in Zola's *Thérèse Raquin*, and as an excommunicated priest, existentially distanced from the divine and further empowered by the raging animal affects that awakened in him. Moreover, it decenters cinematic perception in existential ways by pushing the limitations of the affection-image into the realm of an ironic externalized address that reveals the medium of the cinematic apparatus to the viewer. Park is no doubt an auteur who joyfully plays with the extremes of externalization and of expression, satirically reframing the traditional Gothic vampire film of the West, the *jiangshi* tradition of East Asia, and the Zola-inspired treatise on intensified affects in "a Brechtian mode, a Godardian mode, a Benjaminian mode" as Alexander Galloway writes, which as he concludes, "is not dissimilar to the sorts of formal techniques seen in the new wave, in modernism, and in other corners of the twentieth-century avant-garde."[29]

It is in this direct address that Park asserts two philosophical negations in *Thirst*: (1) a vampire is not a vampire, it is a rush of becomings, and (2) blood is not blood, it is red (red not as a symbol, but as a phenomenon in physics whereby the human eye catches light with a wavelength between 625 and 740 nanometers). The spectral color of red is as real as becoming-animal and must not be limited to the symbolic in *Thirst*. Park's negation of the traditional vampire narrative is activated in the montage; it exposes an embodied naturalism that resembles Deleuze and Guattari's claim that "[m]an does not become wolf, or vampire, as if he changed molar species [...] Of course there are werewolves and vampires, we say this with all our heart; but do not look for a resemblance or analogy to the animal."[30] Park's slice of the vampire world-image denaturalizes the ontology of the vampiric (the "what is a vampire," the "what attributes constitute a vampire compared to other undead figures," the "what makes vampire cinema vampiric") first and foremost, as much as it reifies *the real* aspects of molecular becoming and the physics of color and vision. This is most effectively done by optically overloading the affection-image and pushing it against the optic barriers of color. Park's colorism leans toward the saturation of the red—the making visible of red, the seeing-red—as a way to denaturalize and deterritorialize the existence of color in our (visible) universe:

the colour-image of the cinema seems to be defined by another characteristic, one which it shares with painting, but gives a different range and function. This is the *absorbent* characteristic. *Godard's formula, "it's not blood, it's red" is the formula of colourism* [my italics]. In opposition to a simply coloured image, the colour-image does not refer to a particular object, but absorbs all that it can: it is the power which seizes all that happens within its range, or the quality common to completely different objects. There *is* a symbolism of colours, but it does not consist in a correspondence between a colour and an affect (green and hope…). Colour is on the contrary the affect itself, that is, the virtual conjunction of the objects which it picks up.[31]

Park's strategic use of the red color-image follows the Godardian formula to a tee, especially as he invokes the bloodied lens at moments of Sang-hyun's skepticism (framed as doubt or guilt). Moreover, Park's use of the red color-image becomes more intensified as it clashes with the color-image of white, which Deleuze explains is not merely devoid of color or affect, but overwhelmed by it:

It is indeed doubtful whether one "must" choose the white. In Dreyer and Bresson, celllike and clinical white has a terrifying, monstrous character no less than the frozen white of Sternberg. In any case, it is not only a matter of passion or affect, in so far as, in Kierkegaard's phrase, faith is still a matter of passion, of affect and nothing else […] From its essential relation with the white, lyrical abstraction draws two consequences which accentuate its difference from Expressionism: an alternation of terms instead of an opposition; an alternative, a spiritual choice instead of a struggle or a fight.[32]

As Deleuze explains, the relation between color-images that often frame or link affection-images (like the red sea-image, the blinding white wall of Tae-ju's living room depicted in the third act of the film) is a lyrical, poetic, and expressive interface. This red-white interface reveals that the signs and symbols of divine transcendence (white) or mythic bloodletting (red) are philosophical machines and aesthetic tools of thought that provide an extremely expressive template for exposing the alternatives of the corporeal, the human, the perceived as a supercharged deterritorialized shock of the nonhuman.

Thus, as the color-images of red and white constantly fight for supremacy in the second half of the film—a vicious duel that often frames the conflict between Tae-ju and Sang-hyun—Park eventually ends the film by undermining the traditional dialectical duel between binary antipodes (male/female, life/death, god/human, nature/culture, etc.) by saturating and blending the color-images together into a visual mélange of burned out whites and bloodied reds, which viewers are bombarded by in the last scene. Just as the sun rises, Park once again anchors another becoming (becoming-dust) in the color-images of red and white that are mediated in the intensified and grotesque close-ups and a red sea-image; as Sang-hyun stares out into the ocean, he does not witness the idyllic blue waves cresting over the horizon as the audience does. Instead, he envisions an entire ocean of blood, framed by Park's close-up of his reddened eyes, which then transform into the red sea in actualization. Viewers, complicit in Sang-hyun's entire existential becomings within the film, witness the red sea-image return in again more biological and molecular contexts, with a more nonhuman and ecocritical pulse, similar to the transformation montage that ends with Sang-hyun acknowledging a becoming-vampire of the mites on his skin. Feeling the impulses and resonances of becoming-animal and Sang-hyun's pack affects, we begin to think, "seeing-red means we must see the world in blood, to remember that we are all blood," indicative of Park's wild imagery of whales leaping from the sanguine sea, spurting blood from their blowholes and descending into the depths of Sang-hyun's blood-red eyes. Subsequently after the red sea-image encloses the dominance of affect, fury, and pack affects, the blinding white color-image ends the corporeal becomings of vampire and of animal, and in tearing the skin from their flesh, enacts the final stage of deterritorializing the human: becoming-dust. In becoming-dust, the intensified affection-images melt away in the extreme deployment of lighting and color; what is replaced in the close-up of Sang-hyun and Tae-ju is long takes of cheeks smoldering, of eyes flooding with blood (seeing-red), and of their limbs roasting in their clothing from the overexposed white light. As the blinding white light burns the vampires to smoldering embers with nothing but their shoes remaining, the film ends with a quick cut to black, resoundingly echoing Deleuze's reading of overexposed color-images: "Colour elevates space to the power of the void, when that which can be realized in the event is accomplished."[33] It is in Park's extreme deterritorialization of anthropocentric perception that the film ends with a critical reevaluation of the human and the spirit, as we experience the furious becomings and unbecomings of both vampiric lovers, limiting the vampire to yet another extension of the posthuman experience that not only exposes the desire for becoming-animal, but the reminder that what awaits for us in the end may not only be a red sea, a hell, or a heaven, but simply dust, as Tae-ju seems to articulate at the very end of the film: "When you're dead you're dead (from dust to dust)."

Seeing-Ghosts in the Polaroid: Non-Photography as Cosmic Pessimism in The Wailing

In the wake of Park's radical production of an existential vampire world-image of blood (red), light (white), and dust (black), Na Hong-jin's ghost film, *The Wailing*, is perhaps a more bizarre entry in the discussion of contemporary South Korean cult auteur cinema by Park, Na, etc., and their niche vampire films, even though as Marc Raymond illustrates, Na has been often linked to Park as a stylistic and industrial influence on his films: "[Park] also remains both a model for younger genre directors and a competitive obstacle. A good example of this would be Na Hong-jin, whose 2008 debut *The Chaser* (*Choo-gyeok-ja*) gathered a cult audience and whose most recent film *The Wailing* (*Gok-seong*) topped many domestic critics' list of the best movies of 2016."[34] While influenced by Park, Na's take on the vampire genre borders on the avant-garde, and it offers a profoundly different philosophical solution to the questions of media, communication, and an extreme existence.

To begin, I must state that Na Hong-jin's film is not entirely a vampire film, in that the primary antagonistic force is not a vampire *per se*, but it is clearly a female vengeful spirit (*yeogwi*) that is caught between a spiritual duel between two shamans: a rural Japanese shaman and a Seoul-based city shaman. However, the image of the vampire is integral throughout the film, and it is a curious plot device that again functions as a direct address to reveal the cinematic apparatus to the audience. Specifically, the vampire of the town, that locals claim has been caught in the woods killing and drinking the blood of deer as well as mountainfolk in the town, is depicted like Tae-ju in *Thirst*: as a prime predator who has weaseled his way into a tight-knit rural community. Like the vampires in *Thirst*, the vampire of *The Wailing* continually sees-red, sporting crimson, blood-filled eyes, and is a master shapeshifter, having an uncanny ability to transform between his human form (a quiet Japanese man who has relocated to the tiny mountain town in Korea) to his monstrous, demonic form that only pursues those who cross into his territory. However, Na is quick to cast the vampire as a clever MacGuffin for the audience, and most importantly, for the protagonists, the cops and detectives of the town who are investigating a series of family-based murderer-suicides and the possession of dead members of the community. Only by the final act of the film do we realize that the vampire is an illusion cast over the sleepy rural village by a vengeful female ghost whose motivations for killing and disorienting the entire town are completely unknown. While Park's extreme blood-world of *Thirst* functions as a canvas for articulating the raging affects and furious expressions of becoming-animal, whereby the motivations of the vampires is known and is framed as a conflict between human and animal, Na's ghost story is peculiar in that it is no solid canvas for exploring a duel between human and nonhuman perspectives; it is rather a dispersal, an aerosol, a gaseous evaporation of any human intuition, inclination, or impression of the darkened, indifferent, misanthropic cosmos that cannot truly be understood in either the optic or ontic sense, as film or as philosophy.

The Wailing tells the story of a rural policeman named Jong-goo (Kwak Do-won) who investigates the outbreak of a disease that possesses a victim's body, and transforms them into a vicious killing machine, often leading the victim to murder their closest relatives in the home. Jong-goo and his police department investigate local apothecaries, hunters, and shop-owners who have gone mad and killed their entire families, and struggle with finding any leads, until a rumor begins to float through the town that a Japanese man is the culprit, with many misleading stories about him supposedly raping a young woman (a significant reference to the brutal historical trauma of Korean comfort women in World War II), or that he is a witchdoctor, responsible for casting spells and curses on the townspeople. The rest of the film follows Jong-goo and his family as they navigate a deadly *jiangshi* disease outbreak in the town, and Na's plot quickly becomes tangled in a web of deceptions, feints, and sleights-of-hand that leads viewers and the protagonists down increasingly more disturbing, self-destructive steps toward a cosmic madness, seeming more H.P. Lovecraft than Bram Stoker. Na, like Park, ends the film in complete annihilation, leaving the entire village obliterated by its own deathly madness, drenched in its own blood and hollowed out by the inhuman fury of the town's ghastly matron.

Unlike in *Thirst*, the vampire world-image constructed in *The Wailing* is darkened, fractal, and illusory. Formally, the most intriguing elements of the film are not only the continual twists and turns in what seems like a completely incomprehensible narrative, unhinged and cruel to most casual viewers, but in the way in which Na utilizes yet another direct address in the cinematic discourse in the tradition of photography, which as François Laruelle describes in *The Concept of Non-Photography* as a philosophical process as much as an art form: "Philosophy is perhaps born as a photographic catastrophe—in all senses of the word: as an irruption of the 'empty' essence of photography and as an intoxication."[35] While *Thirst* was overwhelmed with a painterly, illustrative fury that Park engenders in all of his films, Na seems to engage in a dark, documentarian photographical use of the camera, a style that Eugene Thacker refers to as Korean "dark media," which he defines as media-based horror tropes that articulate the terror of technology and otherworldly mediation, as he further explains: "In these stories the innocuous and even banal ubiquity of media objects, from cell phones to webcams, enters a liminal space, where such objects suddenly reveal the ambivalent boundary separating the natural from the supernatural, the uncanny from the marvelous, the earthly from the divine."[36]

The Wailing, from the outset, may not seem specifically like a traditional dark media film; the film is largely low-tech, and it is purposefully excluded from the high-tech world of Seoul in a rural pastoral setting that undermines the dark media tropes of technophobia or haunted mediation. However, the film is, like *Thirst*, an apparatus-revealing, mediation machine that uses the medium of cinema to explore the uncanny elements of photography, which as Thacker writes, fulfills the potentiality of dark media's philosophical richness: "Thus what we are witnessing is not a single, master medium that represents all possible cases of the supernatural, but a variety of media that mediate or remediate other media: a novel about a cursed videotape, a film about haunted webcams, a videogame that uses a paranormal camera."[37] However, when revisiting the film from an alternative perspective, Na reframes the film with this haunted media trope as a way to throw off the puzzled audience and the investigating characters as in any Lovecraft short story: Jong-goo and his deputy first believe that the vampiric contagion that spreads throughout the town is mediated through Polaroid photographs taken by the Japanese stranger, who they accuse of being serial killer and demonic occultist. When Jong-goo and his deputy first interrogate the Japanese man, they find dozens of photographs in his hut of all the victims who died of the disease and then became possessed, killing their entire family. Na specifically employs a slow tracking shot of all the photographs, from up to down, right to left, lingering on the faces of the dead and memorabilia that the Japanese man supposedly took from them, like a ring, a hairpin, a baseball cap, a toy, or even Jong-goo's daughter's shoe.

Moreover, Na's hyperreal, documentarian, shaky camera work alienates the viewers and the protagonists from the event; even Jong-goo's deputy is unable to move after witnessing the stash of photographs, seemingly infected by the mysterious curse or virus. Na then turns to another room in the Japanese man's house that includes occultic paraphernalia: ornately crafted animal skull headdresses, dead chickens hanging from the roof, bloody Polaroid pictures, and an altar that is littered with unusual markings, some of which resemble pentagrams. These two scenes are less cinematic montage than they are photographic collage, which essentially slows the film down and readdresses the terror of the film as an existential threat. The photographic collage induces catatonia in Jong-goo's deputy and destabilizes the film's traditional vampire horror trajectory. Na's framing of both scenes, while short in duration, alters from the affection-image of becoming-vampire to what Deleuze refers to as "the crystal-image," or a fractal slice of the world-image that is temporally rather than spatially mediated, relying more on memory and time than affect and movement.[38] As David Deamer writes, "no longer is there a fixed and solid centre that can process affects as lucid expressions, a centre that can adequately react to and perform acts upon the world; a centre whose thoughts can be reliably traced, depicted and defined." As we can see, these crystal-images call into question the seemingly linear or determined situations and perceptions of the movement-image in this scene through its "[d]ispersed centres, disjunctive temporality and displaced spatiality."[39]

Not only does Na utilize the temporally-embedded crystal-image as a way to overturn traditional movement-image discourses of bodies, subjectivities, affects, and continuity, but as Thacker explains, the decentralized collage-shots reveal the struggle of truth and deception rooted in the film's depiction of photography and the supernatural: "something appears that has no appearance, or something appears that shouldn't appear. Something defies the litmus test of the empirical, or something defies natural law and the production of knowledge."[40] Moreover, following the trend of dark media films like Nakata Hideo's *The Ring* (*Ringu*, 1998) and Kurosawa Kiyoshi's 2001 Cannes Film Festival surprise hit *Pulse* (*Kairo*, 2001), *The Wailing* targets the ontological questions of photographs as gateways into a rhizome of other worlds, as Laruelle writes: "the photo harbours a double discourse: as supplementary representative or double of that which it reproduces, its emanation and its positive substitute; but also as sign of that which it fails to be. Whence the double register necessary in order to describe it: illusion, lack, absence, death and coldness; but also life, becoming, rebirth and metamorphosis."[41] Non-photography then is an effective philosophical framework in understanding how dark media interrogate the imperceptible or ineffable, because like the film, non-photography is "neither a mode of philosophical reflection—even if there is plenty of photography integrated into philosophy—nor a mode of unconscious representation or a return of the repressed."[42] It is like Deleuze's cinema of becoming-animal, a machine for a world-imaging beyond the human, a push away from the interpretative and toward the real. Moreover, Galloway clarifies that a non-photography produces new fractals of the real, the physical, the cosmic: "Laruelle calls such photography a 'hyperphenomenology of the real'; it follows a logic of auto-impression, not expression. Not a cliché snapshot, but an immanent identity of the Real."[43]

In this philosophical context, in reading the chaos, nihilism, and clear hopelessness of *The Wailing*, the photographic discourse becomes one the more unsettling elements of the film. As we can see, Na's photographic collage upends the entire world-imaging role of the horror film, decentering the viewer's sense of perceptual wholeness through a fractal disorientation, instead of through the excess of affective expression or transformative becomings in Park's *Thirst*. All images are under interrogation, every scene feels alien and denaturalized. For example, after the police track down and kill the Japanese man who flees from them during a botched arrest, the viewers learn much later from Il-gwang, the hired Seoul-based shaman, that his divinations were wrong: the demonic, vampiric Japanese man was not that at all. He is revealed to have been a local healer who too sought to keep the invasive primeval *yeogwi* from returning to the town to sacrifice the lives of innocents for unknown reasons. The only way the Japanese forest shaman thought he could defend the town was by taking Polaroid pictures of the living and of the dead who were infected with the ghastly plague so to encase their spirit in an image, so that it would misdirect the possession by the ghost antagonist, seemingly following Laruelle's logic: "a photo testifies to this tendency by which the image 'approximates' reality, concentrates its dimensions, tends toward the cadaveric, to the excessive state where death encounters life and already threatens the certainty of classical dimensions, the theoretical space of 'whole' dimensions of representation."[44] Challenging what is and what is not in the mediation allegories of the cinematic and photographic apparatus, Na further exposes the limitations of undead representation in the cinematographic and photographic experience in his new weird, documentarian, photo-realistic style, again, addressing the veracity of the image itself, the ontics of optics as it were. Narratively, we learn that the ghost of the town implanted images of the Japanese man as an illusory vampire in the minds of random townspeople so as to throw them off the scent of the haunting. The entire thematic structure of the film continually pushes viewers into *seeing-ghosts*, into whether questioning what they saw was real or their imagination, whether or not everyone is the villain or victim, echoing the final statements of the possessed body of the Japanese man who transforms into a demon in the eyes of a priest so to reveal a profound truism, one that is never made false throughout the film: *we see what we want to see.*

This alienating experience of feeling fooled, tricked, and hoodwinked throughout the film is often infuriating, exhilarating, but more often than not, deeply revealing about our expectations about the vampire horror genre that we hope will offer dreams of transformation, expressive embodiment, immortal motivations, and either Gothic or posthuman reflections of our desires to overcome the human in some shape or form, to become-animal, to rage, feast, and howl at the night sky. There is none of that in *The Wailing*. Na, a master of misdirection, reveals that the horror of the film is not in the monster, the killing, or the cruelty of humanity; it is in an exposure of a darkly nihilistic *cosmic pessimism* that colors his illusory, darkened vampire world-image. As Thacker describes, "[t]he view of Cosmic Pessimism is a strange mysticism of the world-without-us, a hermeticism of the abyss, a noumenal occultism. It is the difficult thought of the world as absolutely unhuman, and indifferent to the hopes, desires, and struggles of human individuals and groups."[45] In this world without us, Na offers an entirely alienating and speculative approach to the vampire cinematic tradition. While Park accelerates and intensifies the vampire world-image in the affection-image, Na blacks it out entirely, muddying the waters, and makes-false the cinematic truisms and narrative tropes established in the cinema of movement, of traditionally teleological, Hollywood-style continuity films like *Thirst*, as Deleuze explains:

> Making-false becomes the sign of a new realism, in opposition to the making-true of the old. Clumsy fights, badly aimed punches or shots, a whole out-of-phase of action and speech replace the too perfect duels of American Realism [...] Under this power of the false all images become clichés, sometimes because their clumsiness is shown, sometimes because their apparent perfection is attacked.[46]

In other words, what is made-false in this film is like a refraction of light that transforms into dozens of other shades, that mutates and mixes, blends and bends, and misrepresents the original in its entirety, forcing us to question the reality of the world depicted, as Laruelle writes: "Photography is that activity which, before being an art, produces in parallel an intelligible photographic universe, a realm of non-photographic vision; and a derealization of the World reduced to a support of this realm, which rests on it ever so lightly."[47] Thus, not only is the vampire film itself made-false through Na's narrative twists and turns, also but the fractal collage of dark mediated Polaroids reshapes the world against what is merely mimetic representation. Discoveries transform into more mysteries, answers disperse into questions, flipping the entire cinematic world upside down. Na's antagonist is not the imperial colonial Japanese man, but a ghastly *yeogwi* who possesses Jong-goo's daughter and best friend, leaving most of the village in bloody ruin. Both shamans in the film overturn each other's hard work, and Na even hints at the possibility that both shamans may simply be superstitious frauds who have no real connection to the spiritual realm. While in *Thirst* the vampire functions as the anti-institutional force that seems to ask for more radical experimentation against said institutions, the vampiric illusion in *The Wailing* merely confirms that there is nothing any durable institution like the police, the family, or the religious leaders of a community can do in the wake of the viciousness of the black universe, as Laruelle calls it: "Man, who carries away the Universe with him, is condemned, without knowing why, to the World and to the Earth, and neither the World nor the Earth can tell him why. He is answered only by the Universe, being black and mute."[48]

It is throughout the entire film that Na exposes his darkened cosmic pessimism, leaving the vampire world-image not vibrantly crimson or dazzlingly white, but a darker-than-black shadow of speculation and endless investigation, hermeneutics of the endless cosmic night. Thus, the ghouls of Na's cinematic cosmos are children of the *cosmic* night, a pessimistic peopling that seek to not only speculate, but to know the darkness, to know the night, to actively see what the undead sees. Na's vampire world-image is an elusive one, but just as Park forced any viewer into seeing-red and opening their bodies to intensity, *The Wailing* seems to ask any viewer to open their "eyes in the night, not to look or speculate but to *know*," thus reminding us that "we are this night."[49]

Conclusion

As this essay attempts to illustrate, *Thirst* and *The Wailing* should not simply be read as generic vampire films made in the Republic of Korea, nor should they be thought of as simple vampire films in global, generic, and nationally specific terms. This essay, while it is not against these readings, attempts to avoid reading these films in the context of genre or global reception of the vampire film, nor does it read the films as humanist, theological, political, historical, or literary allegories that reconsider the role of the vampire in South Korean culture. Rather, it attempts to indicate the film-philosophical potency of each horror film by following the aesthetic philosophical works of Gilles Deleuze, Félix Guattari, and François Laruelle. This essay examines both films as *non-vampire* films, or at least, films that challenge and alter the ontology of vampire cinema. Both films express a richly dark and furious media philosophy that is artfully mediated through the speculative aesthetic expressions of color-images and darkly mediated photographs. The intensely existential, posthuman, and nonhuman philosophical engagements that both Korean cult auteurs imbue their vampire film genre with reveal that a cinematic recuperation of *the extreme* must be contextualized as an aesthetic and philosophical project that beckons the viewers to create new models of the intense, the speculative, and most importantly, the cosmic in the cinematic apparatus. And hence, by learning to see-red and to see-ghosts in these films, to feel the grit of blood and dust on my heels as I gaze into the empty, starless expanse, I too, a mere cosmic subject like Park and Na, hope that after exploring these affects of becoming-vampire and fractals of unbecoming-human, that I too might catch a glimpse of way out of this "world-for-us," as Thacker calls it in *Cosmic Pessimism*; beyond this ready-made world of the living, the blood, dust, and shadows of this planet reveal the realm of the other-than-man, a darkened plane where we thirst for rage and scream into the quiet night.[50]

NOTES

1. Chi-Yun Shin, "The Art of Branding: Tartan 'Asia Extreme' Films," *Horror to the Extreme: Changing Boundaries in Asian Cinema*, edited by Jinhee Choi and Misuyo Wada-Marciano, Hong Kong University Press, 2009, pages 85–86.

2. Jinhee Choi and Misuyo Wada-Marciano, "Introduction," *Horror to the Extreme: Changing Boundaries in Asian Cinema*, edited by Jinhee Choi and Mitsuyo Wada-marciano, Hong Kong University Press, 2009, page 6.

3. Choi and Wada Marciano, cited above, page 6.

4. Shin, cited above, pages 86–89.

5. Shin, page 99.

6. Shin, page 98.

7. Choi and Wada-Marciano, cited above, page 6.

8. Shin, cited above, page 99.

9. David Martin-Jones, *Deleuze and World Cinemas*, Continuum, 2011, pages 2–5.

10. Lisa Odham Stokes, "Vampire Movies," *Historical Dictionary of Hong Kong Cinema*, Scarecrow Press, 2007, page 448.

11. Jeffrey Weinstock, *The Vampire Film: Undead Cinema*, Columbia University Press, 2012, pages 67–68.

12. Stephanie Lam, "Hop on Pop: Jianshi Films in a Transnational Context," *CineAction*, number 78, 2009, page 46.

13. Kyu Hyun Kim, "Park Chan-wook's *Thirst*: Body, Guilt, and Exsanguination," *Korean Horror Cinema*, edited by Alison Peirse and Daniel Martin, Edinburgh University Press, 2013, page 203.

14. Christopher Vitale, "Guide to Reading Deleuze's The Movement-Image, Part I: The Deleuzian Notion of the Image, or Worldslicing as Cinema Beyond the Human," from Networkologies: https://networkologies.wordpress.com/2011/04/04/the-deleuzian-notion-of-the-image-a-slice-of-he-world-cinema-beyond-the-human/.

15. Kim, cited above, page 87.

16. Kim, page 213.

17. Steve Choe, *Sovereign Violence: Ethics and South Korean Cinema in the New Millenium*, Amsterdam University Press, 2018, page 263. page 263.

18. Kim, cited above, page 201.

19. Giles Deleuze and Félix Guattari, *A Thousand Plateaus: Capitalism and Schizophrenia*, translated by Brian Massumi, Continuum, 2004, page 264.

20. Deleuze and Guattari, cited aove, page 303.

21. McKenzie Wark, "Furious Media," *Excommunication: Three Inquiries in Media and Mediation*, edited by Alexander Galloway, Eugene Thacker, and McKenzie Wark, University of Chicago Press, 2014, page 193.

22. Deleuze and Guattari, cited above, page 265.

23. Gilles Deleuze, *Cinema I: The Movement-Image*, translated by Hugh Tomlinson and Barbara Habbejam, Bloomsbury Academic, 2013, page 240. Deleuze goes on to explain that the affection-image is any cinematic image "which occupies the gap between an action and a reaction, that which absorbs an external action and reacts on the inside," including a close-up shot, a transversal lateral tracking shot (perfected throughout the Vengeance Trilogy), an expressive or poetic montage overwhelmed by color, or any intensified use of lighting that exposes an explosive reaction to the movement of not only characters, but affects, bodies, and perceptions.

24. Deleuze, *Cinema I*, page 103.

25. Deleuze and Guattari, cited above, page 289.

26. Deleuze and Guattari, page 289.

27. Deleuze and Guattari, page 268.

28. Deleuze and Guattari, page 28.

29. Alexander Galloway, *Laruelle: Against the Digital*, University of Minnesota Press, 2014, page 140.

30. Deleuze and Gauttari, page 303.

31. Deleuze, *Cinema I*, cited above, page 132.

32. Deleuze, *Cinema I*, page 127.

33. Deleuze, *Cinema I*, page 134.

34. Marc Raymond, "From Old Boys to Quiet Dreams: Mapping Korean Art Cinema Today," *Film Criticism*, volume 42, number 1, March 2018, paragraph 10.

35. François Laruelle, "Of Black Universe in the Human Foundations of Color," *Hyun Soo Choi: Seven Large-Scale Paintings*, translated by Miguel Abreu, Thread Waxing Space, 1991, page 3.

36. Eugene Thacker, "Dark Media," *Excommunication: Three Inquiries in Media and Mediation*, edited by Alexander Galloway, Eugene Thacker, and McKenzie Wark, Unicersity of Chicago Press, 2014, page 91.

37. Thacker, "Dark Media," page 91.

38. Gilles Deleuze, *Cinema II: The Time-Image*, translated by Hugh Tomlinson and Robert Galeta, Bloomsbury Academic, 2013, page 123. The crystalline regime of thought is the *time-image*. Crystalline images are abstract, imaginative, and always in flux. Compared to the organic regime, Deleuze writes that "the crystalline regime is completely different: the actual is cut off from its motor linkages, or the real from its legal connections, and the virtual, for its part, detaches itself from its actualizations, starts to be valid for itself." As Markos Hadjioannou writes, "the crystalline regime renegotiates the distinction between real and imaginary leading to what is in fact an indecipherable indiscernibility between the two. The real and the imaginary within the crystal-image becomes facets of the same world. It is no

longer the case that a dream is situated within reality and analysed and justified on the basis of this reality. Rather, within the crystalline regime the dream becomes actual by transforming the real, while the real becomes simultaneously a manifestation of the dream," from "In Search of Lost Reality: Waltzing with Bashir," in *Deleuze and Film*, edited by David Martin-Jones and William Brown, Edinburgh University Press, 2012, page 112.

39. David Deamer, *Deleuze's Cinema Books: Three Introductions to the Taxonomy of Images*, University of Edinburgh Press, 2016, page 14.

40. Thacker, "Dark Media," cited above, page 98.

41. Laruelle, pages 65–66.

42. Laruelle, page 34.

43. Galloway, cited above, page 147.

44. Laruelle, cited above, page 44.

45. Eugene Thacker, "Three Questions on Demonology," *Hideous Gnosis: Black Metal Theory Symposium*, volume 1, edited by Nicola Masciandaro, Glossator, 2010, page 186.

46. Deleuze, *Cinema I*, cited above, page 237.

47. Laruelle, cited above, page 123.

48. Laruelle, page 2.

49. Galloway, cited above, page 150.

50. Eugene Thacker, *Cosmic Pessimism*, Univocal Publishing, 2015.

The Craft of Delicacy in *Cronos*

Rethinking Vampire Films in Latin America

ROBERTO FORNS-BROGGI

Cinematic Lab: Feeling and Thinking in Terms of a Trigger

> To think in terms of trigger implies action, performance, embodied relation, engagement, intervention, and hands-on investigation as a mode of operating with the material that is not merely vintage or a surface.
>
> —Jussi Parikka

> Cronos reworks vampire and Frankenstein narratives into an often intimate, tender comedic meditation on time, love and human existence.
>
> —Keith McDonald and Roger Clark

Cronos is a seminal film that has made me think in a deep way about human condition in today's complicated world. Guillermo del Toro's first major feature film is 26 years old, and it still feels like a fresh movie, one that stirs the imagination and encourages a reflection on the nature of imagination.[1] *Cronos* makes me want to get to grips with it. It also makes me think of cinema as a lab imaginary, a place of experimentation that advances ways to think of time, as a site of shifting scales that make things readable. Del Toro recuperates for cinema a marginalized function to illuminate the animal's deathly residency, and recasts film as a creaturely driven assemblage.[2]

When I watched *Cronos* for the first time in 1994, I did like it, but I did not pay attention to so many little details and aspects. My first film viewing did not produce any speculative practice *in situ*, neither did I consider cinema as a place of trial and error that gathers special powers of scale from the interface with the outside world. Let's say that I did not understand that dark side of these all-too American characters: the powerful industrial predator Dieter De la Guardia (played by Claudio Brook, a leading actor of Mexican cinema), and his ugly nephew Ángel (played by Ron Perlman, a key actor for del Toro's cinema) obsessively concerned with changing the appearance of his nose which is broken several times.[3] I did not see them as part of a playful "revenge for the clichéd but familiar representation of Mexicans in Hollywood movies as moustachioed bad guys."[4] As they were looking for Cronos, the metallic-insectoid device that is "the key of eternal life," it never occurred to me that those finance-rogue characters were, in effect, living metaphors to expose the undead and omnipresent nature of consumerism. I did not think of this vampire story as "a chilling reminder that human life aspires to death and rottenness rather than to changeless permanence."[5] I did not laugh at the parodic and sarcastic aspects of the film as much I do now. What a scene when the old man shaves his moustache and flirts with his wife and exclaims "*¡Es muy bueno!*" What a scene when the dead-body of Jesús Gris is being fixed by an extravagant embalmer who sings and lights the fire of the empty coffin at a crematorium! What a scene when the undead Jesús is welcomed at home and protected by the doll box of his granddaughter! The prized device is hidden in a teddy bear! What a close-up of Jesús when he smiles before a great mortal jump with his bleeding-nose aggressor! What a cinematic phone call when the undead monster pronounces his wife's name! Right there del Toro's characters condense comically the similar feeling of defenselessness and disempowerment of Kafka's protagonist of *The Castle* when he listens to a humming on the telephone line without a meaning that is humanly decipherable.[6]

Now I think deliberately and imaginatively and even obsessively about the insect inside the Cronos device: I pay close attention to those three key moments when the film provides a weird close-up of the inside of this mysterious device. I scrutinize the film with an ecological eye, refocused by this curiosity of a mysterious insect. If you watch this film for a second time, maybe for a third time, you start to feel this strange spell that has haunted so many critics in so many critical reviews and studies of this particular film. What I admire now is *Cronos*'s experimental flavor because my notion of cinema has changed radically as I have studied and made eco-films and experimental films over the last two decades.[7] *Cronos* reminds me that cinema might offer the powers of the Lab of reproducing inside its walls an event or situation that seem to be happening only outside. Experimental cinema is what Phil Solomon affirmed as an effective way to defend and nurture a thoughtful, contemplative and self-aware individual before "the worker bee mentality of the ever busy, ever connected, ever wired and jacked-in-from-morning-till-night electronic buzz seeker."[8] Besides all the written character-izations made about *Cronos*—a modern-day fable vampire film, a *Bildungsroman*, a ghost story, a political horror/fairy tale, a Gothic superhero movie, and a wartime adventure monster movie—I would like to tap into its experimental quality.[9] My love for cinema differs from the mainstream use of films: instead of the false reassurance of instant gratification—something that Hollywood and Netflix share in common in spite of a few mind-blowing films. I rather prefer the slow relaxed state of the aesthetic experience. I am afraid that even in the specialized circles of film critics, few would watch a film and have an epiphany, a revelation that shakes them to the very foundation of their being. Cinema made out of love and craft produces that kind of unique occasion for feeling and thinking that Jussi Parikka calls "a trigger [that] implies action, … investigation."[10] In my case it works as an endless desire to investigate today's complicated relation between humans and technology, and *Cronos* is a powerful trigger to think about "time, love and human existence" in the face of our weakness before digital culture and, simultaneously, our awareness of the benefits or advantages of a more fluid sense of past and future.[11] My take: it is critical to ponder the lack of personal responsibility for loving and caring about people and the planet, and what *Cronos* offers is an imaginative meditation on the loss of what connects us with others and nature under the pressures of the market economy.

I consider *Cronos* to be a good example for teachers like me to encourage the most valuable thing one can do for students, "to interrupt and counter their experiences of the commercial media."[12] It could be a good occasion to have a transformative experience, from what vampires are in the pop culture to something else. As Nick Groom maintains in *The Vampire: A New History*, "Vampires still maintain the power both to convey and to confront the most pressing contemporary issues of our times. They are, in effect, roving thought-experiments lingering in the periphery of comprehension, and even now can help us think through current anxieties from border control to epidemic con-tagion." Vampire films are just the peak of an immeasurable iceberg: there is an intense and self-referential intertextuality that means "it is impossible to disentangle the multitude of manifestations in which vampires today appear." Like Groom, I believe that vampires "personify the fear of moving beyond what is familiar—incarnate a fear of the unknown."[13] *Cronos* can help the reader to ponder and think about this vampiric constellation.

The cinema I love to watch and think of in terms of a trigger is a very interesting interruption of concerns and preoccupations, because it makes them objects of reflection, of encouragement for thinking, and an animated occasion for connecting. Watch *Cronos* and then tell yourself what you think.

I try to avoid the funny way of our collective preference to escape from individual responsibilities.[14] Instead of explaining the plot and offering a summary of abstract-articulated interpretations—I am not saying they are useless, you can check some of them that I cite in this essay—I would rather expose my own enthusiasm for this movie. I enjoy its humor, an aspect that is not much studied: almost all of what is written about it focuses on its power to transgress borders, to rethink genres, to criticize globalization and the sneaky big vampires of the market, and to imagine alternative resistance. I know that Jesús Gris, a Kafkaesque character played by the famous Argentinean actor Federico Luppi could constitute a difficult obstacle to overcome for American audiences. First of all, the protagonist is incapable of killing even a cockroach.[15] Not a Hollywood hero, Gris is a gentle, even Christ-like antique dealer, a loving grandfather who becomes an elderly working-class vampire who fights the elusive forces of global disintegration and the pressures of the vampiric market—as an enormous insect à la Kafka.[16] Changing slightly David Foster Wallace's explanation about the signal frustration in trying to read Kafka with college students, I am afraid that *Cronos* will be next to impossible to get students to see as funny, let one see how its funniness is bound up with the extraordinary power of the story.[17] I hope I am wrong about this.

I want to encourage the contemplation of this film, available in the Criterion Collection and from free-streaming sites. I like to emphasize this uncommon, unpopular art of contemplating cinema as a laboratory to watch an insect-vampire-machine-human that would allow us to grasp the cryptic art of the weak and the urge to survive the threat of bodily dissolution. Through his relationship and closeness with a child character, Jesús Gris presents himself not only as a monstrous representation of the mortal side of human being (vis à vis aging, decay), but also as a living creature that might incarnate an unusual identification for film spectators. When we have to make big decisions in life, we are in a similar situation to this poor vampire. It's a common problem in late twentieth-century vampire stories: Would we have the same courage as Jesús Gris, to renounce our own life in favor of the Other, or would we allow ourselves to become bloodsucker-depredators? We all face such complicated and deep transformations. Underrating this mutating desire for survival exposes the height of our vulnerability, and the depth of its sources. It makes me think of the height of a child. The insect-vampiric-device, besides its abject bloodthirst, is put in a circuitous relation of force fields to create new opportunities to change radically. Guillermo del Toro in multiple interviews has indicated that in *Cronos* the main vampire is a poor devil, the saddest vampire ever made. It is not a star. It is an antidote to celebrity culture and its ever-shrinking, unified world of universal consumption.[18] The monster serves a more symbolic function to illuminate the human condition. Compared to his namesake, Jesus, the protagonist is an imperfect but Christ-like vampire who walks on water in the eyes of his granddaughter, sacrifices himself for the Other, is an ordinary man, does not look for money or power, whose body receives bloody punishment in a Calvary-like manner as he sometimes talks to God, has a cut in his side, at the moment of his first death echoes the famous last words on the cross, resuscitates on the third day, and loves the Other to overcome evil, purify sin, and appease souls. And in order to protect his family, he needs to confront the bloodsucker industrialist who is looking obsessively for eternal life. When Jesús fights Dieter De la Guardia, he is distanced from the Christian symbology and starts to know himself as an abject monster, as slimy as his opponent as he confronts modern, neoliberal alienation.[19] *Cronos* is unique cinematic creation that, with its hybrid amalgamations and tendency to mix everything in an instinctive manner, would have you think on diverse and disparate levels such as the cultural, economic, historical, ecological, biotechnological, political, literary, psychological, religious, and on, but its humor and final self-sacrificing will guide you to an interesting and enduring place of loving contemplation and family accord.

A Rare Cultural Device of Turbulence and Flow

> To spend time in a movie house is to make a "hole" in one's life.
> —Robert Smithson[20]

> One of the forces that makes Guillermo del Toro's work so electrifying is the tension between multiple versions of cultural entropy and persistence.
> —Laurence Davies[21]

Cronos as cultural object—the movie as well as the artifact—moves from interaction to interaction—crafted in an alchemical lab in 1537, recuperated after debris removal through a public space of urban putrefaction, vetted by authorities in 1937, blamable for persecution and violence, interpreted by cinephiles, handled as a commodity in a DVD-Blu-ray crafted box, or perhaps exhibited in a museum—somewhere along the way the film and the artifact have stopped doing what they were intended to do. Or maybe the device penetrates the mind of the viewer from the past, but operates in the present as "the embryo continues to be active in the/tissues of the mature organism, and the child in the psychic life of the adult."[22] Whether gothic science fiction or contested symbolic art, the energy invested in a symbolic object sometimes flows along the intended path, like this monstrous bloodsucking device to prolong life. Often, though, an object's energy diffuses or diverts along unintended trajectories. *Cronos* makes it possible to choose alternative paths that are built into different interpretive arrangements of people, objects, and settings. This potential instability is due to the shared symbolic and material qualities of arrangements that never perfectly stabilize. Cultural entropy suggests that culture is far more complex than designers' instrumental view. *Cronos*, the movie, like the device, is a strange object, and it is not easy to think with. It is an invention that invites the viewer to "give up being a player at the fairground and become an operator within the technical world where one can work on developing alternatives."[23]

Watching *Cronos* could be a unique event that creates deeper opportunities for creative, contemplative, poetic time in our lives.[24] It is a protest against sloppy thinking.[25] It recreates what Carol Becker calls "never-enough-time," a moment of truth when Jesús Gris decided to end the time of his long journey home to himself, when he comes to understand that taking care of Aurora, his granddaughter, was all he was ever intended to do—"for that, in fact, there was always just enough time."[26] In that sense, *Cronos* is more than an ingenious rework of an embedded Mexican Tradition around death. It recreates smartly that disturbing moment of facing your own death as a terrific opportunity to reflect on the most important aspects of your own life.

3-Zooming In

> Through the practice of contemplation, little by little, the muscles and the mind relax and the whole body opens out to become an ear.
> —R. Murray Schafer[27]

> Give me a laboratory and I raise the world.
> —Bruno Latour[28]

The whole time we watch the movie, we wonder what is inside the enigmatic golden device. Just before the first glimpse to its interior, Jesús opens his refrigerator in the middle of the night, drinks a whole jar of water, and sees a glowing red meat dish of guts. He stares at it, more than thinking, craving instinctively for blood. Like a prayer, Jesús utters a plea to the device at his hand: "Please, please, very careful," and then the first legs of the device start to sound like a clockwork mechanism and begins to clinch Jesús body, and Jesús starts to declare nervously and rapidly the Our Father prayer.[29] Aurora sees from upstairs his grandfather trying to put the device to work on his itchy wound. The clockwork mechanism sounds like a rhythmically paused, sinking metallic knife.

The first peep into the interior of the device occurs from minute 24:20,

Cronos (in Spanish, 1993). Jesús Gris (Federico Luppi), antiques dealer in Mexico City and grandfather of Aurora (Tamara Shanath), shows her the Cronos device, which extracts and injects blood when activated and gives one eternal life—as a vampire. Although an important character in the story, Aurora speaks only one word in the film: *abuelo* (Photofest).

for 22 seconds. In the third of several shots, in a blurry image, something organic and red is moving like a larva among the clockwork cogs. In the fourth shot there is a slow pan along that red, insectoid organism. The last seconds barely show the insectoid body among the clockwork mechanisms. Like its creatures, the film works elliptically.

In the second peep, 15 minutes after the first, Jesús is dressing up for the New Year's eve celebration in the bathroom and talks to the device, "Who are you? A God?" "What a good you give me!" This second glimpse lasts only 8 seconds, but it is an important reminder of the inexplicable urge for blood that will occur a few scenes later in a bathroom of the big New Year's Eve party. Jesús misses the opportunity to lick the blood leaked onto the sink by a stranger whose nose was bleeding, so then licks desperately from another little pool of blood on the floor. In the next scene, the kick of Jesús' face puts us into another box, the car of the aggressor, and then in a bigger box marked by city lights. A box in a box in a box, this sequence seems to conduct the rhythm of this film. And the cryptic insect inside is also in a box, a blood-filter in the machine, a vampire in the big city. Are viewers not, likewise, in a Lab imaginary of impositions, fears, and choices?

The third and decisive peep comes less than ten minutes before the end and lasts 24 seconds. Aurora puts the device on the body of the transformed grandfather to revive him again. The shots become clearer. The insect is more visible this time, glowing red and alive. Its close-up lasts two seconds and then we see the cogs, the clockwork mechanisms as wheels, spinning around. These shots are the preamble for the last minutes of the device. We are very close to the end.

It is interesting to keep in mind that those glimpses were made not with a microscope lens, but with an enormous intricate set of wheels. Cinema is an artifice that works as a Laboratory to observe bodily movements, like in the films by Jean Painlevé, known for his wonderful poetic animal documentaries. Painlevé's *The vampire* (1945) uses the vampire figure as a point of transfer, a body of mediation between the natural world beyond morality and the cultural world in which the Nosferatu is a threat to the veins of society. The body of Nosferatu is depersonalized, becoming detached and displaced from being a personal event to being a more general, intensive relay among political, social, and communicative bodies.[30] But del Toro's cinematic lab makes a reversed move, very different from Painlevé's cinematic lab and

Cronos (in Spanish, 1993). In Guillermo del Toro's *Cronos*, the aptly named Jesus (Federico Luppi) is about to be resurrected from his coffin and escape cremation. He goes on to destroy the device and sacrifice himself for the sake of his endangered family—and for righteousness' sake (Photofest).

a way to frame imaginaries of media and biotechnological design as an illuminating approach to understanding the human soul.

Thoughts on Guillermo del Toro's Craft

> *Cronos* is an exploded view of my brain. All my movies are
> one big movie.
> —Guillermo del Toro[31]

Think of *Cronos* as fragments.

Think of *Cronos* as aphorisms, which Guillermo del Toro loves. "Your heart is uncomplicated. It knows what it knows and acts accordingly. Greater wisdom is hard to find." He tweets aphorisms about monsters as well.

Think of films as seeds, and Cronos as the seed of all of del Toro's creative alchemical obsessions. Accented Fantasy and the Gothic Perverse. Twisted genres.[32]

Think of *Cronos* as an early example of intertextual film-making.[33]

Out of all the mentioned sources, references, influences, it is most important to stop at Víctor Erice's *The Spirit of the Beehive* and Juan Rulfo's fiction.

Cronos symbolizes low-budget non–Hollywood independent filmmaking art that wants to reflect on elderly monsters and worn-out economics.

Cronos is a good example of sincerity and consciousness in future key filmmaking.

The true horror of *Cronos* is not in its supernatural events but in the sense of lurking evil beneath the everyday.[34]

Even though *Cronos* does not refer clearly to Pre-Colombian vampires, you might think of the device as made of Aztec gold.

Cronos shows the monster at its most truly frightening: not simply part of real human history with specific dates and places, but also inescapable and at times even banal. Its monstrosity hits harder precisely because of its quiet restraint.[35]

Think about *Cronos* as a crossroads in which one road was never thought of.

Cronos is a difficult object to think with.

Cronos transforms a vampiric fantasy into a feasible thing like an animal's infection.

Cronos exposes in a minimalist scale a cyber-network as a weapons system.[36]

In Chronos we live most of our lives, and watch our bodies fall off. That is why the old and the young make an alliance that reflects the bricolage structure of the film, but also the bricolage nature of our social being.

The relationship between grandfather and granddaughter confers on the film a density of unusual human warmth.[37]

The worst enemy to Chronos is Kairos poetry, or the work of the favorable mixture.[38]

Kairos poetry in a media world is potentially an efficacious tool against expropriation of the moment.[39]

Artistic praxis in media worlds is a matter of extravagant expenditure. Its privileged locations are not palaces but open laboratories.[40]

Our wrist watches and alarm clock time are the same for all of us, but there is a considerable variation in our interior clocks.

We simply do not understand time.

The device can help us to think about time. Crushed time. Imaginative time. Real time. Never-enough-time. Auspicious time. It replaces travel time by time transcendence.[41]

Jesús Gris is a Biblical parable character with political, philosophical, theological, and scientific interrogations about insects and the end of life. An undisciplined vampire. A reworked Gregor Samsa. A trick to rethink the most important things.

Jesús Gris is a responsible agent before this extemporal antecedent of a digital media device.

"Who says that insects are not the favorite creatures of God? Christ walked on water, same as a mosquito," says Dieter De la Guardia.

Insects also are an alternative way to understand communication: the propensity to generate mutations, free from the hold of memory on the socially enforced forms of sedimented institutions and the market.[42]

Aurora, Gris' granddaughter, is a benevolent and liberating figure that helps the monster along his tortuous and brutal journey.

A childish vision serves to question and bear witness to the destructive violence of adults.[43]

Aurora's silence speaks about the perfect cinema, without dialogue. She is a silent and ghostly observer of human fallibility.[44]

The only immortal being is the child.

The spectacle of children experiencing trauma is revealed quietly in its perverse nature: The absence of consciousness, is not knowing how to distinguish life and death, good and evil.

Del Toro's secret purpose is not to flash his heretic "lapsed" Catholic fringe but is to make us aware of our status as children of God, and to turn our feet toward home.[45]

Del Toro's explicit purpose is to achieve a moment of absolute serenity and pure love.

Aurora learned about death thanks to her grandfather's vampire-insectoid metamorphosis. She is still submerged in the time of loss—her father's absence is painful but not explicit. Like the insect inside the device, is felt internally along the film.

Cronos plays with its ghostly theology, rational religion, and spiritual reason in order to make sense of complex impulses such as rage, impotence, the need to hunt, the need to kill, fear of the word, defenselessness, the need to know.

Cronos warns about mortal pathologies. It warns about being bestial, about living lies.

The Cronos device is an active space closer to that of a computer game topology than that of a visual representation.

The desire is a way to rethink our ways of perception and sensation, an invitation to think deeper, to feel viscerally.

Artists, readers, viewers, students, scholars: Be aware of the overwhelming state-corporate apparatus. Open this shapeshifting little box and be more careful with the terrifying proximity of the bodily decay. Vampires can teach us about it.

A careful and contemplative reception of del Toro's craft can invigorate teaching.

Cronos incites meditation: it appeases the machine of desire, and it encourages enjoyment of what we have at hand.

During the time of creativity, we are freed from normal restrictions.

Keep the clock wound: Thinking time is not wasted time.

Film is a fertile ground for thinking about every aspect and every genre of cinematic thinking.

Devices offer personal autonomy, renewal of fitness, and self-realization.

Devices entertain a sinister form of precarity, insecurity, and continual pressure to perform.

Lie of devices: The prospect of living the most intense lives of maximized investment and maximized return.

Truth of devices: they privatize, expropriate, and extract a surplus from everything in sight.

The price of the Cronos device: the debasement of craving for blood and the addiction to the device.[46]

Cronos refuses to satisfy our desire for authentic national culture. It serves as point of departure for reframing our critical questions.[47]

Monster creation is one of the hardest forms of creation. When they are good and powerful they need to draw from a multitude of sources such as myth, literature, nature reference and our own spirit.[48]

Be aware of the Cronos device. It is:

- A mysterious scarab-shaped artifact.[49]
- A beautiful gem in the shape of a Fabergé egg that encapsulates something more valuable.

- An intricate biotechnical invention that has rules written for its use.
- A complex, mystical device, a central puzzle to be resolve by the spectator that provides a key narrative driver.[50]
- The seed of Guillermo del Toro's legacy.
- A clock-artifact with an intricate golden shell adorned with symbols such as the *ouroboros,* the ancient symbol of the serpent eating its own tail and thus forming an unbroken circle of creation and recreation.
- (...) not anxiety at work, but ridicule, not existential uncertainty, but rebuttal of a crass and inadequate system of beliefs.[51]
- A vampiric/insectoid creature that hibernates inside a mechanic exoskeleton, waiting for human blood.[52]
- A blood filter supported by complicated clockwork mechanisms.
- A Spanish device from the Renaissance.[53]
- A platform from the past, a buried treasure.
- A useful pocket-map of anti-relational anti-ethical existence.
- A tragic-comic commanding magnetism.
- A uniquely Mexican baroque cyborg, which has its origins in narratives of colonization, embodies the transgression of boundaries between nature and technology as a microcosm of the cultural fusions and transfusions of the megalopolis, and in particular of the vampiresque operations of multinational capitalism which threaten the loss of temporal depth and cultural memory.[54]
- A case against hyper-individualism.
- A penetrative mechanism that reveals the human body itself as an entity with boundaries that can be breached, infiltrated.[55]
- A powerful synecdoche, a complicated technological *mise-en-scène.*[56]
- A repository of multiple and diverse references to filmic and cultural remnants that come to haunt the film like so many celluloid ghosts.[57]
- A Mexican passport for Guillermo del Toro.
- An all-embracing cipher, a cosmic vessel to be filled and refilled with endless readings and re-readings—a veritable multiplicity.[58]
- A rare cultural device of turbulence and flow.
- A cinematic lab that makes you feel and think in terms of a trigger.
- A seed—A contagion?—for loving cinema with fluently transcultural response, and unprecedently boundless appetite.

Above all, the film *Cronos* is a prompt to love cinema with fluently transcultural responses, and unprecedently boundless appetite.

NOTES

1. Eric White connects *Cronos* to the way literary imagination of E.T.A. Hoffmann, Honoré de Balzac, and Angela Carter employs metaphors for mechanistic and biological automatism as vehicles for reflecting upon the nature of imagination (363–378).

2. Janet Harbord, *Ex-Centric Cinema: Giorgio Agamben and Film*, Bloomsbury, 2016. Harbord's book provides an excellent introduction to Agamben's philosophical archeology and Media Archeology to think of cinema in deeper terms. Particularly her chapter 4, "Cinema as Laboratory: On Insects and the Anthropological Machine"(131–68), helps to expand and enrich the notion of cinema that I employ in this essay.

3. Laurence Davies, "Cronos, or the Pleasures of Impurity," *Gothic Science Fiction 1980–2010*, Liverpool University Press, 2011. Davies indicates that the U.S. appears symbolized by De la Guardia as diseased and sick, oozing liquid from every orifice according to the cutting comment of his nephew Ángel. The American body seems diseased, infectious and repulsive; and indeed the bodies of the three central characters point to the possibility of a collapse of boundaries in both national and bodily terms ("Guillermo del Toro's *Cronos*," 402).

4. Keith McDonald and Roger Clark, *Guillermo del Toro: Film as Alchemic Art*, Bloomsbury Academic, 2014, page 117.

5. Nick Groom, *The Vampire: A New History*, Yale University Press, 2018, page 91.

6. Bernhard Siegert, *Cultural Techniques: Grids, Filters, Doors, and other Articulations of the Real*, translated by Geoffrey Winthrop-Young, Fordham University Press, 2015, page 28. As Siegert points out, the telephonic meditations in *The Castle* are also commentaries on language and embodiment in the age of technological media. "Kafka moves the mythic origin of language (and of culture) from the anthropological domain to that of the nonhuman, where the distinctions between language and noise, animals and humans are abolished." This note and the idea of the Lab imaginary come from a collection of art and theory *across & beyond—A transmediale Reader on Post-digital Practices, Concepts, and Institutions*, edited by Ryan Bishop, Kristoffer Gansing, Jussi Parikka and Elvia Wilk. Eco-films are not only a thematic classification but a way of seeing beyond the confines of narrative and story, of feeling and thinking with the non-human world as well, by seeking deep existential questions, by exploring ambiguity and nuances, and by cultivating an spirit of inquiry.

7. Eco-films are not only a thematic classification but a way of seeing beyond the confines of narrative and story, of feeling and thinking with the non-human world as well, by seeking deep existential questions, by exploring ambiguity and nuances, and by cultivating an spirit of inquiry.

8. Phil Solomon, interview, www.cinemad.iblamdsociety.com/2006/12/phil-solomon.html.

9. McDonald and Clark, cited above, page 10.

10. Jussi Parikka, "Remain(s) Scattered," *Remain* (University of Minnesota Press/Mason Press, 2018), page 22.

11. McDonald and Clark, cited above, page 108.

12. Even though Scott MacDonald affirms that premise to justify a selection of women's experimental films for some specific classes he teaches, the ideas resonate in this essay as an effective way to generate serious, long-term thinking by students (and their teachers). See also "Conclusion: Women's Experimental Cinema. Some Pedagogical Challenges" in Robin Blaetz, ed., *Women's Experimental Cinema: Critical Frameworks* (Duke University Press, 2007).

13. Groom, cited above, pages xv, 55, and 200.

14. David Foster Wallace describes the U.S. culture in a "crude but concise way" as a culture both developmentally and historically adolescent: "Since adolescence is pretty much acknowledged to be the single most stressful and frightening period of human development—the stage when the adulthood we claim to crave begins to present itself as a real and narrowing system of responsibilities and limitations-it's not difficult to see why we as a culture are so susceptible to art and entertainment whose primary function is to escape," from "Laughing with Kakfa," *Harpers' Magazine*, July 1998, page 27.

15. I recommend the excellent and comprehensive book by McDonald and Clark, cited above, which notices and values the comedic power of del Toro's films: "It is important not to underestimate del Toro's use of parody as a source of meaning in *Cronos*, as the film regularly employs a comic sensibility as a key part of its narrative discourse. This emerges particularly in the reworking of earlier filmic vampire conventions," page 118.

16. The Kafka insect-figure is an emblem for the radical temporality and network nature of the body. Jussi Parikka, cited above, understands the insect—including the Kafka's fictional one—as an active space closer to that of a computer game topology than that of a visual representation (101), an intensive temporal space that distributes functions, vectors, and speeds, pages 101–103.

17. There is a possibility that I am totally wrong with this take on humor in *Cronos*. When the film was released in two different formats by Criterion Collection in 2003, the recommendation for a broad audience stated that "*Cronos* is a marvelous debut: cool, creepy and surprising, tempered with a clever gallows humor and anchored by a passion for life and love." Among the supplement's materials (interviews, making of, commentaries by producers) there is a new interview with Guillermo del Toro, who is both passionate and articulate, and he is frank about what he thinks didn't work in the film (and how he learned from it) and describes his feature debut as his only true "lapsed Catholic movie" https://streamondemand athome.com/guillermo-del-toros-cronos-criterion-vod-dvd-blu-ray/.

18. Lauren Berg sees Jesús Gris, *Cronos*'s protagonist, as an emblematic resistance to the devouring power of globalization, in "Globalization and the Modern Vampire," *Film Matters*, Fall 2011, page 10.

19. I found the explanation of the dialogical logic of neoliberalism by Byung-Chul Han very appropriate to understand the importance of the perspective of the Other. Han sustains that the neoliberal alienation is not that of from the world neither from work, but rather a destructive alienation from oneself. The *Cronos*'s protagonist is relearning the language of responsibility, "*to listen to the Other and respond*" when he learns about the nature of the device, chooses to defend his granddaughter, and rethinks his love for his wife instead of embracing the bloodsucking eternal life of vampires. See Han's *The Expulsion of the Other: Society, Perception and Communication Today*, translated by Wieland Hoban (Polity Press, 2018), page 51.

20. Robert Smithson, "Entropy and the New Monuments," in *Unpublished Writings of Robert Smithson: The Collected Writings*, edited by Jack Flam, 2nd edition (University of California Press, 1996), page 17.

21. Davies, cited abovde, page 88. Cultural entropy describes the process whereby the intended meanings and uses for a cultural object fracture into a chaos of alternative meanings, new practices, failed interactions and blatant disregard. If entropy broadly describes a tendency toward disorder, cultural entropy is the tendency toward disorder at the level of meaning, in Terence McDonnell, *Best Laid Plans: Cultural Entropy and the Unvraveling of AIDS Media Campaigns* (University of Chicago Press, 2016).

22. Giorgio Agamben, "What Is the Contemporary?" in *What Is an Apparatus? And Other Essays*, translated by David Kishik and Stefan Pedatella (Stanford University Press, 2009), page 50.

23. Siegfried Zielinski, *Deep Time of the Media: Toward an Archaeology of Hearing and Seeing by Technical Means*, translated by Gloria Custance, MIT Press, 2006, page 260.

24. Malte Hagener, "Cinephilia in the Age of Post-Cinematographic," *L'Atalante*, volume 18, 2014, page 9. Hagener indicates that for the cinephile the film projection is a "unique experience." If we follow this idea that *Cronos* is not a stable text or a reproducible artifact, but a unique event, "film is not anymore a commodity of the entertainment industry or a medium of social communication, but it becomes part of a biography like accidental meetings and other supposedly contingent things of life."

25. Becker, page 53. The phrase belongs to the painter Victor Neep when he was challenged to explain the alleged element of protest in Cezanne's *Still Life with Apples*. The anecdote was referred in Herbert Marcuse's book *The Aesthetic Dimension*.

26. Becker, page 56.

27. R. Murray Schafer, *The Tuning of the World*, Knopf, 1977, page 262.

28. Bruno Latour, "Give me a Laboratory and I Rise the World," *Science Observed: Perspectives on the Social Study of Science*, edited by Karin Knorr-Cetina and Michael Mulkay (Sage, 1983), page 141.

29. S.T. Joshi, "The Magical Spirituality of a Lapsed Catholic: Atheism and Anticlericalism," *The Supernatural Cinema of Guillermo del Toro*, edited by John W. Morehead, McFarland, 2015, pages 11–20. This particular point made me doubt about the atheistic point of view that Joshi confers on the film; despite its several Lovecraftian touches, del Toro's film has a magical spirituality.

30. Parikka, *Insect Media: An Archeology of Animals and Technology*, University of Minnesota Press, 2010, pages 90–94. This is relevant in the biopolitical regime. Biopolitics for Parikka refers both to the question of the distribution of bodies in the intensive, temporal, metamorphotic spaces of modernity and technical media and to the integration of knowledge from animal bodies as part of regimes of control (page 103).

31. Guillermo del Toro, interview on the *Cronos* Criterion DVD.

32. McDonald and Clark, cited above, pages 59, 107.

33. McDonald and Clark, page 10.

34. Alain Silver and James Ursini, *The Vampire Film: From Nosferatu to Interview with the Vampire*, 3rd edition (Limelight, 1997), page 221, quoted in Ann Davies, "Guillermo del Toro's *Cronos*: The Vampire as Embodied Heterotopia," *Quarterly Review of Film and Video*, volume 25, number 5 (2008), page 401.

35. Davies, "Slimy and Subtlety," page 55.

36. This thought comes from Alexander R. Galloway and Eugene Thacker, *The Exploit: A Theory of Networks*, University of Minnesota Press, 2007.

37. Jorge Ruffinelli, Cronos," *Amèrica Latina en 130 Peliculas* (Uqbar Editores, 2010), page 198. Translation provided by the author.

38. Eva Hoffman, *Time*, Picador, 2009, page 187. According to Hoffman, the Greeks acknowledged two distinctive concepts of time: "Chronos, the time of continuity and mutability, and Kairos, the temporality of the auspicious moment of opportunity or crisis—the kind of heightened and irretrievable instant that we need to grab by the horns, or the head."

39. Siegfried Zielinski, *Deep Time of the Media: Toward an Archeology of Hearing and Seeing by Technical Means*, translated by Gloria Custance, MIT Press, 2006, page 272.

40. Zielinski, page 276.

41. McDonald and Clark, cited above, page 109.

42. Parikka, *Insect Media*, cited above, page 147. Here I follow the interesting connections Parikka makes between insects, the human body and technology. She indicates that "the insect potential of transformation, variation, relation, and intensive environmental relations has also characterized technology since recent decades."

43. I follow here the insightful observations by Juan Carlos Vargas about the child vision in the del Toro's Hispanic trilogy, page 195. Vargas besides reinforces the idea of the child character as agent of responsible change and solidarity.

44. McDonald and Clark, cited above, page 114.

45. My speculation is beyond belief, and it goes against all recorded declarations of godlessness by del Toro. Even though del Toro himself has declared that he does not believe there is life beyond death, he also has said "I do believe that we get this clarity in the last minute of our life. The titles we achieved, the honors we managed, they all vanish. You are left alone with you and your deeds and the things you didn't do. And that moment of clarity gives you either peace or the most tremendous fear, because you finally have no cover, and you finally realize exactly who you are." https://www.brainyquote.com/quotes/guillermo_del_toro_872854.

46. Davies, "Slime and Subtlety," page 54.

47. Ann Marie Stock, "Authentically Mexican?" *Mi querido Tom Mix and Cronos: Reframe Critical Questions, Mexico's Cinema: A Century of Film and Filmmakers*, Scholarly Resources, 1999, pages 279–83. Stock makes this observation on *Cronos*'s capacity to reproduce polyphonic dialogues by acknowledging the porosity of borders, the migrancy of populations, and the hybridity of expressive culture.

48. Guillermo del Toro, "13 tweets on monsters," www.themarysue.com/guillermo-del-toro-monster-tweets/, accessed March 18, 2019.

49. Eric White, "Insects and Automata in Hoffmann, Balzac, Carter, and del Toro," *Journal of the Fantastic in the Arts*, Volume 19, Number 3 (2008), page 375.

50. McDonald and Clark, cited above, page 10.

51. Davies, cited above, page 96, resists a purely allegorical approach to the film, stating "to characterize this film, though, as any kind of allegory—political, cultural, sexual, or religious—goes against the grain. Its moods are mercurial, its modes elusive."

52. Gabriel Eljaiek-Rodríguez, "Bloodsucking Bugs: Horacio Qiuiroga and the Latin American Transformation of Vampires," *The Supernatural cinema of Guillermo del Toro*, McFarland, 2015, page 152.

53. Kevin J. Wetmore, Jr., "The Echoes and Intertexts of Lovecraft and Dunsany," *The Supernatural Cinema of Guillermo del Toro*, edited by John W. Morehead, McFarland, 2015, page 27. Wetmore transcribes the beginning voice-over of the film: "In 1536, fleeing from the Inquisition, the alchemist Uberto Fulcanelli disembarked in Veracruz, Mexico. Appointed official watchmaker to the Viceroy, Fulcanelli was determined to perfect an invention which would provide him with the key to eternal life. He was to name it the Cronos device. Four hundred years later, one night in 1937, part of the vault in a building collapsed. Among the victims was a man of a strange skin, the color of marble in moonlight. His chest mortally pierced, his last words, 'Sue tempore.' This was the alchemist."

54. Geoffrey Kantaris, "Cyborgs, Cities, and Celluloid: Memory Machines in Two Latin American Cyborg Films," *Latin American Cyberculture and Cyberliteature*, edited by Claire Taylor and Thea Pitman, Liverpool University Press, 2007, pages 51–52. Kantaris uses Donna Haraway's notion of Cyborg, "as an ambiguous technological artefact which disturbs boundaries-between cultures, between the organic and the artificial—and which collapses temporal and spatial distinctions." Kantaris relates the Latin American cyborg with specific anxieties which connect historically to the experience of colonization, and the erasure of the nation as a space of collective agency and memory, an erasure which seems to be inscribed in the very mechanisms which effect the transition from nation-state to global market.

55. Davies, "Guillermo del Toro's *Cronos*," cited above, page 402.

56. Kantaris, cited above, pages 51–52. Kantaris uses Donna Haraway's notion of the Cyborg "as an ambiguous technological artefact which disturbs boundaries—between cultures, between the organic and the artificial—and which collapses temporal and spatial distinctions" (51). Kantaris relates the Latin American cyborg with specific anxieties which connect historically to the experience of colonization, and the erasure of the nation as a space of collective agency and memory, an erasure which seems to be inscribed in the very mechanisms which effect the transition from nation-state to global market.

57. McDonald and Clark, cited above, page 121.

58. Groom, cited above, page 201. In Nick Groom's words: "Today's vampires retain an affinity with historical vampires—an affinity that can embrace our current relationship with the supernatural."

Only Lovers Left Alive

Expat Vampires and Post-Imperial Cosmopolitanism

Wendolyn Weber

Jim Jarmusch's *Only Lovers Left Alive* is a genre-bending and border-crossing film. More cerebral love story than horror movie, it is western cinema with a global perspective: Jarmusch portrays his vampires in diaspora, as sophisticated expatriates who have left the European Old World and taken up residence in North Africa and the United States. Achingly cool bohemian aesthetes played with considerable physical beauty by Tilda Swinton and Tom Hiddleston, these vampires surround themselves with cultural artifacts and bounce between continents on night flights with strategically timed European connections. Bibliophiles, music aficionados, appreciators of mechanical innovations and scientific inquiry, they seem to exemplify wide-ranging cultural interests. They model the potential for intersection found in modern global cosmopolitanism. Yet their world is also tinged with blight. The new locales they have chosen to haunt are economically depressed and formerly colonized spaces, evoking rich histories of political, economic, and cultural oppression and exploitation. It is a placement and a perspective by which the old narratives of western dominance are put into tension with post-imperial decline.

The vampires, centuries old and thus endowed with the long view on the vagaries of human fortune and endeavor, seem in many respects to transcend the activities of humankind, to offer a detached perspective on it, and yet they also remain intimately intertwined with human history. Observers and collectors, but also anonymous contributors to art and culture, Jarmusch's vampires seem to occupy a special, privileged position as intellectual and artistic purists in a corrupt, declining world. The film consists largely of their

195

Only Lovers Left Alive (2013). The two main characters are Eve (Tilda Swinton), living in Tangier, and Adam (Tom Hiddleston), living in Detroit. Both are extremely knowledgeable about music, literature, and botany. They signal their sophistication with their accessories: gloves and sunglasses (Photofest).

meditations on that state. But the very weight of their longevity implicates and imbricates them in that world as well, and they themselves are, of course, far from innocent.

The film centers on the relationship between Adam and Eve (Hiddleston and Swinton, respectively), longtime lovers and spouses who remain deeply connected even when living apart: Adam currently in Detroit, and Eve in Tangier. The couple also triangulates with two other vampires: Christopher Marlowe (of Elizabethan-era playwriting fame), Eve's close friend and supplier of premium blood in Tangier; and Ava, Eve's troublemaking younger sister. Eve, perceiving that Adam has become deeply depressed and requires her company, joins him in Detroit, but their reunion is quickly disrupted by the unwanted arrival of Ava. While Marlowe represents the couple's kindred spirit, Ava's irresponsible and destructive behavior serves as both a counterpoint and a tipping point to the comfortable and careful balance Adam and Eve maintain in their existence among humankind. The action of the film revolves around these relationships and the necessary response to the consequences of Ava's catalytic presence when she kills Adam's human associate Ian, driving Adam and Eve out of Detroit and back to Morocco.

Only Lovers Left Alive (2013) Eve (Tilda Swinton), who remembers the middle ages, is a (very) long-term friend with fellow vampire Christopher Marlowe (John Hurt), who faked his death in 1594 and went on to write the plays usually attributed to "that Philistine" Shakespeare. Here, he is about to die in Tangier from having imbibed tainted blood (Photofest).

While the placement spans continents, the narrative arc is tight, spanning days, and intimate. Jarmusch relentlessly refuses to provide backstory or exposition but drops references, leaving the viewers to put together the pieces and hypothesize about the rest. The very fact that his vampires are vampires is left unspoken. While the drinking of blood, the occasional flash of a lengthened fang, and the nocturnal habits of the characters are sufficient to establish the connection, Jarmusch also nods to other common vampire traditions, such as the need to be invited in before crossing a threshold. Eve admonishes Ava for having violated the protocol, entering Adam's house uninvited while they were absent; this is no myth like garlic, she insists, but a matter of bringing genuine bad luck. The tradition that a vampire can be killed by a wooden stake to the heart is referenced in Adam's desire to procure a bullet made out of wood—an easier and edgier way for a suicidal vampire to go than stabbing oneself in the chest. *Only Lovers Left Alive* also dispenses with such traditional vampire necessities as coffins and makes additions like the habitual wearing of gloves outside the lair. While the accessory serves as a fashionable mark of otherness when out and about, it also amplifies the threshold-crossing rule, creating a pretty etiquette of guest proffering gloved hands to host. Adam's removal of Eve's gloves on her arrival contrasts nicely with Eve's refusal to take Ava's gloves when she offers them. Ava simply ignores the rebuff and pulls them off, herself.

The exact ages of the vampires, how, when, and by whom they were turned, are also left unstated. Adam makes reference to a man (whose name he has decided to give to a newly-acquired vintage guitar) killed by a Royalist in the English Civil War; it seems to be a personal connection that would then place Adam's human life and subsequent transformation in the first half of the seventeenth century. Eve, on the other hand, seems much older: she speaks of all the great human horrors and calamities that Adam has missed, such as the great plague during the Middle Ages. Marlowe's lifetime can be pinpointed exactly, but when and how he became a vampire is not clear, other than that it only happened when he was at a more advanced human age (as played by the late John Hurt, in his seventies)—well after Marlowe's death in the historical record, in 1593, in a knife fight, at the age of twenty-nine. No hints are given about Ava (played by Mia Wasikowska), other than that the last time she created trouble for Adam and Eve was about a hundred years earlier, in Paris.

The stories of how these vampires became vampires are treated as inconsequential, nor is the plot driven by any concrete narrative revolving around conflicts between humans and vampires. It is a vampire movie that seems intent on not being a vampire movie—while remaining necessarily and fundamentally a movie about vampires. The opening credits proclaim as much, the red gothic-style text emulating the opening titles of the 1958 Hammer film production of *Dracula* (released as *The Horror of Dracula* in the United States), starring Christopher Lee in a sexier makeover of the Bela Lugosi model. Jarmusch draws his referential connection but is clearly not interested in exploring well-trodden paths so much as examining less-frequented implications. He draws our attention to a classic of the vampire film genre (that spawned a number of kitschy sequels), which is not, however, the first of its kind; it is itself a refashioning of the older cinematic original *Dracula*, which is an adaptation of a stage play based on the original novel. The reference is not to sameness but rather to variation. And in many respects, *Only Lovers Left Alive* offers an almost complete inversion of the Dracula formula.

The Dracula of Stoker's novel is a predator who builds harems of vampire "brides" from his prey, and the action is driven by the device that the ancient monster has decided to relocate from his remote Carpathian dwelling to the British metropolis of London. It is a scenario that speaks to the particular anxieties of Victorian England: xenophobia, sexual repression, and patriarchal social mores foremost. With his destruction of vibrant bride-to-be Lucy Westenra and subsequent vamping of married Mina Harker, Dracula attacks the sanctity of marriage itself, dealing a sensationalist blow to a fundamental cultural institution. While the act of vampirism is highly sexualized in Stoker's account, Dracula himself is markedly unattractive, even repulsive. In his first encounter with the count, Jonathan Harker notes his "very marked physiognomy"—one that, with its strongly aquiline nose and massive eyebrows, is markedly not-Anglo, down to his coarse hands, complete with tufts of hair on the palms.[1] His close proximity induces nausea. When Harker stumbles upon Dracula in his coffin, freshly fed, the impression is likewise one of horror: "It seemed as if the whole awful creature were simply gorged with blood. He lay like a filthy leach, exhausted with his repletion."[2] Even when Dracula appears in London as a much younger-seeming man, the effect is not that of handsomeness. As Mina describes him, he is "a tall, thin man, with a beaky nose and black mustache and pointed beard […] His face was not a good face; it was hard, and cruel, and sensual, and his big white teeth, that looked all the whiter because his lips were so red, were pointed like an animal's."[3] Such descriptions speak to the combined messages of Dracula's otherness and the abjection of unrestrained sexual desire.

While the specific horror of Dracula is that he steals the brides of other men, the greater horror is that he replicates his kind in the process. Technically, Lucy has not been destroyed by Dracula, only transformed into a member of the undead. Lucy's violent destruction comes at the hands of her former beloved and would-be saviors and in the cause of halting the spread of vampirism. This is the horror of Harker's realization at Dracula's castle, when he discovers the nature of his host and client: "This was the being I was helping to transfer to London, where, perhaps, for centuries to come he might, amongst its teeming millions, satiate his lust for blood, and create a new and ever-widening circle of semi-demons to batten on the helpless."[4] Dracula is a one-creature wave of unwanted and parasitic immigrants. He is a colonizer who will prey upon the indigenous population and replace it with more of his own. He is the menacing Other and the return of the repressed to imperialist Britain's own colonial project. In the end, he is thwarted. But as Jeffrey Jerome Cohen asserts in his "Monster Theory: Seven Theses," the monster never dies. It always returns.

With every resurrection, however, "the message proclaimed is transformed by the air that gives its speaker new life."[5] Contemplating the modern vampire figure ranging from Stoker's "foreign count's transgressive but compelling sexuality" and Murnau's *Nosferatu*, to Anne Rice's creation of a "pop culture phenomenon" (surpassed in the twenty-first century by Stephanie Meyer's vampire-romance *Twilight* sensation), and Francis Ford Coppola's 1992 blockbuster reboot of the *Dracula* franchise, Cohen notes the prevalence of variation. He argues, "even if vampiric figures are found almost worldwide, from ancient Egypt to modern Hollywood, each reappearance and its analysis is still bound in a double act of construction and reconstruction."[6] The multiple paths that modern vampire narratives have taken reflect that shifting of cultural contexts and variety of symbolic purposes that any given monster might serve. The turn toward romantic vampires as sympathetic protagonists possibly demonstrates an extreme extension of another of Cohen's theses, that "Fear of the Monster Is Really a Kind of Desire": "The same creatures who terrify and interdict can evoke potent escapist fantasies; the linking of monstrosity with the forbidden makes the monster all the more appealing as a temporary egress from constraint."[7] Dracula both thrills and repulses, and the fact that he repulses allows his audience to savor the thrill that much more, without any fear of having overstepped into actual transgression in the process. The vampire narrative that invites sympathy with the monster, on the other hand, offers a fantasy of direct transgression, possibly inviting a valorization of the subversive or a rethinking of the norms that define otherness in the first place. This is not, however, to say that such reversals of the monster's monstrousness may not simultaneously involve reinscriptions of cultural norms in other ways.

   Only Lovers Left Alive offers sympathetic vampires in the characters of Adam, Eve, and Marlowe. Acquiring their sustenance from hospital blood banks instead of human veins, enjoying the worldly experience that comes of extreme longevity and exuding cultural sophistication developed over the course of centuries, they present as eccentric but non-threatening and more cool than any mere mortal could ever hope to be. The drinking of blood from delicate stemmed glasses, flasks, and even an experimental blood-popsicle shifts the vampire feeding aesthetic away from carnal violence towards quirky chic. That the vampires enjoy a drug-like bliss from the blood conjures something more akin to the figure of the artistic opium addict than the ravenous predator: the overhead camera catches each of them dropping back in slow motion, eyelids lowered and blood-tinged lips parted, into their respective cushions after the moment of imbibing. The greater threat, rather, seems to come from the human front, and in the form of a terribly banal, general stupidity. The vampires themselves present as both superior and beleaguered: beset, in the case of Adam, by fatal ennui and disappointment in the human race; and threatened in their food supply by the fact that much of humanity is poisoned, their very blood corrupted with toxins and disease. It is this state of affairs, in fact, that is the prime motivator for seeking blood from sanitary medical sources instead of drinking it straight from human prey. In something of an ironic reversal of the same theme conveyed in Stoker's *Dracula*, where vampirism itself is distinctly akin to a sexually transmitted disease, the sensuality of vampirism is burdened with the threat of blood-borne disease. Humans have poisoned their environment and themselves. And now in addition to the traditional threats of sunlight and wooden stakes, consuming "bad blood" can be fatal for vampires as well.

This fatal corruption of human flesh is reflected in Adam's reference to humans as "zombies," another element of Jarmusch's reversal. Modern zombies are, in the vast majority of their renditions, a decidedly unsexy variant of the undead. They represent the horror both of animated, ambulatory, contagious decay and of the mindless mob. Whether fast zombies or slow zombies, the terror tends to come in their sheer numbers, and most zombie narratives concern the desperate efforts of a surviving humans to somehow hold the line. By embedding his vampire narrative into a referential zombie frame, Jarmusch further bends his genre categories, and the equation of humans with zombies transports the vampires into that privileged position of the heroic minority. Of course the humans are not actually zombies, which might also lead us to consider whether the vampires are actually vampires or in fact symbols working on another layer of signification. That is: if Jarmusch is allowing his vampire characters to employ zombies as a metaphor for lame, mindless, corrupted humanity, then is he inviting us to read his vampires as superhuman, or, at least, as a metaphor for something else outside the parameters of the vampire film?

Jarmusch's framing of Adam and Eve says a great deal. They are highly complementary characters, from their mythic name-pairing to their monochromatic color schemes: he all in black, and she with pale, heavy tresses and cream-colored attire. His home is filled with vintage musical instruments and recording equipment, while her walls are lined with stacks of books. He composes moody, atmospheric pieces while she speed-reads through world literature across times and languages, her fingers running down page after page as though she were absorbing the words not just with her eyes but also with her touch. He is the quintessential romantic artist, and she the ideal audience and connoisseur. From the opening scenes, their connection is made clear. The credits play against the backdrop of a night sky, rotating slowly at first but also gaining speed until the stars become blurs of light that resolve into the image of a record spinning on a turntable. The camera in turn matchcuts to rotating overhead shots of Adam and Eve, reclining in their respective abodes. The song is Wanda Jackson's "Funnel of Love." The singer's spinning head referenced in the song lyrics, the spinning of the record, the spinning sky, and the spinning images of the two lovers all converge in a single simultaneous rotation. Later, the spinning reel-to-reel tapes playing on Adam's stereo system are juxtaposed with a stationary overhead shot of Eve spinning in a dance. The opening scenes cut back and forth between Adam and Eve in Detroit and Tangier, living in parallel. A shot of Adam looking down from his window to people in the street below is paired with Eve looking down from her rooftop to the people and shopfronts in the alley below. Adam ventures out, driving the empty streets of abandoned neighborhoods in Detroit, to procure fresh blood from his supplier; Eve ventures out, weaving her way through the narrow passages of Tangier, to meet up with Marlowe and fetch her supply. The back and forth of parallel experience culminates in a video call between the two, direct contact that culminates in Eve's promise to come to Detroit. Later, a conversation about the cosmos turns to the concept of quantum entanglement and spooky action at a distance; whether or not the suggested analogy works perfectly in accord with the actual physics, the terms resonate both for the connection between Adam and Eve and their dawning awareness, through mutual dreams, of Ava on the horizon.

Location is also significant. The threat of Dracula is that in coming to London, he has invaded the center (of England, of the British empire) from his previous location on the periphery. In *Only Lovers Left Alive*, the situation is reversed. Adam, Eve, Ava, and Marlowe are all, by all indications, British expatriates. Yet Eve refuses even a connecting flight through London, a decision that may or may not have specific, unexplained motivations but that gestures toward a general rejection of Britain's political center and, by extension, its history of imperial projects. Ava has been living in Los Angeles, but Adam has selected Detroit, a formerly prosperous metropolis and a historic center of modern music production that fell on hard times with the decline of the motor industry. The Detroit of the late twentieth and early twenty-first century is famously blighted. The visuals focus on empty streets, abandoned automobile factories, and deserted neighborhoods. Packs of feral dogs roam concrete labyrinths in a post-industrial toxic wilderness. Needing to dispose of Ian's body, Adam and Eve take it to one such abandoned industrial site and drop it into an open pool of acid. From the rundown Victorian house Adam inhabits to the shell of the Michigan Theater he takes Eve to see, the vibe is that of deeply faded former splendor. The theater, once a marvel of design and an opulent venue for the arts, has been reduced to a parking garage. But he also drives her past the house where Jack White grew up, a reminder of Detroit's still-fertile grounds. Though he is fiercely protective of his privacy, his music is out on the underground scene—Ava declares that she has heard it in LA—and Adam finds his anonymous abode increasingly disturbed by doorbell-ringing "rockers" seeking the reclusive musician.

If Detroit represents the gritty alternative to America's more celebrated metropolises, Tangier is the global representative of eccentric (dis)locations. Situated on the northern coast of Morocco and overlooking the Straits of Gibraltar, Tangier has long been a key point of national and cultural intersections. Morocco's geographic placement has led to a long history of colonizations; in modern times, Morocco was subjected to combined Spanish and French control in 1912, but a coalition of European powers converted Tangier to an "International Zone" in 1923 in order to prevent the strategic port from falling into the hands of any one nation. That international status remained until 1956, when Morocco regained independence and reabsorbed the city, making Tangier in the post-war years an extremely appealing destination for European and American expatriates. As Greg A. Mullins describes it, "This 'international' status reinforced the sense that Tangier was a city apart from the world; on the edge of a continent, overlooking two oceans, caught between Africa and Europe, between Islam, Judaism, and Christianity, Tangier was a place where nations, languages, and cultures could mix promiscuously."[8] The nature of that international control also made Tangier a place with relaxed legal enforcement: "it was a kind of free port, with a population equally divided between Europeans and Moroccans and an economy based on smuggling and questionable financial transactions."[9] The drug and sex trades were prominent parts of that economy, and the freedom to experiment with substances and sexual orientations alike was a strong draw for some. Though the period of the Interzone, as William S. Burroughs dubbed it, is long past, the cultural imprint remains. One can see why such a social atmosphere would be a perfect fit for the proclivities of vampires. But the city also has a unique artistic legacy.

Tangier drew a number of artists and writers to its international scene, some passing through and others who stayed for extended periods. American writers Paul Bowles and William S. Burroughs produced some or all of their greatest work in Tangier. The work of these men and others, combined with Bowles' translations/collaborations with Moroccan writers Mohamed Choukri, Larbi Layachi, and Mohammed Mrabet, has led scholars such as Mullins to argue for a particular body and quality of literature characteristic of the Interzone. Burroughs drew other Beat writers, Jack Kerouac and Allen Ginsberg. Jean Genet and Tennessee Williams both spent time in the city; their visits, along with Paul Bowles' extended residence, are recounted in Choukri's memoires of his interactions with them, combined in the single volume *In Tangier*. The Café Mille et une Nuits (Thousand and One Nights) seen in *Only Lovers Left Alive* may be a reference not just to literary intertextuality but also to the restaurant of the same name run by artist and writer Brion Gysin, who moved to Tangier after visiting in 1950, stayed for decades, and served as a tour guide to the Rolling Stones when they visited in the 1960s. The city also seems like a highly appropriate place for Christopher Marlowe, a man who was surprisingly open about his atheistic religious views and homosexuality in a time period when both orientations were potentially deadly to admit.

"Kit" Marlowe offers an important key to the symbolic value of Jarmusch's vampires. In the film Marlowe dismisses Shakespeare as a philistine. The Marlowe of historical record was the dominant playwright in London before Shakespeare. Marlowe's "mighty line" and bombastic plots made him the undisputed master while Shakespeare was still a fledgling talent, but his sudden, premature death mooted the question of whether the two would ultimately have produced one of the great artistic rivalries of all time. Shakespeare stepped into the void left by Marlowe's death and became one of the greatest writers in the history of English literature. Though there is no indication that anyone at that time or for some two hundred years following ever questioned Shakespeare's authorship of the plays, the near-mythic stature of the Bard was perhaps bound, eventually, to invite subversions. A lack of surviving documentary evidence clearly proving Shakespeare's authorship opened the door to doubt, bolstered by suspicions whether this shrewd businessman from an unsophisticated background, lacking both higher education and worldly experiences, could truly have possessed such a brilliant command of the English language and understanding of the human condition. While the vast majority of professional Shakespeare scholars stand by Shakespeare, a robust tradition of alternate-author theories has arisen. Famous artists and thinkers who have expressed doubt in Shakespeare's authorship include Mark Twain, Ralph Waldo Emerson, Orson Welles, Sigmund Freud, and Jarmusch himself. Favored candidates have been Francis Bacon and Edward de Vere, Earl of Oxford, but Marlowe has emerged as a popular possibility as well.

The shocking randomness of Marlowe's death in a tavern brawl and the likelihood that he was a British spy provide ample motivation for conspiracy theorists. Multiple accounts of what happened, a suspicious coroner's report, and the general unreliability of those present at the death left a shaky record. Marlowe was also facing arrest on charges of heretical atheism, a religious stance deemed as a threat to the state. The Elizabethan era was one of complex and dangerous political intrigues. As proposed by Charles Nicholl in *The Reckoning*, a meticulously researched work on Marlowe's death, the characters and connections of those involved make it virtually impossible to believe the official account of a knife fight over who should pay the bill (the "recknynge"). It is far more likely to have been a matter of "another conspiratorial gathering in an age of conspiracy, another session among the informers and persuaders of the Elizabethan police-state" taking a violent turn.[10] But Marlowe's death within a milieu of conspiracy, witnessed and reported by professional conspirators and cloaked in all the trappings of a coverup, creates fertile ground for further conspiracy theories. Marlowe's body was quickly buried in an unmarked grave; might the circumstances not likewise support a faked death and escape to live out the rest of his life safe under an assumed identity?

And then there is Shakespeare. The two men were the same age, so Shakespeare was a late bloomer in comparison to Marlowe. Shakespeare lacked a university education (Marlowe, the son of a cobbler, had received a scholarship to study at Cambridge). His early work was clearly influenced by Marlowe, and collaboration was far from uncommon amongst playwrights in the period. In 2016, the New Oxford Shakespeare's latest edition granted Marlowe co-author status for the *Henry VI* cycle of three plays. Works of literary fiction, filling in the gaps in the historical record, have long hypothesized Marlowe as an early mentor to Shakespeare, from Anthony Burgess's *A Dead Man in Deptford* to the film *Shakespeare in Love*. For those who question Shakespeare's authorship, Marlowe makes an enticing alternative.

Historically-informed fictional accounts of Marlowe's death-faking and second life as a writer under the guise of Shakespeare include Rodney Bolt's *History Play* and Ros Barber's verse-novel, *The Marlowe Papers*. Scholarly non-fiction arguments embracing Marlowe as the true author of Shakespeare's works include Calvin Hoffman's 1960 book, *The Murder of the Man Who Was "Shakespeare"*; Hoffman inspired the work of Samuel L. Blumenfeld, whose *The Marlowe-Shakespeare Connection* came out in 2008. Blumenfeld in turn inspired the creation of the Marlowe-Shakespeare Connection website, "The Web's #1 Blog on Christopher Marlowe," active from 2008 to 2015 and committed to "offer[ing] up hearty servings of delicious intrigue" over Marlowe's potential authorship of Shakespeare's works. "Delicious intrigue" perfectly captures the appeal of the Marlowe hypothesis. The tragedy of great talent prematurely lost and a general distaste for seeing protagonists living dangerously and then actually dying as a result necessitates an intervention: a happy ending (he lived!) that celebrates Marlowe's subversiveness in the process. And he perpetrated the greatest literary hoax of all time!

Shakespeare meanwhile has come to represent the literary establishment. His great success in Elizabethan theater during a time when artistic subversiveness could be dangerous also means that he was adept at staying within bounds, pushing at boundaries and thrilling his audiences without overstepping. Shakespeare was not a man who appears to have suffered greatly for his art; rather, he profited from it very comfortably.

This socially and economically successful side of Shakespeare seems to be Jarmusch's primary target in his version of Christopher Marlowe. Shakespeare the playwright becomes Shakespeare the producer, a "hack" who happily profits from Marlowe's need for anonymity. Marlowe accepts the bargain for the sake of the art; it was the "only way to get it out there." Eve delights in the notion of revealing the great subterfuge and shaking up the literary world, but Marlowe still values his anonymity all these centuries later. The need for art to find an audience is repeated in Adam's explanation for why he gave a piece he wrote, the adagio movement of a string quintet, to the composer Schubert. He speaks also of the artist's need to put something out into the world, to create a reflection and "to see if it would echo back." The piece referenced is of course the most celebrated movement in one of Schubert's most celebrated works. Fame and commercial success, on the other hand, are anathema. Adam repeats this sentiment in his appreciation for the singer Yasmine, heard performing in a Tangier cafe; when Eve suggests that she is sure to become famous, he declares that he hopes not, as she is too good for mere celebrity. Los Angeles, the heart of the commercial art and entertainment industry, is "zombie central" in Adam's reckoning.

The implication is that great art cannot be created out of comfort, or from a position of centrality. It must come from outsiders and from the periphery. The appeal of Marlowe versus Shakespeare is that of the anti-establishment figure. Shakespeare is a "zombie," while Marlowe has become a vampire. The fact that Marlowe is a fragile vampire who ultimately succumbs to a batch of tainted blood exemplifies the sense that in this zombified world the great artists, and great art, are in peril. It also emphasizes the fantasy element of Jarmusch's vampires: an escapist celebration of coolness and cultural sophistication in the form of mythic exceptionalism. The sheer gorgeousness of the film, its actors, and the carefully curated spaces they inhabit makes a powerful argument for the appeal of cosmopolitan cultural literacy. We might read the final scene in these terms, when Adam and Eve, adrift in Tangier, out of blood and fading fast, decide to save themselves by attacking a young Moroccan couple. The message might read something along the lines of "watch out, crass commercial world; we artists and aesthetes won't go down quite so easily." Just as Eve earlier, presciently, replies, "I'm a survivor" to Adam's declaration that she has been ruthless and brutal in a game of chess.

There are, however, also problems with this fantasy. Jarmusch has flipped the script on Dracula, but the signifier does not detach quite so easily from the chain of signification. Dracula's otherness haunts Britain's colonial and imperial project. Jarmusch's expat vampires traverse a post-imperial landscape, but it is one still haunted by the marks of imperialism. Tangier carries colonial and exoticist baggage along with its cosmopolitanism, and the Interzone was far from free of inequality. Even as scholars explore the fluid spaces opened by the writers in Tangier, they acknowledge the colonial and postcolonial context: "Relations between Americans and Moroccans were significantly determined and circumscribed by larger political and cultural forces. These were marked by economic inequalities, orientalist fantasies, and racial attitudes."[11] Adam laments the lost beauties of Detroit's great automobile age but eschews reference to the history of racial segregation embedded in the city's growth or the working classes left behind when the wealth withdrew. Moreover, the very exceptionalism of the vampires themselves reflects the structures of privilege and narratives of superiority that have historically supported colonial projects.

Amanda Anderson has analyzed the complexities of cosmopolitanism in regard to the problems of inequality, differentiating between the positive potential of cosmopolitan world views and the more negative forms it may take. "In general," she suggests, "cosmopolitanism endorses reflective distance from one's cultural affiliations, a broad understanding of other cultures and customs, and a belief in universal humanity." However, "Cosmopolitanism also typically manifests a complex tension between elitism and egalitarianism. It frequently advances itself as a specifically intellectual ideal or depends on a mobility that is the luxury of social, economic, or cultural privilege."[12] This is a set of luxuries that the vampires in *Only Lovers Left Alive* do enjoy. One might argue that if they could not afford to travel and were constantly scrounging for cash, there would be no story. However, neither should one ignore the fact that this is not a concern. Jarmusch's refusal of exposition offers a neat escape from the question, Where did that money come from? But the possession of endless-seeming wads of bills certainly speaks to privilege and is a pointed element of Adam's relationships with his blood supplier and Ian. None of this would work without the money. Surely the economic factor is also a motivation for Ian's often sycophantic behavior. And Ian's bowing and scraping becomes that much more painful when paired with Adam's condescending remark that "for a zombie," Ian is "not bad." Perhaps we are supposed to see this positioning of Adam and Ian as an ironic commentary on western traditions of racism and inequality, but the problem with such moments of ironic mimicry is that they depend on careful framing. And another shift of the frame may well reveal that the ironist is simply reinscribing that which is purportedly being ironized.

Anderson notes that even the "awkward elitism" in certain forms of cosmopolitanism "can manifest different degrees of self-consciousness"[13;] in *Only Lovers Left Alive*, that self-consciousness may come in the character of Ava. Wasikowska plays her to perfect, claustrophobia-inducing effect. Irresponsible and hedonistic, Ava demonstrates none of the self-control of Adam and Eve. She knocks back her glass of blood, blisses out for a moment, and then declares that she wants more. She steals from Adam's supply, and then she kills Ian. (The awkward elitism of Adam's attitude toward Ian is again evinced in his remark, on discovering the body, not that she killed him, but that she drank him.) Ava is sheer appetite. Though she risks her health in the process, she also remains a predator. Ava's shallowness contrasts sharply with Adam and Eve's depth, and her recklessness may initially serve to amplify their cultivation. But she is also the monster that returns as the unwelcome houseguest, as the shadow of the horror-movie vampire. Ava is the fore-shadow of what Adam and Eve will ultimately return to in order to survive, and she is the reminder that any new construction of the monster (as less monstrous, as transgressively appealing) remains entangled in its referential reconstitution of the old.

This final scene also carries a degree of self-consciousness. When Adam and Eve decide to live instead of die and turn to feed on the young Moroccan lovers who have fortuitously appeared before them, another contrast is clear. The vampires are white, western, and exhausted. They have certainly enjoyed a good, long run on this earth. The Moroccan couple is young and vital and innocent. Eve suggests to Adam that they needn't kill the couple; they could turn them, instead. Adam replies that she is being a romantic. Indeed, whether they take the couple's lives or take away their humanity, it is still an act of plundering. It is an imperialist gesture. Significantly, the final shot is from the Moroccans' point of view: the white couple approaching, the lady offering a polite "excuse me," before the bearing of fangs and the cut to black.

NOTES

1. Bram Stoker, *Dracula*, in *Dracula and Frankenstein*, Doubleday, 1973, page 20.
2. Stoker, page 58.
3. Stoker, page 191.
4. Stoker, page 58.
5. Jeffrey Jerome Cohen "Monster Theory: Seven Theses," *Monster Theory*, edited by Jeffrey Jerome Cohen, Minnesota University Press, 1996, page 5.
6. Cohen, pages 5–6.
7. Cohen, page 17.
8. Greg A. Mullins, *Colonial Affairs: Bowles, Burroughs, and Chester Write Tangier*, University of Wisconsin Press, 2002, page 4.
9. Mullins, page 4.
10. Charles Nicholl, *The Reckoning: The Murder of Christopher Marlowe*, University of Chicago Press, 1992, page 326.
11. Allen Hibbard, "Tangier at the Crossroads: Cross-Cultural Encounters and Literary Production," *Writing Tangier*, edited by Ralph M. Coury and Robert Kevin Lacey, volume 169 of *Currents in Comparative Romance Languages and Literatures*, Peter Lang, 2009, page 6.
12. Amanda Anderson, *The Way We Argue Now: A Study in the Cultures of Theory*, Princeton University Press, 2006, pages 72–73.
13. Anderson, page 73.

"Don't ... don't believe the hype!"

Vampiric Evolution and What We Do in the Shadows

Charles Hoge

The vampire can never die. But even when it does, it is a temporary condition, as it only stays dead long enough to mutate. When the vampire returns to life, it has invariably adapted itself to fit the culture that it seeks to invade and prey upon; it has evolved and reinvented itself, in other words, into a more relevant monster with its specific victim-culture in mind. Jeffrey Jerome Cohen, in his seminal "Monster Culture (Seven Theses)," outlines how the vampire has achieved this trans-cultural elasticity: "the undead [always] returns in slightly different clothing, each time to be read against contemporary social movements or a specific, determining event."[1] Cohen argues that the vampire, like all monsters, is a cultural body, and so must shift that body, its appearance, behavior and implications, to match developments within the specific cultures it haunts. Not only is the vampire categorically different in terms of morphology and behavior from iteration to iteration, but even its figurative value is unstable. It never "means" the same thing cross-textually, in other words. Jeffrey Weinstock reminds us that "[i]t's just too simple to say that the vampire is the metaphorical embodiment of devouring female sexuality or alternative configurations of sexual desire or of capitalist exploitation or of viral contagion or of xenophobia" because "any given vampire may clearly lend itself to one particular interpretive possibility, but—as with any text—is never exhausted by a single interpretation."[2] Vampires' ability to feed the specific fears of any culture in which they make an appearance allows them an open multivalence that helps them perform the

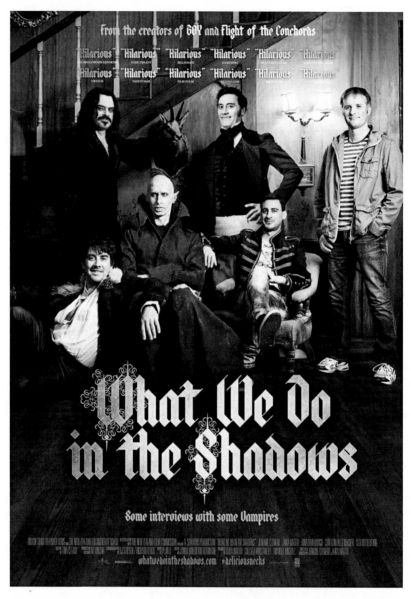

What We Do in the Shadows (2014). The poster collects the ensemble cast of various vampire types: standing, left to right, are Vladislav (862-year-old tyrant), Viago (379-year-old dandy), Stu (loveable techno-geek mortal); and, sitting, Deacon (183-year-old bad boy), Petyr (8,000-year-old, probable ancestor of Count Orlok in *Nosferatu*), and Nick (newly-turned vampire-dude). Like many flatmates, they don't always get along, particularly when it comes to household chores such as washing blood off the dishes (Photofest).

roles of "roving thought-experiments lingering on the periphery of comprehension, and even now [they] can help us think through current anxieties
from border control to epidemic contagion."³ The vampire, ever-changing,
is perpetually relevant. And this monstrous malleability is visible in any environment that vampires can be found, be it folkloric, literary, or cinematic,
and the longevity of the vampire figure is at least in part attributable to this
adaptability.

As a result of this constantly shifting nature, it is impossible to define
an "authentic vampire" from which all others radiate. At what point in space
and time, then, can we mark the "beginning" of such a process in human culture? An inextricable web of relationships involving folklore, literature and
cinema must be examined in order to venture toward an answer to this question, but this essay will explore how the film *What We Do in the Shadows*
(2014), the interactions among its characters, and its unique setting may offer
the most entertainingly succinct avenue toward engaging the quest for vampiric authenticity.

A Monstrous History

Since the vampire is a site at which a culture's fears metastasize in the
embodiment of a supernatural entity, it has an exceedingly murky history,
beginning within a variety of occasionally overlapping folk traditions which
stretch back to unrecorded and unwritten roots. Though often fragmentary,
ancient evidence of vampires can be found as, for example, the parasitic
undead creatures resembling vampires that haunt classical Greek texts. Likewise, surviving narratives detail attacks by predatory human corpses,
recorded by the twelfth-century clerics and chroniclers William of Newburgh
and Walter Map.⁴ More corporeal evidence of the widespread belief in vampires may be inferred from the widespread practice of driving a stake through
the heart of the suspected vampire, either to extinguish its evil undead life
or, more frequently, just to nail it to the ground so it can't leave its grave;
these "vampire graves" have been found across Europe. Evidence of this practice, for example, has been exhumed in Polish and Bulgarian cemeteries that
date back to the tenth century, in Anglo-Saxon burial sites from the sixth
century, and even in an Iron Age bog body found in Ireland, likely to have
been buried around 300 BCE. (It should be noted that there is no current
archeological consensus that these sites are unquestionably vampire-related,
but that the possibility has not been discarded.) The vampire that emerges
from most of these traditions is a horribly bloated human corpse, semi-
corporeal and swollen with the blood of its victims. These vampires did not
possess the pointed canine teeth that would so dramatically characterize later

iterations, so evidence of their predations upon the living left no telltale tooth marks; victims of folkloric vampires, rather, were thought to be those who had succumbed to sudden or otherwise inexplicable wasting diseases—and likely to return from beyond the grave as vampires themselves.

These beliefs and practices, lying in the distant cultural periphery of Enlightenment Europe, provided a sort of palimpsest onto which newly "discovered" eastern European folk vampire-narratives could be infused with new cultural meaning and a new cultural shape. Nick Groom argues that the recognizable form of the vampire coagulated here, in the eighteenth century, as these folk narratives were exhumed and analyzed by emerging Enlightenment scholars: "[v]ampires came into being when Enlightenment rationality encountered East European folklore [and, I would include, residual Western European folk beliefs]—an encounter that attempted to make sense of them through empirical reasoning and that, by treating them as credible, gave them reality."[5] Later, this resuscitated vampire folklore was absorbed and revised to allow for the adoption of the vampire as a literary monster, by writers such as John Polidori (*The Vampyre*, 1819), Thomas Preskett Prest or James Malcolm Rymer (*Varney the Vampyre; or, The Feast of Blood*, 1844–5), Sheridan LeFanu (*Carmilla*, 1872), Florence Marryat (*Blood of the Vampire*, 1897), Bram Stoker (*Dracula*, 1897)—all of whom constructed their own versions of the monster, shaping a literary tradition that has filtered through the twentieth century work of Richard Matheson, Anne Rice, Stephen King, among many others, and which continues to this day. The generic vampire, assembled from this literature, is a singular, eccentric, undead human being, largely indistinguishable from non-undead humans. Finally, the cinema seemed a darkly appropriate environment for the vampire, as "the moving frames of celluloid are already a parable of dark and light, and it is hardly surprising that they have, then, lent themselves especially well to the chiaroscuro of the vampire theme."[6] Indeed, from F.W. Murnau's *Nosferatu* (1922) and Tod Browning's *Dracula* (1931) and continuing, of course, to the present day with films like Jemaine Clement and Taika Waititi's *What We Do in the Shadows* (2014), filmmakers have hungrily adopted the vampire's inclination toward evolution and developed it enthusiastically in myriad intriguing and culturally-specific directions.

While each of these iterations of the vampire spoke to the particular culture, or the constructed storyworld, into which it was placed, none can ultimately claim to reflect (pun intended) the figure of the "authentic vampire." This vast, sprawling, multi-streaming evolution clearly cannot coagulate into a single "type-species" for the vampire. Some scholars attempt to posit Stoker's Dracula on this throne, but his version of a vampire was strongly informed by a collection of sources both folkloric and literary. Furthermore, "interpretation of Stoker's novel has become a sort of cottage industry pre-

What We Do in the Shadows (2014). Viago (Taika Watiti) is a foppish vampire from the seventeenth century who enjoys housekeeping and "robs the cradle" of a merely ninety-six-year-old vampire companion (Photofest).

cisely because the text supports so many approaches and interpretations"[7] marking the novel as more of a playing field for filmmakers and writers, rather than a template that fixes an absolute vampiric shape on their interpretations. So what emerges, then, from a search for vampiric authenticity is an awareness that the vampire is defined perhaps by nothing so much as its profound ability to mutate itself into the kind of monster that its cultures need. Rarely are connoisseurs of vampire narratives treated to the vision of a vampire that has lost its relevance to the culture that it haunts, but, if the vampire is conditionally immortal, its obsolete members, unable to adapt as individuals to changing conditions, must have someplace to go.

Perhaps that place is Wellington, New Zealand.

And so it is with this deep but constantly moving history in mind that a productive encounter with *What We Do in the Shadows* may be engaged. This film operates as a pseudo-documentary, or "mockumentary," and throws together a collection of four very different vampires, taken from various cinematic contexts, as moderately dysfunctional flat-mates living in an old mansion in Wellington, New Zealand. Each vampire has been borrowed from a specific era along the evolutionary spectrum of the vampire and is shaped from a collection of contexts. This diverse collection of supernatural predators demonstrates in itself the inability to define one "authentic vampire" figure. Viago, the ostensible narrator of the film, is a well-mannered, aristocratic, 379-year-old vampire who attempts to keep order in the flat as he acts and dresses the role of the eighteenth-century dandy (though he does seem to predate that placement by more than a century). Vladislav, at 862 years of age, is an overly-sexual warlord tyrant vampire with a literally medieval worldview, a penchant for torture, and an amusingly inflated self-image. Deacon, the youngest of the vampires, at 183 years of age, is a former peasant with a history of making "bad boy" decisions after becoming one of the undead. Petyr is quite simply a horrifying monster, a nonverbal 8000-year-old vampire with demonic eyes and a mouthful of jagged, razor-sharp teeth. In addition, Nick, a hip, twenty-something dude who gets converted to vampirism during the course of the film, is not an original flat-mate, but is nonetheless a very significant presence in the film. This eclectic assortment of vampires is united in agreement, by the way, that they will not eat the camera crew.

It is clear that these vampires do prey on the blood of living humans, as they speak constantly, and we as viewers are allowed to witness several feeding sessions. But, again, the comedic prevails, when we see their vampiric predation in action: Viago bites a young woman he has brought to the house as a date (after setting down an arrangement of towels, obviously to minimize the bloody mess to come), but, after playing music for her to make her last moments alive pleasurable (demonstrating in ridiculous manner a sort of vampiric conscience), he hits an artery on her neck with his teeth and ends up scurrying about trying simultaneously to stop the spraying blood, to feed from the geysering wound, and to keep the floors as clean as possible. Each of these vampires carries with him the unique culture from which he originated (even though none of these origins is specifically mapped in a geographic or historical sense), and their archaic trappings in worldview, language, dress and behavior mark them as obsolete presences in the twenty-first century world of Wellington. But no matter how divergent they appear, they are all certainly vampires and, as such, they are united by certain rules that define the vampire.

The Rules

Vampires, like all monsters, maintain their presence as a coherent trope in part because they operate within a set of rules, even though these can vary from place to place, film to film. These rules serve multiple purposes: they let one know that one is in the presence of a vampire, specifically doing this by identifying parameters in terms of morphology and behavior and defining the powers and the limitations of the vampire. These rules serve to coagulate reader and viewer expectations. But perhaps most importantly, vampiric rules set forth the *apotropaics*, the protective rituals and defensive objects, or in the words of Paul Barber the "methods of turning away evil"[8] whereby the vampire can be protected against and ultimately defeated. The rules in this sense permit one to understand that a vampire can be defeated. And while these rules create an atmosphere of expectation around the vampire, this is inherently problematized by the tendency of any monster to actively resist any efforts to defeat it, or sometimes more importantly, simply to categorize it. A monster is a monster in part because it refuses to "play by the rules" that attempt to define it, and so every monster, including the vampire, constantly threatens to attack and undermine any of humanity's endeavors to understand and classify it. (With this in mind, it is possible to read the humor of a "vampire comedy," a subspecies to which *What We Do in the Shadows* definitely belongs, as based on a violation of the "rule" that a narrative about the murder and predation of innocent human beings by supernatural monsters should not be wildly funny.) Inevitably, the vampire fits well within the Kristevan sense of the Abject, as their perpetual violations of coherent classification make them truly "what disturbs identity, system, order. What does not respect boundaries, positions, rules. The in-between, the ambiguous, the composite."[9] This fundamental tendency toward violent categoric instability also reminds one that there can be no such thing as a universally authentic vampire. Yet, variable and tenuous as these rules may be, and as much as they refuse to provide an easy definition of the vampire as a singular figure, such rules must exist as part of the internal logic of any vampire narrative.

Many of the more prominent "vampire rules" have gravitated into film and literature from deeply-entrenched European folklore, while others have matriculated into the cinema by way of Bram Stoker's novel *Dracula* and its myriad cinematic adaptations, and still others have wormed their way into circulation from influential individual vampire films. Some of these rules have become almost universally recognized: these include the vampire's supernatural nature as formerly dead, its conditional immortality, its need to feed on human blood or at least human energy, its ability to convert victims into vampires themselves, its propensity to sleep in a coffin, and its vulnerability to having a stake driven through its heart. Most of these ideas have been drawn from folkloric sources that predate the vampires of literature and popular culture. A creature that lacks these features is arguably not a vampire. Less universal but frequently present attributes include the vampire's sense of sexuality, its inability to enter a room without first being invited by the living, its failure to cast a reflection in a mirror or other reflective surface, and its pronounced aversions to sunlight, religious icons, silver, running water, garlic, and eating "human food."[10] Most of these secondary features do not have deep folkloric roots (though they are widely believed to have such), but rather are contributions from literary and popular culture sources.

According to the conglomerated storyworld of *What We Do in the Shadows*, a majority of these aforementioned rules seem to be at work, connecting these vampires to both their folkloric and literary/popular culture forebears. These vampires are formerly human (a bit of each flat-mate's backstory is shared with us), are almost immortal (each flat-mate is introduced on screen with a notation of his age, and all of them have lived much longer than even the longest human lifespan; however, Petyr does die in front of us), require human blood to live (much of the film's storyline centers on the acquisition of human blood for sustenance), sleep in coffins (at least Viago does, and Petyr and Deacon apparently sleep in closets), and are vulnerable to stakes through the heart (we see an unused stake in the hand of the dead vampire hunter and actually witness Stu staking "the new guy" vampire at the Unholy Masquerade). However, while each of these rules clearly defines a non-human entity and a figure of frightening horror, the expression of these rules here is almost always treated comedically. That the film is populated with genuine vampires is never in doubt, as all the universal rules are deployed. In fact, the film opens by confirming one of these universals while simultaneously demonstrating the film's comedic spirit: it shows us a scene depicting Viago, levitating, fully and fancily dressed, out of the coffin in which he sleeps. This scene echoes an iconic moment from *Nosferatu* (1922), in which the vampiric Count Orlok rises with corpselike stiffness out of his sleeping coffin. Whereas that scene is played as a horrific moment, with the dead demonic eyes of Orlok glaring out at the viewer, Viago is played much more for comedy, as he initially reaches from his coffin to fumble with the snooze button on his alarm clock before he rises, and when he finally does levitate from the coffin he does so with more of a sleepy stiffness than a horrific stiffness, and with an embarrassed grin on his face.

Many of the non-universal and later-developing rules are also presented here. These vampires cannot enter a room without being invited, which plays out in the film when doormen are considered "cool" if they give the vampires permission to enter a club. These vampires also cannot see their own reflections in mirrors, so, in order to prepare for a night out on the town, they draw crude but well-intentioned pictures of one another so that they can check their looks that way. These vampires, unlike some of their cinematic counterparts, can be photographed, as, most obviously, they are visible on screen in the film we are watching. Moreover, the film presents multiple montage sequences in which we are shown pictures of the flat-mates throughout the years, and we even see their human friend Stu teaching them how to take selfies.[11] All the vampires in this film are able to turn themselves into bats. Additionally, at least one, Vladislav, is capable of shapeshifting into a variety of animals, but we learn that his skills have diminished over the years and that, as Viago tells us, "now he never gets the faces right." This is confirmed later, when we encounter a semi-transformed Vladislav pursuing Nick in the form of a cat with an embarrassed-looking human head on its otherwise feline shoulders.[12] (Interestingly, this apparent failure of Vladislav's abilities might actually allow him to produce a more disturbing transformation, as the cat-with-a-man's face evokes, if slightly, the Sphinx, as well as the sort of hybrid, interstitial "admixed being" whose unclassifiable liminal nature profoundly disturbs the human observer.)[13] With regard to apotropaics, running water and garlic are not shown as vampire-deterrents in this film. Silver is at best a painful annoyance; Viago demonstrates this when he briefly puts on the silver locket that he had been given long ago by his lost love Katherine. His skin sizzles and smokes and he is obvious pain, only able to endure the contact for a few moments. However, we clearly see the destructive power of sunlight, through the nocturnal lifestyles of the flat-mates, the elaborate adjustments to the house they have undertaken in order to keep the sun's rays out, and, most dramatically, the gruesome burning death of Petyr when he is attacked in his sleep by a hapless vampire hunter. The vampires' aversion to crucifixes is a factor in this scene as well, as the cross being brandished in the dead vampire hunter's grasp nearly causes Deacon to vomit and must be covered up before they can continue to assess the scene.

One of the most apparent vampiric features highlighted in the cinema does not seem to be an active factor here, though. Specifically, in *The Vampire Film: Undead Cinema,* Jeffrey Weinstock claims that "the cinematic vampire is always about sex."[14] (One should keep in mind that it is the post–Enlightenment literary and popular culture vampire that is being discussed here, and not the decidedly unsexy and unsexual vampire of folklore.) Our initial moments in the film with Deacon and Vladislav would seem to indicate that this is the case, as the former uses his first words in the film to announce that last night he had shapeshifted into the form of a dog and "had sex," whereas Vladislav is introduced by having the door to his room open to reveal a wild, slow-motion supernatural orgy. However, the next vampire we meet, Petyr, is completely asexual, and we learn later that Viago is motivated more by love than sex, as he is haunted by the memory of his mortal lover Katherine, whose heart he lost to a mortal rival decades ago. And while Vladislav talks about sex a lot, the only actual sexual, or near-sexual, experience we encounter in the film actually occurs at the hand of lovelorn Viago (pun intended), apparently masturbating to thoughts of Katherine; after displaying an old photograph of the young Katherine taped to the inside of his coffin lid, he closes the door, whereupon the coffin begins to rock slightly. Later, when Vladislav admits that he and the other vampires prefer the blood of virgins simply "because it sounds cool," we are given more insight into how there is not really a sexual component to their predation and that these vampires' sense of sexuality is more of a performance than a legitimate, obsessive appetite. Ultimately, it seems that these vampires, unlike the majority of their cinematic brethren (as Weinstock illustrates in a fascinating chapter titled "Vampire Sex") these vampires do not seem to be all about sex.

Another non-universal vampire rule involves their antipathy toward werewolves. The flat-mates clash with a pack of untransformed lycanthropes as they walk home from their night on the town, which escalates no further than name-calling but illustrates the hatred the groups feel toward one another; later in the film, after the chaos at the Unholy Masquerade, they encounter the werewolves again, this time on the night of a full moon, and a full battle ensues as the enraged werewolves transform into their gigantic wolf-forms. (It ought to be noted that these lycanthropes apparently live by a very strictly-enforced social code, and that they are in fact "werewolves, not swearwolves.") While popular culture has explored the werewolf theme prior to *What We Do in the Shadows*, perhaps most dramatically in the *Underworld* film series, it should be noted that significant folkloric precedents exist to support this violent rivalry. Granted, the enmity was less between two supernatural creatures than it was between the folkloric vampire and the natural (not were) wolf, but since werewolves in many European traditions are virtually indistinguishable from natural wolves except in terms of ferocity, perhaps the distinction between the two is not so great after all. In any form, though, the animosity between the vampire and the wolf/werewolf has deep roots. For example, Serbian folklore explains how the wolf is the only creature on earth with the strength to tear apart and eat a vampire.[15] Elwood B. Trigg notes that "[s]ome Rumanian gypsy villages believe that many cemeteries are occupied by white wolves. It is only because of the vigilance and viciousness of these wolves in discovering and destroying the vampires in these cemeteries that living men are kept safe from a complete takeover of the world of the living by the world of the dead."[16] But the relationship is more complicated: Greek folk beliefs cast the wolf as the mortal enemy of the vampire and describe specific rituals that can direct a wolf toward a vampire in order to destroy it, but this culture also believed that a werewolf could transform posthumously and return from beyond the grave in the form of a vampire.[17] Barber suspects that this antagonistic relationship may have arisen from a need to interpret the presence of wolves in graveyards. Recent burials would be an ideal food source for a predator such as the wolf, but "i[f] an observer approached a feeding wolf [in or around a graveyard], he might see the wolf leave and note what was left behind was a typical vampire [as the partially decomposed human corpse was the shape taken by the folkloric vampire], quite inactive, and he might then conclude that either the wolf had killed the vampire or that the vampire had left its old body *behind* and had become the wolf."[18]

To overlay this tradition onto *What We Do in the Shadows* can help to explain why the vampire flat-mates feel such violent antipathy toward the werewolf pack. The werewolves here, though, do not seem to initiate the nastiness between the two groups, and are not in any sense protecting the integrity of a cemetery (the first meeting takes place in the outskirts of the city and the second in a wooded park). Moreover, we do not see any werewolves turning into vampires after their deaths, but, in perhaps a comic twisting of this belief, we do see the human *friend* of the vampires, Stu, converted to a werewolf after he is killed in the battle between the vampires and werewolves. (Most of the "documentary's" camera crew is also mauled and eaten by the werewolves in this scene, but their posthumous fate is unrecorded.) Nonetheless, the vampires in the film do perform the expected rivalry with their lycanthropic neighbors.

Recently converted vampire Nick confronts the camera to discuss his frustrations with the rules of vampirism. For one, shortly after trying to eat a chip at a chip-shop, we subsequently see him see him projectile-vomiting dozens of gallons of blood into an alley as a result; in this way he becomes spectacularly aware of how he can no longer eat "human food." Interestingly, it is this development, a violent dietary restriction that cuts him off from his self-declared "favorite food," that upsets Nick the most about his new vampiric condition. Even though his transformation into a vampire feels "like a hangover times ten" and causes his eyes to bleed copiously in its early stages, it is the sudden inability to eat chips that causes him to declare he is "over" being a vampire; "don't ... don't believe the hype" about the glamorous life of a vampire, he angrily tells the camera crew as he storms away. Even though Nick is the newest vampire and has the least vampiric experience of any of the flat-mates by far, his irritation here with the limitations of his new condition takes on more meaning if he is read as the evolutionary future of the vampiric species.

The Trajectory of the Vampire

The vampire flat-mates are comparatively readable as living, or non-living, representatives of discernible points along the spectrum of vampiric evolution; in other words, they are each embodied remnants of past versions of the vampire. In terms of tracing these evolutionary roots, Petyr is perhaps the most immediately recognizable of these vampires, and certainly the one most clearly drawn from a single source. He is discernibly modeled on Max Schreck's Count Orlok from the 1922 film *Nosferatu*. A montage sequence even depicts a photograph of Petyr on a ship, looking out from a below-decks hatch in much the way that Murnau's Nosferatu, stowed away on the Demeter and preying on its doomed crew, would have done. Furthermore, his pallid blue skin, jagged shark-like dentition, and long razor-sharp talon-fingers, in addition to the fact that he does not say a word in the entire film (or at least any that we can hear), mark him not only as a reflection of Murnau's vampire, but also mark him as being very different from the rest of his flat-mates. (Petyr is the only vampire among the flat-mates that clearly cannot travel out into public without being detected, for example, as he looks too much like an inhuman monster. As clumsy and socially awkward as the rest of the vampires are, they can "pass" as human at least within the nocturnal culture of the city.) Akin to how Petyr stands apart from his flat-mates, the film *Nosferatu* is itself very different from other vampire films. In part this was the result of Murnau's inability to acquire legal permission from Stoker's estate to adapt *Dracula*; a legal need to distance the production from the novel created a series of forced departures from Stoker's narrative (seen most evidently in different character names and changes in plot structure) so that Murnau's film could not be accused of being an unauthorized adaptation. Thus, the ghoulish, corpselike vampire Count Orlok, necessarily not–Dracula, does not transcend the film that introduces him. Tod Browning's *Dracula* (1931) was created with more permission from Stoker's estate than was *Nosferatu*, and so could adhere more closely to Stoker's novel; it is this adaptation that achieved cultural "immortality," as Bela Lugosi's debonair aristocrat Dracula became the default template for the next several decades of vampire films. In short, the frighteningly inhuman Nosferatu subspecies dies after 1922 (at least until the form was borrowed by the 1979 German remake of *Nosferatu* and again for the television miniseries *Salem's Lot*, also in 1979). Perhaps this particular vampiric morphology was no longer necessary as soon as filmmakers no longer were required to create a legally viable narrative distance from Stoker's novel: the time for *Nosferatu*'s Count Orlok had passed.

Finally, Petyr is the only vampire in the group that is killed during the course of the documentary, and it is here, perhaps, that the film makes clear that there is no future for this kind of vampire. The monster that cannot walk among non-vampiric humans is ultimately untenable, as it is the stealth factor (though, admittedly, executed poorly and amusingly by the other vampires in the film), the ability to co-exist undetected in the midst of large concentrations of its prey species, that allows the vampire to endure. Viago and the others joke that they get dressed up to go out on the town amid Wellington's night-life in order to hunt for prey. They describe themselves well as predators in search of prey, highlighted best perhaps with Vladislav's comment that the look he pursues is a specific look he calls "dead but delicious." "We are the bait but we are also the trap," he muses. Even though Vladislav's "dead but delicious" look is medieval, very unlike the style of dress favored by non-vampiric Wellingtonians, he can at least impersonate a human being on the streets of the city, whereas Petyr cannot. Even the little backstory we are allowed for Petyr describes him, via Deacon, as a very Old World type of vampire, occupying a massive "creepy" aristocratic castle and attacking hapless peasants. We see that he clearly could never have joined his flat-mates in such predatory endeavors as trolling the nightclubs of modern Wellington. His dated Nosferatu-like appearance has made him like an aging predatory animal, no longer able to hunt for himself and only capable of snaring prey when it wanders into his flat.

So if Petyr is not a viable iteration of the vampire, what subspecies is lurking at the fringes of possibility to replace him? Since we know that an "obsolete vampire" no longer terrifies humanity, that it must reinvent itself as an updated avatar of a culture's fears and anxieties, what is the "new" kind of vampire in this storyworld to look like?

Perhaps we should look in Nick's direction here.

After Nick, the "newest vampire," is converted by Petyr, he seems to assert himself as a new kind of vampire, unencumbered by the rules and expectations that govern his more-established brethren. For one, he is incapable of keeping his new identity a secret, shouting it out to everyone on the streets of Wellington, talking it up in pubs (fatefully for Petyr, when Nick is overheard by a self-proclaimed vampire hunter) and even transforming his face into that of a frightening bat-demon kind of creature to intimidate a convenience store clerk. "I'm the main guy in *Twilight*," he announces to everyone within earshot. (He is, indeed, the vampire that comes closest to fitting the demographic for vampires in the *Twilight* series. He is also the only vampire in the group that seems to be from the present, twenty-first century world; in contrast, the four flat-mates are aligned with older and deeper histories, as the film's multiple montage sequences show them making numerous cameo appearances in ancient and classical artwork). This insistent self-identification culminates with Nick stumbling drunkenly through the streets at night simply shouting "Twilight!" Deacon angrily corrects him: "Shut up, Nick! You're not Twilight!"[19] Pushing and name-calling ensue, and Nick counters by claiming "I'm Dracula, man!" After a bit more pushing and shouting, Deacon hollers, "you don't even know who Dracula is, you idiot!" Enraged, Nick immediately transforms into a bat (which is a very Dracula kind of thing to do); Deacon follows him, and they fly into the night sky to engage in a brief but violent "bat fight!" in the words of the excited Vladislav. The vampire-to-bat transformation, it should be mentioned, is not a part of older folkloric traditions, but emerges much later, through Stoker and the cinema. In Stoker's novel, the Count haunts Mina in bat-form, and the vampire-as-bat appears in the Browning film *Dracula*.[20] In short, changing into a bat is not something the "old" vampires of folklore did, but is rather an ability affiliated with a "new" vampire. That Deacon and Nick's bat-transformations take place after one vampire claims to be Dracula, and another refutes the claim, also indicates that association with Dracula is important to these vampires.

And there are several ways to look at Deacon's comments here. The first is that he is simply annoyed with how Nick equates being a vampire with essentially being in a movie (after all, both *Twilight* and *Dracula* are the actual names of films). However, it is perhaps significant that Deacon's reaction to Nick's title-shouting is more violent with regard to *Dracula* than to *Twilight*: Nick's alignment with a new, trendy vampire-type necessitates only pushing and insults, but his claim to be the seminal (bat-transforming) film-vampire Dracula angers Deacon so much that he prods Nick into fighting him in bat-form. While it is true that we lack a frame of reference that would tell us if Deacon is referring to Dracula as a novel, a film, or an actual "real-life" vampire, what is clear is that Nick has not earned the right to associate himself with this name. Perhaps Dracula acts as a standard for these vampires. After all, each of the flat-mates carries an element of one if not several of the aspects of Dracula, even if they are not directly traceable to a single source.[21] Petyr, as discussed previously, is clearly an echo of *Nosferatu*, which itself is an adaptation of Stoker's novel, albeit unauthorized. Viago's dapper nature evokes Bela Lugosi's rendition of the sociable Count in Browning's *Dracula*. Vladislav's medieval roots and his rampant sexuality, made evident in his frequent anecdotes and through the bizarre, gravity-defying orgy-image which introduces him to the film, and via the enormous stylized hairpiece he wears to the Unholy Masquerade, aligns him with the highly-stylized, hypersexualized version of Dracula presented in *Bram Stoker's Dracula* (1992).[22]

Finally, Deacon is perhaps most difficult to place as a conventional Dracula figure, but his chosen affiliation with another well-known vampire family might be telling. Deacon's petulant "bad-boy" behavior and fixation with being "cool" appear to hearken back not to *Dracula* so much as they do back to the teenage vampires in *The Lost Boys* (1987); Deacon's tendency to "steal" vampiric pranks from this film heightens the connection. When Nick and his fellow unwitting human sacrifice-to-be Josephina have dinner at the vampires' flat, Deacon "glamours" Nick, using the power of suggestion to promote a kind of visual hallucination—a vampiric ability that was popularized by the HBO series *True Blood*. Specifically, Deacon's trick involves waiting until Nick and Josephina are served "biz-ghetti' (spaghetti) directly from a can, then asking Nick, as he starts eating, if he enjoys eating worms," at which point Nick starts to hallucinate that his plate is, indeed, crawling with earthworms. Deacon admits that "we stole that idea from *The Lost Boys,* but I put a nice twist on it," by which he means that he has added another suggestion whereby he asks "how does it feel to have a snake for a penis?" at which Nick recoils in terror as he hallucinates that his penis has been turned into a "cobra snake." (Nick later attempts to steal this trick from Deacon but is unable to convince Stu that his chips have become worms because, as Vladislav condescendingly reminds him, it only works with foods that already look like worms. We see here that in stealing from Deacon who is stealing from *The Lost Boys*, Nick, the new vampire, is willing to learn more updated popular-culture-generated vampire tricks, even if he has yet to perfect the technique. And we learn that, while an entrenched vampire like Deacon and a new vampire like Nick cannot agree on *Twilight* or *Dracula*, they can find common ground in *The Lost Boys*.) In making Nick hallucinate his penis as a cobra, Deacon happens to forecast Nick's future: namely, that his male organ will become vampirically generative (the fangs of the cobra mirroring those of the vampire) and that he will reproduce his new vampiric "species" in a way that his flat-mates will not.

In addition to understanding the culture of the urban twenty-first century environment, Nick is decidedly unlike Viago, Vladislav, and Deacon, in that the former has no qualms about converting willing mortals to vampirism. The other vampires largely refuse to bequeath their vampiric gift to the living, even when they are literally begged to do so. For example, Deacon continually refuses to convert his loyal familiar Jackie, whose frustration simmers throughout the film, but we find out at the Unholy Masquerade that Nick has fulfilled her wishes and converted her to a vampire. And Jackie's discontent about Deacon's reticence might invite us to think further of what is going on here, as she angrily tells the camera crew that "if I had a penis I'd have been bitten years ago" and, after describing the flat-mates' association as a sort of vampiric circle-jerk, concludes by labeling them as members of a "homoerotic dick-biting club." Indeed, the flat-mates do seem to exhibit a resistance toward initiating a female member into their "club," reminiscent of the all-male vampire Brotherhood of the film *Byzantium* (2012). This apparent resistance might be fueled in part by Vladislav's festering hatred and fear of his ex-girlfriend "The Beast," and it might inspire Viago's inability to realize that he could convert his elderly ex-lover Katherine to vampirism in order to rekindle their relationship. Nick is unhampered by such baggage, though, and converts Jackie in time for her to attend the Unholy Masquerade. His willingness to understand that vampires cannot remain in a "boys' club" if they wish to endure into the twenty-first century, and that female vampires should be included among their ranks, marks him as a sort of inclusive vampire. (There are, however, plenty of female vampires at the Unholy Masquerade, and several are encountered during the flat-mates' night-out in Wellington, including two very young girl-vampires hoping to trap a pedophile, in a probable reference to the film *Let the Right One In* [2008]. Perhaps the flatmates' regressive, misogynistic thinking plagues their household more than others.) That Nick himself is "recruited" to vampirism by Petyr, the oldest vampire, might imply a sense of cyclicity, an awareness of which the other flat-mates have lost. And, indeed, Nick helps to nudge Viago into a more adaptable and welcoming vampiric space, as the final scenes of the film reveal that he has finally "recruited" Katherine to the ranks of the vampire.

If Nick is the new vampire angling to replace the obsolete predecessors, then his semi-coherent claim that he is essentially both *Twilight* and *Dracula* is in some ways a declaration of his ascendency. As a single figure that unites both the old literary vampire and the new cinematic vampire, Nick becomes perhaps the very monstrous adaptation that Cohen states must appear in order to keep a monster-type like the vampire culturally relevant as times change. As a product of early twenty-first century urban Wellington, Nick can blend in with human culture in ways the other vampires, disconnected from the modern world both by geography and culture, simply cannot. Seen this way, glaringly out-of-place-and-time vampires like Petyr, Viago, Vladislav, and Deacon are obsolete: not only are their powers and "reproductive awareness" eroding as the centuries pass, but so is their understanding of their prey-species. They think, act and dress in the archaic trappings from whence they sprang, and they are incapable of seeing that they, unlike their new vampire recruit Nick, do not fit in their current surroundings. And it is here that we should turn to those very surroundings, in an attempt to understand what this collection of vampires might be doing in Wellington, New Zealand.

A Perfect Setting

New Zealand is not internationally known for its vampire lore, though certainly here (as almost everywhere) myriad popular culture iterations of vampires may be encountered. Most New Zealand vampires have been presented comedically. Probably the best-known vampire from this country's television archives is Count Homogenized, a chalky white-skinned vampire with deeply blackened eye sockets and an all-white vampire-style wardrobe, who lusts after milk instead of blood; the Count appeared on the late 1970s children's program *A Haunting We Will Go* and proved so popular he earned his own show in the early 1980s, *It Is I Count Homogenized.*[23] Additionally, many well-received New Zealand horror films that pre-date *What We Do in the Shadows* work very effectively within the horror-comedy genre as well. A few standout titles include Peter Jackson's *Dead Alive* (1992), Peter Jackson's *The Frighteners* (1996), Jonathan King's *Black Sheep* (2008), Guy Pidgeon's *I Survived a Zombie Holocaust* (2014), and Lei Howden's *Deathgasm* (2015). And vampires have specifically been treated in New Zealand cinema via David Blyth's *Moonrise* (1992), released in New Zealand under the title *Grampire* and non-comedically in Glenn Standring's *Perfect Creature* (2007). There is a rich history of horror-comedy here in which *What We Do in the Shadows* certainly participates.

Research for this project revealed no extant folkloric records describing vampires in early colonized New Zealand, or any creatures that behaved in a recognizably "vampiric" manner. Furthermore, it is possible that the colonization of the islands took place at a historical moment in which the vampire was considered an archaic construct of a bygone age, and so vampire folklore did not migrate with the colonists. Moving away from the islands, we find that the indigenous folklore of Australia offers only one potentially vampiric entity, the *yara-ma-yha-who*.[24] However, this small tarsier-like creature, an arboreal fusion of a man and a red-tinted frog with parasitic blood-draining suckers on the ends of its fingers and toes, does not seem to have influenced the vampires that occupy *What We Do in the Shadows*.

The fact that the vampires of *What We Do in the Shadows* become flatmates in this country without a well-known history of vampiric folklore and traditions is not that strange, as vampires, quite simply, are expected to travel widely. According to Ann Davies, "vampires travel a good deal, and vampire films, accordingly, demonstrate an unusual emphasis on geographic and often transnational mobility."[25] In other words, the vampire originates in its home territory but doesn't stay there: when we encounter it, especially in film, "it always appears to be coming from someplace else."[26] We should, in short, expect to find vampires where we do not expect them: Count Dracula's relocation from Transylvania to London is perhaps the classic example of this tendency. Significantly, none of the four "original" vampires that the film introduces us to became vampires in New Zealand: rather, they are all the products of European environments (though, to be fair, Petyr's origin predates the concept of Europe) that created them as vampires long before they occupied the postcolonial space of New Zealand.

The Film as Folklore

What, ultimately, is going on with this film? Folklorist Alan Dundes discusses the various iterations of the vampire figure throughout the landscapes of popular culture (literature and film) and folklore:

[B]oth high and popular cultures are locked and fixed into print and locked into videotape or film. In marked contrast, there are *always* multiple versions of folklore, versions which exhibit variation from one to another. A literary novel or a television program cannot change over time. They are necessarily the same for each new generation. True, the perception or reception of them can vary with succeeding sequences of audiences, but the texts themselves cannot change. Folklore, on the other hand, is in a constant state of flux. No two versions of an item of folklore will be verbatim identical. Multiple existence (in more than one time and/or place) and variation are the hallmark criteria of folklore or oral tradition.[27]

By way of this definition, *What We Do in the Shadows* oddly seems to function both as popular culture and as folklore. Of course, as a film, its storyworld is locked into place and is inflexibly "fixed" on the screen (though the storyworld can be enlarged, enhanced, and complicated by everything from the *What We Do in the Shadows* television series to fan fiction dedicated to the film). However, in Viago, Vladislav, Deacon and Petyr, it provides a collection of vampires that simultaneously and overlappingly reflect the "multiple versions" of the vampire that one would expect to find in folklore. This folkloric status is further enabled in that the film does not begin by privileging any one vampiric iteration over another, and in fact places them geographically within a culture that lacks well-entrenched New Zealand vampire folklore; in this way, these vampires are on a level playing field, each of them awkward and flawed, and, in spite of what Deacon and Nick might think about themselves, none of them laying claim, either directly or otherwise, to occupying the role of "a Dracula," which may be thought of, at least in their storyworld, as an "authentic vampire."

However, this vampiric landscape is not a stagnant one, and the film shows us the sort of vampiric evolution that again would be more expected in a broad study of the vampire figure than in a single film. Here, we may look again to Cohen, who, in "Monster Culture (Seven Theses)," explains how the monster acts as a cultural body, a constellation of constructed, embodied anxieties shaped by the culture that employs it, and that, as such, it always speaks to something other than itself. Since cultural fears are neither stagnant nor universal, the monster that wishes to live through these changes is forced frequently to disappear, appearing perhaps to have been defeated or outgrown by the culture it formerly haunted. However, it is never truly gone. It is only reconstituting itself, fashioning a new version of itself that better reflects the cultural fears and anxieties that are most relevant to the culture into which it returns. The monster, in the words of Cohen, "always escapes," and when it returns, it has shed its archaic or outdated qualities and replaced them with attributes that resonate more frighteningly for the culture that has called it forth. In this way the monster, and specifically the vampire, operates in the manner of a cultural version of natural selection. The film demonstrates this process in how it disposes of Petyr, the vampire least adapted to the cultural fears and anxieties of the twenty-first century, and essentially replaces him with Nick, a vampire much better suited to wander the nighttime streets of Wellington. But *What We Do in the Shadows* also shows us a collection of what this process leaves behind: the iterations, or subspecies, of the vampire that their cultures of origin have outgrown. There are in twenty-first century New Zealand no Gothic castles for Petyr to inhabit, no slavery for Vladislav to take advantage of, no Nazis for Deacon to cavort with. All of these vampires are on their way out, culturally speaking (although perhaps there is some hope for the adaptive Viago we see at the film's conclusion), and this film uses comedy to highlight their obsolescence while simultaneously providing us a glimpse, in Nick, of the "next step" the vampire is going to need to take. And in doing so, the film performs against the unique backdrop of twenty-first century Wellington, New Zealand, to remind us about something we have likely known all along, that there is no permanent, authentic vampire.

NOTES

1. Jeffrey Cohen, *Monster Theory: Reading Culture*, Yale University Press, 1998, page 5.
2. Jeffrey Weinstock, *The Vampire Film: Undead Cinema*, Columbia University Press, 2012, page 13.
3. Nick Groom, *The Vampire: A New History*, Yale University Press, page xv.
4. David Keyworth, *Troublesome Corpses: Vampires and Revenants from Antiquity to the Present*, Desert Island Books, 2007, no page.
5. Groom, cited above, pages 4–5.
6. Leonard Wolf, *A Dream of Dracula: In Search of the Living Dead*, Little, Brown, 1977, page 279.
7. Weinstock, cited above, page 13.
8. Paul Barber, *Vampires, Burial, and Death: Folklore and Reality*, Yale University Press, 1988, page 46.
9. Julia Kristeva, *The Powers of Horror: An Essay on Abjection*, Columbia University Press, 1982, page 4.
10. The notion of the vampire as a sexual being was present in Stoker's novel (but is entirely absent in folkloric sources); Stephen King distills the novel's sexuality into "an infantile oralism coupled with a strong interest in necrophilia" and quotes Erica Jong's characterization of sex with Dracula as a "zipless fuck" (*Stephen King's Danse Macabre*, page 75). This sexuality evolved into Bela Lugosi's depiction of Dracula, in Browning's film, as a vampire with "charm and sexual charisma" (Maberry and Kramer 26), features which later films borrowed and enthusiastically enhanced.
Interestingly, one of the few folkloric vampires with a definite antipathy toward sunlight is the *Chiang-Shih* of China; this exceptionally powerful and bloodthirsty vampire hops instead of walking because its body is so corroded by decomposition (Maberry and Kramer, page 64). The vampire's fear of a brandished crucifix originates with Stoker's novel (Maberry and Kramer, page 9), actually, and was quickly incorporated into vampire films, perhaps most prominently with the influential cycle of *Dracula* films produced by Hammer Studios in the late 1950s and 1960s.
11. In addition to instructing them on selfie-snapping, Stu also shows them online videos of sunrises and how to search the internet for "images of virgins"; Stu even sets up a Skype conversation between Viago and his now-aged servant Phillip. One thinks of the prevalent role of technology in Stoker's *Dracula* (the phonograph perhaps most prominently) when one sees Stu introduce the vampires to the wonders of twenty-first century technology. In the film, however, it is the vampires that are affiliated with "cutting edge" tech, instead of the vampire hunters.
12. Oddly, there is folkloric precedent for vampire cat; Dr. Fernand Mery's 1966 study *The Cat* transcribes a Japanese folktale about the Vampire Cat of Nabeshima, which attacked humans, punctured their throats in vampiric manner, and feasted on the blood that flowed forth (Copper, pages 51–52).

13. Kelly Hurley, "Abject and Grotesque," *The Routledge Companion to the Gothic*, edited by Catherine Spooner and Emma McAvoy, Routledge, 2000, page 139.

14. Weinstein, cited above, page 7.

15. Keyworth, cited above, page 205.

16. Barber, cited above, page 93.

17. Keyworth, cited above, page 205.

18. Barber, cited above, page 93 (italics Barber's, interpolations mine).

19. To be clear, Nick appears intoxicated, but we do not actually see him consuming alcoholic beverages, leaving open the possibility that drinking booze, like eating chips, would violently sicken him, that he is instead drunk on human blood.

20. Browning's decision to include the bat in his film was likely a response to the cultural fascination attached to the recent Western-world "discovery" of the vampire bat, discussed in Chapter 12 of Stoker's novel.

21. In a way, the difficulties in discovering a single-stream "plug-and-play" source for each individual vampire allows this film to participate in the kind of frustration that horror-scholars and students encounter when they attempt to locate a coherent evolution of the vampire figure. There isn't one, as influences overlap, elements appear and disappear, and terminologies mutate and become amorphous. As a result, finding a sense of coherent linear progress in vampire-evolution is simply not possible. This is of course one of the aforementioned hallmarks of studying monstrosity, the resistance to systems and classification, so this film represents a tangled, sometimes unreadable web of relationships between vampire figures that operates in much the same way as the trajectory of the study of the vampire itself.

22. It is important to note that these cross-textual connections are not offered as inflexible interpretations, as the filmmakers are certainly under no obligation to create easy interpretive linkages to their characters when decisions to enhance the comedic elements of the film might encourage them to take different creative directions.

23. Irene Gardiner, "NZ on Screen: A History of Vampires in NZ," *New Zealand Herald* 20 June 2014, paragraphs 3–5.

24. Bernard Heuvelmans, *On the Track of Unknown Animals*, translated by Richard Garnett, Kegan Paul International, 1995, pages 230–34.

25. Weinstock, cited above, page 12.

26. Weinstock, cited above, page 11.

27. Alan Dundes, "The Vampire as Bloody Revenant," *The Vampire: A Casebook*, edited by Alan Dundes, University of Wisconsin Press, 1998, page 160.

Vampire Privilege

Class, Gender and Sex in Serbian Metaphysical Horror

Tatjana Aleksić

Blood and sex are easily recognized as the most common motifs in the majority of vampiric narratives, yet there is another motif that facilitates the vampire's wanton behavior with impunity, and that is class privilege. Most vampire narratives indeed are about an upper class vampire whose extraordinary, aberrant, and deadly sexuality exploits, endangers, or destroys ordinary mortals. The historically known case of the "vampirism" of Countess Elizabeth Bathory, crossed with the sadistic cruelty of Prince Vlad Tepes, are the prototypes for the lethal appetites of their Hollywood versions like Nosferatu, Count Dracula and a host of later predatory arrivals. An archaic representative of European aristocracies, Nosferatu-Dracula slowly penetrates western industrial societies, although his exotic accent and strange mannerisms never allow for his full social integration. Instead, Dracula admits himself through a seductive ensnaring of inexperienced upper class maidens. Faced with the novelty and intensity of their desire the girls' fates are exemplary—some prudently shelter themselves within a bourgeois marriage, like Mina, who weds her accountant fiancé and goes on to enjoy her dull but safe existence. On the other hand, Lucy obliviously surrenders herself to her newly discovered sexuality, dies a fallen woman, and gets redeemed only after being staked by a host of western males.[1]

Everything in the popular vampiric narrative reeks of the oft-iterated morality tale of not meandering beyond the secure confines of one's culture, class, or experience, as well as that the rule of law is safe in the hands of cultivated upper class males. Yet, not many critics have demonstrated much interest in the class issue itself that so obviously underlies the vampire narrative, with Count Dracula as an aristocratic, imperialist colonizer whose quiet bloodsucking is merely a personification of lethal capitalism ferociously protected by the western elites.[2] That the vampire creature embodies the seductiveness of upper class enlightened existence is almost unquestioningly assumed from Nosferatu to Lestat to sparkling Edward—as is the fact that their threat can only be deflected by antagonists of corresponding social standing.[3] Society is both threatened and sustained by the elites, while lower class collaterals end up being as irrelevant for modern vampire narratives as they were to Countess Bathory herself, who allegedly destroyed hundreds of peasant girls but faced legal sanctions only after mistakenly killing an aristocrat.[4] The standard vampire narrative thus reads like an apology for social privilege that is sanctioned unless it becomes so excessive to threaten the bedrock of social order itself. Social elites may be draining the life out of common mortals, but they are also the only ones capable of standing up to, say, foreign immigrant vampires, like Dracula.

Long before noble vampires became so dangerously alluring in the Western imagination, they were considered a fact of life among Eastern European peasantry.[5] The vampires had no manners, spoke no foreign tongues and did not look nice either. There are very few modern narratives with or about such archaic unappealing vampires, however, and in this essay I will focus on two of them in an attempt to reclaim the vampire power from contemporary erudite elites back to its more ancient chthonic origins. The two films I discuss in this essay were directed by Serbian Djordje Kadijević, whose rich opus is, for better or worse, forever marked by his several films done in the genre of "metaphysical fantasy," as he insists on calling it, refuting the genre of "horror" as too trivial and inadequate in conveying the sense of dread the human race feels when faced with inexplicable phenomena.[6] Both these films are loosely based on nineteenth century Slavic fiction that in Kadijević's interpretation barely resemble their literary roots. In chronological order, the first one is *Leptirica* (usually translated as *The She-Butterfly*, sometimes as *The Butterfly Woman*), which first appeared in 1973, and which not only gave this author nightmares for years but is allegedly "responsible" for an actual death of a TV spectator.[7] *The She-Butterfly* is based on an 1880 story "After Ninety Years," written by the Serbian Realist author Milovan Glišić, which gave birth to the legend of the best known Serbian vampire, Sava Savanović, who in 2012 was even featured in *The Guardian* and *National Geographic*, and boasts a Facebook following.[8] Kadijević's next excursion into the metaphysical did not happen for almost two decades, until in 1990 he made *Sveto mesto* [*A Holy Place*], based on the better known story by Nikolai Gogol, "Viy" (1835). Kadijević sees few reasons why he should have been the first adapter, and he remains a rare Yugoslav or post–Yugoslav author who made so-called "horror" films before the 1980s, when the genre took off, especially given that a

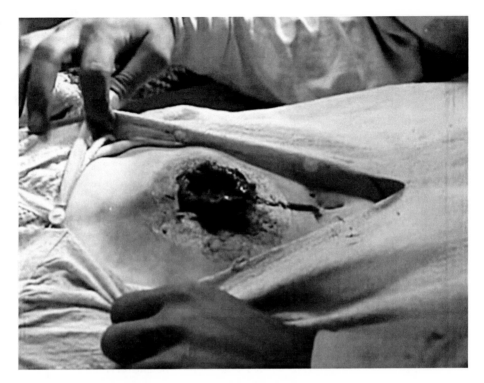

The She-Butterfly (*Leptirica*, 1973). In this Slavic film Strahinja (Petar Božović), an impatient groom, violates the seclusion of his fiancée (Mirjana Nikolić) only to discover that she is a monster bearing a horrific wound rather than the beautiful bride he was anticipating.

capitalist vampire seems such an irresistible model of a class enemy that one wonders why vampire movies were never made in communist cinematographies.[9] Kadijević speculates that the horror genre in Yugoslav socialist cinema production was considered too frivolous to offer relevant commentary on the development of a socialist society, and the production of such movies was not encouraged.[10]

The Gender Abject

The film *The She-Butterfly* derives from the archetypal narrative of an orphaned, poor itinerant young man who arrives at a remote place threatened by disaster, falls in love with the daughter of the land's ruler, but in order to obtain her he must achieve an extraordinary accomplishment to avert the disaster. Such a "hero" in *The She-Butterfly* is Strahinja (derived from the word for "fear"), where a young orphaned man in quest of his destiny volunteers to save his adoptive community from hunger that looms because the long-forgotten vampire, Sava Savanović, kills everyone who attempts to grind flour in the local watermill. In return, the villagers promise to help him marry Radojka, the daughter of the village lord, whose malevolent father aggressively opposes the match. This is the point where Kadijević abandons Glišić's story, which leads to a happy ending and a communal celebration of the young couple's marriage. In contrast, Kadijević creates some of the most spine-chilling scenes ever seen on film. Strahinja survives the vampire's nocturnal attack by his agility and cunning, and lives to tell the tale to the villagers who gather at the mill expecting to discover yet another corpse. The villagers trace the vampire's grave, stake the vampire through the coffin, but clumsily let a butterfly out, which gets caught by Radojka's father. Thinking little of the butterfly, villagers help Strahinja elope with Radojka, on condition that they remain separated before the wedding rites have been performed. However, our hero is too impatient to observe the custom, sneaks upon Radojka while she is asleep, and subsequently pays a heavy price for his impetuousness.

Kadijević's film complicates both Glišić's short story and its mythical subtext by adding a strong underlying focus on domestic violence in the household of the village lord, which he perpetrates especially against Radojka, his eldest daughter. Although Glišić's story contains mentions of father's rigorous upbringing and harsh punishments against Radojka when he discovers her tryst with Strahinja, the girl's father is never brought into a direct connection with vampirism. There is a recurrent motif, however, that never gets an explanation in the story: in every encounter with other characters Radojka's father is described as yawning and looking tired. Others talk, but he yawns—probably because he is kept awake at night for some reason. The readers also learn that he keeps his eldest daughter in the barn and does not let her sleep in the house with the rest of the family. After the young lovers elope, he threatens to hunt them down, but the efforts that the community puts into appeasing him pay off in the end, and subsequently the vampire and its alter ego, the eponymous butterfly, disappear from the village altogether. Kadijević's film, however, insinuates that father's controlling behavior and his treatment of Radojka could be read through the taboo relationship that is likely the real cause of the anathema on the village. Moreover, Strahinja is not merely an archetypal hero who destroys the vampire, saves the village from hunger, and wins a bride. Instead his sexual eagerness, that could possibly be read as a stand-in for male predatory sexuality, must be punished in the end. Kadijević organizes the scene in which the couple are separated as a semi-benevolent siege of the female element, with the girl locked up in a house, guarded by an elderly matron, while the village males surround the house loudly joking and drinking. Once everyone falls asleep the impatient groom hurries to taste matrimonial bliss ahead of time.

What awaits him in Radojka's bed is an ambiguous sight that generates lust, fear and disgust, and that extends for about five minutes of screen time during which the viewer can never tell with certainty what they are witnessing. A horrific open wound is located right where the young man expects to discover Radojka's youthful beauty, and it becomes the sight/site of disgust, before it turns into a sight/site of horror. Here is the crux at which the paternal/patriarchal and communal prohibition against use of Radojka's body has been violated, and Strahinja must confront not only the punishment for his transgression but also the ugly secret behind the object that can be "enjoyed"— the pleasure that seems to be the prerogative of the family patriarch—and for this reason is necessarily placed off limits. The abominable transformation of Radojka's body figures as a revelation of what Kristeva designates as an "unnamable otherness—the solid rock of jouissance," and that in the patriarchal system undeniably carries a gendered, feminine, identity: "What we designate as 'feminine,' far from being a primeval essence, will be seen as an 'other' without a name, which subjective experience confronts when it does not stop at the appearance of its identity."[11] Similar to what Lacan used to define as *real*, this metaphysical force is not something that has a shape or can be dealt with—it is known merely by the effects it has on the subject, and Strahinja learns its true essence only at the moment when his death has already begun.

In the closing sequence, which consists of inarticulate gasping and moaning—very much like lovers consummating their affair, Radojka, now with a hairy face and vampire teeth, rides Strahinja out of the village and to the coffin in which the vampire was staked the day before. Radojka's screams to Strahinja to "take it out" and his pulling the impaling stake out of the vampire's coffin barely masks the act of sexual penetration. His final thrust of the stake at Radojka-as-vampire, however, leads to his death, while it never becomes clear who or what the vampire really is, or where it resides, the only certainty being that the ploy of the rootless man and his peasant accomplices was always doomed to fail. That haunting uncertainty at the end of the film is precisely the source of the metaphysical horror that makes this film worth watching even at an age in which the horror genre has surpassed everything we used to know about fear.

Kadijević's eclectic approach in *The She-Butterfly* is a rare occasion on which a film narrative about the vampiric phenomenon revisits its ancient roots that derive from a variety of sources, like the Slavic lore about werewolves and witches, administrative accounts of the eighteenth century "vampire epidemic" among Serbian peasants, or medical reports about vampires' decomposing bodies that trouble the local community,[12] peppered throughout with moments of humor and simplistic peasant characters. Interestingly, a direct origin of the butterfly motif from the film's title is particularly difficult to trace, as references to butterflies in Slavic lore are at best obscure. A more circuitous route can be found in the meanings that the ancient Greek word ψυχή used to carry, designating both the concept of "soul," or "breath," but also that of a "butterfly," although this linguistic link seems to have been lost in Modern Greek language. This etymology further implies a duality of phenomena related to the existence of butterflies, invoking the beauty of the developed insect, but also ugliness and negativity of its moth form.[13] Kadijević's film brands this connection into the viewer's memory, emphasizing the sense of dread with ominous sounds of nocturnal birds, and hinting at unnatural relations between Radojka and her father that are set to tip the delicate balance on which the community sustains itself. The vampire and the threat to the community thus need not be sought in external elements and foreign dangers, because it, the *vampire*, has always resided within the village's most prosperous family. There is no greater horror than the one coming from what appears to be ordinary and Kadijević situates this primeval sense of metaphysical dread within what is considered familiar, and, most of all, beautifully innocent.

Sexual Violation

Kadijević returns to the subject of decadent elites and their abuses of power and wealth two decades later with his film *A Holy Place*, in which he further intensifies the incest motif he had introduced in *The She-Butterfly*. *A Holy Place* is loosely built on Nikolai Gogol's story *Viy*, the name that signifies a demon from the Ukrainian tradition. The film follows the plot of the story to a certain point: three theological students find themselves lost in the wilderness on their return to the seminary and need a place to spend the night. They arrive at a shed inhabited by an old woman who lets them stay in her barn. During the night she approaches one of them and hag-rides him, deaf to his pleas rejecting her apparent sexual advances. He defies her with exorcism, beats her unconscious and exhausted, discovers she has turned into a beautiful girl. The novice returns to his school only to find out that his dean is requesting him to stand at a wake for a landowner's beautiful daughter, who crawled home beaten up and died soon afterwards. Her only dying wish was that he should personally read psalms for her in church for three nights. What follows is the mythical repetition of three nights of ever magnifying horrors for the novice priest, which ultimately kill him. Gogol's story ends with the novice's friends commenting on his death as a consequence of his fear of demons—the conclusion being that his faith was too weak to endure the test.

Kadijević's intervention into Gogol's narrative reiterates the strong erotic subtext of *The She-Butterfly*, which is further intensified with overt references to incest, sadism and homoeroticism. The first such erotic intervention arrives in the opening scenes, when after being hag-ridden the novice priest, Toma, overpowers the hag and finds himself lying over a beautiful young woman in her place. When Gogol's novice finds himself in this position he runs away in fright, but Kadijević's Toma attempts making love to the girl until she apparently dies. When Toma is later summoned to her father's property, he discovers the family's many dark secrets and hears perverse gossip about the deceased girl's insatiable and unhealthy sexual appetites. During this visit to the late girl's estate, however, the viewer gets further insight into Toma's less than appropriate behavior for someone who has dedicated his life to serving God, as he is not shy of looking into the maid's bosom, or indulging himself in debauchery with other servants at the farmstead. The girl, Katarina, seems to have been a literal devourer of men and women alike, specializing in seducing men in her father's service and then stomping their virile members to pulp. The film culminates in Toma's discovery of a compromising painting that testifies to an incestuous relationship between Katarina and her father, the relationship which is said to have sent her mother to an early grave. It is never completely clear whether the incestuous relationship should be interpreted as sexual molestation on the part of the father, which would serve as an explanation for Katarina's sexual vampirism, or whether it is merely another proof of her disturbingly corrupt nature.

Toma's discovery that the hag who rode him was in fact Katarina's mother—and ultimately Katarina herself, as they change shapes between each other—adds to his sense of loathing and horror. At this point, however, he is unable to abandon his religious service at the girl's wake since Katarina's father threatens him with severe consequences if he does not observe his duty. Whichever decision he makes, Toma jeopardizes an aspect of his existence: if he does not observe the landlord's request he will lose his social standing and be excommunicated from his order; yet if he complies with the orders he risks losing his life to the underworldly mother-daughter tandem. He decides to prioritize his vocation over his fears of female revenge and proceeds to spend three nights alone in church reading above Katarina's coffin. Katarina's ultimate revenge against Toma, and we are to understand against male predatory sexuality, takes place on the third night, when Toma is tricked into leaving the relative safety of his religious paraphernalia and must confront her unprotected. She crushes his masculinity to an extent that is painful to watch. The following morning Toma is found indecently lying under Katarina's dead body. He is accused of dishonoring her and is murdered on the spot.

Sexual Innuendos

Although the two films were made almost two decades apart from each other, Kadijević's interest in the specific topic of sexual taboo and monstrous female revenge against a stand-in for the actual violator creates something like a thematic continuity between them. It is clear that he to a large extent subscribes to Freudian interpretations of male repressed sexuality as trigger for the female characters' vampirism. Strahinja and Toma, his principal male characters, who are also the main victims of the women's vicious revenge, demonstrate conspicuous symptoms of sexual anxiety in encounters with their female antagonists. Both men make illicit contacts with the female bodies while the women are considered to be in the state of sleep paralysis (Radojka), or even dead (Katarina). The positions of helplessness in which their bodies are about to be violated literally reproduce the famous 1781 painting *The Nightmare* by Henry Fuseli, depicting a woman lying over a bed in state of deep sleep, while a leering incubus sits on her chest, and a horse's head (a night mare) peeks through heavy curtains. The female protagonists, however, do not remain passive victims who succumb to violation, and they in fact turn into monsters and lash out against the men on the point of being assaulted. By returning their Medusa-like gaze to the men they stop them in their tracks, visually "castrating" them and making the sexual contact impossible. Their gaze horrifies the perpetrators as much as what they find in place of their sex disgusts them.

As we are discussing Freudian approach to these narratives, it is appropriate to point out that Ernest Jones in his study *On the Nightmare* (1931) ties diverse nocturnal phenomena and fantastic creatures, vampires included, to sexual anxieties. Jones defines nightmare as "dependence of morbid anxiety on repressed Libido," claiming that "Nightmare is a form of anxiety attack, that it is essentially due to an intense mental conflict centering around some repressed component of the psycho-sexual instinct." He describes nightmare as a disease of sexual nature in which men are "troubled with incubus, or witch-ridden (as we call it): if they lie on their back, they suppose an old woman rides and sits so hard on them, that they are almost stifled for want of breath."[14] Kadijević's female protagonists look and act as embodiments of precisely such a "night mare": Radojka hag-rides Strahinja to his death, and Katarina-as-her-mother hag-rides unsuspecting novices in *A Holy Place*. Ultimately, Katarina crushes men's genitals as a mare might with her hooves.[15]

However, the underlying reason Kadijević's itinerant would-be heroes prove susceptible to such subconscious subversions is due to themselves being perversions of the archetypal hero-on-the-quest. In classical myths of male initiation, the innocent, virtuous and highly ethical hero must suffer a number of hardships and temptations until he destroys the underlying cause of social problems and consequently restores balance to the community. In the process

The Nightmare (1782). Henry Fuseli's painting of an incubus atop a sleeping female (with an exposed neck) suggests the vulnerability of females to sexual assaults at night—and dreams thereof. Horses also are associated with nighttime visits in folkloric fantasies, but it is sleeping men that they take for rides. In this depiction of sleep, notes Lorna Hutchison, all is in implicit motion including the subject of the monstrous. According to art critic Nicholas Powell, the mare in the word *night-mare* derives from the Anglo-Saxon word for a chest crusher, not from the word for a female horse (courtesy Detroit Institute of Art).

he routinely proves his own maturity and virility by finally winning a bride and the right to sexual intercourse. Strahinja (his name deriving from the word for *fear*) and Toma (suggesting the Christian Apostle "doubting" Thomas) are odd candidates for the completion of the quest, not merely because they are immature and unaware of the expectations that society places ahead of them, but as their names already indicate, they prove ultimately unworthy of the goal. Neither Strahinja nor Toma are thus exactly innocent victims, as they both sexually inappropriately approach or molest the women—Strahinja, as we deduced, was hurrying to taste marital bliss before it was appropriate to do so, while Toma's transgressions were even graver, as he almost rapes Katarina and is directly responsible for her death.

The real culprits and legitimate targets of the vampires' reprisals, however, remain virtually untouchable, due in equal parts to their paternal influence over the young women, as well as their social standing within the community. Given that the father figure is out of reach, the female monstrous directs its retribution at socially powerless substitutes—orphaned and uprooted men, neither of whom belongs to the community in which they meet their end. By thus providing social justification for the brutal revenge served by the female monsters, Kadijević's films appear to test the sense of social entitlement given to men to subdue and control the female body and sexuality, as well as to tease the limits of their self-control when tempted by these raw forces. Ultimately, neither of these films makes it clear as to who is the real sexual demon: the men who believe they are authorized to assault defenseless women, or the chthonic female creatures whose primordial powers society has always feared and sought to repress.

The Female Monster and the Social Order

Teratologies frequently establish vampires and other monsters as representative of some kind of inversion or disruption of the repressive normalcy of social dictates, whose ugliness evinces the actual monstrosity of mundane existence. Trying to define the role of the vampire in relation to the social order, Erik Butler determines that the vampire's ambiguous social role is very much reflected in the corrupt and inconclusive nature of its own being. According to Butler, vampires "move between and undo borders otherwise holding identities in place. At this monster's core lies an affinity for rupture, change, and mutation. Because of its inimical relationship to stability, tradition, and order, the vampire embodies the transformative march of history."[16] True to this the vampires in my films respond to patriarchal brutality in a rather brutal manner, but what does their vampirism ultimately achieve? Do these female vampires and hags in any significant way disrupt the social system that stands in permanent opposition to but is simultaneously threatened by their infernal forces? It is tempting to read Radojka's vampirism, or Katarina's nightmarish stomping on male genitals as a revenge of molested victims against violent male sexuality-by-proxy. However, I invite the actions of our Slavic *succubi* to be interpreted as angry but nevertheless inadequate responses to patriarchal violence. Although Kadijević's female monsters appear to disturb the patriarchal law that relegates them to the demonic and underworldly, excluded from the site of narrative production, neither his films nor the stories they are based on are really focused on the female vampires themselves, nor do they promote anti-patriarchal views.

Quite the opposite is true, as Kadijević prefers to focus on the natural equilibrium, inextricable from social balance, and which is in turn disturbed by something that the contemporary viewer could recognize as gender violence. This natural-social hierarchy in both films is ruptured because the unnatural sexual relation has been brought back into the community's midst, from which, at least according to Freud, it was to have been expelled at the point of the re-establishment of social order. The one closely depends on the other and any loss of balance creates a threat to the entire community. Once the vampire is slain or otherwise driven away, the order gets reestablished and community triumphs, just as Glišić states at the end of his story "After Ninety Years." Kadijević, however, prefers to end his film with a more ominous lingering presence that threatens to never go away—perhaps because life once ruptured can never be patched whole again. One way in which Kadijević is unable to distance himself from the prevalent way of depicting female monsters is his use of menacing female sexuality as a threat to social order.[17] Kadijević takes it a step further because his female victim-monsters do not merely terrify society with their contaminated sex, but they also choose to assault suspect or potential male sexual predators. We need to remember that in the alleged lesbian relationship between Katarina and her house maid, the maid lives to tell the tale and keeps her job, unlike all of Katarina's male victims who are driven to insanity and deprived of their virility.

It therefore comes as not just slightly underwhelming that this attack on the phallus—literal and metaphorical—seems to be inadequate in making much difference in the system of cosmic, or even human justice. The female vampires and hags are not capable of overturning the patriarchal order, but rather revolt against their own violation within it. They are likewise incapable of avenging themselves against the father figures, who in both films are the principal perpetrators of sexual and other forms of violence against their persons, and instead select substitutes from among socially uprooted and powerless subjects—servants, orphans, itinerants.[18] These marginal and frequently nomadic characters, who are neither bound by the laws of the communities they arrive in, nor will their absence be felt anywhere else, fill the position of what Agamben defines as a *homo sacer* figure, who "cannot be sacrificed, yet may be killed."[19] As stand-ins for the actual perpetrators of violent acts against the female bodies, Strahinja and Toma absorb the rage of the community caused by the unnaturalness of the violent acts and die to help restore a delicate balance that assures community's continuity.

For this reason it does not matter that neither Strahinja nor Toma perpetuated any crimes in reality and that their guilt is at that point more potential than actual. Community being more interested in its own survival than in the pursuit of justice, it welcomes any sacrifices that facilitate its recovery from crisis. No further reparations are sought and no other culprits will be punished beyond the restoration of the original order and the resolution of the temporary crisis—Katarina's death in *A Holy Place*, and hunger in *The She-Butterfly*. It is important to emphasize that the female monsters themselves appear to be sacrificed to that same order, as they continue their evil existence at the margins of society, exiled, shunned and threatening to all except their true violators, who are powerful enough to avoid their clout. They rebel and rage against patriarchal violence, even against patriarchal institutions—let us not forget that Toma is a church initiate—but their anger never reaches the very center of social violence, the main pillars of social order itself, abusive fathers or church paters. Violence remains inscribed in the very foundations of society: it is part of family life, it is enshrined in religious practices, and our narratives seem to state that there is no cosmic or terrestrial power strong enough to deal with it.

Is Baba Yaga a Feminist?

My female vampires, as I like to call them, disturb the seat of power, but are unable to dethrone it. All the sex and seduction we frequently encounter in vampire narratives, to the extent that they become their own purpose, in the stories I present have a logical explanation: These women *become* monsters because masculine brutality and injustice against their persons turns them into vampires. They seem to attack apparently decent folk; however, to a mindful observer they help denude what true monstrosity is: the ability to commit injustice and violations against others with impunity, occluded by the front of a respectable model citizen. Yet, their ontology being so alien to the human community all they invoke in the common folk is fear. We could derive their existence from a long line of female monsters, abundant as much in Slavic as in other traditions and mythologies. Commonly represented as a female who died an unnatural death or incurred God's wrath, these vengeful spirits roam free and make demands upon the community. Kadijević does not give much thought to the "purity" of his female vampires' identities, and he lets their ontologies fluctuate freely among several types of monsters known from pan–Slavic mythology. Radojka the butterfly girl is a shapeshifter who can assume the form of the male vampire Sava Savanović, a hag, or a hairy faced werewolf. In reality it does not really matter *what* she is precisely, because in traditional tales these monsters typically have rather indistinguishable realms, functions, or even appearances. The ontology of Katarina and her mother, however, is more consistent with the function and appearance of a hag, a witch, or Baba Yaga—that ambivalent female monster of Russian and Ukrainian folklore. In a recent critical collection dedicated to the complexity of Baba Yaga, Jack Zipes describes her:

[She is] not just a dangerous witch but also a maternal benefactress, probably related to a pagan goddess. [She] is inscrutable and so powerful that she does not owe allegiance to the Devil or God or even to her storytellers. In fact, she opposes all Judeo-Christian and Muslim deities and beliefs. She is her own woman, a pathogenetic mother, and she decides on a case-by-case basis whether she will help or kill the people who come to her hut that rotates on chicken legs.[20]

Operating almost like a force of nature, with the ignorance and disregard for social morality or individual ethics, Baba Yaga appears to be neither a protectress of specific social groups, nor their enemy. How does she select her victims, or those she may occasionally choose to protect from an even greater evil? Sibelan Forrester explains that Baba Yaga may have a role in initiation rituals of young social members and in teaching them traditional values and rules of cohabitation within the community.[21] We could argue that Kadijević assigns a similar role to his beauties/hags/vampires in *The She-Butterfly* and *A Holy Place*. Radojka and Katarina are not merely victims of Strahinja's and Toma's unbridled sexuality, a role that is in our age increasingly perceived as predatory rather than just being inevitable due to a rush of male hormones, but in their dual vampiric aspect of old hags/witches they also act as guardians and defenders of social ethics, brutally punishing any excursions into socially unacceptable behaviors that ultimately threaten the stability of the community. In this way these female vampiric figures acquire a complexity whose multifaceted contradictoriness is sometimes difficult to comprehend, being simultaneously victims of patriarchal violence, supernatural avengers, and upholders of those same social norms that made them victims in the first place.

It is possible that a more ancient text could throw better light on both the role that these female monsters uphold in a social setting while simultaneously being actively marginalized due to their monstrosity and raw sexual powers, which no social setting tolerates. The text in question is Aeschylus' *Oresteia*, whose third segment, *The Eumenides*, sees the Olympian pantheon help absorb the Erinyes, or Furies, into the texture of post–Uranian Greek society. The ending of the play sees Athena and Apollo, those good children of daddy Zeus, cajole the frightening hags Erinyes, whose time has expired with the establishment of the enlightened Olympian pantheon, to stop persecuting Orestes for the unnatural offense of having killed his mother Clytemnestra—because her death was merely a retribution for an even greater crime, that of her having killed his father Agamemnon. Their divine, rational and patriarchal intervention is the move that puts an end to the archaic vendetta system and introduces legal distribution of justice, but by distinguishing between the lives of a father and a mother with such patriarchal bias it metaphorically enshrines the crime of matricide, or femicide in general, as the foundational event of the social and civilizational structure.[22] After some rhetorical persuasion the Erinyes are ready to abandon their former mission of persecuting matricides in exchange for social acceptance; from that moment they will be assimilated into the pantheon as guardians of the city of Athens. Who could blame them for agreeing to such a compromise if it grants assurances that people will no longer fear their terrifying dysmorphia but will instead worship them as minor deities?

Protecting Social Values

Regardless of all the promise of subversion through the gender, class or sexual matrix, the vampire narrative ultimately leads to an anti-climactic conclusion. The ending of Stoker's *Dracula*, which is so universally West-centric that it deserves its status as a classic, promises that Western law and order will prevail and life will continue as they always have before the intruding Eastern vampire's temporary disturbance. Dracula's sexual innuendos, seductions and nocturnal visitations to young middle class maidens were nothing but lines of least resistance that the social intruder practiced in order to infiltrate the promise of the English way of life. His apparent sexual contamination of elite women from the elite is thus merely a ploy through which the dead seriousness of politics gets exposed. It is easy to read the ritualized staking of Bram Stoker's Lucy by a company of enlightened men, as suggesting that libertine abandon will not be tolerated in society that represses any disruptions of its onward rush toward progress and wealth. Lucy is the domestic enemy, contaminated by an alien agent, and her destruction settles the case without the need for any further examination of the foundations on which society sustains itself. Erik Butler explains:

> The ritualized extermination of the vampire, an embodiment of social chaos and contagion, offered the salutary illusion that there was a cause of problems within the community that might be eliminated to the benefit of all—a view preferable to admitting that everyone was powerless. The destruction of a common, domestic enemy who had been contaminated by foreign influence promised a return to normal.[23]

What causes this sense of helplessness that Butler claims is justifiable but unmentionable by community, covering it up with the sacrifice of the monster within? Perhaps the endings of Kadijević's two films, which fail to provide sufficient hope that the circle of evil and violence will ever stop, could help in fathoming the origin of the "helplessness" and fear that Butler talks about, and the true nature of the monster itself. The *She-Butterfly* ends with Rado-jka's disappearance from the screen although the effects of her actions are in plain sight: a close-up of Strahinja lying on the ground next to the abandoned stake/phallus he was wielding at Radojka the moment before. The closing scenes of *A Holy Place* are even more bizarre, given that they run as an almost identical iteration of the opening hag riding spectacle, except that this time Toma is missing from the young men's company and another man gets treated to the same horror Toma endured first time around. No one mentions Toma any longer and it seems that nobody even learned anything from his experience, given that the same company of novices revisit the same house, ask the same question, and receive the identical treatment as during their previous stay at the hag's lair.

A question that poses itself in both films is whether these endings deliberately disperse hopes for the restoration of normalcy with their open paths to more young men's deaths and the hushing over of the fathers' incestuous crime, or whether these events precisely *are* the normalcy that reoccurs with its own unalterable rhythm. But if in fact such a stand-off between the social offenders and the vampiric avengers actually *is* the normalcy whose restoration is sought, we could read these endings as not suggesting a clear victory for either party but instead a comfortable compromise that calms the social protest (vampiric disturbance) and reestablishes the peace that is uneasy but always preferable to anarchy and disorder. The vampire thus does not get annihilated but rather lingers at the boundaries of social acceptance as both an example and a nominal warning against further transgressions and transgressors of a similar kind. However, transgressors continue to get tolerated and marginal individuals continue to be sacrificed to what is complacently contemplated as "the way of the world," the continuation of life undisturbed, unaltered, as it always has been and always will be. The vampire is a "plague" that promises to expand beyond any limits and borders unless the entire community—the village in *The She-Butterfly*, the estate workers in *A Holy Place*, or the representatives of the enlightened West in *Dracula*—reunites in the defense of its purported values. With each iteration of the cycle social norms receive a new validation as something worth living and dying for. And once the monster becomes semi-absorbed into the mainstream with the intention of protecting the system, it becomes clear why, as Butler insists, "the vampire never wholly subverts the borders it transgresses and in fact it reinforces them."[24]

NOTES

1. That the imagery of Lucy's staking resembles a gang rape is hard to miss, as is the fact that this ritual is performed by western males as a sort of disciplining for her transgression with an unwanted "illegal" alien.

2. Franco Moretti, "The Dialectic of Fear," *New Left Review* 136 (1986): 74–78.

3. *True Blood* seems to have varied this issue a little bit.

4. What Dracula does at night in the villages around his castle is never told because the story focuses on the English protagonists. Exceptions, however, include Mircalla-Carmilla from *The Vampire Lovers* (1970), shown satisfying her hunger with peasant girls while taking care of a young English girl she does not dare hurt, and the Count's initial victim in *Dracula*

3D (2012), a sexually active peasant girl who becomes a jealous-minded resident of the castle.

5. A rich source of folklore and commentary on this topic can be found in Paul Barber's *Vampires, Burial and Death* (2010), as well as in Alan Dundes' edited collection *The Vampire: A Casebook* (1998).

6. Dejan Ognjanović, *Više od istine* [*More Than Truth*], Orfelin, 2017, pages 321–22.

7. The director claims that he was called a "terrorist" by the Yugoslav press of the time because a person in former Yugoslavia allegedly died while watching this film (Ognjanović, *Više od istine*, 204–05).

8. Some British papers caught on to the internet joke that claimed Sava Savanović was made homeless after the collapse of his watermill—the same one that features in Kadijević's film—and was angry and on the loose. See the 2012 piece by Deborah Hyde in *The Guardian*: "Vampire legends that refuse to die," https://www.theguardian.com/science/blog/2012/dec/04/vampire-legends-refuse-die-undead; *National Geographic News* offers a short interview with a "vampire expert," Sasha Ingber, "The Bloody Truth about Serbia's Vampire," 17 December 2012, https://news.nationalgeographic.com/news/2012/12/121217-vampire-serbia-supernatural-garlic-fangs-science-weird/.

9. A rare exception is an amusing Cuban cartoon series *Vampiros en la Habana* (1985) made by Juan and Ernesto Padron, which employs the threat of a capitalist vampire coming from the U.S. as its main story line. The entire series is currently available on YouTube.

10. Ognjanović, cited above, page 200.

11. Julia Kristeva, *Powers of Horror: An Essay on Abjection*, translated by Leon Oudiez, Columbia University Press, 1982, pages 58–59.

12. Paul Barber, *Vampires, Burial and Death*, 2nd edition, Columbia University Press, 2010, pages 5–20.

13. Alma Atonakou and Triarhou Lazaros, "Soul, Butterfly, Mythological Nymph: Psyche in Philosophy and Neuroscience," *Arquivos de Neuro-Psiquiatria* 75.3 (2017), pages 177–78.

14. Ernest Jones, "On the Nightmare," Hogarth Press, 1931, pages 75, 77–78.

15. Compare this night hag to Nicholas Powell's explanatory note on the actions and meanings of a night mare: "Nightmare comes from the [Germanic] Anglo-Saxon *neaht* or *nicht* (night) and *mara* (incubus or succubus). *Mara* is the agent form of the verb *merran* and literally means 'a crusher.'" For context see Powell's *Fuseli: The Nightmare*, Viking, 1973, especially pages 49–50.

16. Erik Butler, *Metamorphoses of the Vampire in Literature and Film*, Camden House, 2010, page 1.

17. Barbara Creed, *The Monstrous-Feminine*, Routledge, 1993

18. René Girard elaborates on the sacrificial substitutes in *Violence and the Sacred* (1972).

19. George Agamben, *Homo sacer: Sovereign Power and Bare Life*, translated by Daniel Heller-Roazen, Stanford University Press, 1995.

20. Jack Zipes, "Unfathomable Baba Yagas," *Baba Yaga*, edited by Sibelan Forrester, et al., University of Mississippi Press, 2013, pages vii–viii.

21. Sibelan Forrester, et al., editor, *Baba Yaga*, University of Mississippi Press, 2013.

22. I have written extensively on this topic in Tatjana Aleksić *The Sacrificed Body: Balkan Community Building and the Fear of Freedom*, University of Pittsburgh Press, 2013.

23. Butler, cited above, page 42.

24. Butler, cited above, page 2.

Unqueering Child Vampire Love in *Let the Right One In*

JAMES AUBREY

Let the Right One In is promoted on its American DVD case as "Best. Vampire film. Ever." (*Washington Observer*).[1] For once the claim is not just commercial hyperbole but indeed reflects a wide consensus among critics and audiences. More than most other vampire films this one, from Sweden in 2008, is melancholy in tone, even grim, with a pair of complex, sympathetic characters at its center—one a twelve-year-old boy and the other a girlish vampire who appears to be the same age. Along with *Psycho* and *The Exorcist*, *Let the Right One In* has also been listed as one of the "Top Five Scary Movies" ever, but that claim is dubious because the film's appeal is not in its scares or its thrills but in its subtle characterizations in a realistic style, without the usual sensationalism and supernaturalism of the vampire film genre.[2] No capes or fangs in this film but, instead, a vampire that plays with puzzles and doesn't like to kill. It's the human boy next door who has violent urges, plays with a knife, and keeps a crime scrapbook.

The film opens with illuminated snow falling in darkness, an appropriate setting for a *noir*-ish film set in Sweden, land of long winter nights. The shooting locations in and around the identifiable Stockholm suburb of Blackeberg help to establish a realist aesthetic—"dirty realism," one critic has called it.[3] It's not that the town center is unclean or run down, it's just unbeautiful. Twelve-year-old Oskar (Kåre Hedebrant) lives with his mother in a beige apartment complex that another critic has described as a Soviet-era "housing blocks ... that convey the sense of a failed community," with "'a living-dead look of its own.'"[4] In the first scene Oskar, in his underwear, silently looks out his bedroom window at the snow. Outside, underneath, someone pauses

Let the Right One In (*Låt den rätte komme in*, 2008). The Swedish publicity poster features the symbolic raised hand, often pressed against a wall or a glass barrier between human and vampire (Photofest).

to urinate while a man and a child move in and immediately put up a poster over their window in the apartment next to Oskar's. Within minutes we see the man go out and kill a random passer-by and start to drain his blood into a jerry can; however, he is interrupted and, in his hurry to flee, loses the contents. Once he has returned to the apartment, Oskar hears angry shouting through the wall. The next evening, when it is already dark in northern latitudes during the winter, Oskar's mother is hesitant to let him go outside to play because of the previous night's murder—a warning that immediately precedes the appearance in the courtyard of the girl from next door, standing on a climbing structure. She is lightly dressed for the freezing conditions and emotionally cold in her greeting: "Just so you know, I can't be your friend." The boy professes not to care. Despite their declarations of separateness, they become friends when they discover a mutual interest in puzzling, over a Rubik's Cube. When Oskar tells the girl, named Eli (Lina Leandersson), that he is twelve years old, she tells him that she also is twelve but doesn't know when she was born, only that she has been "twelve for a long time." That remark and her companion's blood collecting and the blocking of light into their apartment window make evident to the audience what Oskar doesn't yet guess: Eli must be some kind of vampire.

The audience is also learning that Oskar is a lonely, unhappy child. In the first scene at his school, he is pushed against his locker by another student, who calls him "piggy" and flicks his nose. In a later scene, outside, the violence

Let the Right One In (*Låt den rätte komme in*, 2008). **Oskar (Kåre Hedebrant, right) and Eli (Lina Leandersson) are lonely tweens (except that Eli has been "twelve for a long time") who find at first companionship, then safety, and finally love and revenge against a hostile environment—in something like the spirit of Romeo and thirteen-year-old Juliet, who are quoted at one point in the film. Here Oskar has awakened Eli in time for her to have attacked her would-be killer, after which they are about to exchange a (bloody) kiss for the first time.**

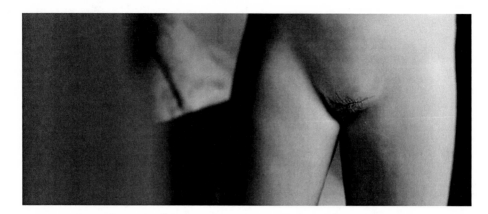

Let the Right One In (*Låt den rätte komme in*, 2008). The only indication in the film adaptation that Eli in the novel was once a boy is a ¼-second shot of scar tissue in his genital area. The significance of that glimpse does not otherwise discourage most viewers, who perceive the pre-pubescent romance of boy and vampire to be heterosexual—a view that the film does not otherwise discourage.

intensifies as Oskar is struck repeatedly by several boys with a switch. At home Oskar's divorced mother seems to enjoy brushing her teeth with him, but usually she is exasperated with him over something or other. He has some fun on a weekend with his divorced father at his house away from the town, but their good times are interrupted when the father's drinking buddy shows up, prompting Oskar to leave and hitchhike back to the apartment. His parents show no awareness that Oskar feels alienated, harbors violent fantasies, and maintains a scrapbook of crime puzzles and advertisements for weapons. However, as viewers come to understand his feelings of rejection, they also overlook Oskar's potential sociopathy. As events play out, Eli becomes Oskar's friend and protector and rescues him from the bullies, tearing them to pieces in a climactic scene at the local swimming pool, where they are trying to drown Oskar. But this is not a simple tale of revenge. Oskar and Eli are lonely, complex characters—not simple markers for violent conflict. By the end of the film the isolation and bullying become subordinated to a kind of love, as the two kiss for the first time and, in the last scene, are running off together, leaving Blackeberg behind. Eli has learned to value a human as a friend rather than as an accomplice or a victim; Oskar has learned to value a vampire as a friend and prospective lover. Both seem to have learned that partnerships— even erotic ones—can come in odd forms. Thus the film is layered: generically it is a coming of age story with a vampire aspect and a revenge plot that becomes, ultimately, a love story.

  Let the Right One In is based on the 2004 vampire novel *Låt den rätte komme in*, by John Ajvide Lindqvist, his first novel.[5] Director Tomas Alfredson invited Linqvist to write the screenplay for the film adaptation—not always a good idea because writers often don't understand the visual medium. Wisely, Alfredson insisted on certain changes to the story for the two-hour, commercial adaptation he envisioned.[6] In the novel, for example, Oskar has a friend, Tommy, whose elimination from the film simplifies the story and makes Oskar seem more lonely. Another change was the elimination of a prolonged, sensational episode in the novel after Eli's older companion, who has allowed Eli to feed on him as he is dying, revives at the morgue as a vampire with an erection, who stalks Eli and attempts to rape her until his heart is ripped out by Tommy.[7] This episode would certainly have distracted from the main story and subplots, and its elimination helped keep the film's tone serious.

Another change from the novel that made the story more realistic was to have Eli seem like a believable, sad twelve-year old. She appears prepubescent, without breasts or body hair. Her pupils can alter strangely, but she does not display any of the conventional female vampire features such as fangs or voluptuousness, nor do we see her shift shape into, say, a bat. Her abilities seem preternatural rather than supernatural. She says that she can fly, but she is never shown doing so. She is shown to be strong and quick, adept at climbing a building or a tree—but some humans also can do that. There is a faint, hardly audible sound of wings from off-camera during two scenes, but Eli is never shown in flight, which would have undercut viewer identification with her essentially human character. Showing the dismemberment of the bullies from under the water allows a viewer to imagine that she might just be dragging them along the side of the pool rather than flying, as in the novel, where Eli can evidently grow wings. The penultimate page describes blood on the ceiling of the pool, as if "made by someone who was ... flying"—as if "Oskar Eriksson had been rescued by an angel."[8] Linking Eli with traditional beings that fly is a rhetorical move that Alfredson's film wisely plays down to the point of disappearance, with the result that Eli remains a realistic looking girl, whose vampire characteristics allow her to remain almost human, subject to indigestion, loneliness, or even to death by sunlight or a knife to the heart.[9] Oskar is made to seem even more vulnerable, with a quiet voice, an awkward gait, and a downward gaze. He even has a persistently runny nose, which the filmmakers could easily have eliminated. Much of the appeal of *Let the Right One In* can be attributed to this naturalistic approach, without the sensational fangs and other bodily transformations of most vampire movies, thus enabling the spectator to become sutured more deeply into the film's world.

Eli's origin as a vampire is not addressed in the film. Except for vampire traditions, there is no reason to suppose that Eli is an undead revenant from the grave but, as is customary in vampire lore, she evidently must feed periodically on human blood, and if Eli does not subsequently break her victim's neck—if the victim is not drained or killed but only bitten—they will turn into a vampire—as happens to the minor character Virginia (Ika Nord), who chooses to die by exposing herself to sunlight rather than to live on as a vampire. Eli evidently contends with similar scruples, killing for blood only when she cannot arrange for someone else to kill for her, as viewers can infer from the angry tone she takes with Håkan when he returns from his murder without blood for her. Unlike traditional vampires—more like Anne Rice's reluctant vampire Louis—Eli has a conscience, a fact that further humanizes her in the mind of a reader or spectator. There is, however, one shot—one moment in the film that connects Eli with a flashback in the novel that provides the history that is absent from the film. The shot is about ¼ of a second in duration, a close-up shot of Eli's genital area, observed by Oskar as he spies on her after she has taken a shower and is putting on a dress. If one pauses to examine this shot (of a sculpture, not of the actress), it is clear that the area where Eli's penis was, is now jagged scar tissue—not pubic hair, as a first-time viewer might mistakenly believe. Eli is a castrated, penisectomied, transvestite male. The novel explains that his name was Elias when, two hundred years before, he was unsexed by a man in a wig performing some sort of ritual with a bowl of blood.[10] The novel doesn't explain how this 18th-century surgical mutilation has turned Elias to an unaging vampire; perhaps the man was himself a vampire and also bit his victim. Nor does the novel explain why Elias decided subsequently to present himself as a female. Perhaps a girlish appearance aided in the luring of victims. Perhaps he always had felt more like a girl. The film retains only a momentary glimpse of the mutilated genital area to hint at Eli's original, mysterious transformation to a vampire. In any case, the shot goes by so quickly that most viewers miss its implications, but it exists, and one implication is clear: Eli is queer in multiple ways, and the romantic attraction between Oskar and Eli is queer love, even if Oskar wouldn't understand what that means. For most viewers the characters are thought to be boy and girl, and the film is generally received as a heteronormative love story, felt to be more straight than queer. If Alfredson had intended otherwise, he needed to develop Eli's backstory—as Lindqvist does in his novel, which not only explains the transsexual aspect of Eli's character but reinforces it with a stylistic move: immediately following Eli's unsexing in flashback, Lindqvist switches pronoun references to Eli from the feminine *hun* to the masculine *han*, from that point onward.[11] This aspect of the novel may reflect what seems to be a particular interest in Sweden in gender dynamics and politics; by the late twentieth century enough Swedes had adopted the gender-neutral pronoun *hen* in place of the gender specific pronouns *han* and *hun* that *hen* was added to the National Encyclopedia in 2011.[12] Alfredson's decision to include the brief genital shot in the film may reflect a wish to pay tribute to Swedish progressive thinking about sex and gender, or it may have been an homage to Lindqvist's novel.

Lindqvist's interest in sexual dynamics is further evidenced in his novel, where Eli's older companion's character is developed more fully. His name is Håkan, and in the second chapter of the book he is described picking up a young boy for oral sex. The reader then learns that Håkan first met Eli on a playground only two years before and has been providing her with blood in exchange for her occasional "tenderness."[13] Their relationship is similar to that of Humbert and twelve-year-old Lolita, the title character in Nabokov's 1955 novel, who manipulates her older companion with sexual favors.[14] In the film adaptation, however, Håkan can seem to be a protective, fatherly figure, whom Eli pretends is her "*papa*" when she asks for him at the hospital. The only hint of Håkan's possible sexual attraction to Eli is when Håkan expresses jealousy over Eli's friendship with Oskar: "Could you not see that boy tonight?" he asks, and Eli responds with a caress to his face. At that point, early in the film, we know only that this middle-aged man is obtaining blood for a young girl, who might be his daughter, so Håkan's objection could seem to be merely that of a protective father. Director Alfredson has acknowledged that he did not want the novel's pedophilia theme retained in the film adaptation because "it would have taken up too much space" in the narrative.[15] As a result, however, many viewers assume that Håkan has been Eli's protector for a long time, perhaps since he also was twelve. Alfredson has also said that that interpretation of the character wasn't something he had in mind, but that he likes the idea. The 2010 American re-make of the film, with the more succinct title *Let Me In*, encourages this interpretation of Håkan's character by showing an old-looking photo booth picture of the girl vampire, Abby (Chloë Grace-Moretz) with a boy about her age, wearing glasses like those of "the father" (Richard Jenkins).[16] Alfredson's decision to eliminate Håkan's homosexual pedophilia makes both him and Eli more sympathetic to both straight and gay audiences—and makes the film more commercial, of course.[17]

"Be me, a little," Eli urges Oskar, after he is injured by the bullies at his school. She reminds him that he was fantasizing about violence when she met him, and that he would hurt the others if he could. Eli promises to help him if he will hit back harder than he has been hit. Subsequently, during an ice skating excursion, Oskar strikes out against Connie, the chief bully, by hitting him in the ear with a stick—a weapon that recalls the switch used by the bullies to punish Oskar, earlier. Simultaneously, the frozen body of Jocke, an earlier victim of Eli, is discovered in the ice. This narrative juxtaposition of the two victims could be a hint that Eli is deliberately grooming Oskar to be violent on her behalf, as her next provider—an interpretation that would make Eli less sympathetic but more realistic as a character with a self-serving motive to befriend Oskar. Or, a more charitable interpretation would be that her advice is well meant, from friend to friend: the classic advice to "stand up to bullies."

Despite the sociopathy of vampires, generally, the growing friendship between Oskar and Eli could be a model of sociability on a small scale—a twosome rather than a village society—but admirable for the mutual loyalty involved. The film certainly encourages identification with the two of them rather than with the larger society of Blackeberg, represented in the film by a group of friends: Lacke, Jocke, Gösta, Morgan, and Virginia. Four of the group are seen first at a restaurant, where they sociably invite Håkan to join them for a drink, because they think he would welcome companionship. They don't understand that he rejects their invitation and leaves because he is afraid of being linked with Eli and their previous attempts to procure blood. Håkan's wariness extends to his preparing to mutilate his face with acid if caught in one of his regular murders. The sociable warmth that Håkan is rejecting reflects a Scandinavian value known as *hygge*, a concept sometimes translated as "coziness"—an ideal in Swedish culture, and an antidote to the occasional stereotype of Nordic countries as dark, cold, and populated by brooding Hamlets.[18] When a friend of Oskar's father interrupts their game of tic-tac-toe, he comments that "It's nice and cozy in here." Oskar's father invites him in for drinks, which in Sweden customarily requires finishing the bottle. His father being oblivious to Oskar's need for filial companionship, Oskar feels rejected and leaves, hitchhiking back to Blackeberg and to his friend, Eli, for a private get-together in a dingy storage room below their apartments. The Blackeberg social group meanwhile is losing its would-be cozy relations. One evening at the restaurant, Virginia and Lacke reveal their troubles as they argue in public. Virginia storms out only to fall victim to an abortive attack by the hungry Eli. The next evening, having been bitten but not killed, Virginia begins to turn into a vampire. When she tries to rejoin the social group, this time at Gösta's flat, she is attacked by his cats, which evidently can sense her undead state of being, in keeping with the folkloric belief that "cats must be kept away from corpses, because they will attack them."[19] In keeping with the film's sub-agenda of social critique, Virginia's disruption of the get-together is an example of failed Swedish sociability. Like the ineffectual teachers and parents in the film, the barflies without a bar are a what John Calhoun has called "forgotten wards of a welfare state," and "a failed community."[20] Their dreary lives (and only two are still alive at the end) provide a context that serves to strengthen audience identification with outsiders such as Oskar and Eli.

Let the Right One In further invites this kind of nationalist social interpretation by having Eli wear a hat of blue and yellow, the colors of the Swedish flag, for what makes Sweden exceptional, according to the book *Scandinavians*, is its "very high degree of social cohesion."[21] One manifestation of that value is what has been called the *jante low*, or "law of jante," an idea about group behavior first put forward by a sociologist in the 1930s. This ethnographic principle holds that in Sweden community members pressure each other not to try to stand out from others.[22] Oskar violates this principle in school when, to the annoyance of his classmates, he correctly answers a difficult crime question posed by a visiting policeman. Connie turns around to stare at Oskar and bullies him in the hall after the class. The scene helps to establish that school constitutes Oskar's unhappy social world, and that the bullies are tribalist-types who exclude loners such as Oskar. The involvement later of Connie's older brother makes the bullying literally a family affair. The idea that schools reinforce *jante* sociability is further suggested by various images of forced team activities such as coed soccer, basketball, and a shot of an empty goal for European team handball. The ice skating excursion is shown as a highly organized social event, and even swimming class involves marching in place by Oskar, Martin, and some girls at the side of the pool. Later, alone in the water, Oskar faces a vigilante group conspiracy to punish him. His rescue by Eli is not only fighting back; the triple homicide constitute a declaration of their independence from society, and their revenge becomes a form of rebellion. Like some Swedish version of *Bonnie and Clyde*, Eli and Oskar's friendship turns into criminal love on the run, but it doesn't end in doom. Indeed, in a 2012 short story Lindqvist envisions Oskar and Eli thirty years later, in Barcelona, both still looking twelve years old, both obviously vampires.[23]

The title of the film is mildly problematical, both cumbersome and misleading. In this context, the phrase *let the right one in* refers to the European folkloric tradition that a vampire cannot enter a prospective victim's house unless invited in. This familiar vampire trope resonates with the moment in Chapter 2 of the novel *Dracula* when the title character greets Jonathan Harker: "Welcome to my house! Enter freely and of your own will!"[24] Leonard Wolf has suggested that the implied conditionality for a vampire to enter a prospective victim's house derives from the medieval belief that the Devil can transact only with willing customers, allowing them agency and, thus, denying them the excuse that "The devil made me do it."[25] Elizabeth Klinger notes that the prohibition also has the unfortunate tendency to encourage blaming of the victim.[26] The simplest explanation, of course, is that the film is merely adopting one of the conventions established by Dr. Van Helsing in Chapter 18 of Stoker's novel: "[Dracula] may not enter anywhere at the first, unless there be some one of the household who bid him to come; though afterward he can come as he please."[27] Lindqvist's novel and screenplay, however, aren't really about these entrances, so the title is misleading, but the film shows what might happen if a vampire were to cross the threshold to a victim's household anyhow, without an invitation. In the most dramatic scene in the film, Eli shows the result when she responds to Oskar's silent beckoning to her, to come into his apartment without having been expressly invited. Eli reluctantly but loyally enters and begins slowly to bleed from her pores and out her ears and eyes, until a horrified Oskar saves her from probable self-destruction by shouting, "You can come in!"[28] By this point in the story the two have already invited each other into their lives, so Eli is worthy of Oskar's invitation, but Lindqvist's story is not about which vampire is "right" rather than wrong to let in. When the two leave Stockholm at the end of the film, their future promises romance—so Eli is indeed the right one for Oskar. Contrary to the title, however, the story is not about how to choose a vampire.

Let the Right One In is also somewhat long for a film title. The phrase is a quotation from a Morrissey song about dreams rather than about vampires, originally translated into Swedish for the title of the novel: Låt den rätte komme in. Lindqvist provides the whole verse, in English, as an epigraph at the beginning of Part Five:

> Let the right one in
> Let the old dreams die
> Let the wrong ones go
> They cannot do
> What you want them to do.[29]

Lindqvist must have found the last line appealing because it resonates with the idea of a vampire crossing a threshold, particularly if the word one were understood to refer to a vampire. The last line also resonates: when Eli kills three of the four bullies at the swimming pool, she is doing what Oskar on some level would "want" her to "do"—as he has been fantasizing about doing since the opening scene of the film when he is seen stabbing a tree with his knife—that is, to exact violent revenge. In addition, by having shown Eli to be vulnerable at Oskar's threshold, Lindqvist heightens suspense over her fate, later, when Lacke finds her asleep in the bathtub (filled with blood in the novel) and prepares to kill her with his knife.[30] Perhaps the Morrissey line best applies to Oskar's dream-fantasy in which he is letting her into his life, is removing the invisible boundary between them by granting her permission to enter his apartment—and stop bleeding—so that she can do what he "want[s] her to do." Even if the title's relevance is questionable, as if the story were about choosing the right vampire, the Morrissey line must have inspired the scene of Eli's bleeding forth—perhaps the most original and memorable moment in the film, perhaps in all vampire cinema.

A secondary way of referring to the issue of threshold permission and, by extension, of exclusion and boundary crossing, is the pattern of images of hands in the film. The second shot of the film depicts Oskar in his bedroom, looking at the snow falling outside, with the palm of his hand leaving a print on the glass of the window. In a later scene, Eli puts her hand on the glass window of the swimming pool. This *mise en scène* will recur seven other times in the film, including hands against the wall between their rooms and during the doorway moment when Oskar holds up his hand to indicate the invisible boundary between his apartment and Eli standing outside, uninvited, waiting to come in. A repeated image can constitute symbolic meaning, and these hands on the invisible boundary separating them seems to represent the existential boundary between any of us and others—not just between Oskar and his classmates or Oskar and his parents or Oskar and Eli. After their mutual trust develops, Oskar asks Eli to confirm their friendship by cutting the palms of their hands with Oskar's knife and pressing their wounds together, symbolically exchanging blood with one another in a bloody handshake. When some of Oskar's blood ends up on the floor, Eli, who is hungry, cannot resist dropping to her hands and knees to lick up the blood, in a scene derived from the novel *Dracula* when Renfield similarly licks the blood of Dr. Seward off the floor of the asylum.[31] Eli regains self-control and runs off to avoid attacking Oskar out of blood lust, but there is symbolism in Oskar's idea of joining their hands in blood partnership. The glass blocking their hands elsewhere symbolizes the obstacles between Eli and Oskar, not only in the existential sense that everyone is alone, but also in the sense that humans and vampires are essentially distinct. On an interpersonal level, their separate hands represent potential friendship, or even potential love as indicated when Eli and Oskar lie chastely in bed together and she reaches her hand for his and holds it until they fall asleep. On an ethical level the film is about the individual need on some level to connect, even if doing so may violate Swedish social norms of inclusion and, by implication, exclusion. Oskar and Eli are extreme examples of a radical separateness that is transcended by the end of the film.

The developing love relationship between Oskar and Eli fundamentally drives the narrative. Notwithstanding vampire film theorist Jeffrey Weinstock's pronouncement that "the cinematic vampire is always about sex," Oskar and Eli are sexually innocent.[32] Both characters look pre-pubescent: neither has adult body hair. Their conversations about sexual matters sound amusingly naive. They don't engage in any sexual activity, not even in the scene where they are in bed together. Their ages are given as twelve—conventionally a pre-sexual age in other stories such as *Romeo and Juliet*, whose Juliet is thirteen when she and Romeo sleep together; or in *Lolita*, whose title character becomes sexually active at twelve but is represented as, at first precocious, then as a victim of pedophilia; or in *Moonrise Kingdom* where the twelve-year-old runaways do not become sexually intimate.[33] This kind of very young love is what interests Lindqvist and Alfredson, not adolescent vampire love, a popular trope since the 1992 *Buffy the Vampire Slayer*, whose eponymous high school cheerleader, pursued by an older male vampire, inspired a popular American television series.[34] Bella in *Twilight*, published in 2005, is seventeen and in high school and, like Eli and Oskar, sexually chaste, but her more advanced age introduces a sexual element to her love-longing that is absent from *Let the Right One In*.[35] That is not to say that Oskar and Eli are too young to be in love. Indeed, one study has argued that any longing for each other between children should be categorized as a form of queer love, outside of the heteronormative mainstream but on the spectrum of love possibilities, nonetheless.[36] Love between vampire children would be doubly queer, and Oskar and Eli's love would be triply queer since both are biologically male. In any case, by the end of the film, Oskar and Eli are in some kind of love. After Oskar has helped Eli dispatch Lacke in her bathroom, she embraces Oskar and they enjoy a lengthy, bloody but exquisitely romantic kiss. Their affection seems mutual. In the final scene (which is not in the novel) they are shown escaping on a train, in a private compartment, as Oskar affectionately taps out the Morse code for the word *puss*, Swedish for "little kiss," on the trunk in which Eli is concealed. In terms of the bullying-revenge subplot, Eli has not only rescued Oskar, Eli has taught him to channel his violent fantasies in a new direction as her partner and probable blood provider. Their future promises serial homicides, but viewers don't think about that. In terms of the love plot, the story has a happy ending.

Lindqvist evidently was inspired in part by Shakespeare, for the film and the novel both quote *Romeo and Juliet*, the classic tale of impermissible love between youngsters whose parents don't get along. After Oskar and Eli have spent the night together, while Oskar is still asleep, Eli writes him a good-bye note quoting Romeo's remark to Juliet as he is leaving her room at dawn: "I must be gone and live, or stay and die."[37] Eli writes in Swedish, of course: "ATT FLY ÄR LIVET, MEN AT DRÖJA DÖDEN—DIN, ELI," but the English subtitles reproduce Shakespeare's English from Act 3, Scene 5, line 11—minus the closing, "Yours, Eli." A literate vampire is unusual.[38] Perhaps over the centuries Eli has acquired some book learning along with the money and valuables she has obtained from victims, but more likely Lindqvist wanted to remind readers that his story has roots in literature, that his characters are not embodiments of good and evil in some spiritual war, but are more like the children of early modern families in a pre-modern feud: Romeo and Juliet also were misfits in an adult culture.

Like a vampire, the 2004 story of *Let the Right One In* has an afterlife. In 2007 the novel *Låt den rätte komme in* was translated from Swedish into English by Ebba Segerberg, with the more succinct and more apt translation of the title as *Let Me In* in place of the Morrissey line. However, in 2008, when the film was released with English subtitles for distribution outside Sweden, the title was translated literally into English as *Let the Right One In*.

Perhaps Lindqvist preferred the literal translation of the title, or perhaps the subtitle writer merely translated the Swedish title literally without considering the earlier translated book's title in English, *Let Me In*. When the film became successful, however, St Martin's Press changed the title of the English paperback book to match the movie title, *Let the Right One In*, and put Lina Leandersson as Eli on the cover. In 2010, when Magnolia Pictures remade the Swedish film as an American adaptation, set in New Mexico with Chloë Grace Moretz as the Eli character, Abby, the filmmakers added a scene that normalizes the older man (Jenkins), as the Oskar character, Owen (Kodi Smit-McPhee), discovers an old photo-booth print of Abby with a boy her age, evidently meant to be "the father" some forty years before as Eli's committed partner (not a pedophile). The remake also omits the brief genital image, thus unqueering the story even further. Because the remake had adopted the original English book title *Let Me In*, to tie in with the new film's release, St. Martin's again re-titled the novel as *Let Me In* and changed the cover to show two children holding hands. In 2011 a graphic novel-prequel to the American remake called *Let Me In: Crossroads* was published, with Abby and the father accumulating corpses in an old house in Indiana. A chapter from this graphic novel was included with the 2011 DVD release of *Let Me In*. In 2013 St. Martin's published a short story-sequel by Lindqvist to his own novel titled "Let the Old Dreams Die," in which a detective assigned to the swimming pool murders of 1982 comes across a photo of Eli and Oskar taken thirty years later in Barcelona; they both still look twelve years old, so Eli has evidently turned Oskar into a companion vampire.[39] In 2014 the Scottish National Theatre in Edinboro produced a stage version of *Let the Right One In* with a script by Jack Thorne that moves the story from the suburbs to the woods, where Eli hides and Oskar finds refuge. In 2015 St. Ann's Warehouse produced the same play in Brooklyn using actors who appear much older than twelve—more like twenty, judging from the photo of them that accompanied a *New Yorker* review.[40] As with Bella and Edward in *Twilight* film series, the original chaste relationship between Eli and Oskar has been developed into a story of mature, heteronormative love between lonely eccentrics who choose to live as vampires. The 2014 New Zealand mockumentary *What We Do in the Shadows* contains what is surely an homage to the book version of *Let the Right One In* when an adult vampire at a bus stop asks two vampire girls who appear to be about Oskar's and Eli's age whether they are planning to kill any child molesters that night. One replies, "Yeah, we're meeting a pedophile."[41] In 2017 Turner Network Television planned to re-tell the story as a television limited series starring Kristina Frøseth (age 22), but the production was cancelled shortly before the pilot was to air that August. The decision probably was commercially based, perhaps out of concern that vampires were going out of fashion given that *The Vampire Diaries* had ended earlier that year and *The*

Originals was about to conclude its 92-episode run. Nevertheless, the existence of an audience for vampire stories evidently remained sufficient for FX to go ahead in 2019 with its ten-episode television series *What We Do in the Shadows*, continuing the premise of the 2014 film but adding a major female character and moving the setting from New Zealand to New York.

In any case, more than other versions of the story, the 2008 film *Let the Right One In* creates the darkest mood with convincingly natural, prepubescent characters playing out a realistic, queer but emotionally straight narrative in a tight, two-hour format. Like Kubrick's *The Shining*, Alfredson's *Let the Right One In* is brilliant film adaptation of a lesser novel, and the best telling of its story—so far.

NOTES

1. Tomas Alfredson, *Let the Right One In*, Magnolia Home Entertainment, 2009.
2. "Top Five Scary Movies," *The Metropolitan*, MSU Denver, 29 October 2015, page 14.
3. J.M. Tyree, "Warm-blooded: *True Blood* and *Let the Right One In*," *Film Quarterly* 63.2 (2009–10): 31–37.
4. John Calhoun, "Childhood's End: 'Let the Right One In' and Other Deaths of Innocence," *Cineaste* 35.1: 29; Michael Sragow is quoted by Rochelle Wright in "Vampire in the Stockholm Suburbs: *Let the Right One In* and Genre Hybridity," *Journal of Scandinavian Cinema* 2.3 (2010): 65.
5. John Ajvide Lindqvist, *Let the Right One In*, translated by Ebba Segerberg, St. Martin's, 2007.
6. Tomas Alfredson and John Ajvide Lindqvist, commentary track on *Let the Right One In*, Blu-ray disc from Momentum Pictures, UK, 2010.
7. Lindqvist, pages 389–96. The idea of a revenant with an erection has a basis in folklore, based on the tumescence of corpses in certain stages of decomposition, described by Paul Barber in *Vampires, Burial, and Death*, Yale University Press, 1986, page 9.
8. Lindqvist, page 471. Serinity Young, in *Women Who Fly: Goddesses, Witches, Mystics, and other Airborne Females*, Oxford University Press, 2018, traces the history of the idea of flying females, including angels (but not vampires).
9. Alfredson, cited above, claims to have interviewed "thousands" of prospective actors to play the twelve-year olds. Casting a girl as Eli helped to generate a sense that she is female, hints to the contrary notwithstanding.
10. Lindqvist, pages 347, 351–54.
11. Lindqvist, page 307.
12. Nina Bahadur, "Swedish Gender-neutral Pronoun, 'Hen,' Added to Country's National Encyclopedia," www.huffingtonpost.com/2013/04/11.
13. Lindqvist, pages 59, 215–16.
14. Vladimir Nabokov, *Lolita*, Putnam, 1955, page 67, establishes Lolita's age as twelve.
15. Commentary track, cited above.
16. Matt Reeves, director, *Let Me In*, Magnolia Pictures, 2010. The title *Let Me In* is the original English translation of the Swedish title *Låt den rätte komme in*. The publisher changed the title to *Let the Right One In* to tie in with the film when it became popular. The title was changed back to *Let Me In* when the American version came out, for the same reason. The novel's title is now, once again, that of the Swedish movie, *Let the Right One In*.
17. Jeffrey Weinstock has observed that "there has been little tolerance—in keeping with cinematic history in general—for *male* homoeroticism" [italics in original], in *The Vampire Film: Undead Cinema*, Columbia University Press, page 51.
18. Meik Wiking, *The Little Book of Hygge: Danish Secrets to Happy Living* (HarperCollins, 2017), page 6.; Tom Shippey, "Friends of Darkness and the Cold: Scandinavia: The

Contradictory Lands of Angst, Sex and Social Cohesion," review of *Scandinavians: In Search of the Soul of the North*, by Robert Ferguson, *Times Literary Supplement* 2 December 2016, page 5.

19. Barber, cited above, page 27.

20. Calhoun, cited above, page 29.

21. Tyler Marshall, "Stifling Penchant: Conformity—a Must in Scandinavia," *Los Angeles Times* 14 December 1988: no page, articles.latimes.com/1988-12-14/news/mn-278_1_welfare state.

22. Shippey, cited above.

23. John Ajvide Lindqvist, "Let the Old Dreams Die," *Let the Old Dreams Die,* translated by Ebba Segerberg, St. Martin's, 2013, pages 371–93.

24. Bram Stoker, *Dracula*, edited by Glennis Byron, Broadview Press, 1998, page 46.

25. Leonard Wolf, editor, *The Essential Dracula*, ibooks, 2004, page 223n.

26. Leslie Klinger, editor, *The New Annotated Dracula*, Norton, 2008) page 43n.

27. Stoker, cited above, page 279.

28. Lindqvist, *Let the Right One In*, cited above, pages 344–45. There is a precedent in the USA-Mexico co-production *Alucarda* (1975), when blood flows from the eyes of a nun who is distressed to see her female ward participating in a Satanic orgy. The ward's name, Alucarda, is Dracula spelled backward, with an added Spanish feminine ending.

29. Morrissey, "Let the Right One Slip In," quoted in Lindqvist, page 441.

30. Eli sleeps during the day in her bathtub, under a blanket, rather than in a coffin. Lindqvist's idea that the bathtub would be full of blood perhaps derives from the legend of Countess Elizabeth Bathory, who bathed in the blood of young virginal girls to preserve her youth. There is also a precedent in Sheridan Le Fanu's short story *Carmilla* (1871) in which a vampire's coffin, when opened, is found to be filled with blood.

31. Stoker, 177–78. The scene where Renfield licks up Dr. Seward's blood from the floor has been replicated in many vampire films, most excessively in Andy Warhol's *Blood for Dracula* (directed by Paul Morrissey, 1974), where Dracula himself drops to the floor to lick up the hymeneal blood of a virgin recently deflowered there.

32. Weinstock, cited above, page 7.

33. William Shakespeare, *Romeo and Juliet,* Bedford/St. Martin's, 2003, pages 53–54 (Act 1, Scene 3, line 13), establishes Juliet's age as "not fourteen" when she has her first sexual experience (with Romeo), as her nurse swears by her own "maidenhead at twelve year old" (line 3); Lolita's age is twelve (Nabokov, cited above), but her sexual activity is to be considered premature; in *Moonrise Kingdom* (2012) two twelve-year-olds run away and camp out together for several days but do not have sex.

34. *Buffy the Vampire Slayer* began as a film in 1992 starring Kristy Swanson; the subsequent success on television of *Sabrina the Teenage Witch* in 1996 probably helped inspire the nine-year television series *Buffy the Vampire Slayer* (1997–2005) and its spinoff, *Angel* (1999–2004), which probably helped inspire the novel *Twilight* (2005) and its sequels, and the five film adaptations (2008–2012), which in turn probably helped inspire the television serials *The Originals* (2008–2013) and *The Vampire Diaries* (2009–2012).

35. Stephanie Meyer, *Twilight* (Little Brown), 2005. In the 2008–2012 film series based on the book, the lovers marry and have sex and have a child (in that order).

36. Kathryn Bond Stockton, *The Queer Child: Or Growing Sideways in the Twentieth Century* (Duke University Press, 2009).

37. Shakespeare, cited above, page 111 (Act 3, Scene 5, line 11).

38. Another exception would be the vampire Eve in the film *Only Lovers Left Alive* (2013), who over the centuries has become widely read in various languages and in one scene is shown speed-reading Arabic.

39. Lindqvist, "Let the Old Dreams Die," cited above, pages 371–93.

40. Gareth McConnell, photo of Rebecca Benson and Cristian Ortega in the stage play, review of *Let the Right One In*, *The New Yorker* 26 January 2015, page 7.

41. Jemaine Clement and Taika Waititi, directors, *What We Do in the Shadows*, Shadow Pictures, 2014. A mockumentary pretends to be a documentary, is not necessarily mocking the subject matter.

Museological Horror
in *Ganja and Hess*
and *Da Sweet Blood of Jesus*

CHERYL D. EDELSON

In a recent article published in *The Conversation*, Robin R. Means Coleman argues that African Americans are enjoying a Golden Age of Black horror after enduring a hundred years of cinematic misrepresentation and marginalization. Means Coleman, the author of *Horror Noire: Blacks in American Horror Films from the 1890s to Present*, argues that while "Black actors have always had a role in horror films, ... something different is taking place today: the re-emergence of true black horror films. Rather than simply including black characters, many of these films are created by blacks, star blacks or focus on black life and culture."[1] This is a far cry from the erasure of black artists in early twentieth century horror films and the relegation of African Americans to peripheral roles in classical Hollywood horror movies—primitive jungle natives (one thinks of *King Kong*, 1933) and comic relief on the part of Mantan Moreland, Willie Best, and others. Few-and-far-between exceptions such as *Chloe, Love Is Calling You* (1934) and *Monster from Green Hell* (1957) look forward to *Night of the Living Dead* (1968), George Romero's indie zombie flick that stars Duane Jones as a resilient and courageous black protagonist who leads a group of survivors against hordes of the undead. *Blacula* (1972) and *Sugar Hill* (1974) continued this trend in the 1970s, "treat[ing] blacks as whole and full subjects." Although *The Shining* (1980) represents the persistence of sacrificial black characters, and *Angel Heart* (1987) and *The Serpent and the Rainbow* (1988) regress into the exoticism that plagued midcentury Hollywood horror, the last two decades have seen a black horror film renaissance. Filmmakers such as Ernest Dickerson (director of *The Purge, Bones, Demon Knight*) and Rusty Cundieff (*Tales from the*

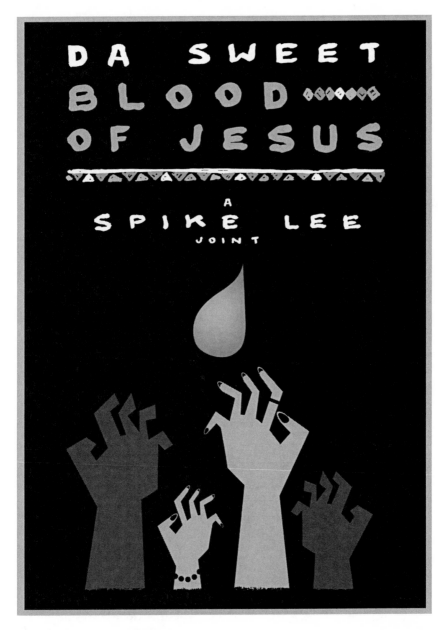

Da Sweet Blood of Jesus (2014). Directed by Spike Lee, this film is a re-make of *Ganja and Hess* (1973), also with African American lead actors. Lee's title is an homage to the 1940 film *The Blood of Jesus*, directed by Spencer Williams (Photofest).

Hood and *Tales from the Hood 2*) have continued the gains of the Blaxploitation era and inspired a new generation of black horror directors, including Meosha Bean, Nikyatu Jusu and Deon Taylor. The contemporary Golden Age is nowhere more clear than in the work of Jordan Peele, who directed the Academy Award winning *Get Out* (2017) as well as the Dopplegänger film *Us* (2019). Bearing in mind these achievements, Means Coleman states, "The horror genre is maturing and becoming more imaginative and inclusive—in who can play hero and antihero, and who gets to be the monster and savior."

Means Coleman also celebrates Bill Gunn's 1973 *Ganja and Hess,* an arthouse horror film that was suppressed in Hollywood despite winning the Critics' Choice Award at Cannes. In what has become a paradigmatic story of the African American experience in Hollywood, Gunn was hired by Kelly-Jordan Enterprises to write "Vampires in Harlem," a Blaxploitation flick in the "vein" of *Blacula.* As suggested above, *Blacula,* directed by African American filmmaker William Crain, has been recognized as an important milestone of Black horror cinema. In *Ganja and Hess,* however, Gunn went beyond Blaxploitation conventions to make an avant garde vampire thriller that stands, in Means Coleman's words, as a "gorgeous and deliberative treatise on race, class, mental illness and addiction." Lauded by film critics and quoted in movies such as Julie Dash's *Daughters of the Dust* (1991), *Ganja and Hess* was remade by Spike Lee in 2014 as *Da Sweet Blood of Jesus.* Taken together, *Ganja and Hess* and *Da Sweet Blood of Jesus* stand as landmark African American vampire films that also engage the conventions of the lesser known subgenre of museological horror. Lee's controversial remake of *Ganja and Hess* reads as a work of museological cinema that further illuminates the inner workings and significance of *Ganja and Hess.* In keeping with its allusive title, *Da Sweet Blood of Jesus* interprets *Ganja and Hess* as a reworking of Spencer Williams's *The Blood of Jesus* (1940), the most famous and successful race film of all time and one that has itself been read as an influential work of Black horror. In doing so, however, Lee also integrates allusions to Roy Ward Baker's *The Vampire Lovers* (1970), a Hammer Horror production often regarded as the most famous example of the lesbian vampire film.

Ganja and Hess stars Duane Jones, of *Night of the Living Dead* fame, as Hess Green, a well-to-do Doctor of Geology and Anthropology researching the ancient African Myrthian people. Dr. Green is working on behalf of the Institute of Archaeology, which gives Green an assistant, George Meda (played by Gunn himself). Meda turns out to be an extremely volatile figure: after annoying Hess over dinner with flattery and off-color stories, Meda later attempts to hang himself from a tree on Hess's property. Later that night, Meda breaks into Hess's bedroom and stabs his host before shooting himself with a revolver. Hess awakens from the attack to a new and terrifying situation: he craves blood and slakes his thirst on Meda's corpse (which he sub-

Da Sweet Blood of Jesus (2014). Dr. Hess Greene (Stephen Tyrone Williams) examines the ancient African knife that he has been stabbed with, which has turned him into a vampire (Photofest).

sequently stores in his basement freezer). Meda has stabbed Hess with a Myrthian dagger from the anthropologist's personal collection; the weapon transmits a pathogen that transforms Hess into an immortal blood-addict (the word "vampire" is never used, and many of the common vampire conventions such as fangs and aversion to daylight are missing from this film). In order to feed his new habit, Hess raids blood banks and preys upon prostitutes, pimps, and the impoverished. When Meda's wife Ganja (Marlene Clark) shows up at Hess's doorstep, the two get acquainted and begin an amorous relationship. After their marriage, Hess uses the Myrthian dagger to transform his lover into a blood-addict like himself. The couple reach new heights of predation, inviting a young man into a sexual interlude with Ganja before feeding on him and dumping his body (though Ganja worries that he is still alive). After a time, Hess becomes disgusted with his blood addiction and learns from Myrthian texts that one may be freed of the condition by accepting Jesus and then exposing oneself to the shadow of the cross. While Hess goes through with this ritual, converting to Christianity at his chauffeur's church, Ganja opts out of suicide as salvation. She takes advantage of Hess's wealth to continue her predatory lifestyle. In a powerful concluding sequence, Ganja smiles at a young lover, the former victim who has indeed survived, running nude from the swimming pool to the house and leaping over the body of Hess's manservant Archie (Leonard Jackson).

Despite its recognition at Cannes, *Ganja and Hess* was re-edited and distributed under different titles (*Blood Couple, Double Possession, Black Evil,* and *Black Vampire*). The film was a box office failure, but an original print remained intact, available for individual screenings at the Museum of Modern Art. In 1980, Gunn's original was screened as *Ganja and Hess* at the Independent Black American Film Festival in Paris. Gunn was invited to speak at the screening. This rediscovery led to the film's eventual preservation and widespread distribution in the form Gunn intended.[2] Since that time, many critics, among them James Monaco, Mantia Diawara, Phyllis Klotman, Harrison M.J. Sherrod, Jerry Rafiki Jenkins, and many others have recognized the importance of *Ganja and Hess*. Ishmael Reed, who collaborated with Gunn on the film *Personal Problems* (1980), describes *Ganja and Hess* as "a successful and surrealist subversion of the horror genre, with some interesting flashbacks to Africa and the idea of a black psychiatrist, which is different from the kind of role that blacks get to play in Hollywood ... [it is] one of the most beautiful and unusual films ever produced in the United States."[3] Resonating with Reed's contemporary work *Mumbo Jumbo* (1972), *Ganja and Hess* not only evokes the cinematic vampire but also the academic character of the archaeologist/collector and the concomitant setting of the museum (in its public and domestic iterations). In this sense, *Ganja and Hess* joins (and outdoes) other horror pretexts in questioning and subverting the Enlightenment project of hegemonic control through appropriation and collection (a project that tends to be valorized in the genres of adventure and the detective story).

Museums have frequently appeared in Gothic fiction and film as a stage for terrifying ruptures of normality. H.P. Lovecraft's short story "The Horror in the Museum" (1933) is an early example of this sensibility; the tradition continues in films such as *The Mummy* (1932), *It!* (1966), *Damien: The Omen II* (1978), and *The Relic* (1997). Within Enlightenment ideology the emergence of a monstrous or polymorphic Other presents a direct affront to and attack upon the museum's archival regime. In "Of Other Spaces," Michel Foucault identifies museums as a form of the heterotopia; in contrast to idiosyncratic collections of the seventeenth century, heterotopic museums and libraries derive from "the will to enclose in one place all times, all epochs, all forms, all tastes, the idea of constituting a place of all times that is itself outside of time and inaccessible to its ravages...."[4] Arguing that museums cannot be confined to one epoch or ideology, Beth Lord sums up this interpretation of the museum as "an Enlightenment institution whose power to collect and display objects is a function of capitalism and imperialism, and whose power to form individuals is exercised through the careful ordered deployment of knowledge within an institutionally controlled and publicly monitored space."[5] As Ruth Hoberman argues, however, Museum Gothic dramatizes "the tension between the museum's power to create order and the disruptive potential of the objects" displayed: "Placed within the static confines of the glass case, these objects seem silenced, the history of their production and cultural role supplanted by the museum's classificatory system." In Museum Gothic tales, the narrative conflict arises from the struggle between the heroic curator and the disruptive object—including the irresistible allure that the object exerts upon various antagonists: "The curator," Hoberman suggests, "unlike the financially suspect dealer and the sexually suspect collector, provides the benevolent oversight no longer available from an impoverished aristocracy."[6] In this sense, the Museum Gothic resonates with the museological dimension of cinema itself. As Ella Shohat and Robert Stam point out, "cinema has not simply articulated itself as the product of science, but has also positioned itself as the practitioner of a new interdisciplinary science that could make 'other' worlds accessible":

> It could chart a map of the world, like the cartographer; it could tell stories and chronicle events, like the historiographer; it could "dig" into the past of civilizations like, like the archaeologist; and it could narrate the customs and habits of exotic peoples, like the ethnographer.[7]

Shohat all but names cinema as a museological form that lays out the world in terms of Enlightenment regimes of display. Although in some measure complicit with this project, horror films also work to question and subvert museology, teasing out the latent unease associated with the museum and transforming its bright spaces into Gothic settings of fear and uncertainty. Freund's *The Mummy* is paradigmatic: in this Hollywood classic, the museum becomes an arena in which European academics struggle against a villain that embodies abjection and the irrational. But it isn't much of a contest, for Ardeth Bey (Boris Karloff) penetrates the defenses of the museum and continually uses this site as a staging area for his nefarious plans. Although there is a happy ending, it is not the Enlightenment heroes who win; the heroine Helen Grosvenor (Zita Johann) is saved by another supernatural entity, the goddess Isis. "As a colonial thriller, *The Mummy* fails," writes Caroline Siri Johnson, "The hegemony is pushed back in favor of the foreign undercurrent of female sexuality."[8]

Johnson compares *The Mummy* to Ishmael Reed's novel *Mumbo Jumbo*: "*Mumbo Jumbo* and *The Mummy* both radically undermine the existing canon of the white male media in subtle, pervasive and permanent ways: *Mumbo Jumbo* overtly and *The Mummy* inadvertently."[9] One of Reed's many subplots concerns a group of radical activisits, the "Mu'tafikah," dedicated to liberating stolen artifacts from New York City's Metropolitan Museum, which Reed renames the "Center of Art Detention." *Mumbo Jumbo* was published in 1972, the same year that *Ganja and Hess* was released; and in many ways, *Ganja and Hess* holds elements of both *The Mummy* and *Mumbo Jumbo*—it is a Museum Gothic vampire film that deploys radical techniques and thematics for a critique of Western Enlightenment culture. From its first sequences, *Ganja and Hess* engages museological horror. As a "Doctor of Geology" and "Doctor of Anthropology," Dr. Hess Green is firmly recognized as an Enlightenment protagonist devoted to discovery, acquisition, collection, and interpretation of cultural artifacts. His project of research on the fictional Myrthians of Africa represents a new take on a conventional motif—instead of white European academics unearthing and decoding African culture, we now have a Black man engaged in this pursuit. The gesture recalls Pauline Hopkins's novel *Of One Blood: Or, The Hidden Self* (1901–1903), in which an African American medical student participates in an archaeological dig in Ethiopia. This scenario becomes for Hopkins an opportunity to explore issues of Du Boisian "double consciousness."[10] While Hopkins pioneered use of the black archaeologist in Gothic/fantastic fiction, Gunn was perhaps the first filmmaker to feature an African American in a cinematic role of this kind. Like Hopkins, Gunn does not simply place the black character in a professional role historically reserved for whites; he goes beyond this tactic to use this characterization as a vehicle for complex and disturbing inquiries. On one hand, Hess represents the Afro-centrist gesture of claiming Enlightenment academia as a platform to redirect imperialist/colonialist social science (this in keeping with the example of Hopkins's characters). As such, however, Dr. Green also falls into complicity with the white power structure.

Consistent with these ambiguities, the museum in *Ganja and Hess* is not presented as an orderly and illuminated space but rather a shadowy maze. As Hess and Jack Sargent walk through the galleries, their conversation can only be heard in fragments that compete with Luther's voice-over narrative on the theological implications of Hess's situation. Moreover, we are treated to close-ups of Salvatore Albano's sculpture *The Fallen Angels, Or The Rebel Angels* (1893) and Chevalier Féréol de Bonnemaison's painting *Young Woman Overtaken by a Storm* (1799)—the latter a portrait of suffering that dissolves into a close-up of Meda pointing his revolver into a mirror.[11] The images become symbolic reflections of the inner states of the characters; for example, the Bonnemaison painting immediately prefigures Meda's mounting psychological crisis. Later in the film, Hess has a nightmare in which Sargent and Meda, wearing garish masks, appear in a surreal version of the museum; the latter beckons to him and laughs. As Gisselle Liza Anatol suggests, this dream sequence represents "the Western study, acquisition, and implied objectification of ancient cultures" as opposed to the "lived experience and emotional connection to those cultures" indicated by the contiguous dream in which the Myrthian Queen (played by Mabel King) beckons to Hess.[12] But the nightmare version of the museum is not too different from its daytime exposition—it is clear that Hess suspects his participation in the dominant museology as a form of corruption or damnation.

As Hess leaves the museum with Meda, the camera dwells on a sign posted to the museum's gate: "The nucleus of this collection was assembled and donated by the anonymous arts recovery society." This signage refers to the efforts of Ivan C. Karp, an art dealer, later associated with Andy Warhol and pop-art, who founded the Anonymous Arts Recovery Society in an attempt to save architectural pieces from demolition. Beginning in 1966, he collaborated with the Brooklyn Museum to house, display, and preserve sculptures and other adornments that might otherwise be lost.[13] Gunn dwells on this signage in order to underscore the film's meditations on the politics of collection and display, a concern that also informs his treatment of Hess's mansion. Like many elites, Hess has used his wealth to create a private museum, one that comes to have even more pronounced Gothic overtones. Virtually every shot of Hess's home captures artwork and decor items collected from many world cultures, including those of Europe, Asia, Africa, and the United States. Hess's dinner with Ganja exemplifies the museological character of his home. Serenaded by Mabel King's "March Blues,"[14] Hess wines and dines Ganja surrounded by Chinese vases and African statues. Amid the crystal and silver of Hess's dinner table, we see a copy of *Afrique noire: Géographie, civilisations, histoire* (1958), a history of French colonial Africa by Marxist historian Jean Suret Canale. This set-dressing conveys a sense of the domestic collection that Hess has attempted: he gathers diverse artistic and intellectual works—radical Marxist scholarship on Africa side-by-side with the trappings of bourgeois wealth. While the Anonymous Arts Recovery Society rescues art objects without provenance, Hess strips his artifacts of their histories and contexts. Sherrod points out, this "Wunderkammer" is filled with objects that are "temporarily treated as ahistorical vessels devoid of any ethnic symbolism." He goes on to suggest that Hess collects people as well as inanimate objects. He stores the frozen body of Meda in his cellar and, as Ganja wryly jokes, Archie is tantamount to a plumbing fixture that "came with the house."[15] Under this reading, Ganja herself would seem to be another collectible. In a reversal of roles, however, Ganja and Hess trade places.

Writing on the domestic museum of Pierre Loti, Anthony Purdy argues, "If Loti is at home in the museum, it is because it is there that his life coheres and makes sense, that his collection collects him."[16] With its subjectively recontextualized objects, Hess's mansion is very much akin to Loti's heterotopic home, as Purdy describes it. In *Ganja and Hess*, however, the idea of the collection collecting the collector becomes horrifically realized when the Myrthian dagger, one of the "anonymous" artifacts that Hess has "recovered," becomes the instrument of his own objectification. For Sherrod, this item is the vampire's fang that colonizes Hess's body with disease and denudes him of his "ontological status as a human," a process suggestive of slavery.[17] In one sense, Hess goes right on collecting, snapping up Ganja as another acquisition and one that will help normalize his blood addiction. After forcibly converting Ganja into a vampire, Hess enjoys the spectacle of her having sex with the rec center director and feeding on his blood.

But this object d'art has a history and subjectivity that she will not yield. After she discovers Meda's body, Ganja shares her own past, which includes other attempts at objectification. As a child, Ganja was treated as a "disease"; but she vowed to turn this trope back on her mother: "And I think that day, I decided that I was a disease and I was gonna give her a full case of it, that whatever it was I was, she was gonna have it." Although she is visually associated with Hess's Beaux Arts and African statuary, Ganja demonstrates a high degree of agency; as in her relationship with her mother, Ganja refuses objectification—the collectible collects the collector by marrying him and assuming his wealth. When Hess decides to free himself through ritual suicide, Ganja stands by, declining to join her husband as he suffers the ultimate objectification. In the final scenes of the film, we find that Ganja has mourned Hess and moved on with her life. Reflecting on the final scene, in which Ganja watches her lover jump over the corpse of Archie, Diawara and Klotman interpret her as a "contemporary black woman ... tired of being subservient to the church and to black men": "She's glad that Meda and Hess, the self-destructive artist and the bourgeois patriarch, are gone.... She's in command."[18] Minding the context of museological horror, we might also see that Ganja the object has now become the collector as she assumes proprietorship of the domestic museum and enjoys the spectacle of one male acquisition cavorting over the body of another.

Citing Jewelle Gomez and other critics, Anatol approaches the conclusion of *Ganja and Hess* with ambivalence, noting, "It is ambiguous whether her [Ganja's] refusal [to join her husband] is to be read as an act of female independence and agency, or an act of betrayal of her life companion—another example of the untrustworthy black woman."[19] Differing opinions aside, it is undeniable that *Ganja and Hess* is an important work of African American cinema that has attracted a great deal of critical commentary. Perhaps the most memorable, if controversial, interpretive statement on *Ganja and Hess* comes to us in the form of Spike Lee's 2014 remake *Da Sweet Blood of Jesus*. Although there are some significant revisions, this movie so closely follows *Ganja and Hess* that Lee gave Bill Gunn co-writer credit. Dennis Leroy Kangalee has written, "Instead of remaking a haunting delicate film into a virtuosic, ironic 'art film,' why not simply just acknowledge the original? Is a remake necessary? Spike Lee would have done us all a favor if he had simply written a monograph on *Ganja and Hess* and called it a day."[20] Armond White goes further arguing that Lee has created a cinematic commentary that abuses his pretexts: "Impertinent Lee squeezes two classic films about African American life in his Afro-hipster vise: He rebukes the Southern gospel of Spencer Williams's 1941 *The Blood of Jesus* and travesties Bill Gunn's 1973 quasi-occult art film *Ganja and Hess*. Both movies, made for specialized audiences, explored spiritual aspiration within the struggle against racism. Lee works those personal, little-known films to show off his own celebrated rascality."[21] Invective notwithstanding, White is one of the few critics to recognize the importance of Williams's evangelical race film as another important pretext for *Da Sweet Blood of Jesus*. I would argue that *Da Sweet Blood of Jesus* operates as a self-reflexive work of museological horror, exhibiting and commenting on *The Blood of Jesus* and *Ganja and Hess* as well as a third pre-text: Roy Ward Baker's Hammer Horror film *The Vampire Lovers* (1970).

Like *Ganja and Hess*, *The Blood of Jesus* is at bottom the story of a couple: Razz Jackson (Spencer Williams) and his wife Sister Martha Ann (Cathryn Caviness). Sister Martha is a fervent member of a local African American Baptist congregation and longs for her rascally husband to "get some religion." When Razz accidentally shoots his wife with a hunting rifle, she lapses into a coma and undergoes an out-of-body experience in which an angel (Rogenia Goldthwaite) guides her through a spiritual journey and ordeal. After witnessing the spirits of martyrs wandering a graveyard, Martha is conducted to the Crossroads between Zion and Hell. Judas Green (Frank H. McClennan), acting on behalf of Satan (James B. Jones), introduces Martha into a new reality, first as a patron of the swanky 400 Club and then as a dancer (and pickpocket) at a roadside juke-joint run by Rufus Brown (Eddie DeBase). Although she is intrigued with this exciting milieu, Martha ultimately rejects this pitfall and flees the roadhouse with angry patrons in hot pursuit. She ends up back at the crossroads, where Satan has installed a blues combo on a flatbed truck, luring souls to Hell instead of Zion. Prostrate at the foot of the cross/signpost, Martha is about to be stoned by the roadhouse patrons for stealing; the voice of God intervenes demanding, "He who is without sin, cast the first stone." The mob disperses; and as the titular blood of Jesus drips from the cross onto Martha's face, she awakens in her bed, fully recovered from the gunshot wound. Not surprisingly, Martha's miraculous recovery has stirred Razz to conversion. As Means Coleman argues, *The Blood of Jesus* is not only the most prominent race movie of all time, but also a seminal work of African American horror cinema. She recognizes in Williams's 1941 movie several themes that would become central to "Black horror" films of the 1990s—the choice between good and evil, the temptations of Northern urban life as opposed to Southern rurality, and the prominence of a female heroine as "moral arbiter and savior." Martha is not the "wicked Voodoo priestess"

Da Sweet Blood of Jesus (2014). In this photograph Spike Lee is directing Dr. Green's wife, Ganja (Zaraah Abrahams, on the right), and Dr. Green's ex-girlfriend, Tangier (Naté Bove), who will soon become their victim—and, later, Ganja's vampire mate (Photofest).

figure commonly foisted on African American women; to the contrary, she is a Black protagonist who is both feminine and central, deserving of the love and adoration of her newly converted husband Razz.[22]

In many ways, *The Blood of Jesus* parallels *Ganja and Hess*: each film features a troubled heterosexual relationship that lies at the heart of a supernatural drama that involves life, death, undeath, sex, damnation, and salvation. Furthermore, all of these Gothic horror motifs transpire in complex ways amidst African American history and culture. While *Ganja and Hess* arguably represents the greatest artistic achievement to emerge from the Blaxploitation genre, *The Blood of Jesus* is acknowledged as the most important race movie. Taken together, these two films grapple with the Great Migration and the tension between Northern (urban) and Southern (rural) Black culture as well as Du Boisian "double consciousness" and the search for African "roots." Experiencing *Ganja and Hess* on its own, one might not think of Williams's *The Blood of Jesus* and *Ganja and Hess* as comparable films.[23] Part of Spike Lee's achievement in *Da Sweet Blood of Jesus* is to provoke thought about the relationship between these two films. In this respect, *Da Sweet Blood of Jesus* does not simply reiterate or even amplify the peculiar Museum Gothic of *Ganja and Hess* (which it certainly does); instead, the film represents an even more self-reflexive take on this subgenre. Acting as a curatorial auteur, Spike Lee re-presents *Ganja and Hess* in such a way as to educate viewers about its relationship to *The Blood of Jesus*.

Da Sweet Blood of Jesus closely follows the plotline and dialogue of *Ganja and Hess*. Stephen Tyrone Williams plays Hess Greene, an anthropologist studying African culture—this time the Ashanti as opposed to the fictional Mythians. Another minor revision lies in the relocation of Hess's Westchester "forty acre" estate to Martha's Vineyard; we are told that Dr. Greene's parents owned the first black firm on Wall Street. As in the Gunn original, Hess is stabbed with the infectious African dagger; the assailant is here Lafayette Hightower (Elvis Nolasco), a curator from the museum where Hess works. After Lafayette shoots himself, Hess is revived as a vampiric figure and he feeds on Lafayette's body, which he later stores in a freezer. He goes on to steal blood from a doctor's office and feed on an HIV-infected prostitute, who then turns into a blood addict. Ganja (Zaraah Abrahams) turns up in Martha's Vineyard, looking for Lafayette and the doctor and she become lovers. In an important revision, Lee replaces Ganja's male lover with a woman, Hess's old flame Tangier Chancellor (Naté Bova); she and Ganja have a sexual interlude before Ganja kills and feeds on her. In Lee's version, Ganja kills Hess's servant, Seneschal Higginbottom (Rami Malek) earlier in the narrative. It is during this time that Hess sets in motion his plan to kill himself in the shadow of the cross. After witnessing Hess's demise, Ganja survives to enjoy the Martha's Vineyard estate with a resuscitated Tangier at her side.

Although Lee maintains the heterotopic character of Hess's home, he handles this crucial aspect of the set dressing in a different way. In *Ganja and Hess*, Dr. Greene's weird house owes more to the Wunderkammer, as Sherrod suggests, or even the Gothic mansion and the ruinous vampire's castle. A key element of Gunn's original is the juxtaposition of different cultural artifacts, evoking the question of whether Hess invites comparison of African and African American culture with that of Europe and Asia or rather detaches these artifacts from their original context and reorganizes them in subjective fashion (in keeping with the example of Pierre Loti's collection). Lee tidies up Hess's home and gives it a makeover with all African artifacts, such as the crossed assegais that hang above his fireplace. One other conspicuous design element introduced by Lee is the life-size black-and-white photograph of an Ashanti warrior that hangs behind Hess's chair in the dining room. This suggestive prop recaptures something of the interrogative nature of *Ganja and Hess*: while Dr. Greene clearly wishes to identify with this powerful figure from his ancestral homeland, this mode of connection aligns him more with Western Enlightenment regimes of knowledge and is fraught with the distancing that always attends ethnographic photography. Worse yet, Lee's Hess comes across as a black bourgeois poseur who has decontextualized all of these African artifacts and images, transmuting them into posh bric-a-brac. In a particularly ironic gesture, Lee has Hess maintain his curatorial affectations to the end—in contrast to Gunn's Hess, the Stephen Tyrone Williams character kills himself with a conspicuous vintage folk-art cross rather than a knocked-together makeshift affair, which, like Meda's noose, may conjure images of "Jim Crow violence."[24]

If Hess has transformed his home into a pretentious museum of African art, then *Da Sweet Blood of Jesus* should also be understood as a cinematic museum that displays and interprets the African American film canon. However, Lee's exhibit is more didactic than Hess's interior design. By titling his film *Da Sweet Blood of Jesus*, Lee invites us to consider the intertextual dialogues between *Ganja and Hess* and Spencer Williams's *The Blood of Jesus*. Although these two films would appear to have little in common, a closer look reveals many parallels. Both feature a marriage in which the husband mortally wounds the wife, initiating a Gothic drama of salvation and damnation. In each case, the drama is encoded with specific elements of Black cultural history: while damnation is equated with Northern urban sophistication, salvation aligns the Southern rural experience. Further, each film concludes with the triumph of the female protagonist, though in very different ways. As suggested above, Sister Martha survives her spiritual trial by resisting temptation and her virtue is rewarded by the conversion of her wayward husband Razz. In *Ganja and Hess*, Ganja also survives her ordeal; but she does so by refusing her husband's suicidal form of redemption and by mastering the supernatural and material forces by which he sought to control her.

Lee of course remains true to the spirit (and much of the letter) of Bill Gunn's *Ganja*; but this character also represents Lee's major revisions. The most significant change, of course, is the replacement of the male dinner guest/paramour with Hess's former girlfriend Tangier. After Hess introduces Ganja to Tangier, the women converse, dance, and end up having sex. Rough play turns deadly when Ganja strangles Tangier and feeds on her blood. Burying Tangier, Ganja expresses her apprehension that her victim is still alive. In the film's last shot, a nude Tangier joins Ganja on the beach as she looks out on the sunset. Although quite different from Gunn's film, this original element serves to illuminate the way in which *Ganja and Hess* interprets *The Blood of Jesus*. As Means Coleman suggests, Williams's Sister Martha is a seminal Black horror film protagonist who gets to enjoy the "pedestal" historically reserved for figures such as Ann Darrow (Fay Wray) in *King Kong*. As regards *Ganja and Hess*, Means Coleman states that the vampire heroine of this movie "not only survives her encounter with the monster, but happily chooses to become one": "She does not expect a knight in shining armor to come to her rescue; as such, she has developed ways to ensure her own survival, and even to thrive."[25] By recasting Ganja as a lesbian vampire, Lee finds a way to amplify the Black horror heroines set forth by Williams and Gunn, respectively. Ultimately, Ganja 2014 does not need a man in any way, shape, or form. She allows Hess to kill himself and then carries on with Tangier, who has survived her vampiric attack. "With Tangier and Ganja," writes Amanda Hobson, "their seduction of one another is mutual. By exploring their sexualities, unconnected from the heteronormative paradigm, Ganja and Tangier are able to explore identities as sexual beings.... Their sexual fluidity and their ability to adapt to the circumstances of life allow them to persevere when others are unable to do so." By underscoring Ganja as a "hypersexualized female vampire," Lee joins Spencer Williams and Bill Gunn in taking the Black female horror protagonist one step further into agency and autonomy.[26]

Lee's Ganja therefore replicates Gunn's vampire heroine, but does so with new tones derived from other influences. In the final scene of the film, as Ganja stands side-by-side with the naked Tangier, she is wearing a white gown, her bare shoulders scantily covered by a diaphanous black cape tied at the throat. These costume elements serve as museum labels that explain Lee's curatorial gestures in *Da Sweet Blood of Jesus*. While the dress in its outdoor *mise en scène* recalls the climactic sequences of Williams's *The Blood of Jesus*, the gauzy black cape appears borrowed from Ingrid Pitt's wardrobe in *The Vampire Lovers*, which is often regarded as the most famous example of the lesbian vampire film. The first film of the Hammer House of Horror Karnstein trilogy, which also includes *Lust for a Vampire* (1971) and *Twins of Evil* (1971), *The Vampire Lovers* casts Pitt as Mircalla Karnstein, a vampire who seduces and vampirizes the daughters of wealthy families. Although she is killed at the end of the film by General Spielsdorf (Peter Cushing), the father of one of her victims, Mircalla lives on as an exempla of the lesbian vampire's propensity for disturbing conventional gender roles as well as the boundaries between life and death, human and animal, solid and fluid.[27] In similar fashion, although the vampiric relationship between Ganja and Tangier began as a spectacle for Hess, they transcend the homoerotic spectacle initiated by Hess[28] and subsume the narrative, supplying the movie's final tableau.

With his *Variety* review of *Da Sweet Blood of Jesus*, Scott Foundas joins other critics in appraising Lee's vampire film as a failed remake of *Ganja and Hess*: "Four decades on, 'Ganja' still packs a primal punch, whereas Lee's version serves as a gory yet oddly bloodless affair that's been made with a lot of craft and energy but ultimately little sense of purpose."[29] Rather than condemning or dismissing *Da Sweet Blood of Jesus* as a "bloodless" vampire film, it is perhaps more revealing to think about the movie as a cinematic museum in which the exhibits have been scrubbed of blood. As in Hess's well-appointed home, Lee's "craft and energy" have gone into the creation of a bright and orderly space that allows us to see and understand the ways in which *Ganja and Hess* looked back at *The Blood of Jesus* and *The Vampire Lovers*. In this sense, *Da Sweet Blood of Jesus* is reminiscent of Alice Walker's "Everyday Use" (1973). In this fiction, Wangero (née Dee) is an urbane and sophisticated African American woman who returns to her rural family home, with her boyfriend, in search of heirlooms. She is particularly interested in a quilt sewn by successive generations of the women in her family. While Dee's sister Maggie, a girl disfigured by burn scars, wants the quilt for "everyday use," Dee wants to hang the quilt on the wall as a piece of folk-art that will serve as home decor. At the end of the story, Dee's mother sides with Maggie and deems the quilt something that was meant to be used by the family. Lee's Hess has much in common with Wangero—like this pretentious character, he attempts to preserve his cultural past through commodification,[30] transforming useful African objects into trendy ornamentation (a gesture less pronounced with the decadence of Gunn's Hess). However, as David Cowart suggests, this critique of Dee/Wangero turns back on the author herself: "Walker ... actually doubles the self-mocking portrait of the artist, projecting herself as both the benighted Maggie and the sophisticated but shallow Wangero."[31] Walker exposes the flaws of Dee/Wangero's misguided attempts to preserve the past, but she herself engages in a similar effort by translating everyday language and experience into artistic fiction. Lee might hold up his version of Hess to scorn and ridicule; but Lee too has indulged in displaying his cinematic past, and he in some measure implicates himself with his portrait of Hess. The result of this curatorial effort is a "bloodless" museum piece that appeals to the head rather than the hitting us in the gut.

NOTES

1. Robin R. Means Coleman, *The Conversation*, no page.

2. Manthia Diawara and Phyllis R. Klotman, "Ganja and Hess: Vampires, Sex, and Addictions," *Black American Literature Forum*, volume 25, number 2, 1991, pages 299–314.

3. Caroline Siri Johnson, "The Limbs of Osiris: Reed's *Mumbo Jumbo* and Hollywood's *The Mummy*," *Melus*, volume 17, number 4, 1991, pages 105–15.

4. Michel Foucault, "Of Other Spaces."

5. Beth Lord, "Foucault's Museum: Difference, Representation, and Genealogy," *Museum and Society*, volume 4, number 1, 2006, page 2.

6. Ruth Hoberman, *Museum Trouble: Edwardian Fiction and the Emergence of Modernism*, University of Virginia Press, 2011, page 51.

7. Ella Shohat and Robert Stam, *Multiculturalism and the Media*, Routledge, 2008, page 114.

8. Johnson, cited above, page 114.

9. Johnson, cited above.

10. Scott Trafton, *Egypt Land, Race and Nineteenth-Century American Egyptomania*, Duke University Press, 2004, page 242.

11. Diawara and Klotman, cited above. Thanks to Professor Kevin L Ferguson for helping me to identify the Bonnemaison painting.

12. Giselle Liza Anatol, "Narratives of Race and Gender: Black Vampires in U.S. Film," *Dracula's Daughters: The Female Vampire on Film*, edited by Douglas Brode and Leah Dayneka, Scarecrow Press, 2014, page 200.

13. John Freeman Gill, "Ghosts of New York," *Atlantic* June 2010, n.p.

14. John K. Muir, *Horror Films of the 1970s*, McFarland, 2007, page 248.

15. Harrison Sherrod, "The Blood of the Thing (Is the Truth of the Thing): Viral Pathogens and Uncanny Ontologies in *Ganja and Hess*," *Beyond Blaxploitation*, edited by Lawrence Novotny and G.R. Butters, Wayne State University Press, 2016.

16. Anthony Purdy, "At Home in the Museum: Pierre Loti, Self-Collected, Self-Possessed," *Image and Narrative*, volume 16, February 2006, n.p.

17. Sherrod, cited above.

18. Diawara and Klotman, pages 299–314.

19. Anatol, cited above, page 201.

20. Dennis Leroy Kangalee, "Flowers for Bill Gunn: Remembering an Outlaw Artist," *Shadow and Acts*, 20 April 2017.

21. Armond White.

22. Robin R. Means Coleman, *Horror Noire*, Routledge, 2011, pages 75, 78.

23. Means Coleman, page xix.

24. Sherrod, cited above, no page.

25. Means Coleman, cited above, page 134.

26. Amanda Hobson, "Dark Seductress: The Hypersexualization of the Female Vampire," *Gender in the Vampire Narrative*, edited by Amanda Hobson and U. Melissa Anyiwo, Sense, 2016, pages 2–28.

27. Barbara Creed, *The Monstrous-Feminine: Film, Feminism, Psychoanalysis*, 2014, page 61.

28. Hobson, cited above, pages 23–24.

29. Scott Foundas, "Film Review: Da Sweet Blood of Jesus," *Variety* 23 June 2014.

30. David Cowart, "Heritage and Deracination in Walker's 'Everyday Use,'" *Studies in Short Fiction*, Volume 33, Number 2, Spring 1996, page 171.

31. Cowart, page 177.

"It's more like a disease"

Compensatory Masculinities and Intersectional "Otherness" in The Transfiguration

Cain Miller

Introduction

Throughout their history on screen, cinematic vampires have represented "the Other" that stands in opposition to the dominant ideologies connected to Western culture such as heteronormativity, Judeo-Christianity, and
white supremacy. Examples of this include the racial Otherness encoded into
various vampiric figures such as the anti–Semitic character design of *Nosferatu*'s (1922) Count Orlok and the African American slavery allegory presented
in *Blacula* (1972), as well as the sexual Otherness presented through characters
like the lesbian-coded Countess Marya Zaleska in *Dracula's Daughter* (1936),
the queer coupling found in Anne Rice's *Interview with the Vampire* (1976)
and its 1994 film adaptation, the trend of lesbian vampire films throughout
the 1970s like *Vampyros Lesbos* (1971) and *Daughters of Darkness* (1971), and
more recent comedic interpretations such as *Bite Marks* (2011) and *Vamperifica* (2011). Traditional horror narratives typically conclude with the monstrous Other being vanquished by a white patriarch, thus removing the figure
that threatened the dominant ideological structure and consequently restor-
ing normality. While past cinematic vampires have predominantly served as
metaphors for sexual and racial Otherness, there has been less attention given
to how these facets intertwine. Far fewer films have featured vampiric characters who represent a "double Othering," i.e., figures who face multiple means
of marginalization, whether it be a combination of racial, sexual, gendered,
and/or socioeconomic factors. Consequently, less academic attention has

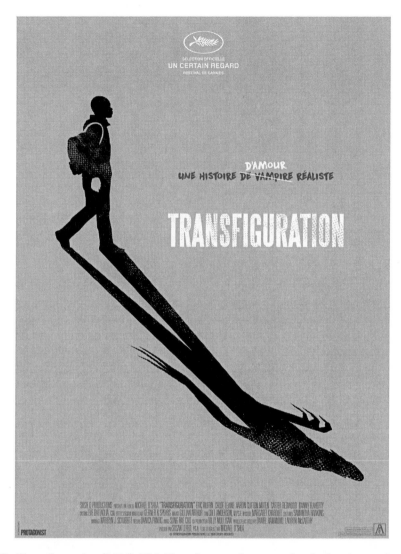

The Transfiguration (2016). This French poster borrows the shadow image from *Nosferatu* (1922), a film much admired by Milo (Eric Ruffin), an African American teenager who is so obsessed with vampires that he behaves like one (Photofest).

been placed on the cinematic vampire's relation to intersectionality, specifically in regard to topics such as masculinity and gender performativity. One notable exception to this notion is Michael O'Shea's 2016 horror-drama *The Transfiguration*, whose protagonist faces a multitude of maltreatments in relation to his race, sexuality, gender identity, and economic status, and as a result engages in a number of vampire-inspired killings as a means of performing his masculinity, in order to cope with systemic oppression. This essay will analyze how *The Transfiguration* uses the vampire figure as a symbol for intersectional, multiple Otherness, specifically in relation to the struggles black men face in defining their masculinity when faced with societal oppression and how an individual can develop their own methods of masculine performativity when they are a social misfit within their already marginalized demographic.

Gender Performance and Intersectionality

When discussing the concept of masculinity, it is important to first address the topic's development out of Antonio Gramsci's theory of cultural hegemony. In particular, hegemonic masculinity, a phrase coined by R.W. Connell, is characterized by a man's ability to subordinate women as a means of legitimizing the patriarchy.[1] Hegemonic masculinity is thus established as a dominant ideology within Western culture. Mike Donaldson further notes that a man's attainment of hegemonic masculinity is typically signified by his role as the dominant "breadwinner" within a traditional domestic sphere.[2] This masculine symbol of authority is reliant upon the man's ability to achieve financial prosperity, as this indicates success within his patriarchal-capitalist structure. In turn, hegemonic masculinity inherently favors men who are heterosexual and white, as a result of their compliance with the other dominant ideologies of heteronormativity and white supremacy. As a result, non-hegemonic masculinities tend to arise in different cultural circumstances.

Connell argues that masculinity is not a singular characteristic that all males display in the same fashion. Rather, men can form their own respective masculinities depending on their "institutional context," most notably in relation to their family life, profession, and living environment.[3] Karen D. Pyke expands upon this idea and argues that one's masculinity is innately connected to their race, sexuality, and social class. Pyke argues that these certain socioeconomic "hierarchies" lead to "fragmented" masculinities that deviate from hegemonic masculinity. These unconventional masculine identities are often displayed by men of color, non-heterosexual men, and working-class men due to their cultural subordination. These practices are defined as "compensatory" masculinities.[4] In response to various societal oppressions, marginalized men can develop compensatory masculinities as a way to assert their male authority due to the fact that they are unlikely to obtain hegemonic masculinity.[5] As Victor Rios and Rachel Sarabia note, compensatory masculinities are often displayed by "street-life-oriented young men" who engage in "deviant-behaviors" to show defiance against the dominant power structures linked to hegemonic masculinity.[6]

One of the most well-known examples of a compensatory masculinity is "cool pose." Developed by Richard Majors and Janet Mancini Billson, cool pose is characterized by emotional stoicism and aloofness as a means of rebellion against the hegemonic structure.[7] Cool pose is a masculine practice associated with black males that is often conceived in response to racial oppression. In regard to the systemic discrimination people of color have faced throughout the history of Western civilization (and of course in other cultural contexts as well), Majors and Billson affirm that black men become "psychologically castrated—rendered impotent in the economic, political, and social arenas that whites have historically dominated."[8] Having realized that the concept of "the American dream" is primarily suited for white individuals, persons of color often face the grim reality that their efforts to attain hegemony will not provide them with the same rewards as their white counterparts because the racial hierarchy of Western culture actively works against them. With hegemonic masculinity seemingly out of their grasp, black men (particularly those who live in lower socioeconomic conditions in urban cities) rely on cool pose as a compensatory tool.

These oppositional practices can consequently be expressed through illicit, violent actions. Lynette D. Nickelberry and Marilyn Coleman further elaborate on this notion, stating that "with legitimate forms of economic attainment denied to many African American men, some, although not most, resort to illegal and dangerous means of economic access ([such as] drug dealing) deemed, from their perspective, necessary for survival." In relation to displays of violence, Ronald E. Hall and Jesenia M. Pizarro provide further elaboration: "As a result of societal limitations, Cool Pose acted out via homicide by lower socioeconomic black males has been perceived by them as an effective strategy for the rescue of their manhood and the management of their self-presentation." Thus, cool pose can be exhibited through acts like theft, drug dealing, and gang violence.[9]

Importantly, Majors and Billson describe cool pose as an "expressive performance" comprised of specific behaviors, speech, and body language to signify a man's "pride, strength, and control."[10] This relates to the established hypothesis in gender studies which is that one's gender is demonstrated through social configurations rather than solely based on their biological sex. Through their discourse over the concept of "doing gender," Candace West and Don Zimmerman argue that a person's gender is not something that they are intrinsically born with, nor does it merely stem from one's male/female anatomy. Rather, gender is a construction; an identity that a person forms as a result of interacting with others within various social institutions.[11] Hence, aspects of gender such as masculinity and femininity are something that a person *does* in correlation with their respective social circumstances (e.g., the culture into which they are born).[12] Judith Butler expands upon this claim through her theory of gender performativity. While noting that social contexts indeed aid in the construction of one's gender, Butler further argues that gender can be displayed through performance. Thus, one's gender is portrayed through a person's "stylized repetition of acts" that signal their masculinity or femininity.[13] Relating back to compensatory masculinities, cool pose is performative because it relies on a man's stoic and/or aggressive actions to denote his masculinity.

Yet Butler also notes that it is possible for a person to perform their gender "wrong." If one does not display the socially expected, essential traits of their gender (e.g., moving outside of the gender binary and performing unconventional qualities of masculinity or femininity) they risk being punished by their respective social institution.[14] This same notion is also present in compensatory masculinities. According to Majors and Billson, if a young black male does not display the common characteristics of cool pose, he risks being ostracized by his "cool" peers.[15] As a result, men of color who experience this social exclusion must develop their own unique compensatory masculinities which inherently differ from the masculine practices of others within their demographic.

Vampires and Masculinity

Produced independently and shot on location in New York City, *The Transfiguration* revolves around Milo (Eric Ruffin), a black teen living in a low-income urban neighborhood. Due to the area's lower socioeconomic conditions, many of its residents develop compensatory masculinities. Most notable of these are a group of gang members and their leader, Andre (Carter Redwood), who frequently gather outside of Milo's apartment building. Andre and his gang display cool pose through their aggressive behaviors and acts of violence. Milo, however, does not share in these displays of cool pose. Milo, who is soft-spoken and has noticeably poor social skills, spends most of his time isolated from others, typically reading, drawing, or journaling. Due to his separation from other social groups, Milo does not form the relationships that can be important in coping with oppression. As Brandon A. Jackson argues, "Partly due to their isolation from the larger society, a manifestation of racist politics and practices, working-class Black men come to rely on one another as their main source of emotional and social support. These tight-knit relationships help the men survive economic insecurity, violence, and other hardships associated with poverty and the inner city."[16] These "tight-knit relationships" are displayed in Andre's gang who label Milo as a "freak" because he does not participate in similar compensatory masculine practices.

The Transfiguration (2016). The reclusive Milo (Eric Ruffin) becomes friends with Sophie (Chloe Levine), another teenage loner in New York City. Although Milo becomes caught up in gang activity, he helps Sophie to escape.

Milo does not receive social bonding in his home life either, as both of his parents are deceased and he is raised by his older brother, Lewis (Aaron Clifton Moten), a military veteran. Lewis has experienced economic emasculation because he was unable to find work following his service. Furthermore, Lewis evidently suffers from post-traumatic stress disorder (PTSD), given that he shows little regard for Milo's well-being and spends most of his time indoors watching television. As a result, Lewis sells drugs to support both of them while remaining emotionally distant from Milo. The brothers' relationship is damaging to both of their well-beings because, as Jackson further claims, "support from family is especially important for these men. Given that many face an uphill battle in terms of their own mobility, for those Black men interested in navigating the social and economic ladder, emotional support from their family is all they had to rely on."[17] Due to his inability to form social bonds with those around him, Milo represents an outsider within his already marginalized community. As a result, Milo develops his own compensatory masculine identity: he believes that he is a vampire.

Traditional characteristics of the vampire figure present complicated, and often contradictory, connections to masculinity. A conventional vampire character such as Dracula (both in film and in literature) is commonly displayed as an aristocrat who embodies economic prosperity. A nobleman, Dracula has commonly been interpreted as an allegorical figure for capitalism, given that he leaves his flamboyant castle to quite literally feed on nearby village peasants. In his analysis of Bram Stoker's original novel, Franco Moretti argues that "Dracula is a true monopolist: solitary and despotic, he will not brook competition. Like monopoly capital, his ambition is to subjugate the last vestiges of the liberal era and destroy all forms of economic independence.

He no longer restricts himself to incorporating (in a literal sense) the physical and moral strength of his victims. He intends to make them his forever. Hence the horror, for the bourgeois mind."[18] At first glance, the vampire figure, at least in the context of *Dracula*, demonstrates hegemonic masculinity because he represents capitalist ideologies. However, vampires also possess characteristics that oppose Western hegemony, most notably their non-heteronormative sexualities. Dracula's character heavily revolves around his abnormal sexuality. As David J. Skal states, the Count is "a 'castrated' seducer who cannot penetrate in the conventional way; all sex energy is displaced to his mouth."[19] Thus, Dracula engages in many non-heteronormative actions, most notably through his implied bisexuality given that he penetrates both men and women. Queer sexuality has always been a recognizable component of the vampire, dating all the way back to Joseph Sheridan Le Fanu's 1872 novella *Carmilla*. In her work over the "vampire dandy" archetype, Vicki Karaminas states that "vampires are a construct of many binary definitions, including good and bad, light and darkness. Belonging to an undefined category outside of these polarizations, vampires enable the questioning of these barriers, and they represent a polymorphic and mobile sexuality that eludes the restrictions encoded in traditional gendered roles."[20] These "mobile" sexualities indeed go against the dominant ideology of heteronormativity, and they also present a contrast to hegemonic masculinity, as heterosexuality is to be expected of dominant patriarchal figures.

The vampire's relationship to hegemony is further complicated by the monster's varying connections to race. While vampires might often be physically portrayed as pale to indicate their being undead, the lore has nonetheless offered many different metaphors for other races, most notably African Americans. Texts like *Blacula*, *Ganja & Hess* (1973), and the *Blade* franchise (1998–2004) use the motif of vampirism to address topics like slavery, institutionalized religion, and biracial identity, respectively. In the context of gender studies, *Blacula* is particularly noteworthy because the titular character (William Marshall) represents an oppressed figure (a former African prince named Mamuwalde, who has been enslaved by the white, vampiric Count Dracula) who uses compensatory violence to combat hegemonic forces such as the Los Angeles Police Department. The vampire's representation of racial and sexual Otherness plays a significant role in relation to horror spectatorship, in that viewers who respectively belong to marginalized demographics often *relate* to the monstrous Other antagonist. Building on the common claim that black audiences have historically always made up sizeable portions of horror film crowds, Harry Benshoff argues that "identifying with monsters out to topple dominant social institutions (that oppress both movie monsters and real-life minorities) can be a pleasurable and a potentially empowering act for many filmgoers."[21] This argument helps to explain Milo's fixation with vampires, as he collects various books and films about vampirism. As he relates to the vampiric Others within these texts, Milo adopts a vampire persona that allows him to develop his own compensatory masculinity. Rather than engaging in the open displays of violence and aggression typically associated with cool pose, Milo discreetly murders residents of his city.

With regard to his consumption of vampire media, Milo shows particular fondness for *Martin* (1978), a pseudo vampire film that reappropriates gothic imagery as a means of commenting on topics like mental health, poverty, and sexuality. Directed by George A. Romero, *Martin* revolves around its title character (John Amplas) who believes that he must drink human blood to keep himself alive. Opting for an unapologetically downbeat tone, Romero places his vampire lead not in the lush countryside, but rather in an impoverished Pittsburgh cityscape. Thus, Martin does not represent a capitalistic aristocrat like Dracula who feeds on the poor. Rather, he is a victim of economic oppression who uses his vampiric killings as a means of "escapist indulgence" to counter the hardships he faces.[22] Martin's vampire persona also serves as a metaphor for his queer sexuality. As is common for the vampire figure, Martin attacks both men and women, though his murders carry noticeably amplified sensual imagery, particularly in relation to his male victims. After a botched home invasion, Martin manages to sedate Lewis (Roger Caine), one of the city's residents, and drags his body to an adjacent wooded area. Martin then penetrates Lewis's neck with a wooden stick, removes his own shirt, and sucks Lewis's blood directly from his throat—a symbolic act of fellatio. Martin's queer identity is further stressed by his uncle, Tateh Cuda (Lincoln Maazel), who attempts to abolish Martin's "vampirism" through the use of Christianity by forcing him to attend church and even bringing forth a Catholic priest to perform an unsuccessful exorcism. Cuda represents a conventional "Van Helsing" patriarch who seeks to abolish the vampiric Other for its noncompliance with dominant Western ideologies. In the end, Cuda is indeed successful in eradicating Martin, as he violently drives a stake into his nephew's chest during the film's abrupt climax.

Milo claims to like *Martin* because he believes that it portrays, in his words, a "realistic" depiction of vampirism. Milo's belief that *Martin* displays vampirism in an accurate manner is likely the result of the fact that Milo himself uses his vampire persona to express his own queer desires. While not explicitly stated, Milo is queer-coded because his victims are both men and women, though he shows a particular interest in killing older white men. In the telling opening of the film, an adult male is shown in a public bathroom. After hearing faint sucking noises originating in a nearby stall, the man approaches and crouches below it, finding two people inside. Believing them to be engaged in a homosexual act, the man quickly leaves. The camera then cuts to a shot of Milo sucking the blood from the neck of a dead businessman whose throat has been slashed. The camera then cuts to a close-up of Milo, now looking down at his victim, with blood smeared across his lips. Here, similar to *Martin*, blood symbolizes semen, another example of abjection, as it is the result of Milo's figurative fellatio. After he kills his victim, Milo steals money from the man's billfold as a means of compensating for his lack of economic prosperity. Milo's queerness is expressed further in a later scene that also takes place in a public bathroom. In a long-take medium shot, Milo stands at a urinal and attempts to make eye contact with an older man standing next to him. This showcases Milo "cruising," implying that this is how he isolates most of his victims. Furthermore, Milo's killing of men in hidden, isolated environments indicates his attempted suppression of his queer identity.

Past depictions of black queer sexuality in the vampire subgenre have led to certain problematic themes. In his analysis of *Blacula*, Leerom Medovoi draws attention to the titular character's first act of violence within the narrative: his murder of an interracial gay couple. Medovoi states: "Mamuwalde's and Luva's stately visit to Castle Dracula in 1780 stresses their nobility as a heterosexual couple where the husband commands political, intellectual and filial respect. By contrast, the visit of Bobby and Billy, a mixed-race gay couple whom the film depicts as degenerate and ridiculous, comes to figure slavery's damaging effect on black character.... Bobby, the black queen, and the first contemporary black man to appear in the film, comes to embody the loss of African pride and a degeneration into modern sexual decadence."[23] Through Medovoi's argument, *Blacula* seemingly bemoans black queer identity and frames it as something to be ashamed of, and ultimately exterminated. Similarly, Milo feels the need to suppress his queer desires. *The Transfiguration* lends itself to queer readings beyond solely its textual characteristics, as it was released through Strand Releasing, a distribution company known for its vast library of LGBTQIA titles. In the past, Strand has distributed films from prominent queer auteurs like Gregg Araki, Tom Kalin, Bruce LaBruce, and, most significant in this context, Marlon Riggs and Isaac Julien whose respective pivotal films *Tongues Untied* (1989) and *Looking for Langston* (1989) still serve as iconic cinematic texts that address black queer identity.

Beyond his queer sexual identity, Milo's vampiric killings also represent another means of masculine performativity. In a shot-for-shot re-creation of a scene from *Let the Right One In* (2008), (another text that Milo cites as one of his favorites), Milo lies under a bridge at night, pretending to be hurt. He is eventually approached by a homeless man played by Troma Entertainment co-founder Lloyd Kaufman in a subtle cameo. When the man crouches down to observe the teen, Milo then penetrates the man's neck with a small blade and proceeds to drink his blood. Several characteristics of this scene signify the notion of performance. First, the visual design, which bears an almost uncanny resemblance to the original cinematography in *Let the Right One In*, indicates that this is a "constructed" situation. This same perception is mirrored in the scene's sound design. When the jogger crouches to observe Milo, the camera cuts to an extreme close-up of Milo's closed eyes. When Milo opens his eyes, the action is met with a startling non-diegetic synthesizer score. This musical motif stands in stark contrast to the sound design found throughout the rest of the film, as most other scenes rely on the diegetic sound effects of the city without the inclusion of non-diegetic music. This unfamiliar element of music signals a theme of theatricality within the scene, opting for a more stylized approach that starkly contrasts with the more neo-realist tones displayed throughout the rest of the narrative. Last, Milo's role within the intertextual re-creation places him as an "actor" within the action. By mimicking the original filmic actions of Eli (Lina Leandersson), the young vampire from *Let the Right One In*, Milo dons her vampiric persona as a means of performativity. Together, these elements demonstrate how Milo quite literally performs his masculinity, yet unlike the gender performativity commonly associated with cool pose, Milo's compensatory violence is modeled after the actions enacted by the Othered characters found within his vampire films. Perhaps most significant with regard to Milo's "acting" is the fact that Eli's vampirism is often read as being metaphorical for her transgender identity. In *Let the Right One In*, Eli bears a sizeable scar where her genitals should be and bluntly tells her companion Oskar (Kåre Hedebrant) that she is "not a girl" when he makes advances towards her. The novel on which the film is based provides more exposition with regard to Eli's gender, stating that Eli was originally a biological male, Elias, who was castrated by a vampire. Putting these admittedly problematic narrative aspects aside, Eli's gender identity nonetheless holds importance in relation to Milo's actions. Not only is Milo performing his masculinity through intertextual recreation, he does so by embodying a trans character, thus adding a deeper element of fluidity with regard to his gender identity.

Milo eventually befriends Sophie (Chloe Levine), a teen girl who lives in Milo's apartment building with her abusive grandfather. Like Milo, Sophie also enjoys vampire texts, though she prefers popular titles like *Twilight* (2008) and *True Blood* (2008–2014). Milo dislikes these texts because they are, in his words, "unrealistic." He shows particular disdain for *Twilight* by claiming the ever-popular "vampires don't sparkle" argument. His claim that the vampires in *Twilight* are "unrealistic" is linked to the series' connection of vampirism to masculine perfection. As Ananya Mukherjea writes about these "vampire boyfriends," "They are, in short, fantasy men—both very hard and very soft and fantastically flawless in a way that even very few fictional human men could possibly be.... These are sophisticated men who tend to live in mansions and tricked-out urban lofts and drive fast, shiny vehicles.

Such socioeconomic privilege augments their supreme masculine dominance, along with their physical prowess, fighting skills, chivalrous manners, and eternal, gorgeous youth."[24] *Twilight* inherently situates the vampiric Edward Cullen as a white, upper-class gentleman boyfriend who does not adhere to the vampire's typical representation of Otherness. Consequently, Edward represents traditional expectations of men who display hegemonic masculinity. Given that obtaining hegemonic masculinity is difficult for Milo, he feels that Edward's vampirism is not believable.

Milo and Sophie soon form a romantic relationship, finding consolation in sharing their respective traumatic pasts. Sophie lost both of her parents and spends much of her time self-harming and engaging in sexual activity with older men. Milo reveals that he lost his father to an illness and his mother to a suicide, the latter of which he witnessed in person. When Sophie states that she also thinks of suicide, Milo claims that he cannot physically take his own life, saying that "it's just the way it is." Milo's feelings on suicide are tied to his supernatural persona, though they also signify his belief that he is stuck in his impoverished environment and that there is no escape from the hardships into which he was born. When discussing the topic of vampirism, Milo states that he does not believe in the supernatural mythology often linked to the vampire figure, such as their inability to eat garlic or be exposed to the sun. Milo also does not believe that one becomes a vampire by being bitten on the neck. Instead, Milo claims that vampirism is "more like a disease" that a person contracts. Through this comparison, Milo relates his supposed vampirism to the various oppressions he faces. Similar to how one contracts a disease, Milo feels subordinated within his environment, unable to control the harm and hardships that afflict him.

Although Milo is initially portrayed as apathetic toward those he kills, this changes towards the end of the narrative. In a later scene, Milo follows a man (Larry Fessenden) to his home with the intention of killing him. Upon arriving at the man's home, however, Milo encounters the man's young daughter. Milo impulsively kills the young girl, and then her father, and drinks the man's blood. Unlike his past murders, Milo is noticeably affected by his killing of the girl, as he feels remorse over the fact that she was not initially intended to be a victim. At this point, Milo begins to question his compensatory masculine practices. As Milo and Sophie's relationship develops, Milo consistently hides the fact that he murders residents of the city, and also attempts to keep Sophie away from the gang members who congregate outside their apartment. This proves challenging after Milo witnesses the gang members murder a white teenager, an open expression of their compensatory masculinities through cool pose. Milo is then questioned by several white police officers who attempt to persuade him to rat out the gang. Here, the police officers represent hegemonic masculinity, as they are part of a dominant systemic power structure (i.e., law enforcement). Milo does not report the gang and the police let him go. Afterwards, the gang express cool pose by verbally threatening Milo, insinuating that they will physically harm him if he reports their murder.

Trapped between the hegemonic masculinity of the police and the compensatory masculinities of the gang, Milo ultimately relies on his compensatory vampiric persona as a solution. Milo frames the gang for his murder of the father and daughter, leading to their arrest. Other members of the gang retaliate by killing Milo in a drive-by, a final act of compensatory violence. As a symbol of the vampiric Other, Milo is indeed eradicated just as one would expect in a traditional horror narrative. Unlike the traditional horror narrative, however, Milo is not killed by a dominant patriarchal "Van Helsing" character familiar to the genre. Rather, Milo is murdered by members of his own community: inner-city black men who face similar racial and economic oppressions similar to his. Importantly, Milo's death is implied to be a staged suicide. After reporting the gang to the cops, Milo seemingly knows that other gang members will respond by killing him. This is evident in the scene prior to Milo's death, in which he sits in a park and draws a picture of the sun in his journal. With sunlight being a traditional threat to conventional vampires, Milo is aware that his demise is approaching. Milo ultimately chooses suicide for two reasons. First, although he feels as though he needs to drink blood in order to survive, Milo no longer wants to kill due to the newfound guilt consuming him after having murdered the young girl. Second, Milo does not want to face the continuing socioeconomic hardships and oppositional masculine forces that threaten him. As a result, Milo believes that death is his only means of escape.

Critical Reception

Despite having received generally favorable reviews, some critics evidently did not decipher the socioeconomic factors/gender politics presented in *The Transfiguration*. In his review for *The Guardian*, Nigel M. Smith expressed disappointment in Ruffin's performance and Milo's characterization in general, arguing that his emotional coldness made him "impenetrable" and that the character only came to life when he enacted a murder. Smith concludes by stating: "It's a shame then that O'Shea seems completely disinterested in the attacks themselves. Each one is staged with little-to-no flair, save for an electronic score that swells louder with each bite."[25] Indeed, *The Transfiguration* does not display much "flair" though it would be hard to argue that the film intends to market itself on visual pizzazz. Rather, *The Transfiguration* communicates its various intersectional social themes through its subtlety. Milo is stoic in his everyday life and only "springs to life" during his murders because that is his act of compensatory performance. These scenes are even accompanied by theatrical musical scores that starkly contrast with the quieter nature of the rest of the film, thus emphasizing Milo's masculine performativity.

In her review of *Little White Lies*, Manuela Lazic expressed similar contempt at the film's understated tone, and showed particular disdain for the film's ending. In her analysis of Milo's death, Lazic argues that "Eventually, Milo accepts that he could never change and finds a radical solution to stop himself. However, this appears random and illogical since the entire film up to this point portrays him as disturbed and needing Sophie's help."[26] This is a questionable interpretation of Milo's suicide. Milo does not suddenly opt to stage his death without reason, nor out of fear that he cannot control himself around Sophie. He coordinates his suicide due to the threats from the police and from the gang because he realizes that he is stuck between their malevolent intentions. In relation to the narrative's conclusion, Lazic takes further issue with the film's title, stating that, "a transfiguration into sanity is expected, but Milo instead remains a 'vampire,' and not a more complete one than he was at the beginning. There has been no real transfiguration in any direction, only a reinstating of this 'disease.' The pessimistic conclusion remains at odds with the director's romantic eye for portraying the two kids together, as well as Milo's growing humanism."[27] While the film's title has indeed sparked confusion among viewers, it does play an important role in correlation with the ending. The term "transfiguration" is defined as when something changes into something else of greater beauty. Hence, one might imagine that the title indicates that Milo will in fact become more "human" and stop his killings. Milo does actually begin this transformation towards the end of the narrative, as evident in his feelings of guilt regarding the young girl that he killed. The title is thus used ironically, as Milo was beginning to show signs of change, only for him to be killed before his actual "transfiguration" could be completed.

Conclusion

While it does offer a wide array of complex portrayals of race, gender, sexuality, and socioeconomic class, *The Transfiguration* is not without its thematic drawbacks. Michael O'Shea is not an individual of color, thus some of his depictions of race bear problematic qualities. Andre and his gang, for example, are given little to do other than display cool pose in its traditional form. Andre's gang are used as clear sources of fear throughout the narrative due to their overt aggressiveness and frequent verbal and physical harm of

Milo and Sophie—the latter of whom they derogatorily refer to as "White Bitch." Consequently, the gang members are arguably diminished to antagonistic "Buck" stereotypes. Furthermore, the film's conclusion also promotes questionable themes. Prior to Milo's assisted suicide, he gifts Sophie the money he collected from his deceased victims. This action allows Sophie to leave the city and live with her aunt, thus escaping the crime and violence found in Milo's neighborhood. This ending mirrors an old cinematic trope in which a black character loses their life (often in the form of self-sacrifice) in order for their white counterparts to survive and succeed. This trope has appeared in other notable horror texts like *Alien* (1979) and *The Shining* (1980). In this context, Milo, firmly aware that his death is approaching, provides Sophie, a white character, with his own money in order for her to prosper elsewhere. Despite these problematic undertones, one could argue that this conclusion further stresses the stagnation people of color face while living in lower socioeconomic environments. Here, the film's only prominent white character is also the only person to escape the city's hardships while every black character ends up in prison or dead as the result of gang violence.

By straying from a traditional "good defeats evil" horror narrative, *The Transfiguration* serves as a look into the various levels of violence that can stem from systemic racial oppression. Furthermore, this text shows how an ostracized figure can form a personalized masculine identity when faced with these oppressions. As contemporary horror texts continue to address themes of masculinity in relation to gender, sexuality, race, socioeconomic class, able-bodiedness, and mental health, it is important for media scholars to examine how these various intersectional topics are displayed within the genre.

NOTES

1. R.W. Connell, "The Big Picture: Masculinities in Recent World History," *Theory and Society*, vol. 22, no. 5, 1993, pages 597–623. *SpringerLink*, https://doi.org/10.1007/BF00993538.

2. Mike Donaldson, "What is Hegemonic Masculinity?" *Theory and Society*, vol. 22, no. 5, 1993, pages 643–57. *SpringerLink*, https://doi.org/10.1007/BF00993540.

3. Connell, page 602.

4. Karen D. Pyke, "Class-Based Masculinities: The Interdependence of Gender, Class, and Interpersonal Power." *Gender & Society*, vol. 10, no. 5, 1996, pages 527–49. *SAGE Journals*, https://doi.org/10.1177/089124396010005003.

5. Victor Rios and Rachel Sarabia, "Synthesized Masculinities: The Mechanics of Manhood Among Delinquent Boys," in *Exploring Masculinities: Identity, Continuity, and Change*, edited by Tristan Bridges and C.J. Pascoe, New York, Oxford University Press, 2015, pages 166–177.

6. Rios and Sarabia, pages 166–68.

7. Richard Majors and Janet Mancini Billson, *Cool Pose: The Dilemma of Black Manhood in America*, Simon & Schuster, 1993, pages 4–5.

8. Majors and Billson, page 1.

9. Ronald Hall and Jesenia M. Pizarro, "Cool Pose: Black Male Homicide and the Social Implications of Manhood." *Journal of Social Services Research*, vol. 37, no. 1, 2010, page 88.

10. Majors and Billson, pages 3–4.

11. Candace West and Don H. Zimmerman, "Doing Gender." *Gender & society*, vol. 1, no. 2, 1987, pages 125–151.

12. West and Zimmerman, page 140.

13. Judith Butler, "Performative Acts and Gender Constitution: An Essay in Phenomenology and Feminist Theory." *Theatre Journal*, vol. 40, no. 4, 1988, page 519.

14. Butler, page 528.

15. Majors and Billson, page 4.

16. Brandon A. Jackson, "Beyond the Cool Pose: Black Men and Emotion Management Strategies." *Sociology Compass*, vol. 12, no. 4, 2018, page 6.

17. Jackson, page 7.

18. Franco Moretti, "The Dialectic of Fear." *New Left Review*, vol. 136, no. 1, 1982, page 74.

19. David Skal, *The Monster Show: A Cultural History of Horror*. Farrar, Straus and Giroux, 2001, page 129.

20. Vicki Karaminas, "The Vampire Dandy: Reconceptualising Masculine Identities in Fashion, Cinema, and Literature." *Lambda Nordica*, vol. 14, no. 3–4, 2009, page 129.

21. Harry M. Benshoff, "Blaxploitation Horror Films: Generic Reappropriation or Reinscription?" *Cinema Journal*, vol. 39, no. 2, 2000, page 32.

22. Williams, Tony. "Martin." *The Cinema of George A. Romero: Knight of the Living Dead*, by Tony Williams, 2nd ed., Columbia University Press, 2015, page 81.

23. Medovoi, Leerom. "Theorizing Historicity, or the Many Meanings of *Blacula*." *Screen*, vol. 39, no. 1, 1998, page 7.

24. Ananya Mukherjea, "My Vampire Boyfriend: Postfeminism, 'Perfect' Masculinity, and the Contemporary Appeal of Paranormal Romance. *Studies in Popular Culture*, vol. 33, no. 2, 2011, pages 12–13.

25. Nigel M. Smith, "The Transfiguration Review: Downbeat Black Vampire Tale Lacks Bite." *The Guardian*, 15 May 2016, https://www.theguardian.com/film/2016/may/15/the-transfiguration-review-cannes.

26. Manuela Lazic, "The Transfiguration—First Look Review." *Little White Lies*, 15 May 2016, https://lwlies.com/festivals/the-transfiguration-first-look-review/.

27. Lazic, cited above.

Filmography

Alien. Directed by Ridley Scott. Brandywine Productions, 1979.

Angel Heart. Directed by Alan Parker. Carolco International N.V., 1987.

Audition (Odishon). Directed by Miike Takashi. Basara Pictures, 1999.

Barry McKenzie Holds His Own. Directed by Bruce Beresford. Reg Grundy Productions, 1974.

Beautiful Vampire (Byutipul baempaieo). Directed by Eunkyung "Jude" Jung, 2018.

Bite Marks. Directed by Mark Bessenger. Blakk Flamingo Pictures, 2011.

Black Sheep. Directed by Jonathan King. New Zealand Film Commission, 2008.

Blacula. Directed by William Crain. American International Pictures, 1972.

The Blood of Jesus. Directed by Spencer Williams. Amegro Films, 1940.

Bloodlust. Directed by John Hewitt and Richard Wolstoncroft. Windhover Productions, 1992.

Bloodspit. Directed by Duke Hendrix. Jigsaw Entertainment, 2008.

Bloody Dracula (Khooni Dracula). Directed by Harinam Singh, H.S. Films, 1992.

Braindead, see *Dead Alive.*

Bram Stoker's Dracula. Directed by Francis Ford Coppola. American Zoetrope, 1992.

Byzantium. Directed by Neil Jordan. Demarest Films, 2012.

The Caretaker. Directed by Tom Conyers. Little Man Screaming, 2012.

The Cat and the Canary. Directed by Paul Leni. Universal Studios, 1927.

Chloe, Love Is Calling You. Directed by Marshall Neilan. Pinnacle Productions, 1934.

The Closed Door (Band darwaza). Directed by Shyam Ramsay and Tulsi Ramsay. Ramsay Films Combine, 1990.

The Company of Wolves. Directed by Neil Jordan. Incorporated Television Company and Palace Pictures, 1984.

Crazy Safari (Fie zhou he shang). Directed by Billy Chan. Win's Movie Productions, 1991.

Cronos. Directed by Guillermo del Toro. CNCAIMC, 1993.

The Crying Game. Directed by Neil Jordan. Palace Pictures and Channel Four Films, 1992.

Da Sweet Blood of Jesus. Directed by Spike Lee. Forty Acres and a Mule Filmworks, 2014.

Damien: The Omen II. Directed by Don Taylor. Twentieth-century Fox, 1978.

Daughters of Darkness (Les lèvres rouges). Directed by Harold Kümel. Showking Films, 1972.

Daughters of the Dust. Directed by Julie Dash. American Playhouse, 1991.

Dead Alive. Directed by Peter Jackson. Wingnut Films, 1992. Also known as *Braindead*.

Deathgasm. Directed by Lei Howden. Metalheads, 2015.

The Door (Darwaza). Directed by Shyam Ramsay and Tulsi Ramsay, Ramsay Productions, 1978.

Dracula. Directed by Tod Browning. Universal Pictures, 1931.

Dracula. Directed by Bhooshan Lal. Bhooshan Films, 1999.

Dracula: Pages from a Virgin's Diary. Directed by Guy Maddin. Domino Films, 2002.

Dracula 3D. Directed by Dario Argento. Multimedia Film Production, 2012.

Dracula's Daughter. Directed by Lambert Hillyer. Universal Pictures, 1936.

Encounters of the Spooky Kind (Gui dagui), directed by Sammo Hung, 1980.

Evil of Dracula (Chi o suu bara), directed by Yamamoto Michio, 1971.

A Fool There Was. Directed by Frank Powell. Fox Film Corporation, 1915.

The Frighteners. Directed by Peter Jackson. Wingnut Films, 1996.

Ganja and Hess. Directed by Bill Gunn. Kelly/Jordan Enterprises, 1973.

Get Out. Directed by Jordan Peele. Universal Pictures, 2017.

A Girl Walks Home Alone at Night. Directed by Ana Lily Amirpour. Shahre Bad Picture, 2014.

Grampire, see *Moonrise*.

The Host (Gwoemul). Directed by Bon Joon-ho. Showbox Entertainment, 2006.

I Survived a Zombie Holocaust. Directed by Guy Pidgeon. 38 Pictures, 2014.

Interview with the Vampire: The Vampire Chronicles. Directed by Neil Jordan. Screenplay by Anne Rice. Geffen Pictures, 1994.

It!. Directed by Herbert J. Leder. Gold Star Films, 1967.

Ju-on: The Grudge. Directed by Takashi Shimizu. Pioneer LDC, Nikkatsu, Oz Co., and Xanadeux, 2002.

King Kong. Directed by Merian C. Cooper. RKO Radio Pictures, 1933.

The Lake of Dracula (Noroi no yakata: Chi o su me). Directed by Michio Yamamoto. Toho Company, 1971.

The Legend of the Seven Golden Vampires. Directed by Roy Ward Baker. Hammer Films, 1974.

Let the Right One In (Låt den rätte komme in). Directed by Tomas Alfredson. EFTI, 2008.

Lust for a Vampire. Directed by Jimmy Sangster. Hammer Films, 1971.

Midnight Vampire. Directed by Yeung Kung-Leung. Nanyue Film Company, 1936.

Mr. Vampire (Jianshi Xiansheng). Directed by Ricky Lau. Bo Ho Film Company, 1985.

Monster from Green Hell. Directed by Kenneth G. Crane. Gross-Karsne Productions, 1957.

Moon Child. Directed by Takashi Hirano. Shochiku, 2003.

Moonrise. Directed by David Blyth. Tucker Production Company, 1992. Also known as *Grampire.*

Moonrise Kingdom. Directed by Wes Anderson. Indian Paintbrush, 2012.

The Mummy. Directed by Karl Freund. Universal Pictures, 1932.

Neighbours: They Are Vampires. Directed by Shyam Ramsay, Ramsay Entertainment, 2014.

Night of the Living Dead. Directed by George A. Romero. Image Ten, 1968.

Nosferatu: Symphony of Horror (Eine Symphonie des Grauens). Directed by F.W. Murnau. Jofa-Atelier Berlin-Johannisthal, 1922.

Nosferatu: The Vampyre (Nosferatu: Phantom der Nacht). Directed by Werner Herzog. Werner Herzog Filmproduktion, 1979. In German or in English.

Ondine. Directed by Neil Jordan. Wayfare Entertainment, 2008.

One More Dracula (Aur ek Dracula in Hindi, originally *Dracula 2012* in Malayalam). Directed by Vinayan. Akash Films, 2013.

Only Lovers Left Alive. Directed by Jim Jarmusch. Recorded Picture Company, 2013.

Outback Vampires. Directed by Colin Eggleston. Somerset Film Productions, 1991. Also titled *The Wicked.*

The Palace (Mahal). Directed by Kamal Amrohi. Bombay Talkies, 1949.

Pandemonium. Directed by Haydn Keenan. Smart Street Films, 1987.

Perfect Creature. Directed by Glenn Standring. Twentieth Century Fox, 2007.

Pulse (Kairo). Directed by Kurosawa Kiyoshi. Daiei Eiga, 2001.

Reign in Darkness. Directed by David W. Allen and Kelly Dolen. Rapidfire Productions, 2002.

The Relic. Directed by Peter Hyams. BBC, 1997.

Rigor Mortis. Directed by Juno Mak. Kudos Films, 2013.

The Ring (Ringu). Directed by Nakata Hideo. Basara Pictures, 1998.

Robo Vampire. Directed by Godfrey Ho. Filmmark International, 1988.

Salem's Lot. Directed by Tobe Hooper. Written by Stephen King and Paul Monash. Warner Brothers Television, 1979.

The Serpent and the Rainbow. Directed by Wes Craven. Universal Pictures, 1988.

The She-Butterfly (Leptirica). Directed by Djordie Kadijević, Beograd: Radio-televizija Beograd, 1973.

The Shining. Directed by Stanley Kubrick. Warner Brothers, 1980.

Silence (Khamoshi) Directed by Chakri Toleti, 2019.

This Story of Love (Pyaar kii ye ek kahaani). Created by Ekta Kapoor. Television, 2001.

Sugar Hill. Directed by Paul Maslansky. American International Pictures, 1974.

That Terrible Night (Wohi bhayanak raat). Directed by Vinod Talwar, Talwar Productions, 1989.

Thirst. Directed by Rod Hardy. F.G. Film Productions, 1979.

Thirst. (Bakjwi). Directed by Park Chan-wook. C.J. Entertainment, 2009.

This Story of Love (Pyaar kii ye ek kahaani). Created by Ekta Kapoor. India Television, 2001.

Three … Extremes, directed by Miike Takashi, Park Chan Wook, and Fruit Chan. Lionsgate Films, 2004.

Train to Busan (Busanhaeng), directed by Yeon Sang-ho. Next Entertainment World, 2016.

The Transfiguration. Directed by Michael O'Shea. Transfiguration Productions, 2016.

True Blood. Showrunner Alan Ball. Home Box Office, 2008–14.

Twilight. Directed by Catherine Hardwicke. Summit Entertainment, 2008.

Twins of Evil. Directed by John Hough. The Rank Organization and Hammer Films, 1971.

2001: A Space Odyssey. Directed by Stanley Kubrick. MGM, 1968.

Us. Directed by Jordan Peele. Monkeypaw Productions, 2019.

Vamperifica. Directed by Bruce Ornstein. Blood River Productions, 2011.

The Vampire. Directed by Robert G. Vignola. Kalem Company, 1913. The sole existing print is housed in the George Eastman Museum's film archive.

The Vampire (Ang Aswang). Directed by George Musser. Manila Talkaone, 1933.

Vampire Cop Ricky (Hebhyeol hyeongsa na do-yeol). Directed by Si-myung Lee. Chungeorahm Film, 2006.

The Vampire Diaries. Created by Julie Plec and Kevin Williamson. Warner Brothers Television, 2009–2017.

The Vampire Doll (Chi o suu ningyo). Directed by Yamamoto Michio. Toho Company, 1970.

The Vampire Lovers. Directed by Roy Ward Baker. Hammer Film Productions, 1970.

The Vampire Moth (Kyuketsuga). Directed by Nakagawa Nobuo, 1956.

The Wailing (*Gok-seong*). Directed by Na Hong-jin. Twentieth Century Fox, 2016.

We Are the Night (*Wir sind die Nacht*). Directed by Dennis Gansel. Celluloid Dreams, 2010.

What We Do in the Shadows. Directed by Jemaine Clement and Taika Waititi. Unison Films, 2014.

The Wicked. See *Outback Vampires.*

Willard. Directed by David Mann. Bing Crosby Productions, 1971.

You Are My Vampire (*Geudaen naui baempaieo*). Directed by Hoi Lee. South Korea, 2014.

Bibliography

Abbas, Ackbar. "The New Hong Kong Cinema and the 'Déjà Disparu.'" *Discourse*, volume 16, number 3, spring 1994), pp. 65–77.

Abbott, Stacey. *Celluloid Vampires: Life after Death in the Modern World*. University of Texas Press, 2007.

Abel, Marco. "22 January 2007: Film Establishment Attacks 'Berlin School' as Wrong Kind of National Cinema." *A New History of German Cinema*, edited by Jennifer Kapczynski and Michael D. Richardson, Camden House, 2012, pp. 602–08.

Adams, Phillip. Interview. *Not Quite Hollywood: The Wild, Untold Story of OZploitation!*, directed by Mark Hartley, City Films Worldwide, 2008.

Aeschylus. *The Oresteia*, translated by Robert Fagles, Penguin, 1984.

Agamben, Giorgio. *Homo sacer: Sovereign Power and Bare Life*, translated by Daniel Heller-Roazen, Stanford University Press, 1995.

_____. What Is the Contemporary? *What Is an Apparatus? And Other Essays*, translated by David Kishik and Stefan Pedatella, Stanford University Press, 2009.

Alfredson, Tomas. Interview. *Let the Right One In*, Blu-ray disc from Magnolia Home Entertainment, USA, 2009.

Alfredson, Tomas, and John Ajvide Lindqvist. Commentary track on *Let the Right One In*, Blu-ray disc from Momentum Pictures, UK, 2010.

Almond, Barbara R. "Monstrous Infants and Vampyric Mothers." *International Journal of Psychoanalysis*, volume 88, 2007, pp. 219–35.

Als, Hiltojn. Review of Jack Thorne's stage play *Let the Right One In*. *The New Yorker*, 9 February 2015, pp. 72–73.

Amirpour, Ana Lily, and Eric Kohn. *A Girl Walks Home Alone at Night: Essay and Graphic Novels*, Radio Comics, 2014, enclosed with DVD.

Anderson, Amanda. *The Way We Argue Now: A Study in the Cultures of Theory*, Princeton University Press, 2006.

Antonakou, Alma, and Triarhou Lazaros. "Soul, butterfly, mythological nymph: psyche in philosophy and neuroscience." *Arquivos de Neuro-Psiquiatria*, volume 75, number 3, 2017, pp. 176–79.

Armknecht, Megan, et. al. "Identifying Impressions of Baba Yaga." *Marvels and Tales: Journal of Fairy Tale Studies*, volume 31, number 1, 2017, pp. 62–79.

Auerbach, Nina. "My Vampire, My Friend: The Intimacy Dracula Destroyed." *Blood Read: The Vampire as Metaphor in Contemporary Culture*, University of Pennsylvania Press, 1997.

_____. *Our Vampires, Ourselves*, University of Chicago Press, 1995.

Augustine, Saint. *City of God*, circa 413–426 CE, Random House, 1950.

Bahadur, Nina. "Swedish Gender-neutral Pronoun, 'Hen,' Added to Country's National Encyclopedia," www.huffingtonpost.com/2013/04/11.

Balmain, Colette. "East Asian Gothic: A Definition." *Palgrave Communications*, volume 3, number 1, 2017, pp. 1–10.

_____. *Introduction to Japanese Horror Film*, Edinburgh University Press, 2008.

Banerjee, Poulomi. "Why Dracula fails to get a bite of India but atmas, dayans make us shiver." *Hindustan Times* 12 November 2017, https://www.hindustantimes.com/art-and-culture/dracula-didn-t-come-to-india-why-atmas-and-dayans-have-us-spooked/story-TNYKHxXVtsjDEOO6TcrwsK.html.

Barber, Paul. *Vampires, Burial, and Death: Folklore and Reality*, 1988. Yale University Press, 2010.

Barnes, John. *The Writer in Australia: A Collection of Literary Documents 1856–1964*, Oxford University Press. 1969.

Barry, Ian. Interview. *Not Quite Hollywood: The Wild, Untold Story of OZploitation!*, directed by Mark Hartley. City Films Worldwide, 2008.

Bawden, Tania. "Director's Golden Stake in Vampire Film." *InDaily* 5 May 2017. indaily.com. au/news/local/2017/05/05/directors-golden-stake-vampire-film/.

Beatty, Bernard, and Vincent Newey. *Byron and the Limits of Fiction*, Liverpool University Press, 1988.

Bechdel, A. *Dykes to Watch Out For*, Firebrand Books, 1986.

Benshoff, Harry M. "Blaxploitation Horror Films: Generic Reappropriation or Reinscription?" *Cinema Journal*, volume 39, number 2, 2000, 31–50. JSTOR, www.jstor.org/stable/1225551.

Beresford, Bruce. Interview. *Not Quite Hollywood: The Wild, Untold Story of OZploitation!*, directed by Mark Hartley, City Films Worldwide, 2008.

Berg, Lauren. "Globalization and the Modern Vampire." *Film Matters*, Fall 2011, pp. 8–12.

Bishop, Ryan, Kristoffer Gansing, Jussi Parikka, and Elvia Wilk, editors. *Across & Beyond: A Transmediale Reader on Post-digital Practices, Concepts, and Institutions*. Stenberg Press, 2016.

Bloom, Harold. Introduction. *Viva Modern Critical Interpretations of Bram Stoker's Dracula*, Viva Books, 2010, 1–2.

Blumenfeld, Samuel L. *The Marlowe-Shakespeare Connection: A New Study of the Authorship Question*, McFarland, 2008.

Bondanella, Peter, and Federico Pachioni. *A History of Italian Cinema*, 2nd edition, Bloomsbury Academic, 2017.

Boon Chan Media Correspondent. "New Life in Death; Rigor Mortis' Juno Mak Has Given Himself a New Image as a Critically Acclaimed Film-Maker." *The Straits Times* (Singapore) 27 November 2013, *Nexis Uni*. advance-lexis-com.ezproxy.valpo.edu/api/perma link/01e6a475-b20e-4fc9-9201-e8bea7bff89b/?context=1516831.

Boyer, Sabrina. "'Thou Shalt Not Crave Thy Neighbour': *True Blood*, Abjection, and Otherness." *Studies in Popular Culture*, volume 33, number 2, spring 2011, pp. 21–41.

Breger, Esther. "'We Like Vampires Because We Hate Death': Interview with the Director of *A Girl Walks Home Alone at Night*." *The New Republic Daily* 24 November 2014, pp. 1–5.

Brennan, Richard. Interview. *Not Quite Hollywood: The Wild, Untold Story of OZploitation!*, directed by Mark Hartley, City Films Worldwide, 2008.

Bryson, Bill. *In a Sunburned Country*, Broadway, 2001.

Buffini, Moira. *A Vampire Story*, 2008. Samuel French, 2016.

_____. Interview. *Byzantium*, cited above, UK Blu-ray special feature.

Bunson, Matthew. *The Vampire Encyclopedia*, Crown Publishers, 1993.

Butler, Erik. *Metamorphoses of the Vampire in Literature and Film*, Camden House, 2010.

Butler, Judith. "Performative Acts and Gender Constitution: An Essay in Phenomenology and Feminist Theory." *Theatre Journal*, volume 40, number 4, 1988, pp. 519–31, JSTOR, doi: 10.2307/3207893.

Byrne, James. "Wigs and Rings: Cross-Cultural Exchange in the South Korean and Japanese Horror Film." *Journal of Japanese & Korean Cinema*, volume 6, number 2, 2014, pages 184–201.

Byron, Lord. See Gordon, George, Lord Byron.

Çakir. Deniz. "*A Girl Walks Home Alone at Night* Is the Feminist Horror Movie of Our Dreams. Literally," Medium.com. 1–6.

Calhoun, John, "Childhood's End: 'Let the Right One In' and Other Deaths of Innocence," *Cineaste* 35.1: 27- 31.
Camper, Cathy. "Essay: 'Yaoi' 101: Girls Love 'Boys' Love.'" *The Women's Review of Books*, volume. 23, number 3, 2006, 24–26.
Choe, Steve. *Sovereign Violence: Ethics and South Korean Cinema in the New Millennium*, Amsterdam University Press, 2018.
Choi, Jinhee, and Mitsuyo Wada-Marciano, editors. *Horror to the Extreme: Changing Boundaries in Asian Cinema*, Hong Kong University Press, 2009.
Chu, Karen. "Hong Kong Filmart: Vampire Genre Gets Chinese Spin." *The Hollywood Reporter* 19 March 2013, www.hollywoodreporter.com/news/hong-kong-filmart-vampire-genre-429815.
Cohen, Jeffrey Jerome. *Monster Theory: Reading Culture*, Minnesota University Press, 1996.
Connell, R. W. "The Big Picture: Masculinities in Recent World History." *Theory and Society*, volume 22, number, 1993), pp. 597–623, *SpringerLink*, https://doi.org/10.1007/BF00993 538.
———. *Masculinities*, 2nd edition, Polity Press, 2005.
Connolly, A. "Psychoanalytic Theory in Times of Terror." *Journal of Analytical Psychology*, volume 48, 2003, pp. 407–31.
Conrad, Joseph. "An Outpost of Progress," *Cosmopolis* July 1897.
Copper, Basil. *The Vampire: In Legend and Fact*, Citadel Press, 1993.
Coulthart, John. "Nosferatu: Phantom der Nacht." *Horror! 333 Films to Scare You to Death*, edited by James Marriott and Kim Newman, 2nd edition, Carlton Books, 2010, p. 213.
Creed, Barbara. *The Monstrous-Feminine: Film, Feminism, Psychoanalysis*, Routledge, 2015.
———. *Phallic Panic: Film, Horror, and the Primal Uncanny*, Melbourne University Press, 2005.
Davies, Ann. "Guillermo del Toro's *Cronos*: The Vampire as Embodied Heterotopia." *Quarterly Review of Film and Video*, volume 25, number 5, 2008, pp. 395–403.
———. "Slime and Subtlety: Monsters in del Toro's Spanish-Language Films." *The Supernatural Cinema of Guillermo del Toro*, edited by John W. Morehead, McFarland, 2015, pp. 41–57.
Davies, Laurence. "Cronos, or the Pleasures of Impurity." *Gothic Science Fiction 1980–2010*, edited by Emily Alder and Sara Wasson, Liverpool University Press, 2011, 87–99.
Deamer, David. *Deleuze's Cinema Books: Three Introductions to the Taxonomy of Images*, University of Edinburgh Press, 2016.
Deleuze, Gilles. *Cinema I: The Movement-Image*, translated by Hugh Tomlinson and Barbara Habberjam. London: Bloomsbury Academic, 2013.
———. *Cinema II: The Time-Image*, translated by Hugh Tomlinson and Robert Galeta, Bloomsbury Academic, 2013.
Deleuze, Gilles, and Félix Guattari. *A Thousand Plateaus: Capitalism and Schizophrenia*, translated by Brian Massumi, Continuum, 2004.
Desjardins, Sylvain-Jacques. "A Monstrous Task," *McGill Reporter*, interview by Lorna Hutchison with David Williams at McGill University, Montréal, 5 November 1998, reporter-archive.mcgill.ca/Rep/r3105/williams.html.
Diawara, Manthia, and Phyllis R. Klotman. "Ganja and Hess: Vampires, Sex, and Addictions." *Black American Literature Forum*, volume 25, number 2, 1991, pp. 299–314.
Donahue, Micah K. "*Translatio Vampyri*: Transamerican Vampires and Transnational Capital in Guillermo del Toro's *Cronos*." *Comparative American Studies: An International Journal*, volume 14, number 2, 2016, pp. 126–38.
Donaldson, Mike. "What Is Hegemonic Masculinity?" *Theory and Society*, volume 22, number 5 1993, pp. 643–57, *SpringerLink*, https://doi.org/10.1007/BF00993540.
Douglas, Drake. *Horror!*, Macmillan, 1966.
Dundes, Alan, editor. *The Vampire: A Casebook*, Wisconsin University Press, 1998.
Edwards, Catherine. "Berlusconi's back: Understanding the Enduring Popularity of Italy's 'immoral' former PM." 31 January 2018, www.thelocal.it/20180131/silvio-berlusconi-back-italy-election-forza-italia.
Edwards, Emily. "Searching for a Room of One's Own: Rethinking The Iranian Diaspora in

Persepolis, Shahs Of Sunset and *A Girl Walks Home Alone At Night.*" *Glocalism: Journal Of Culture, Politics And Innovation* 2017, number 3, pp. 1–29.

Eljaiek-Rodríguez, Gabriel. "Bloodsucking Bugs. Horacio Quiroga and the Latin American Transformation of Vampires." *The Supernatural Cinema of Guillermo del Toro*, edited by John W. Morehead, McFarland, 2015, pp. 146–62.

Forrester, Sibelan. "Baba Yaga: The Wild Witch of the East." *Baba Yaga*, edited by Sibelan Forrester, et. al., University of Mississippi Press, 2013, pp. xxi–li.

Foster, Michael Dylan. *The Book of Yokai: Mysterious Creatures of Japanese Folklore*, University of California Press, 2015.

Gackt. "Mizérable." Nippon Crown Co., 1999.

Gackt, and Hyde. "Orenji no Taiyo." *Crescent*, Burnish Stone Recording Studios, 2003.

Gallagher, Sharon M. *The Irish Vampire: From Folklore to the Imaginations of Charles Robert Maturin, Joseph Sheridan Le Fanu and Bram Stoker*, McFarland, 2017.

Galloway, Alexander. *The Interface Effect*, Polity, 2012.

_____. *Laruelle: Against the Digital*, University of Minnesota Press, 2014.

Galloway, Alexander R., and Eugene Thacker. *The Exploit. A Theory of Networks*, University of Minnesota Press, 2007.

Gardiner, Irene. "NZ on Screen: A History of Vampires in NZ." *New Zealand Herald* 20 June, 2014, no page.

Genslinger, Neil. Review of *Dracula 3D*, *New York Times* 3 October 2013. www.nytimes.com/.../argentos-dracula-3d-is-the-latest-entry-about-the-count.html

Gerard, Emily. From "Transylvanian Superstitions." *Dracula*, edited by Glennis Byron. Broadview, 1998, pp. 439–47.

Giuffrida, Angela. "Berlusconi pledges to deport 600,000 illegal immigrants from Italy" 5 Feb. 2018, www.theguardian.com/world/2018/feb/05/berlusconi-pledges-to-deport-600000-illegal-immigrants-italy-election.

Glišić, Milovan. "Nakon devedeset godina" [After Ninety Years: The Story of Serbian Vampire Sava Savanović], translated by James Lyons, CreateSpace Independent Publishing Platform, 2015.

Glob, P.V. *The Bog People*, translated by Rupert Bruce-Mitford. Faber & Faber, 1969.

Godden, Mark, choreographer. Royal Winnipeg Ballet *Dracula* production, 1998; staged again in Winnipeg in 2016 for the company's 77th season.

Gogol, Nikolay. "Viy," translated by Claud Field, CreateSpace Independent Publishing Platform, 2017.

Gopal, Sangita. *Conjugations: Marriage and Form in New Bollywood Cinema*, University of Chicago Press, 2011.

Gordon, George, Lord Byron. "Fragment of a Novel." *Mazeppa*, 1819.

_____. *The Giaour: A Fragment of a Turkish Tale.* 1814. San Bernardino: no publisher identified, 2016.

Gordon, Joan, and Veronica Hollinger. "Introduction: The Shape of Vampires." *Blood Read: The Vampire as Metaphor in Contemporary Culture*," University of Pennsylvania Press, 1997, pp. 1–7.

Groom, Nick. *The Vampire: A New History*, Yale University Press, 2018.

Hagener, Malte. "Cinephilia in the Age of Post-Cinematographic." *L'Atalante*, number 18, 2014, pp. 7–16.

Halberstam, Judith. *Skin Shows: Gothic Horror and the Technology of Monsters*, Duke University Press, 1995.

Hall, Ronald E., and Jesenia M. Pizarro. "Cool Pose: Black Male Homicide and the Social Implications of Manhood." *Journal of Social Services Research*, volume 37, number 1, 2010, pp. 86–98. Taylor & Francis doi:10.1080/01488376.2011.524530.

Han, Byung-Chul. *The Expulsion of the Other: Society, Perception and Communication Today*, translated by Wieland Hoban, Polity Press, 2018.

Hantke, Steffen. "Postwar German Cinema and the Horror Film: Thoughts on Historical Continuity and Genre Consolidation." *Caligari's Heirs: The German Cinema of Fear after 1945*, edited by Steffen Hantke, Scarecrow Press, 2007, pp. vii–xxiv.

Harbord, Janet. *Ex-Centric Cinema. Giorgio Agamben and Film*, Bloomsbury, 2016.

Hardy, Rod. Interview. *Not Quite Hollywood: The Wild, Untold Story of OZploitation!*, directed by Mark Hartley, City Films Worldwide, 2008.

Hartley, Mark, dir. *Not Quite Hollywood: The Wild, Untold Story of OZploitation!*, City Films Worldwide, 2008.

Heuvelmans, Bernard. *On the Track of Unknown Animals*, translated by Richard Garnett, Kegan Paul, 1995.

Hibbard, Allen. "Tangier at the Crossroads: Cross-Cultural Encounters and Literary Production." *Writing Tangier*, edited by Ralph M. Coury and Robert Kevin Lacey, *Currents in Comparative Romance Languages and Literatures*, volume 169, Peter Lang, 2009 pp. 1–12.

Hine, David. "Silvio Berlusconi, the Media and the Conflict of Interest Issue." *Italian Politics*, volume 17, 2001, pages 261–75. *JSTOR*, www.jstor.org/stable/43041922.

Hoberman, Ruth. *Museum Trouble: Edwardian Fiction and the Emergence of Modernism*, University of Virginia Press, 2011.

Hoffman, Calvin. *The Murder of the Man Who Was "Shakespeare,"* Grosset and Dunlap: 1960, marlowe-shakespeare.blogspot.com.

Hoffman, Eva. *Time.* Picador, 2009.

Homans, Jennifer. *Apollo's Angels: A History of Ballet*, Random House, 2010.

Homer. *The Odyssey*, translated by Robert Fagles, Viking Penguin, 1996.

Hudson, Dale. "Vampires and Transnational Horror." *A Companion to the Horror Film*, edited by Harry M. Benshoff, Wiley-Blackwell, 2014, pp. 463–82.

Hughes, Robert. *The Fatal Shore*, Knopf, 1987.

Humphries, Barry. Interview. *Not Quite Hollywood: The Wild, Untold Story of OZploitation!*, directed by Mark Hartley, City Films Worldwide, 2008.

Hurley, Kelly. "Abject and Grotesque." *The Routledge Companion to the Gothic*, edited by Catherine Spooner and Emma McAvoy, Routledge, 2007.

Hyde, Deborah. "Vampire Legends That Refuse to Die." *The Guardian* 4 December 2012, https://www.theguardian.com/science/blog/2012/dec/04/vampire-legends-refuse-die-undead.

Hyland, Robert. "A Politics of Excess: Violence and Violation in Miike Takashi's *Audition.*" Choi and Wada-Marciano, pp. 199–218.

Ingber, Sasha. "The Bloody Truth About Serbia's Vampire." *National Geographic* 17 December 2012, https://news.nationalgeographic.com/news/2012/12/121217-vampire-serbia-super natural-garlic-fangs-science-weird/.

Inoue, Yoshitaka. "Contemporary Consciousness as Reflected in Images of the Vampire." *Jung Journal: Culture & Psyche*, volume 5, number 4, 2011, pp. 83–99. Jisho.org.

Jackson, Brandon A. "Beyond the Cool Pose: Black Men and Emotion Management Strategies." *Sociology Compass*, volume 12, number 4, 2018, pp. 1–14. *Wiley Online Library*, doi:10.1111/soc4.12569.

Johnson, Carol S. "The Limbs of Osiris: Reed's *Mumbo Jumbo* and Hollywood's *The Mummy.*" *Melus.* Volume 17, number 4, 1991, pp. 105–115.

Jones, Ernest. *On the Nightmare*, Hogarth Press, 1931.

Joshi, S.T. "The Magical Spirituality of a Lapsed Catholic: Atheism and Anticlericalism." *The Supernatural Cinema of Guillermo del Toro*, edited by John W. Morehead, McFarland, 2015, pp. 11–21.

Kane, Tim. *The Changing Vampire of Film and Television: A Critical Study of the Growth of a Genre*, McFarland, 2006.

Kantaris, Geoffrey. "Cyborgs, Cities, and Celluloid: Memory Machines in Two Latin American Cyborg Films." *Latin American Cyberculture and Cyberliterature*, edited by Claire Taylor and Thea Pitman, Liverpool University Press pp. 50–69.

Karaminas, Vicki. "The Vampire Dandy: Reconceptualising Masculine Identities in Fashion, Cinema, and Literature." *Lambda Nordica*, volume 14, number 3–4, 2009, pp. 123–59. https://www.lambdanordica.org/index.php/lambdanordica/article/view/275.

Keyworth, David. *Troublesome Corpses: Vampires and Revenants from Antiquity to the Present*, Desert Island Books, 2007.

Kim, Kyu Hyun. "Park Chan-wook's *Thirst*: Body, Guilt, and Exsanguination." *Korean Horror Cinema*, edited by Alison Peirse and Daniel Martin, Edinburgh University Press, 2013, pp. 199–216.

King, Stephen. *The Shining*, Doubleday, 1977.

Kinoshita, Chika. "The Mummy Complex: Kurosawa Kiyoshi's *Loft* and J-horror." *Horror to the Extreme: Changing Boundaries in Asian Cinema*, edited by Jinhee Choi and Mitsuyo Wada-Marciano, Hong Kong University Press, 2009, pp. 103–22.

Klinger, Leslie, ed. *The New Annotated Dracula*, Norton, 2008.

Knee, Adam. "The Pan-Asian Outlook of *The Eye*." *Horror to the Extreme: Changing Boundaries in Asian Cinema*, edited by Jihnee Choi and Mitsuyo Wada-Marciano, Hong Kong University Press, pp. 69–84.

Kraniauskas, John. "Cronos and the Political Economy of Vampirism: Notes on a Historical Constellation." *Cannibalism and the Colonial World*, edited by Francis Barker, et al., Cambridge University Press, 1998, pp. 142–57.

Kristeva, Julia. *The Powers of Horror: An Essay on Abjection*, translated by Leon Roudiez. Columbia University Press, 1982.

Lam, Stephanie. "Hop on Pop: Jiangshi Films in a Transnational Context." *CineAction*, number 78, 2009, pp. 46–51.

Laruelle, François. *The Concept of Non Photography*, translated by Robin Mackay, Sequence Press, 2011.

_____. "Of Black Universe in the Human Foundations of Color." *Hyun Soo Choi: Seven Large-Scale Paintings*, translated by Miguel Abreu, Thread Waxing Space, 1991 pp. 2–4.

Latour, Bruno. "Give Me a Laboratory and I Raise the World." *Science Observed: Perspectives on the Social Study of Science*, edited by Karin Knorr-Cetina and Michael Mulkay, Sage, 1983, pp. 141–70.

Lazic, Manuela. "The Transfiguration—First Look Review." *Little White Lies*, 15 May 2016, https://lwlies.com/festivals/the-transfiguration-first-look-review/.

Le Fanu, Joseph Sheridan. "Carmilla." *In a Glass Darkly*. Richard Bentley and Sons, 1872.

Lee, Edmund. "Juno Mak Resurrects His Career in Rigor Mortis." *South China Morning Post* 23 October 2013, www.scmp.com/magazines/48hrs/article/1334595/juno-mak-resurrects-his-career-rigor-mortis.

Leigh Danny. "The Skateboarding Iranian Vampire Diaries; Director Ana Lily Amirpour Talks About Feminism, Porn and Her Eerie 'Fairy Tale' *A Girl Walks Home Alone at Night*." *The Guardian* 11 May 2015.

Leupp, Gary P. *Male Colors: The Construction of Homosexuality in Tokugawa Japan*, University of California Press, 1995.

Limpar, Ildiko. "Masculinity, Visibility, and the Vampire Literary Tradition in *What We Do in the Shadows*." *Journal of the Fantastic in the Arts*, volume 29, number 2, 22 March 2019, *Gale General Onefile*.

Lin Chunyan [林春燕]. "中西文化碰撞下的奇观——20世纪80年代香港僵尸恐怖片特色探寻" ["Visions of East-West Encounters: Exploring the Hallmarks of 1980's Hong Kong Vampire Horror Films"]. 青年文学家 [*Literati Youth*], number 26, 2013, *China National Knowledge Infrastructure*. www.cnki.com.cn/Article/CJFDTotal-QNWJ201326063.htm.

Lindqvist, John Ajvide. "Let the Old Dreams Die." In *Let the Old Dreams Die*, translated by Ebba Segerberg, St. Martin's, 2013, pp. 371–93.

_____. *Let the Right One In*, translated by Ebba Segerberg, 2004, St. Martin's, 2007.

Liu, Mandy Yee Man [廖綺雯]. 重讀八、九十年代的「恐怖喜劇」: 殭屍電影與香港後殖民 [*Reevaluating "Horror Comedies" of the 80's and 90's: Vampire Films and Postcolonial Hong Kong*]. MPhil Thesis, Lingnan University, 2014.

Lodge, Guy. "Sundance Film Review: *A Girl Walks Home Alone at Night*." *Variety* 24 January 2014, variety.com/201 4/film/reviews/sundance-film-review-a-girl-walks-home-alone-at-night-1201069599/).

Maberry, Jonathan, and David F. Kramer. *They Bite: Endless Cravings of Supernatural Predators*, Citadel, 2009.

MacCarthy, Fiona. *Byron: Life and Legend*. Farrar, Straus and Giroux, 2002, pp. 109–24.

Macdonald, D.L., and Kathleen Scherf. Introduction. *The Vampyre: A Tale. The Vampyre and Errnestus Berchtold; or, The Modern Œdipus*, by John William Polidori, Broadview, 2008, pp. 9–31.

Mackellar, Dorothea. "My Country." *The Witch-Maid and Oher Verses*, 1908, Dent, 1914, pp. 29–31. Permission to quote is by arrangement with the licenser, the Dorothea Mackellar Estate, c/-Curtis Brown (Aust) Pty Ltd.

MacLeod, Celeste Lipow. *Multiethnic Australia: Its History and Future*, McFarland, 2006.

Magistrale, Tony. *Abject Terrors: Surveying the Modern and Postmodern Horror Film*, Peter Lang, 2005.

Majors, Richard, and Janet Mancini Billson. *Cool Pose: The Dilemma of Black Manhood in America*, Simon & Schuster, 1993.

Manfredino, Carla-Rosa. Review of *Blackbird, Bye Bye*. *Times Literary Supplement* 14 December 2018, p. 25.

Marshall, Tyler. "Stifling Penchant: Conformity—a Must in Scandinavia." *Los Angeles Times* 14 December 1988: no page. articles.latimes.com/1988-12-14/news/mn-278_1_welfare state.

Martin-Jones, David. *Deleuze and World Cinemas*, Continuum, 2011.

Marx, Karl. *Das Kapital*, translated by Samuel Moore, Pacific, 2010.

May, Tiffany. "Hong Kong Umbrella Movement Leaders Are Sentenced to Prison." *The New York Times* 23 April. 2019, www.nytimes.com/2019/04/23/world/asia/hong-kong-umbrella-movement.html.

McConnell, Gareth. Photo of Rebecca Benson and Cristian Ortega in the stage play *Let the Right One In*, The New Yorker 26 January 2015, p. 7.

McDonald, Keith, and Roger Clark. *Guillermo del Toro: Film as Alchemic Art*, Bloomsbury Academic, 2014.

McDonnell, Terence E. *Best Laid Plans: Cultural Entropy and the Unraveling of AIDS Media Campaigns*, University of Chicago Press, 2016.

McKenzie Movies." *Continuum: Journal of Media & Cultural Studies*, volume 28, number 5, 2014, pp. 629–39.

McLeod, Ken. "Visual Kei: Hybridity and Gender in Japanese Popular Culture." *Young*, volume 21, number 4, 2013, pp. 309–25.

Means, Coleman Robin R., *Horror Noire*, Routledge, 2011.

Medovoi, Leerom. "Theorizing Historicity, or the Many Meanings of *Blacula*." *Screen*, volume 39, number 1, 1998, pp. 1–21. Oxford Academic, https://doi.org/10.1093/screen/39.1.1.

"Melusine." http://en.wikipedia.org/wiki.

Meyer, Stephanie. *Twilight*. Little, Brown, 2005. Subsequent novels in the series are *New Moon* (2006), *Eclipse* (2007), and *Breaking Dawn* (2008).

Miller, George. Interview. *Not Quite Hollywood: The Wild, Untold Story of OZploitation!*, directed by Mark Hartley, City Films Worldwide, 2008.

Miller, Julie. "Jim Jarmusch on *Only Lovers Left Alive*, Tilda Swinton, and Vampire 'Mythology.'" *Vanity Fair* 8 April 2014, vanityfair.com.

Monteiro, Venâncio, and Núria Augusta. "Gender Bending in Anime, Manga, Visual Kei and Lolita Fashion: Representations from Portugal." *Prisma Social: Revista de Ciencias Sociales*, number 7, 2011.

Monton, Vincent. Interview. *Not Quite Hollywood: The Wild, Untold Story of OZploitation!*, directed by Mark Hartley, City Films Worldwide, 2008.

Morat, Daniel. "Einleitung." *Weltstadtvergnügen. Berlin 1880–1930*. Edited by. Daniel Morat et al. Göttingen: Vandenhoeck & Rupprecht, 2016, pp. 9–27.

Moretti, Franco. "The Dialectic of Fear." *New Left Review*, volume 136, number 1, 1982, pp. 67–85. knarf.english.upenn.edu/Articles/moretti.html.

Morrissey, Stephen Patrick. "Let the right one slip in." *Viva Hate*, HMV, 1988.

Mubarki, Meraj Ahmed. *Filming Horror: Hindi Cinema, Ghosts and Ideologies*, Sage Publications, 2016.

Muir, John K. *Horror Films of the 1970s*, McFarland, 2007.

Mukherjea, Ananya. "My Vampire Boyfriend: Postfeminism, 'Perfect' Masculinity, and the Contemporary Appeal of Paranormal Romance. *Studies in Popular Culture*, volume 33, number 2, 2011, pp. 1–20, JSTOR, www.jstor.org/stable/23416381.

Mullins, Greg A. *Colonial Affairs: Bowles, Burroughs, and Chester Write Tangier*, University of Wisconsin Press, 2002.

Murguia, Salvador. "Bloodthirsty Films." *The Encyclopedia of Japanese Horror Films*, Rowman & Littlefield, 2016, pp. 26–28.

Murray Schafer, R. *The Tuning of the World*, Knopf, 1977.

Nabokov, Vladimir. *Lolita*, Putnam, 1958.

Nelson, Rob. "Dario Argento's *Dracula*." *Variety* 21 May 2012, variety.com/2012/film/reviews/dario-argento-s-dracula-1117947598/.

Nicholl, Charles. *The Reckoning: The Murder of Christopher Marlowe*, University of Chicago Press, 1992.

Nickelberry, Lynette D., and Marilyn Coleman. "Exploring African American Masculinities: An Integrative Model." *Sociology Compass*, volume 6, number 11, 2012, pp. 897–907, *Wiley Online Library*, doi:10.1111/j.1751–9020.2012.00498.

Ognjanović, Dejan. *Više od istine: Kadijević o Kadijeviću* [More than truth: Kadijević about Kadijević]. Novi Sad: Orfelin, 2017.

O'Halloran, W. *Early Irish History and Antiquities and the History of West Cork*, 1916, Library Ireland.

Palmer, Alex. "The Case of Hong Kong's Missing Booksellers." *The New York Times Magazine*, 3 April 2018, www.nytimes.com/2018/04/03/magazine/the-case-of-hong-kongs-missing-booksellers.html.

Parikka, Jussi. *Insect Media: An Archeology of Animals and Technology*, University of Minnesota Press, 2010.

_____. "Remain(s) Scattered," *Remain*, University of Minnesota Press/Mason Press, 2018, pp. 1–48.

Paterson, Andrew Barton (Banjo). "Clancy of the Overflow." *The Works of "Banjo" Paterson*, Wordsworth, 1993, pp.13–14.

Pender, Anne. "The Mythical Australian: Barry Humphries, Gough Whitlam and 'New Nationalism.'" *Australian Journal of Politics and History*, volume 51, number 1, March 2005, pp. 67–78.

_____. *One Man Show: The Stages of Barry Humphries*, ABC-HarperCollins. 2010.

Phillips, A.A. "The Cultural Cringe." *Meanjin*, volume 9, number 4, summer 1950, pages 299–302, reproduced in *Meanjin* Sep. 5, 2017.

Poggioli, Sylvia. "2018 Puts Pope Francis to the Test." All Things Considered, 27 December 2018, National Public Radio archive.

Polidori, John William. *The Vampyre: A Tale*. 1819, Cavalier Classics, 2016.

Pollan Michael. *The Omnivore's Dilemma: A Natural History of Four Meals*, Penguin, 2006.

Powell, Leah Carson. "Night Hag." *Folklore: An Encyclopedia of Beliefs, Customs, Tales, Music, and Art*, edited by Charlie T. McCormick and Kim Kennedy White, 2nd ed., ABC-CLIO, 2011, volume 3, pp. 909- 10.

Press Kit. *A Girl Walks Home Alone at Night*, directed by Ana Lily Amirpour, Say Aah Productions, 2015.

Punter, David and Glennis Byron, *The Gothic*, Blackwell, 2004.

Pyke, Karen D. "Class-Based Masculinities: The Interdependence of Gender, Class, and Interpersonal Power." *Gender & Society*, volume 10, number 5, 1996, 527–49, *SAGE Journals*, https://doi.org/10.1177/089124396010005003.

Raymond, Marc. "From Old Boys to Quiet Dreams: Mapping Korean Art Cinema Today." *Film Criticism*, volume 4, number 1, March 2018, no pagination.

Rayns, Tony. "Rigor Mortis." *Sight & Sound*, volume. 25, number 4, April 2015. 82–83.

Rice, Anne. *Interview with the Vampire*, Knopf, 1976.

_____. *Queen of the Damned*, Warner Books, 1988.

Rider, Steven Jay; Tony Williams. Introduction. *Horror International*, edited by Steven Jay Schneider and Tony Williams, Wayne State University Press, 2005, pp. 1–14.

Rios, Victor, and Rachel Sarabia. "Synthesized Masculinities: The Mechanics of Manhood "Among Delinquent Boys." *Exploring Masculinities: Identity, Continuity, and Change*, edited by Tristan Bridges and C.J. Pascoe, Oxford University Press, 2015, pp. 166–77.

Rooney, David. "Dario Argento's *Dracula 3D*: Cannes Review." *The Hollywood Reporter* 5 May 2012, www.hollywoodreporter.com/review/dario-argento-dracula-3d-cannes-326991.

Rosner, Heiko. "Toni Erdmanns Erben." *Cinema* November 2016, Verlag, p. 119.
Ruffinelli, Jorge. "Cronos." *América Latina en 130 películas. Uqbar Editores*, 2010. 198–99.
Ryan, Mark David. "Whither Culture? Australian Horror Films and the Limitations of Cultural Policy." *Media International Australia*, volume 133, number 1, 2009, pp. 43–55.
Saintcrow, Lilith. "Angry Chicks in Leather" Pat's Fantasy Hotlist. fantasyhotlist.blogspot.com/2008/12/ad-lib-column-llith-saintcross.html.
Samson, Carol. Interview by James Aubrey in Denver, 15 July 2017.
Satrapi, Marjane. *Persepolis*, Pantheon Books, 2000.
Shakespeare, William. *Romeo and Juliet: Texts and Contexts*. Ed. Dympna Callaghan Bedford/St. Martin's, 2003.
Shin, Chi-Yun. "The Art of Branding: Tartan 'Asia Extreme' Films." *Horror to the Extreme: Changing Boundaries in Asian Cinema*, edited by Jinhee Choi and Mitsuyo Wada-Marciano, Hong Kong University Press, 2009, pp. 85–100.
Shippey, Tom, "Friends of Darkness and the Cold: Scandinavia: The Contradictory Lands of Angst, Sex and Social Cohesion, review of *Scandinavians*, by Robert Ferguson, *Times Literary Supplement*, 2 December 2016, p. 5.
Shohat, Ella, and Robert Stam. *Multiculturalism and the Media*. London: Routledge, 2008.
Siegert, Bernhard. *Cultural Techniques: Grids, Filters, Doors, and Other Articulations of the Real*, translated by Geoffrey Winthrop-Young, Fordham University Press, 2015.
Skal, David J. *The Monster Show: A Cultural History of Horror*, Farrar, Straus and Giroux, 2001.
Smith, Babette. *Australia's Birthstain: The Startling Legacy of the Convict Era*, Allen and Unwin, 2008.
Smith, Nigel M. "The Transfiguration Review: Downbeat Black Vampire Tale Lacks Bite." *The Guardian* 15 May 2016, www.theguardian.com/film/2016/may/15/the-transfiguration-review-cannes.
Smithson, Robert. "Entropy and the New Monuments." *Unpublished Writings in Robert Smithson: The Collected Writings*. Edited by Jack Flam, 2nd edition, University of California Press, 1996.
Sobcyzinski, Peter. "*Dracula 3-D*" RogerEbert.com, 4 October 2013, https://www.rogerebert.com/reviews/dracula-3d-2013.
"Some Facts About the Basic Law." *Basic Law Homepage* 17 March 2008. www.basiclaw.gov.hk/en/facts/index.html.
Squires, Nick. "Silvio Berlusconi says immigrants not welcome but 'beautiful girls' can stay" *The Telegraph* 13 February, 2010, www.telegraph.co.uk/news/worldnews/europe/italy/7223365/Silvio-Berlusconi-says-immigrants-not-welcome-but-beautiful-girls-can-stay.html.
Stanton, Geoff. "Dead Heart: Australia's Horror Cinema." *FilmInk*. 31 October 2018, www.filmink.com.au/dead-heart-australias-horror-cinema/.
Stock, Ann Marie. "Authentically Mexican? *Mi querido Tom Mix* and *Cronos* Reframe Critical Questions." *Mexico's Cinema: A Century of Film and Filmmakers*, edited by Joanne Hershfield and David R. Maciel, Scholarly Resources, 1999, pp. 267–86.
Stockton, Kathryn Bond. *The Queer Child: Or Growing Sideways in the Twentieth Century*, Duke University Press, 2009.
Stoehr, Kevin L. "*Nosferatu.*" *101 Horror Movies You Must See Before You Die*, edited by Steven Jay. Schneider, Barron's, 2009. 253–54.
Stoker, Abraham. *Dracula*, edited by Glennis Byron, 1897, Broadview, 1998.
———. *The New Annotated Dracula*, edited by Leslie S. Klinger, Norton, 2008.
Stokes, Lisa Odham. "Vampire Movies." *Historical Dictionary of Hong Kong Cinema*, Scarecrow Press, 2007, pp. 448–50.
Suvin, Darko. "On the Poetics of the Science Fiction Genre." *Science Fiction Criticism: An Anthology of Essential Writings*, edited by Rob Latham. Bloomsbury Publishing, 2017, pp. 116–25.
Szeto, Miranda May, and Yun-chung Chen. "Hong Kong Cinema in the Age of Neoliberalization and Mainlandization." *A Companion to Hong Kong Cinema*, edited by Esther M.K. Cheung, et al., Wiley-Blackwell, 2015, pp. 89–115.
Tang Wenyu [唐文玉]. "中国文化恐怖符号浅谈—20世纪80年代香港电影僵尸形象包含的

文化" ["Brief Remarks on Horror Symbols in Chinese Culture: The Cultural Significance of the Vampire Figure in 1980's Hong Kong Films"]. 北方文学 [*Northern Literature*], number 7, 2014, p. 101, *VIP*, www.cqvip.com/read/read.aspx?id=662484466.

Thacker, Eugene. *Cosmic Pessimism*, Univocal Publishing, 2015.

_____. "Dark Media." *Excommunication: Three Inquiries in Media and Mediation*, edited by Alexander Galloway, Eugene Thacker, and McKenzie Wark. University of Chicago Press, 2014, 77–150.

_____. "Three Questions on Demonology," *Hideous Gnosis: Black Metal Theory Symposium*, volume 1, edited by Nicola Masciandaro, Glossator, 2010, pp. 179–219.

Theroux, Paul. *The Happy Isles of Oceania: Paddling the Pacific*, Mariner, 2006.

Thorne, Jack, playwright. *Let the Right One In*, Nick Herne Books, 2013.

Tierney, Dolores. "Transnational Political Horror in *Cronos* (1993), *El espinazo del diablo* (2001), and *El laberinto del fauno* (2006)." *The Transnational Fantasies of Guillermo del Toro*, edited by Ann Davies, et al., Palgrave MacMillan, 2014. 161–82.

"Top 5 Scary Movies." *The Metropolitan* [MSU Denver] 29 October 2015: 14.

Toro, Gabe. "Review: Dario Argento's Dracula 3-D" *Indiewire*, 1 October 2013, www.indiewire. com/2013/10/review-dario-argentos-dracula-3d-93078/.

Trafton, Scott. *Egypt Land, Race and Nineteenth-Century American Egyptomania*, Duke University Press, 2004.

Tsui, Clarence. "China's Horror-Film Curbs Rebound as Directors Find Ways to Fill Screens with Sex and Gore and Cynical Audiences Lap It Up." *Post Magazine*, 22 June 2017, www.scmp.com/magazines/post-magazine/arts-music/article/2099451/chinas-horror-film-curbs-rebound-directors-find.

"26 Most Successful Horror Film Franchises." IMDb.com. Updated 12 Sep. 2016. https://www. imdb.com/scary-good/most-successful-horror-franchises/ls063226860/?ref_=ls_mv_close.

Tyler, Marshall. "Stifling Penchant: Conformity—a Must in Scandinavia." *Los Angeles Times* 14 December 1988, articles.latimes.com/1988-12-14/news/mn-278_1_welfare-state.

Tyree, J.M. "Warm-blooded: *True Blood* and *Let the Right One In*." *Film Quarterly*, volume 63, number 2, winter 2009–10, pp. 31–37.

Vander Lugt, Kris. "From Siodmak to Schlingensief: The Return of Horror as History." *Generic Histories of German Cinema—Genre and Its Deviations*, edited by Jaimey Fisher, Camden House, 2013, pp. 157–72.

Vargas, Juan Carlos. "Between Fantasy and Reality: The Child's Vision and Fairy Tales in Guillermo del Toro's Hispanic Trilogy." *The Transnational Fantasies of Guillermo del Toro*, edited by Ann Davies, et al., Palgrave MacMillan, 2014, pp. 183–97.

Veg, Sebastian. "Hong Kong's Enduring Identity Crisis." *The Atlantic* 16 October 2013, www. theatlantic.com/china/archive/2013/10/hong-kongs-enduring-identity-crisis/280622/.s

Vitale, Christopher. "Guide to Reading Deleuze's The Movement-Image. Part I: The Deleuzian Notion of the Image, or Worldslicing as Cinema Beyond the Human." *Networkologies*, networkologies.wordpress.com/2011/04/04/the-deleuzian-notion-of-the-image-a-slice-of-the-world-or-cinema-beyond-the-human/.

Vossen, Ursula. Einleitung: *Filmgenres Horrorfilm*, edited by Ursula Vossen, Reclam, 2004, pp. 9–26.

Wada-Marciano, Mitsuyo. "J-horror: New Media's Impact on Contemporary Japanese Horror Cinema." *Horror to the Extreme: Changing Boundaries in Asian Cinema*, edited by Jinhee Choi and Mitsuyo Wada-Marciano, Hong Kong University Press, 2009, pp. 15–37.

Walker, Alice. *Everyday Use*. New York: Rutgers University Press, 2006.

Wark, McKenzie. "Furious Media." *Excommunication: Three Inquiries in Media and Mediation*. Edited by Alexander Galloway, Eugene Thacker, and McKenzie Wark. University of Chicago Press, 2014. 151–210.

Washington Examiner. Review of *Let the Right One In*, quoted on Blu-ray disc cover, www. magnetreleasing.com, 2009.

Weinstock, Jeffrey. *The Vampire Film: Undead Cinema*, Columbia University Press, 2012.

West, Candace, and Don H. Zimmerman. "Doing Gender." *Gender & society*, volume 1, number 2, 1987, pp. 125–51, *SAGE Journals*, https://doi.org/10.1177/0891243287001002002.

White, Eric. "Insects and Automata in Hoffmann, Balzac, Carter, and del Toro." *Journal of the Fantastic in the* Arts, volume 19, number 3, 2008, pp. 363–78.

Williams, David. *Deformed Discourse: The Function of the Monster in Mediaeval Thought and Literature*, University of Exeter Press, 1996.

Williams, Mark. *Ireland's Immortals: A History of the Gods of Irish Myth*, Princeton University Press, 2016.

Williams, Tony. "Martin." *The Cinema of George A. Romero: Knight of the Living Dead*, 2nd edition, Columbia University Press, 2015, pp. 80–89. *JSTOR*, www.jstor.org/stable/10.7312/will17354.11.

Windt, Uri. Interview. *Not Quite Hollywood: The Wild, Untold Story of OZploitation!*, directed by Mark Hartley, City Films Worldwide, 2008.

Wolf, Leonard. *A Dream of Dracula: In Search of the Living Dead*, Little, Brown, 1977.

Wolf, Leonard, editor. *The Essential Dracula*, ibooks, 2004.

Woolley, Stephen, producer. Interview. *Byzantium*, cited above. UK Blu-ray special feature.

Wright, Rochelle. "Vampire in the Stockholm Suburbs: *Let the Right One In* and Genre Hybridity." *Journal of Scandinavian Cinema*, volume 1, Number 2, 2010, pages 55–70.

Xu Tongxin [徐桐炘]. "錢小豪負面教材當磨練" ["Chin Siu-ho Takes Lesson of Endurance from Negative Experiences"]. *China Times* 20 March 2017, www.chinatimes.com/newspapers/20170320000491–260112?chdtv.

Yeats, W.B. "Byzantium." *The Poems*, edited by Daniel Albright, 2nd edition, Dent, 1994, pp. 298–99.

_____. "Sailing to Byzantium." *The Poems*, edited by Daniel Albright, 2nd edition. Dent, 1994, p. 250.

_____. "The Second Coming." *The Poems*, edited by Daniel Albright, 2nd edition, Dent, 1994, p. 238.

_____. "Under Ben Bulben." *The Poems*, edited by Daniel Albright, 2nd edition, Dent, 1994, pp. 373–76.

Young, Paul. "The Victorians Created Our Meat-Eating Crisis. Can they also teach us how to escape it." *The Independent*, 16 February 2019, www.independent.co.uk/life-style/food-and-drink/meat-eating-vegetarian-victorians-factory-farming-a8741136.html.

Young, Serinity. *Women Who Fly: Goddesses, Witches, Mystics, and Other Airborne Females*, Oxford University Press, 2018.

Zadeh, Hossein Eidi. "15 Essential Films for an Introduction to Italian *Giallo* Movies." *Taste of Cinema*, 14 October 2014, www.tasteofcinema.com/2014/15-essential-films-for-an-introduction-to-italian-giallo-movies/.

Zeddies, T. "Behind, Beneath, Above and Beyond: The Historical Unconscious." *Journal of the American Academy of Psychoanalysis*, volume 30, number 2, 2002, pp. 211–29.

Zielinski, Siegfried. *Deep Time of the Media. Toward an Archaeology of Hearing and Seeing by Technical* Means, translated by Gloria Custance, MIT Press, 2006.

Zipes, Jack. "Unfathomable Baba Yagas." *Baba Yaga*, edited by Sibelan Forrester, et al., University of Mississippi Press, 2013, pp. vii–xii.

About the Contributors

Tatjana **Aleksić** is an associate professor of comparative and Slavic literature at the University of Michigan. She works on gender, sexuality and cultures of violence and is the author of *The Sacrificed Body: Balkan Community Building and the Fear of Freedom*. She is the editor of *Mythistory and Narratives of Nation in the Balkans* and coeditor of the forthcoming *Mediated Resistance: Independent Reporting and the Yugoslav Dissolution*.

U. Melissa **Anyiwo** is a professor and coordinator of African American studies at Curry College, Massachusetts. Her research is on race, gender and visual archetypes in the vampire narrative, and she is currently co-chair of vampire studies at the National Popular Culture Association. Her published work includes the edited collections *Buffy Conquers the Academy*, *Race in the Vampire Narrative*, *Gender in the Vampire Narrative* and *Gender Warriors: Reading Contemporary Urban Fantasy*.

James **Aubrey** is a professor of English at Metropolitan State University of Denver, where he teaches British and world literatures, critical theory and film studies. He has published numerous articles and three books on British novelist John Fowles, including *Filming John Fowles*. Besides teaching vampire films regularly, he has taught cinema of India as a study abroad course and took a Fulbright group of educators to India in 2018.

David John **Boyd** has a Ph.D. from the University of Glasgow in comparative literature (text-image studies). He has published on Japanese manga and anime, and his research includes the works of Walter Benjamin and Gilles Deleuze, regarding their diverse discourses on world visual culture and media philosophies of temporality, semiotics and global history. His other interests include global youth culture and cosmopolitan fan cultures, and how they contribute to the production of everyday avant-gardeism and vulgar Marxism(s).

Anurag **Chauhan** is an assistant professor at Guru Ghasidas University in central India, where he teaches various courses in English at both the graduate (Baccalaureate) and postgraduate (M.A., M. Phil, and Ph.D.) levels. He has supervised numerous theses and dissertations. From 2011 to 2012 he was Fulbright Scholar-in-Residence for two semesters in a joint appointment at two institutions in Denver,

Colorado, where he taught courses in literature, postcolonial theory, and cinema from India.

Cheryl D. **Edelson** is a professor of English and dean of humanities, arts and design at Chaminade University of Honolulu. Her research and teaching interests include film and television studies, the gothic, and popular culture. She wrote the introduction to and coedited the collection *The Interior Landscapes of Breaking Bad*. Her work has appeared in *Pacific Coast Philology*, *The Methods of Breaking Bad: Essays on Character, Narrative, and Ethics*, and *Neo-Victorian Gothic: Horror, Violence, and Degeneration in the Re-Imagined Nineteenth Century*.

Roberto **Forns-Broggi** is a professor of Spanish at Metropolitan State University of Denver, where he teaches advanced courses including Latin American cinema and Latin American essays. His own essays on ecological perspectives applied to literature, art, film and new media investigate alternative epistemologies and their influence on reading and writing practices. In 2016 he published *Knots Like Stars: The ABC of Ecological Imagination in Our Americas*. He is the author of the forthcoming bilingual *Workbook on Environmental Writing and Film in Latin America*.

Charles **Hoge** researches horror, monstrosity, dark folklore and Victorian culture. He teaches at Metropolitan State University of Denver and has published on ludology in *Doctor Who* fanfiction (*Transformative Works and Cultures*), medieval influences in *I Am Legend* (*Reading Richard Matheson: A Critical Survey*), phantom dogs in *Under the Volcano* (*Malcolm Lowry's Poetics in Space*) and the strange footprint left across eighteenth century England by the dodo's extinction (*University of Toronto Quarterly*).

Lorna **Hutchison** earned her Ph.D. from McGill University, Montreal. She is a visiting professor of English at the University of Colorado at Denver, where her teaching includes ecocriticism for graduate students. Her publications include *Children and Cultural Memory in Texts of Childhood*. She has lectured on various films including *Spirited Away*, *Bollywood/Hollywood* and *Cronos*.

Fontaine **Lien** is an assistant professor of Chinese at Valparaiso University, where she teaches Chinese language, literature and film. She has broad research interests in global speculative fiction including Chinese *zhiguai* literature and the French *fantastique*. Her focus is on contemporary Chinese cinema, science fiction and fantasy, and she is working on a book project that explores the classical roots of these contemporary genres.

Jade **Lum** is a Ph.D. student and graduate assistant in English at the University of Hawai'i at Mānoa, where she also received her Master's degree in English with a focus on literary studies. Her research interests include fairy tale studies, gender studies, adaptation studies and visual and new media storytelling, particularly film and video game studies. She also enjoys researching Asian popular culture and media.

Cain **Miller** is a lecturer in film studies at Texas A&M University. He possesses an MA in popular film and media studies from Southern Methodist University and a

BA in radio, television, and film from the University of North Texas. His research primarily focuses on gender studies with particular emphasis placed on the portrayals of masculinity in film and media. He specializes in the horror genre, cult films, and exploitation cinema.

Vincent **Piturro** is a professor of film and media studies at Metropolitan State University of Denver and holds a Ph.D. in comparative literature. His areas of study include vampires, science fiction, documentaries, Italian cinema and international cinema. He hosts an annual Science Fiction Film Series in conjunction with the Denver Museum of Nature and Science and the Denver Film Society.

Wendolyn **Weber** is a professor of English at the Metropolitan State University of Denver, specializing in comparative literature, literary and cultural theory, and medieval languages and literatures. Her scholarship includes work on gender, violence and monstrosity in medieval and popular culture, and her teaching includes courses on monsters and monstrosity, monster theory and vampire films.

Graeme A. **Wend-Walker** lives in San Marcos, Texas, and is an associate professor at Texas State University. His interests include science fiction, fantasy, horror, YA and children's lit, postsecularism and critical theory.

Kai-Uwe **Werbeck** is an associate professor of German and an affiliate faculty member of film studies at UNC Charlotte. His research interests include German postwar film and literature, global horror cinema and media studies. He has published widely on German literature from Rolf Dieter Brinkmann to Heinrich Böll. He is working on a monograph on (West) German horror film after 1945.

Index